CHRISTIAN P. POTHOLM
Bowdoin College

THE THEORY AND PRACTICE OF AFRICAN POLITICS

PRENTICE-HALL, INC., ENGLEWOOD CLIFFS, NEW JERSEY 07632

Library of Congress Cataloging in Publication Data

POTHOLM, CHRISTIAN P.
    The theory and practice of African politics.

    Bibliography: p.
    Includes index.
    1. Africa—Politics and government.
2. Political science—Africa.   I. Title.
JQ1873 1979.P67   320.9'6'03   78-8758
ISBN   0-13-913533-2

THE THEORY AND PRACTICE OF AFRICAN POLITICS
Christian P. Potholm

Frontispiece: From C. Gregory Knight and James Newman,
Contemporary Africa: Geography and Change
(Englewood Cliffs, N.J.: Prentice-Hall, 1976).

Printed in the United States of America

10 9 8 7 6 5 4 3 2 1

Prentice-Hall International, Inc., *London*
Prentice-Hall of Australia Pty. Limited, *Sydney*
Prentice-Hall of Canada, Ltd., *Toronto*
Prentice-Hall of India Private Limited, *New Delhi*
Prentice-Hall of Japan, Inc., *Tokyo*
Prentice-Hall of Southeast Asia Pte. Ltd., *Singapore*
Whitehall Books Limited, *Wellington, New Zealand*

To my partners,
Sandra, Erik, and Pebbles

CONTENTS

4 POLITICAL THEMES IN RECENT AFRICAN LITERATURE, 108

Part TWO
THE PROCESS OF AFRICAN POLITICS

5 THE POLYARCHAL SPECTRUM, 139

6 THE AUTHORITARIAN SPECTRUM, 176

7 THE MARXIST MODERNIZERS AND THE FUTURE, 212

Part THREE
COMPREHENSIVE BIBLIOGRAPHY

AFRICAN POLITICS IN PERSPECTIVE, 247

COUNTRY BY COUNTRY ANALYSIS, 269

PREFACE

In writing a book about African politics today, it is as important to indicate what you are *not* covering as it is to state what your are, since the fifty African countries represent such diversity and multiplicity of interactions as to make coverage in a single volume impossible.

The Theory and Practice of African Politics is not a country by country analysis. Nor does it purport to draw on the considerable political material of North Africa. And it makes no attempt to deal, except tangentially, with the remaining areas of the continent still under European control. Further, the work consciously avoids the intricacies of inter-African relations.

What it does seek to do is to give the reader an introduction to the theory and practice of African politics. That is, what are the philosophical and theoretical wellsprings of contemporary politics on the continent? What are the historical antecedents of the political patterns that have emerged since independence, and what seem to be the most relevant themes for the future?

This study grew out of my earlier work, *Four African Political Systems,* which was written in 1968, and my interaction with both students and practitioners of African politics since then. Several field trips to Africa, sponsored in part by a Rockefeller Foundation Conflict in International Relations scholarship and a Fullbright-Hays grant, enormously broadened my understanding of politics in Africa. I am most grateful for their support. I am also indebted to Bowdoin College and, in particular, to Dean Alfred Fuchs and the Mellon Fellowship Committee for their additional assistance.

Many people contributed to the making of this book. My family, to whom the work is dedicated, accompanied me several times to Africa and shared with me the trials and stimulations of writing a book about contemporary African politics. I am also very grateful for the valuable contributions of my colleagues, who not only helped me frame the parameters of research, but who also challenged many of my assumptions and conclusions.

Morton Schoolman greatly enhanced the work with his chapters dealing with the theoretical underpinnings of politics in Africa. John Rensenbrink, Arthur House, Christopher Mojekwu, Tom Henrikson, Nizaralli Motani, John Campbell, Dennis King, Gail Hines, and Leslie Anderson also added their ideas and talents to various chapters. Grace Lott, Gladys Peterson, and

Virginia Richardson typed portions of the manuscript, and undoubtedly made it far more readable than it was initially. Marianne Russell was also of considerable assistance in the final outcome and, beyond that, a joy to work with as well as to behold.

I would also like to thank the staff of Prentice-Hall, especially Bart Bleisdell, Stan Wakefield, Serena Hoffman, and Colette Conboy, for keeping the production process so sparkling and surprising.

A final note about timing. Any attempt to describe the course of contemporary politics in Africa is likely to suffer the ravages of time. In fact, it is wisest to hold that the phenomenon I describe and the hypotheses I put forward will obtain "for the foreseeable future," that being defined as the period of time prior to the observations being overridden by events!

Christian P. Potholm

Gaberone, Botswana   1975
Whale Rock, Maine   1977
Kigali, Rwanda   1978

THE CONTEXT OF AFRICAN POLITICS

Themes in Traditional African Political Systems

Those interested in the African political heritage face considerable difficulties in ascertaining the philosophical bases of that heritage. On the one hand, the indigenous African political systems that existed prior to the arrival of the Arabs and Europeans exhibited enormous structural variety and continent-wide diversity. On the other hand, when confronted with the problem of discovering the content of the political philosophy underlying these forms, the scholar interested in African political thought must rely on a variety of evidence: oral traditions that survived within the societies in question, archeological and linguistic patterns, the descriptions of the first foreign visitors to these cultures, and especially the African political forms themselves.[1]

[1]An earlier draft of this chapter was presented at the International Studies Association meeting in Edinburgh, Scotland, August 1976, and excerpts of it have appeared in C. Mojekwu, V. Uchendu, and C. Van Hoey (eds.), *African Society, Culture and Politics* (Washington, D.C.: University Press of America, 1977).

If, however, in the absence of extensive written records—either because the societies in question were preliterate or because the records were subsequently lost—one assumes that African peoples adopted political systems that reflected the political thought of the group, then the African philosophical heritage takes on a richness and a multiplicity that has heretofore gone unappreciated.

The varied history of Africa before the intrusion of outside forces offers a vivid portrait of diversity and political choice. This is particularly the case when one considers the extensive migrations across the length and breadth of Africa. As the Bantu-speaking peoples moved across central Africa and into the southern portion of the continent, and major groups of both Negroid and Hametic peoples migrated into the eastern portion of Africa, new societies were constantly being formed. Some groups split off from the main bodies of the migrations; others remained in place; still others moved in new directions. Given the vast open spaces of the African continent, the relatively fertile and hospitable land, and the sparsely populated nature of much of the southern portion of the entire continent, these iron-age people could often pick and choose the location for their settlements. As they formed and reformed their societies, they chose their political forms as well.

For those interested in the range and scope of African political thought, it therefore makes sense to look at the political forms that manifested themselves in the African context and take them as expressions of political philosophy. As such, the forms can be regarded as indicators of the basic societal values that underpinned the political system and permeated the political value systems of the group. By beginning with the premise that various African peoples developed their political systems to conform to the political philosophies operative within their societies, we can deduce the nature and scope of that political thought through the forms themselves. In this way, this chapter seeks to demonstrate the extent to which the great structural variety of African forms reflects certain basic assumptions that Africans made about the nature of human collectivities, the nature of societal interaction, and the desired relationship between power and authority. By sharing common purposes and the political means to attain them, African peoples made choices as to the form of political system to adopt.

In addition, not only the forms themselves, but their varied geographical and even ecological settings provide us with illuminating insights into the nature of African political thought. Just as in Renaissance Italy during the thirteenth and fourteenth centuries, when a great variety of structural forms —monarchy, democracy, dictatorship, theocracy—coexisted within a relatively small geographical area and often under similar socioeconomic conditions, so too in traditional African societies we find a great variety of political forms within relative spacial and temporal proximity of one another.

We would argue that this very diversity is of considerable importance in understanding African political thought. It is also one reason why attempts to catalogue traditional African political systems on the basis of the kind of food-producing process that underlay their societies have not been very successful. In fact, it is precisely the diversity of political forms with their concomitant philosophies that must be regarded as one of the critical variables in African history, to say nothing of contemporary patterns of politics in Africa.

To examine the nature of African political thought in its traditional setting by relying in large part upon the forms themselves may at first seem difficult. But on reflection, this process of investigation is no different than if we were attempting to study the political thought of the ancient Greeks without the aid of the writings of Plato and Aristotle. Such an inquiry would be more difficult to mount to be sure, but it would in no sense be impossible. Having their written observations, often helpfully arranged in a holistic philosophy, certainly facilitates our understanding of the central themes in Greek political thought, and it is extremely useful in going into the reasoning behind the adoption of one form rather than another. But the absence of such a body of written material would in no way preclude our coming to grips with the underlying political themes as lived by the Greeks. If we had only descriptions of sixth-century B.C. Athens, Sparta, Corinth, and Syracuse, we would, in fact, paint quite a rich and perceptive portrait of the philosophical assumptions on which the various forms were based, and could develop by deduction the philosophical rationale behind them. After all, democracy, despotism, and other forms of government have become part of our human heritage not simply because we have written accounts of the rationale behind them, but because the forms themselves have endured, reappearing in time and space throughout the course of human history.

So it is with the African forms. The most persistent political patterns that have occurred throughout African history, in virtually all parts of the continent, among people of various linguistic and racial types, tell us of their enduring quality. Their very appearance in numerous places far removed from one another, among peoples with entirely different cultural and historical backgrounds indicates the strength of the philosophical underpinnings, which have appealed to the diverse groups that subsequently adopted them. The recurring themes of African political thought, manifested in discernible forms by which people choose to guide their destiny—indeed in many cases staking their very lives on the successful functioning of those systems—can give us considerable insight into the scope and depth of African political thought. And, as this chapter also attempts to suggest, the recurrence of certain political forms is of enormous consequence, not just for the theory, but also for the practice of government in Africa today.

It is to these recurring themes that we now turn. In terms of methodology and procedure, we are not making any attempt in this brief chapter to touch on all the themes in African political thought. Indeed we have even deliberately avoided such crucial themes as egalitarianism which will be covered in subsequent chapters. Rather, we are concentrating on those themes that set the stage for our understanding the scope and history of African political thought: the inherent pluralism of African political philosophy, the constant tension between centralization and diffusion of political power, the limitation on arbitrary use of political power, the interaction between religion and political philosophy, and the African tendency to correlate age and wisdom within the political context.

PLURALISM

Although it became rather fashionable in the 1960s and early 1970s to accent the philosophical unity of Africa—indeed to stress the solidarity of the entire Third World—and although there may well be some political advantages in international diplomacy to the holding of this self-image, in point of fact, there is enormous ethnic, cultural, linguistic, and historical diversity within Africa. In a neutral context, such an indication of diversity would seem prosaic. But because of the colonial experience shared by so many African countries (an experience unfortunately not over for some African peoples) and because of the desire on the part of so many Africans to shape their own destinies, the search for unity required an underlying belief in the commonality of "the African experience."

Indeed, the most persistent theme in African history is the very diversity of its peoples. And nowhere is that diversity more keenly appreciated than in an examination of the great structural variety of traditional African political systems. There were societies in Africa that based the holding of political power on the mechanism of kinship. Some political systems incorporated the notion that positions of authority should be inherited. Others insisted that political power should be earned. Still others felt that political power should be shared by various interest groups within society. Some African political systems insisted that political power belongs to one group within society—a class, an organization, or even a racial caste. Some African political systems were democratic; others were despotic. Some placed great reliance on religious authority to guide the destiny of the political ruler; others were more nearly secular.

In short, the diversity of traditional African political forms and the basic political pluralism that characterized African political thought in its traditional settings is both manifest and considerable. In fact, as one observer has noted ". . . there is a wider range in traditional African political systems than exists today among the industrialized nations in spite of the oft proclaimed communist-democratic dichotomy."[2] In the context of independent Africa, numerous political leaders have chosen to portray traditional African society as being homogeneous. Often it has been claimed that these societies share identical assumptions about the nature of human collectivities and hence the new nations. When national leaders have insisted on a return to such patterns of conformity which exist only in theory, there have been most serious consequences for the political systems.

Elsewhere we have asserted that such assumptions about the nature of traditional African political life have had considerable pejorative impact on the newly independent African states.[3] The failure to recognize the importance of the traditional structures and forms for the process of modern government has cost many leaders their positions. In fact, one could well argue that the mix of traditional political systems within the framework of national boundaries has been of as much significance in shaping the destiny of the new states as the more popular, but less precise, concept of tribalism. Often ethnic strife has been exacerbated—or in some cases muted—precisely because of the nature of the traditional political system of that subnational unit. In other words, the basic pluralism of African traditional political systems remains a fact of life, one that statesmen and politicians ignore at their peril.

It is now a rather commonplace observation that the earliest Arab and European observers of the African political scene were ethnocentric in many of their judgments of the forms they encountered. All but a few severely misjudged the complexity and sophistication of numerous African systems, particularly those we now term segmented. But even if these early explorers did not appreciate the textural richness of the African political environment, even their fragmentary observations indicate useful evidence as to the diversity they encountered. The journals of Livingston, Baker, Stanley, and Burton, to name but the most prominent, clearly attest to the hundreds and thousands of different communities, in various parts of Africa, based on different food-producing systems, and peopled by widely differing ethnic groups.

It was not until well into the twentieth century that major efforts were made to analyze the multitude of African peoples on the basis of their sociopolitical organization. Such pioneers as Fortes and Evans-Pritchard attempted to range across the African context to categorize the traditional political systems they encountered in the course of their anthropological investigations. Their *Afri-*

[2]Peter C. Lloyd, "The Political Structure of African Kingdoms," *Political Systems and the Distribution of Power,* American Sociology Association Monograph No. 2 (New York: Praeger, 1965), p. 107. Of course communist political leaders would presumably argue that their systems were "democratic" as well.

[3]C. P. Potholm, "Politics in Africa: Patterns of Growth and Decay," *Four African Political Systems* (Englewood Cliffs, N.J.: Prentice-Hall, 1970), pp. 272–96. For a useful overview of African traditional societies, see Robert W. July, *Precolonial Africa* (New York: Scribner's, 1975).

can Political Systems was designed to develop a classificatory scheme based on the amount of control enjoyed by the political center, the regulation of force within the society, and the relationship between kinship and political authority.[4] In their view, African political systems fell into three major groupings: hunting bands, segmentary lineage societies, and primitive states. Hunting and food-gathering bands, as exemplified by the Kung, the Bergdama, and the Mbuti, exhibited political configurations, and membership in the group was based entirely upon kinship. Segmentary lineage societies, on the other hand, were regarded as "stateless" political systems in which political authority was dispersed throughout individual segments which were coequal. Examples of the segmentary lineage pattern were the Masai, Luo, Ibo, Nuer, Tallensi, and Nandi. Primitive states differed considerably from either of these other two forms since they had well-defined political institutions and centralized authority. The Zulu, Bemba, Asante, and Baganda were offered as primary examples of this pattern.

The Fortes and Evans-Pritchard scheme suffered from a lack of completeness and overlooked many of the important variations of these three basic types, but it did focus on one of the most persistent themes in traditional African political thought—the tension between centralization of political power and its diffusion. We shall be returning to this issue in the following section, but for the moment the reader should be aware that, at the time of its publication and for many years after, *African Political Systems* both stimulated anthropologists to examine their basic assumptions about the nature of African political communities and served as a reference point for further analysis by both Europeans and Africans.

Schapera, for example, in his *Government and Politics in Tribal Societies,* departed from the Fortes and Evans-Pritchard formula by challenging what he took to be an overemphasis on kinship groupings and by developing the notion that a political community in the African context is simply "a group of people organized into a single unit managing its affairs independently of external control."[5] Concentrating primarily on the ethnic groups found in southern Africa, Schapera was interested in the process by which traditional African political systems in that region developed through conquest, immigration, the acceptance of refugees, and the formation of new units. He was able to underscore the great diversity and pluralism in that part of the continent and to distinguish various political systems on the basis of the nature of their political authority, the rights and obligations of that authority, and the way in which leaders attained it.

---

[4]M. Fortes and E. E. Evans-Pritchard (eds.), *African Political Systems* (London: Oxford University Press, 1940).

[5]I. Schapera, *Government and Politics in Tribal Societies* (London: C. A. Watts, 1956), p. 8. This view is certainly not without relevance for the creation of modern states in Africa following decolonization.

Mair examined in considerable detail those African political systems that were segmented. Concentrating on East Africa, she developed a variety of classifications that differed from the "pure" form outlined by Evans-Pritchard. Although the title, *Primitive Government,* showed a certain amount of ethnocentricity, it did emphasize the variations on the segmented theme as encountered among the Masai, Kipsigi, Nandi, and Meru.[6] Analyzing age-sets or training regiments, which cut across segment lines and which acted as a unifying force within segmented societies, she accented the quasi-military character of the age-sets and, more important from our point of view, the process of political socialization that takes place within them—namely, the raising of in-group consciousness by expanding one's loyalty beyond one's individual segment. Formed every ten to fifteen years, the age-sets divided society vertically into boys, warriors, and elders but unified it horizontally by bringing all males of the same age together for common experiences. After the training period of three to four years, the men returned to their individual segments, but when group action was required, the age-sets were reformed. Although political authority remained diffused among the segments, there was an inclination toward a generontocracy in terms of decision making; within the age-sets there was a good deal of emphasis on achievement, especially in warfare.

Another interesting form of traditional political system, which was an additional modification of the segmented pattern, was found among the Nyakyusa in what is now Tanzania. In the case of the Nyakyusa, the age-sets themselves were not dispersed but formed the basis for communal living. Generational villages were set up and members of the particular age-set lived together, joined by the females from their corresponding unit.

As more and more anthropologists recognized the need for a dynamic analysis of African societies in terms of the interaction between their political forms and societal process, an entire subfield of political anthropology came into being within the discipline. Max Gluckman, Jan van Velsen, Victor Turner, Marc Swartz, and Edgar Winans, to name but a few, all made attempts to come to grips with the underlying realities of traditional African political systems.[7] There is not space here to summarize their findings, but even when the anthropologists turned their attention to the political process, they often confused structure with process, overestimated the ritual aspects of political

---

[6]Lucy Mair, *Primitive Government* (Baltimore: Penguin Books, 1962).

[7]Max Gluckman, *Politics, Law and Ritual in Tribal Society* (Chicago: Aldine, 1965); Jan van Velsen, *The Politics of Kinship* (London: Manchester University Press, 1964); Victor Turner, *Schism and Continuity in an African Village* (Manchester: Manchester University Press, 1957); Edgar Winans, *Shambala: The Constitution of a Traditional State* (Los Angeles: University of California Press, 1962); and Marc J. Swartz, Victor W. Turner, and Arthur Tuden (eds.), *Political Anthropology* (Chicago: Aldine, 1966). For an engaging if simplified account of this phenomenon, see E. J. Murphy, *The Bantu Civilization of Southern Africa* (New York: Thomas Crowell, 1974).

offices, and, on occasion, failed to appreciate the deep-seated complexities in such apparently "simple" systems as those termed segmented.

Nor were the anthropologists alone in this significant failure to adequately examine the nature of traditional political systems in terms of their possible impact on modern African politics. By and large, political scientists, especially American and British, often ignored Africa until the late 1950s and then concentrated on the largest ethnic units or the emerging "national" politics. Perhaps the most serious difficulty with much of the political science investigation was unwillingness or inability to come to grips with the underlying importance of the traditional political forms and their subsequent impact on the new nations of Africa.

But if the western and western-trained anthropologists did not adequately grapple with all of the practical issues raised by the very existence of African traditional political systems, their work, taken in the aggregate, is most useful in underscoring the diversity and pluralism to be found in Africa.

In terms of outlining the human richness of the continent, two works stand out: Melville J. Herskovits, *The Human Factor in Changing Africa,* and Jacques Maquet, *Civilizations of Black Africa.*[8] Reacting to what he took to be "the confusion of physical form with cultural and linguistic usage," Herskovits attempted to outline six prominent cultural patterns existent in the nineteenth century: the Khosian, East African Cattle, East Sudan, Congo, Guinea Coast, and Western Sudan,[9] each with different clusters of political structure, aesthetic expression, lineage patterns, social stratification, modes of food production, and metaphysical views to form these composites.

For our purposes, the Herskovits book is most useful in outlining the great cultural variety to be found in Africa and providing a general background for the traditional African settings of political systems. At the same time, it falls far short of a systematic analysis of these political systems and tends to ignore widespread diversity within each cultural area. For example, there are both pastoralists and agriculturalists within the East African cattle area and an even greater degree of structural variety of political forms.

Maquet, too, ignores much of this political diversity as he blends art, religion, method of food production, and social structures to form an outline of six major African civilizations. The first is the civilization of the bow, as exemplified by small hunting bands such as the Mbuti, Kung, and Narem. The second, which he terms the civilization of the clearings, includes such groups as the Kissi, the Mongo, and the Hamba. Other civilizations include the granaries (exemplified by the Kuba, Luba, Kongo, Bemba, and Lozi), the civilization of the spear (including the Zulu, Ankole, Masai, Nuer, and

---

[8]Melville J. Herskovits, *The Human Factor in Changing Africa* (New York: Vintage Books, 1967); and Jaques Maquet, *Civilizations of Black Africa* (New York: Oxford University Press, 1972).
[9]Herskovits, *The Human Factor,* pp. 56–112.

Kikuyu), as well as the civilization of the cities (personified by such peoples as the Youruba, Asante, and those of Dahomey).

While Maquet and Herskovits amply illustrate the vast range of African societies to be found on the continent, their analyses of political systems are far from adequate. Maquet, for example, includes such diverse political systems as those of the Zulu, Nuer, and Masai all under the same categorical heading. Even more distressing is the extent to which both held the political system in traditional African societies to be the dependent variable, a direct outgrowth of the environment in which the system is found. In point of fact, there is no such discernible pattern in Africa, and it is not possible to draw a direct connection between one type of environment and a particular form of government. Segmented systems are to be found throughout Africa, regardless of the cultural area or civilization focus. Within a relatively small area, one may find segmented, centralized, and hunting bands. Moreover, during periods of great turmoil, such as experienced in southern Africa during the early nineteenth century *Mfacane* (the "crushing") following the period of Zulu expansion, essentially similar peoples with linguistic, cultural, and historical affinities opted for widely differing political systems, often within close proximity of one another and within a short temporal frame.

We shall be examining the diversity of African political forms in the section that follows; our objections to the political observations of the anthropologists should not obscure the usefulness of their evidence which demonstrates the wide diversity that is the central fact of the African heritage.

CENTRALIZATION AND DIFFUSION
OF POLITICAL POWER

When confronted with the diversity outlined above, the observer of the African political scene must ask: what do all these political systems have in common, how do they differ? If similar systems have evolved far removed from one another in time and space, and if widely differing systems exist side by side, then one can well argue for the element of choice. That is, Africans, far from passively accepting the political systems, chose forms, altered them, and developed entirely new ones.

The multiplicity of forms, which has baffled many observers, can be made manageable by the application of a relatively simple classificatory scheme. Eisenstadt is most helpful in this regard.[10] Although he includes numerous non-African examples and develops portions of his analysis based on them, his work goes far beyond other scholars in ordering the multiplicity of forms

[10]S. N. Eisenstadt, "Primitive Political Systems: A Preliminary Comparative Analysis," *American Anthropologist,* 61 (1959), 200–220.

encountered in the traditional African context. The section that follows draws heavily on his basic outline, even as it attempts to expand and amplify it and to include many African examples that lay beyond the scope of his analysis.

In African political thought, a constant philosophical argument underlies the selection of political forms: the tension between *diffusion* of political power within a society and its *concentration*. Across the length and breadth of Africa and throughout its history, different leaders and political thinkers disputed what constituted the ideal form of government. As if agreeing with Solon on being asked what was the best form of government ("For what people and for what epoch?"), many Africans argued for different forms depending upon time and circumstances. Indeed, there was probably a rough balance between the number of traditional African political systems that opted for diffusion of power versus the number opting for centralization of that power.[11] African concern with the diffusion of power within segments of the same society represents a striking difference from the main body of western political thought, in which the diffusion of power has not been a favored assumption among political philosophers, at least until very recently.

In the African context, the chief distinction between societies has been between segmented types—in which political power was diffused through different groupings of the same society—and centralized forms—in which there is an identifiable political center. In the segmented type, there was a cultural nation, a linguistic nation, but not a political one in the sense of having a strong central political authority or, in many cases, even a central authority at all. Although the functions of a political system were performed, there was no central political structure, no political process for coordinating the activities of the various units except on a sporadic, *ad hoc* basis. Underlying the segmented form was the philosophical assumption that political power ought to be localized, fragmented, and dispersed, not focused on any central political authority.

In contrast, the centralized alternative had power concentrated at the center, with all groups (whether linked by kinship or not) owing allegiance to the political authority. Although there was a considerable variety of centralized forms within this pattern, the existence of a single political authority who was the recognized figure at the center of a discernible structure remained the key variable in comparison to the segmented types.

The Band

In our examination of this theme of African political thought, we begin by outlining various examples of these two political typologies, beginning with the segmented varieties. The first segment type is the *band organization*. The

---

[11]It is quite likely that several hundred years ago, segmented societies far outnumbered the more centralized forms.

hunting and food-gathering band was the predominant political pattern in Africa nearly 20,000 years ago. Now it is confined to a small number of widely dispersed groups: the Jie of Uganda, the Anaguta of Nigeria, the Namadi of Mauritania, the Tindiga and Bahi of Tanzania, the Twa of Rwanda, the Mbuti of Zaire, and the Kung of the Kalahari desert.

Although hundreds and even thousands of individuals may have belonged to the same linguistic and cultural group, they were broken down into small bands of 10 to 12 people, all of whom were related. Thus political relationships were coterminous with kinship relations so that the society and polity were one. The bands seldom interacted with each other and there was no leader of the entire group. Within the band, political power was exercised on an intermittent basis. There may have been a headman for an individual band, but decisions were usually made by all adult males sitting face to face. There were no ongoing political structures and little territorial basis for the band.[12] The leader may have organized the hunt and chosen the campsite but had no special prerogatives.

There was a blending of social, political, and economic systems. Indeed the survival of the band and the constant search for food predetermined much of the activity. Roles were allocated according to sex and age. In terms of its organization, the band can be represented in the following diagram:

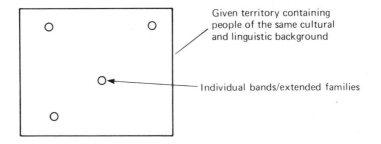

Given territory containing people of the same cultural and linguistic background

Individual bands/extended families

The small size of the band, its egalitarian nature, and the intermittent nature of its political process raise some interesting questions about the nature of political leadership. In food-gathering and hunting societies, particularly those living in harsh environments, leaders were made, not born (although some headmen may be sons of headmen). Perched on the edge of oblivion, the hunting band could not afford the luxury of bad leadership, for a foolish or headstrong leader could cause the demise of the band. In order to survive, the band must have good leadership over an extended period of time. One could well argue that it was not until there were food surpluses caused by the Nilotic

---

[12] At the same time, individual bands of Kung, for example, do have "their" waterholes and this limited territory is recognized by other bands. Nevertheless, the band does not owe its existence to a particular piece of territory as we associate with a modern state which has its particular "place."

revolution of 7,000 years ago that human collectivities developed the luxury of bad leadership. Nevertheless, despite its polyarchal configurations, the hunting band has been superseded as a political form by most other types, and the band is now confined to but a small percentage of African groups.

The Classical Segmented System

A far more widespread pattern is that of the *classical segmented system*. The classical form differed from the band in terms of the size and scope of individual segments, the amount of interaction among them, and the often rich and dynamic interplay between political authority and social cohesion. In the classical segmented system there was one cultural nation, the members of which recognized their affinities to it and their unity vis-à-vis other peoples, but the nation was broken down into a number of smaller units whose basis of membership was clearly kinship (although the kin grouping coagulated far larger units than extended families). Despite the sense of belonging to one nation, the segments were often in competition with one another, and numerous African writers have stressed the fissiparous nature of classical segmented systems.[13]

An interesting mechanism for damping intranational conflict and reducing the scope of violence once it breaks out is found among the Somalis. A pastoral and fiercely independent people, the Somali nation of nearly five million is divided into large clan families (such as the Dir and Hawiye), clans, primary lineages, and "dia paying" groups. The dia paying group represented the smallest acknowledged segment of Somali political life through a compact that warriors entered into for both the payment and receipt of blood compensation. Within Somali society, a conflict that resulted in the shedding of blood was resolved by the paying of a blood price in livestock. Individual warriors thus joined dia paying groups in order to seek protection and reduce their individual liability, much as people in more modern societies take out insurance.

The classical segmented system was found virtually everywhere in Africa: the Kru of Liberia and Sierra Leone, the Ibo of Nigeria, the Lobi of Upper Volta, the Nuer in the Sudan, the Kikuyu in Kenya, the Tallensi in Ghana, the Tonga of Zambia, and the Somali in Somalia, Ethiopia, and Kenya. For practical purposes, the clan was the basic unit for both life and politics. Depending on the society, a clan may have had a leader, a group of leaders, or a committee of elders, but there was no political authority for the entire nation. Some political offices within the clan were hereditary; others were elected.

---

[13]Works that illustrate both this competition and the difficulty of uniting the various segments in the face of an outside threat include Elechi Amadi, *The Great Ponds* (London: Heinemann, 1969); Flora Nwapa, *Efuru* (London: Heinemann, 1966); James Ngugi, *A Grain of Wheat* (London: Heinemann, 1967); and Chinua Achebe, *Things Fall Apart* (London: Heinemann, 1958).

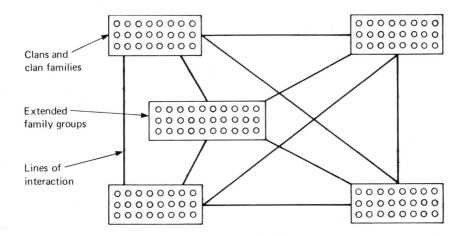

Among the classical systems, there was cultural, linguistic, and religious homogeneity but a weak territorial base. To live in a particular territory in no way conferred group membership on an individual. The home of the group was where the group was. In the southern Sudan, for example, various segmented systems were residentially interspersed as the Nuer, Dinka, and Shilluk. Groups of one system could be separated from other groups of the same system by an entirely different people.

As might be expected, the classical segmented systems, although often defeated by the colonial powers (in part as a result of being unable to coordinate resistance), presented occupying powers with considerable difficulties when they attempted to impose puppet leaders on entire cultural nations.[14] Judged by the ubiquitous nature of the classical pattern, many African societies found the dispersal of political authority a most satisfactory political philosophy and placed great stress on individual subgroup autonomy.

The Universalistic Segmented System

From our examination of hunting bands and classical segmented systems we can conclude that for those Africans who adopted these forms, the overriding concern was for the decentralization of political power, the egalitarian nature of the political process, and individual subgroup autonomy. The *universalistic segmented system* has these same concerns but suggests an additional pattern whereby there is a need for a common socialization process. Thus individual segments retain their political autonomy, but members of the various segments are brought together by a common process. Among a number of African peoples, this form was extremely popular. The cultural nation was

---

[14]Robert Tigner, "Colonial Chiefs in Chiefless Societies," *Journal of Modern African Studies,* vol. 9, no. 3 (1971), pp. 339–59.

divided into segmented subgroups; the people found within each territorial
unit were not necessarily limited by kinship groupings. But through the institution of age-sets, individuals from each segment left that segment to join with
their peers. Thus we can represent the pattern as follows:

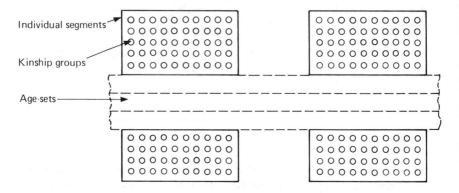

This blend of subgroup autonomy and common socialization was a distinctive feature of the Masai of Kenya and Tanzania, the Sandawe and Nyakusa
of Tanzania, and the Nandi, Kipsigi, and Meru of Kenya. Often the age-sets
were complicated, many-faceted organizations, with corresponding units for
men and women. Among the Nandi, for example, there were seven age grades,
self-renewing every 15 years.

Within these systems, political roles were generally allocated on the basis
of achievement. Often there were two sets of leaders, the village elders and the
warrior chiefs. This role allocation itself underlines an interesting assumption
about human collectivities and the nature of political leadership. Among the
people who adopted the universalistic segmented system, it was assumed that
a certain leader was good for one situation, such as peace, where certain
qualities were essential to preserve the societal order, settle disputes, and
generally harmonize the running of society. On the other hand, in a war
situation, the qualities that would make a leader—and hence a segment—
succeed would be of a different order. A frank recognition of this dichotomy
seems to be a common feature of the universalistic pattern and an interesting
component to African political thought.

In addition to the war chiefs and village elders, some of the universalistic
segmented systems also had the office of war prophet. This figure, who stood
at the interface between the political and the religious, had the very important
function of determining the proper time to go to war. Combining sagacity and
mysticism, the war prophets were often key figures in the determination of
public policy, especially the timing of its implementation. Called *laibon* among
the Masais, *orkoiyot* among the Nandi, and *mugwe* among the Meru, these
war prophets acted as a unifying force for the most part. There was often

considerable competition to become a war prophet, and this competition in and of itself often led to intersegmental strife. For example, a particularly violent upheaval within Masai society during 1889–1890 was due in large part to competition between several *laibon.*

The Ritually Stratified Segmented System

Another variation of the segmented system was the *ritually stratified.* This form was like the classical version but with some differentiation among religious offices and some social stratification based on the possession of certain sacred objects. The individual segments were more or less self-sufficient in economic and political terms but interacted for ritual concerns. There was considerable competition for ritual purposes. It is important to note that the central religious figure was both a symbol of national unity and the actual head of the nation for religious ceremonies, but enjoyed no political power.

For example, among the Shilluk of the Sudan, there was a "king" who was the symbolic referent for the nation, but who had no political power and could not order individual segments about. Whoever held the sacred objects was automatically the king. In Zaire, the Teke also had a "divine" king who was a ritual specialist but who also had no political power. Among the Ankole of Uganda there was a good deal of competition among the nobles, primarily for ritual positions.

The Ankole, divided as they were into two classes (the Bahima and Mairu, nobles and commoners), offer a striking amendment to the view that all African traditional societies were essentially classless. Although a substantial majority of African ethnic groups was egalitarian in terms of social classes, a number of groups were stratified to a considerable extent. Some prominent examples would be the Swazis and Zulus from southern Africa, the Amharas of Ethiopia, and the Anuak of the Sudan. Not only did these societies exist, but social stratification continued over a long period of time, presumably together with the concomitant philosophical rationale for such divisions.

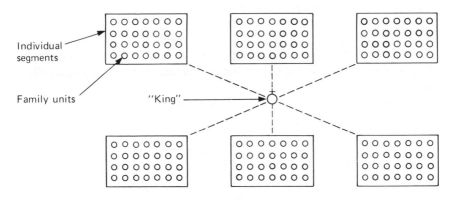

The Autonomous Village System

A final variation of the segmented pattern is that of the *autonomous village system*. In West Africa, as among the Ibibios of Nigeria and the Baule and Bakwe of the Ivory Coast, this pattern took the form of urbanized communities with relative ethnic homogeneity but with some breakdown in kinship linkages associated with urbanization. In East Africa, particularly among the Swahili speaking peoples, this took the form of recognized city-states.

Along the Indian Ocean, a series of city-states evolved based on trade. Although these shared a common culture and language, the area was not under any centralized political authority. Instead, individual city-states existed in autonomy, often with a wide variety of political forms. Some of the city-states enjoyed a republican form of government, others were run by despots, while still others were ruled by the bargaining process among commercial elites. All city-states had strong territorial bases (and these might expand or contract with the fortunes of war and trade) and a heterogeneous population, which might include numbers of non-Africans. Although these city-states shared a common historical and cultural affinity, there was an assumption of basic diversity and competition, often leading to warfare and conquest. Rather like the Renaissance city-states of Italy and the Greek city-states of the sixth century B.C., the Swahili units could identify and share a common cultural core, but the course of human events in the area was more likely to be determined by political and economic competition.

There were at least three prominent types of city-states, based on the amount of political centralization *within* the individual units for there was no overarching political office for all the city-states. Type one was a city-state under despotic control:

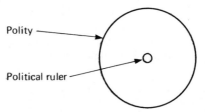

Type two consisted of a political unit run by a council; the council might be elected or might have seized power, but the leadership was in any case collective:

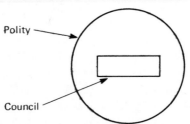

Type three might have a strong central political authority that accepted the notion of collective leadership but provided for a recognized head of the polity, a "first among equals":

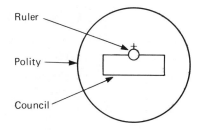

These various manifestations of the segmented system should give the reader a sense of its widespread character and its appeal to Africans. Clearly among the people who adopted this pattern, there was at least an implicit philosophical assumption that the government that governs least governs best, and that local autonomy was a political goal worth pursuing. If this meant fragmentation and internal division, even in the face of outside threats, if this meant often ponderous efforts to achieve cooperation among the units, nevertheless, millions of Africans felt that these were prices they were willing to pay in order to enjoy what they took to be the benefits of diffused political power.

Yet if millions of Africans adopted and maintained political systems based on the diffusion of power, so other millions, often within the same geographical area and with the same means of food production to sustain them, chose centralized forms of government with political power concentrated at the apex of the political system. These Africans assumed that the concentration of political power served the good of society better than the fragmentation of the segmented systems and that the loss of subgroup autonomy was a worthwhile price to pay for the strength and coordination that often accompanied a more centralized form. Certainly the early explorers, whether Arab or European, were far more impressed with the centralized forms—the great empires of Ghana, Songhai, and Mali from the eleventh to the sixteenth centuries, and later the kingdoms of Bakongo, Buganda, and Asante.

The Pyramidal Monarchy

At least three major variations of the centralized form occurred in Africa. The first of these, the *pyramidal or federated* variety, had a strong central authority and a recognized head of state, but also featured considerable subgroup autonomy. Within the subgroups, there was considerable self-regulation. Membership in the total community depended upon membership in one of the subgroups. There were no age-sets and the central political authority depended on the subgroups to raise armies, collect taxes, and the like. The central political authority was considered to be first among equals. The inner council was a major decision-making body consisting of the leaders of the various subgroups. A visual representation of the pyramidal form had the following characteristics:

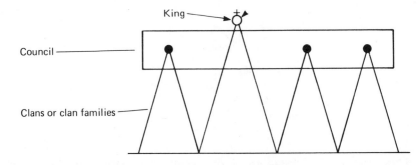

The king was almost always the head of one of the clan families. In the pyramidal arrangement there was often considerable social stratification, for the series of interlocking units were not always socially equal. This form of government existed all across Africa with such prominent examples as the Asante in Ghana, the Bemba in Zambia, the Xhosa in South Africa, the Haya, Hehe, and Shambala in Tanzania, the Oyo in Nigeria, the Baluba of Zaire, and the Alur and Lange of Uganda.

The Asante of Ghana remain one of the most interesting examples of this pattern. The leader of the Asante, the *asantehene,* was chosen by the council, which consisted of the heads of the various subgroups. Each subgroup leader had his own council, treasury, court, and military levees. The asantehene could be sure only of his own subgroup's support unless the council agreed on united action. Further, it was the council that invested the king with the office and its symbols (such as the golden stool), and it was the council that could strip the king of his power through the process known as *destoolment.* Throughout most of the history of the Asante, the council was a most potent force in the politics and economics of the nation.

However, the Asante system was not immutable and as the nation waxed strong on the slave trade, acquiring firearms and using them to expand Asante control over neighboring tribes, several asantehenes, most notably Osei Kwade, Osei Kwame, and Osei Bensu (who ruled from 1764 until 1824), attempted to expand the power of the political center. This well-documented attempt to enhance the power of the king is known collectively as the Kwado-wean revolution. It resulted in successive asantehenes taking more power at the expense of the subgroups, expanding the central bureaucracy and appointing chiefs to government of the subject peoples such as the Dagomba, the Mampensi, and the Gonja.[15] These chiefs were directly responsible to the

[15]J. K. Fynn, *Asante and Its Neighbours 1700–1807* (London: Longmans Group, 1971).

asantehene and had no independent standing. With the arrival of the British and the century-long struggle for control of the area (which lasted from 1806 until 1901), these trends toward centralization were reversed and the Asante never developed into a hierarchical kingdom, as occurred elsewhere in Africa.

In discussing the development of African political forms, it is important to remember that this federated type coexisted with both segmented and more highly centralized systems; so it cannot be said that one evolved from one type or one failed to evolve into another. Nor is there objective evidence to prove that one form was "better" than another, since one can argue that all forms served some societies well and all failed to solve some problems. Although one can point to the superiority of one form or another in a given instance, it is impossible to make an overall judgment setting one form over another. For the purposes of political philosophy, however, the pyramidal or federated form stands as a philosophical counterpoint to both the segmented types and the more centralized hierarchical form.

The Associational Monarchy

In addition to the pyramidal type outlined above, there is a second form of *federated monarchy, one with associational bases.* It was similar to the pyramidal type in terms of having a central political structure together with strong subgroup autonomy with its concomitant emphasis on the checks on royal power. Also there were no age-sets. Instead, there were a series of associational groups that cut across clan lines. These societies formed a link between the clan or village and the central political authorities. The societies assumed some political and administrative functions, such as the collection of debts, and there was considerable competition for the high posts within the societies. In many cases, electoral competition took on highly modern aspects.

This pattern occurred most notably in West Africa in what is now Sierra Leone, Liberia, and the Ivory Coast. One of the most conspicuous examples

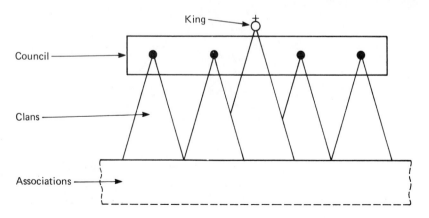

is found among the Mende of Sierra Leone. There the Poro society for men and the Sande society for women served as unifying institutions within the cultural nation. Made up of over one hundred levels or orders, the Poro and Sande societies cut across clan lines and required a three- to four-year initiation. Individuals were able to use their connections within the societies to extend social and economic contacts beyond their kin group or home village. The Kepelle of Liberia is another prominent example of this type.

The Centralized Monarchy

In contrast to both the federated and associational form, the *centralized or hierarchical monarchy* was distinguished by a strong central political administration, a firm territorial base, and heterogeneous membership. It was a widespread pattern in traditional African political systems, found among the Fipa of Tanzania, the Zulu, Nguni, Swazi, and Tswana of South Africa, the Hova-Merina of Madagascar, the Mossi of Upper Volta, and many others.

Membership in this type of system was not based solely upon kinship, nor did an individual have to join one of the subgroups. Instead, one joined by pledging direct allegiance to the king. The king had his own administration made up of both nobles and commoners. There were age-sets loyal to the king and he had the power to tax and call forth work parties for communal labor. Subgroup autonomy was limited, although some subordinate chiefs had considerable power. There was a king's council, whose membership was deter-

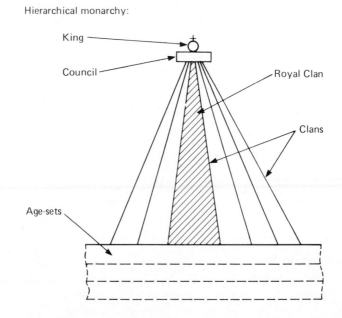

Hierarchical monarchy:

mined by the king. The central political authority stood at the apex of the nation. This type of system exhibited strong absorptive capabilities, the ability to amalgamate conquered peoples; it often permitted cultural pluralism.

The Zulus of the nineteenth century present us with a vivid account of this type of system and also indicate one difficulty with it—the succession mechanism. The kingship was hereditary but not by primogeniture. Rather, among the Zulus and the neighboring Swazis, the king was succeeded by the "eldest son of the king's favorite wife." Since the king may have had over a hundred wives, the succession situation was fraught with dangers and unrest, and regicide was not unknown. In both the kingdoms of Benin (which existed from the fourteenth to the nineteenth century in what is now Nigeria) and Fon (in what is now Benin), there were additional important examples of this type. In Benin, the oba or king stood at the head of a huge bureaucracy and presided over an extensive urban area. In the case of the Fon, the kingdom was divided into three definite classes—royal, commoner, and slave. The king enjoyed a royal bureaucracy of considerable size, a large standing army, and control over the economy.

Likewise among the Buganda of Uganda, the king or *kabaka* was vested with considerable power—to make war, to tax, to settle disputes, and to allocate land. In addition, he was the chief ritual specialist and controlled an extensive bureaucracy. The king's administration was divided into two parts. The saza chiefs who held sway over specific areas might or might not be hereditary, but they served at the king's pleasure. In addition, the kabaka appointed fiefholders to collect taxes, regulate tolls, and supervise the army and the largest navy in tropical Africa.

If we examine what is commonly referred to as the golden age of African empires, the period between the seventh and the sixteenth centuries in the west African savanna region, we see the most prominent examples of the hierarchical forms. The empires of Mali, Songhai, and Ghana were essentially hierarchical for most of their existence, even though many of their client states were of the segmented and pyramidal varieties. Subjugating a variety of other states with different ethnic, linguistic, and historical backgrounds, these empires flourished precisely because they were able to superimpose their political system on their conquests and to integrate them into the body politic.

The major advantage of the hierarchical system would seem to be in the area of its absorptive capability and its ability to marshal its resources in a way denied virtually all segmented systems. For example, at its height, the empire of Mali was able to put more than one hundred thousand men into the field in a military campaign. The enormous logistical prerequisites for such an effort would clearly be beyond most segmented systems. On the other hand, the loss of subgroup autonomy and the ability of the political center to dictate across a whole range of human activities were costs to be borne by those who favored the centralization of authority and the often greater physical security that went with it.

On balance then, as one scans the range of African political forms, one is struck over and over by the constant tension between those societies that favored the dispersal of political power and those that favored its concentration. Both strands of political thought have numerous supporters. Both served numerous societies well or ill, depending upon circumstances and quality of leadership. But in the last analysis, neither proved to be so superior to the other that the debate has ended. We shall be returning to this theme at the end of the chapter, for the dichotomy between those who favor—on philosophical or practical grounds—the concentration of authority and those who favor the diffusion of political power represents one of the continuing themes in contemporary African political life.

LIMITATIONS ON THE USE OF POLITICAL POWER

Western political thinkers are used to regarding constitutional checks and balances and formal institutionalization of a separation of powers as prerequisites for effective restraints on governmental power. Often they have assumed that formalization of these restraints is essential to prevent, or at least mitigate, the unrestricted use of power. In African societies, these checks on the use of political power were not often written down and not often formalized but they were no less real. They existed in virtually every African political system and must be regarded as being highly effective.

But their effectiveness was not always apparent to outsiders. Early European explorers seemed to be describing essentially two types of African political systems—those that were despotic and those that bordered on anarchy. As we have indicated earlier, many Europeans were unduly impressed with the centralized forms and what seemed to be the arbitrary use of power by African rulers:

> It is almost as though all of Africa south of the Sahara were permeated, as it were, by a mental blueprint of a despotic political structure.[16]

This cavalier statement could be simply dismissed as being silly were it not for the fact that many Europeans accepted it and other statements like it at face value. Now there can be little doubt that there were African political systems ruled by leaders who behaved arbitrarily and whose actions could aptly be called despotic. But a far more pronounced strand in African political thought consisted of a series of checks on the abuse of political power by rulers.

Africans generally considered society to be a community, with leadership designed to proceed toward the common good, with leaders tied directly to the

[16]George P. Murdock, *Africa: Its Peoples and Their Culture History* (New York: McGraw-Hill, 1959), p. 37.

people they led. This important aspect is clearly seen in the Sotho proverb, "A chief is a chief by the people; a people are a people through the chief." Throughout Africa a king or chief was bound by law to the society he led and separable from his office in the event of malfeasance or infirmity. Moreover, a leader could not rely on the regulative capability of his office to sustain him for long if he behaved completely irresponsibly or arbitrarily: "coercion is a luxury which not all societies can afford."[17]

In our analysis of traditional African political systems, we have discerned a substantial number of restraints on political behavior, whether within segmented systems or in more centralized forms.[18] One category of restraints concerns the nature of political officeholding in traditional society. The ruler or rulers, whether king, chief, or group of elders, were regarded as serving the society; they were there to punish law breakers, arbitrate disputes, and insure domestic tranquility. But they were to do so *within* the framework of existing custom. This body of custom gave them sanction and legitimacy, but it also imposed considerable restrictions on their behavior. Becoming a ruler meant assuming the responsibility of leading society *according to custom.*

Among the Mbuti, for example, a person who tried to rule outside the customary norms was ridiculed. Also, most African traditional communities exhibited a strong accent on the sharing of wealth, communal ownership or access to land, and a marked thrust toward what we would regard as basic welfare concerns. This ethos particularly shaped the political process. The political authority was expected to "watch over his subjects" and to be generous. A leader was regarded as poor indeed if he waxed prosperous while his subjects went hungry; generosity was regarded as a vital sign of superior leadership.

A second category of restraint impinged from the kinship net that surrounded the leader. The leader arose out of a certain lineage, he was responsible to it as a group, and he was expected to take advice from his kinsmen in terms of their views of society and law. Often, this check on political action was securely institutionalized. Among the Swazi and the Baganda, for example, a ruler's mother was regarded as having a sacred duty to admonish and rebuke him should he stray from the accepted norms of the society. Among the Sotho, the chief was to watch out for public safety and welfare, but he was in turn to be watched by his agnatic kinsmen, who were to advise him should he go wrong. Interestingly enough, among the Tallensi of northern Ghana, it was felt that one couldn't argue with one's ancestors (challenge the cake of custom) without putting one's very life in jeopardy.

Another strong restraint on the abuse of political power was exercised by

[17]Jacques Maquet, *Power and Society in Africa* (New York: McGraw-Hill, 1971), p. 95.

[18]For an interesting discussion of some restraints found among the Swazi, Baganda, Asante, and Nupe, see John Beattie, "Checks on the Abuse of Political Power in Some African States: A Preliminary Framework for Analysis," *Sociologus,* vol. 9, no. 2 (1959), pp. 97–115.

the elders in a given community. They were often regarded as an alternative source of legitimacy, and a political leader was obliged to get their opinions. As Oginga Odinga has written:

> A chief did not issue orders. He sounded out the elders and when he said "This is my decision" he was announcing not his personal verdict but an agreed point of view. His function was not to lay down the law, but to consult and arbitrate to learn the consensus of opinion and to keep the unity of his people.[19]

Councils were instrumental in curbing the power of leaders. Among the Swazis, for example, the king was always referred to as the Ngwenyama-in-council to signify his reliance on this body to sanction his actions. Among the Sotho peoples, the national *pitso* was an assembly open to all and its approval was vital for any major policy decision. Of course individual African leaders could ignore these political bodies, but only at their peril. Indeed, the evidence suggests that most rulers in African traditional systems felt that they had to rule by the consent of the governed.

If the ruler exceeded his authority, he could be removed from office. Even among the centralized monarchies such as the Asante, there were recognized procedures for removing the king. By the destoolment process, Asante kings were replaced by the council if they attempted to rule arbitrarily.[20] In many systems considerable power was vested in councils and other bodies, which served to keep the leaders in check. For example, among the Shambala a council of commoners not only watched the king's actions, they also nominated his successor. In short, the expectation that political leaders would accept advice from their councils and advisors is a most persistent theme in African political thought and action.

Associations and age-sets also functioned as institutional checks on the abuse of political power. We have previously outlined their functions in a variety of African societies. Where they existed, the political authority, in both formal and informal ways, was forced to take into account the wishes of the collective membership as well as those of the most prominent individuals within them. In addition to "talking until they agree" with councils and elders, the leaders had to bring these institutions into the decision-making process. The checks on a leader's scope of action could become quite significant. Among the Benin of Nigeria for example, the Oba was faced with an impressive array of institutions with which he had to validate public policy: important palace associations (the *iwebo, iweguae,* and the *ibiwe-eruerie*); town chiefs

---

[19]Oginga Odinga, *Not Yet Uhuru* (New York: Hill and Wang, 1967), p. 12.
[20]See K. A. Busia, *The Position of the Chief in the Modern Political System of Ashanti* (Oxford: Oxford University Press, 1951); and E. W. Smith, *The Golden Stool* (London: Halloran Publishing House, 1927).

representing forty to fifty wards; and finally the *uzama,* a body of seven hereditary chiefs with whom the Oba had to consult.

Less formal, but by no means less important a check on the course of individual political leadership, was dynastic rivalry. Unlike many European kingdoms that relied on primogeniture, most African political systems that had hereditary offices based the selection on the choice of a royal or family council. This caused considerable instability and jockeying of political power within those systems and countless plots and intrigues (as well as exciting interregnums). In this sense the succession mechanism can be viewed as dysfunctional. On the other hand, a leader knew he could be replaced, and that other siblings could acquire legitimacy; this undoubtedly led to a fear that support could be withdrawn and transferred to other candidates for the position. The arbitrary exercise of power, if sustained over a long period of time, increased the chances that the dynastic rivalry would threaten the ruler. Most African leaders depended on the support of major institutions and prominent figures within the society and were acutely aware of this dependence. The existence of rival claimants to the throne simply underscored that dependence.

One of the most extreme ways of reacting to the abuse of power by a political authority was emigration. Especially in central and southern Africa, the tradition of "hiving off" to escape unpopular or despotic leadership was widespread. Given the sparsely populated nature of the area, this was a viable option for those seeking to avoid a particular leader. Of course, the emigrants might be pursued and killed by that authority, but this was clearly beyond the ability of many political authorities. Particularly during the period of Zulu expansion, new political groups sprang up in southern Africa to avoid conquest or even to escape the harsh rule of Chaka. Such nations as the Sotho, Swazi, and Ndebele owed their expansion during this period to numerous refugees from the upheavals caused by the Zulu kingdom and from the kingdom itself.

Indeed, the formation and/or expansion of many political entities in southern and central Africa were the direct result of emigration. Some tribes grew because they were in a key location, others enlarged through conquest and absorption, while still others gained by accepting refugees from other ethnic groups. Among the Lunda, for example, between the sixteenth and eighteenth centuries, the mechanism of positional succession and perpetual kinship (whereby a successor inherited both the office and the kinship lineages of the deceased) helped to amalgamate the nation and assist its considerable expansion, both through conquest and the absorption of individuals and groups who had fled from elsewhere.[21]

A final check on the abuse of power that we should consider at this point is sorcery or black magic. We shall be developing the interrelationship between

[21]Jan Vansina, *Kingdoms of the Savanna* (Madison: University of Wisconsin Press, 1968).

religion and politics in the next section, but there we are concerned with the specific political ramifications of religious belief on the limitation of political power. In many African societies, leaders were afraid that they would be the target of sorcery if they deviated from accepted norms. Of course many became targets irrespective of their political actions, but the assumption that even the lowliest and weakest commoner could call on enormous supernatural powers was a consistent and potent check on the arbitrary use of power. For example, when the Swazi king Ubunu died in 1890, the Queen Mother appealed to the British to let the royal impis kill witches "for just one day," blaming them for the death of her son. Often the fear of sorcery could get out of control and itself become the source of arbitrary action, as with the paranoia of Chaka that resulted in the killings of hundreds, if not thousands, of innocent people. But more germane for our purposes, many African societies that functioned without widespread bloodletting maintained the tradition that supernatural forces could be enlisted against despotic or even unpopular leaders.[22]

Thus, even a cursory glance at African traditional political systems indicates the extent to which the diminution of political power and checks on its arbitrary use were widespread in African political thought. Despots rose and fell, but they did so against the prevailing political climate in most societies. African traditional society, although it often demanded strong leadership for protection and security, also constantly returned to the theme that political power should be subject to a number of formal and informal checks on its use.

RELIGION AND POLITICAL PHILOSOPHY

In this section, we are not concerned with why individuals turn to religion in Africa, whether as a way of staving off the chaos of the universe or of giving them confidence in the face of death. Rather, we are interested specifically in the relationship between religious belief and the social order. Nor is it being suggested that the intertwined nature of religion and politics is an essentially African phenomenon. For as Parrinder has so aptly expressed, the intermingling of religion and politics is an almost universal phenomenon, one hardly confined to Africa.[23]

The intertwined nature of religion and politics is evident everywhere in African traditional political thought. The chief or political leader was almost always viewed as a representative of the ancestors who had gone before. On one hand, the chief political figure served as a link with the spirit world—the

[22]For variations on this theme, see Dominic Mulasisho, *The Tongue of the Dumb* (London: Heinemann, 1971) in which Chief Mpona is held responsible for natural disasters and is himself considered a witch.

[23]Geoffrey Parrinder, *Witchcraft: European and African* (London: Faber & Faber, 1963). See also his *Religion in Africa* (Baltimore: Penguin Books, 1969). A more recent work is Norman Cohn, *Europe's Inner Demons* (New York: Basic Books, 1975).

space-time continuum that made African cosmology so immediate.[24] He was thus tied to what had gone before and what was to come. In addition, as mentioned earlier, the cake of custom both supported the leader and circumscribed his actions. By his participation in the religious rites of passage—birth, adolescence, and death—his legitimacy was reinforced by the persuasive and pervasive nature of religion in Africa.

It is now generally held by serious students of religious systems throughout Africa that many, if not most, African societies believed in a High God or Supreme Deity who created the world.[25] This more recent view contrasts sharply with the notions of many European observers in the eighteenth, nineteenth, and early twentieth centuries who saw African religions as essentially animistic or polytheistic. It now seems clear that the existence of spirits and lesser gods obscured this central fact of African religion. Furthermore, for Africans in a traditional setting, religion and life were inseparable; the sacred and the profane merged both within time and at any moment in time. By defining man's place in the universe and within society, religion was a key element in preserving the stability of African political traditions. Especially in such segmented systems as the Tele of Zaire or the Nuer of the Sudan, religious ritual was enormously supportive to the noncentralized forms of government.

By regulating conduct, African religions supported those authority figures who were charged with the preservation of societal order. It is true that in many societies isolation and a strong sense of cultural and linguistic unity also tended to support the existing order. We could cite innumerable examples, but this phenomenon has been amply witnessed in a great variety of systems, most notably the Dinka of the Sudan, the Kalabari of Nigeria, and the Azande of Sudan, Central African Empire, and Zaire. Religion and politics were fused —whether one speaks of divine descent of leaders, the supportive aspects of magico-religious ceremonies, or the interface of the religious and the political at the various mysterious circumstances of confirmation, whether of individuals or of the group. Often the political authority officiated at public religious rites, reflecting both his place in the cosmos and the society.

There is another side to the religious interplay with society. One normally speaks of good magic and bad magic in relation to their impact on society: good magic makes it rain for the crops and produces societal harmony; bad magic adversely affects food production and causes harm. In most African societies, it was assumed that "nothing harmful happens 'by chance': everything is 'caused' by someone directly or through the use of mystical power."[26]

With this assumption, sorcery or "bad" magic can be seen to have an enormously pejorative impact on society. That is why sorcerers were feared

---

[24]He was thus an embodiment of the previous order.
[25]K. A. Busia, *Africa in Search of Democracy* (New York: Praeger, 1967), p. 4.
[26]John S. Mbiti, *African Religions and Philosophies* (Garden City, N.Y.: Doubleday, 1970), p. 262.

(hence they served as a check on the exercise of political power) and why their activities could be highly divisive within society. The belief in widespread sorcery in a particular society was very unsettling, often with the result that individuals could never feel completely safe. Most of the time, individuals dealt with their difficulties on a bilateral basis, that is, by coming to diviners and medicine men to get them to work good magic to contravene the bad.

But sometimes the pejorative impact could be cumulative and have profound political consequences, ultimately placing responsibility for the turmoil on the chief, either by blaming him or by doubting that his power was sufficient to ward off evil. Since the notion of community runs so strongly throughout all African societies, and since the maintenance of order was such a primary goal, political leaders were forced to attempt to curtail antisocial actions by developing countervailing influences of a magico-religious nature. Political authorities sought out ritual specialists in order to enlist their support. For a political authority in traditional African society to have a good ritual specialist was like having a good tax collector or an effective general in one's army:

> The witch-doctor has a power like that of witches. By this power he recognizes those who are using witchcraft, and heals those who are bewitched. But the power is very delicate and is fraught with danger to the possessor. For if the witch-doctor gave way to the temptation to use his power against an enemy, he was caught inescapably in the grip of his own force and became a witch himself.[27]

This is one reason why political leaders, either by their office or their use of ritual personnel, attempted to keep the society from unraveling in the face of supernatural forces. For many of the kingdoms, the sacred nature of the office was built into the political process; the asantehene of the Asante, the kabaka of Buganda, the Ngwenyama of Swaziland, even the litunga of Barotseland, all were thought *to have been vested* with supernatural powers.[28] Those kings who wore the mantle of the supernatural well were also astute political leaders, and the sacred and the profane were clearly positively merged.

Perhaps one of the most powerful accounts of the interplay between religion and politics, between political authority and spirituality, is to be found in Laye's *The Radiance of the King*.[29] Although in large part allegorical and primarily intended to draw conclusions about the nature of blackness, the novel is also a penetrating description of the supernatural aura diffused through figures of political importance in Africa.

Although there is not space in this chapter to discuss the subject, the reader should be aware of the enormous importance of religion in the political strug-

[27]Parrinder, *Witchcraft*, p. 183.

[28]For an overview of the kinship phenomenon in contemporary Africa, see Rene Lemarchand (ed.), *Kingship in Africa* (London: Frank Cass, 1975).

[29]Camara Laye, *The Radiance of the King* (Paris: Librairie Plon, 1956).

gle against the onset of colonial rule and its eventual overthrow. Even today, politics in Africa is infused with religious interplay, particularly on the local level.[30] In traditional African political settings, this phenomenon was even more pronounced and more enduring. That religion and politics are, and *ought* to be, intertwined is another persistent theme in traditional African political thought.

THE IMPORTANCE OF GERONTOCRACY
IN AFRICAN POLITICAL THOUGHT

The last theme with which we shall deal in this chapter is the African assumption that age and wisdom are correlated. Virtually every society under review, irrespective of political system and location, maintained that age conferred wisdom and that there was something special about the political knowledge of an older person. Particularly in segmented systems and especially in peacetime settings, the role of the elders was considerable. Running the gamut from settling domestic quarrels to setting public policy, the older men within any society exercised political power all out of proportion to their numbers. Indeed, a large portion of the output—at least in terms of decision making—of any given system was attributable to the elders.

How is this explained? Generally speaking, traditional societies developed in Africa as communities of families. Even when the collectivity expanded, kinship lineages were of paramount importance in determining societal rank. Many African communities were more or less isolated for long periods of time and not subject to a rapid incidence of traumatic shocks from the outside.[31] Such a context fostered not only social conformity, but also societal norms that did not change much over time. Although it would be a gross oversimplification to say that knowledge was not cumulative or that society was static, nevertheless, for most societies the pace of change was slow. Consequently, it was possible for an individual to accumulate most of the knowledge of his society within his or her lifetime.

Therefore the basic African assumption that age denoted accumulated knowledge and wisdom was essentially correct. As a societal norm emerged, it was further assumed that the elders, who had accumulated this store of knowledge, could pass it on to the young. Elders, who had lived their lives despite high mortality rates and warfare, therefore became the repositories of knowledge and wisdom within their respective societies. Knowledge became wisdom, and wisdom, power.

[30]See for example John Paden, *Religion and the Political Culture in Kano* (Los Angeles: University of California Press, 1973).

[31]The slave trade and colonization were of course traumas of the first order.

The youth were inculcated with the learning of their elders, and as they advanced through life they in turn became elders. Life had a definite rhythm and progression. Among the Arusha of Tanzania, for example, both the youth and the elders were each divided into two grades. Each grade of youth or elder brought with it certain ornamental restrictions, food and weapon restrictions, and, above all, decision-making restrictions. Only the senior elders, it was assumed, had earned the right to make the decisions that would affect the lives of all.

African political practices reflected this strand of thinking. Even though a gerontocracy was not an ideal form of society, even though the youth often disagreed with the elders' decisions, more often than not they accepted the principle that the elders were correct in making the decisions.[32] It was this concept of legitimacy, based on age that held the political and social fabric together. Often decisions were made slowly, ponderously. Often change was inhibited by the cultural emphasis on the wisdom of age. But the assumption of the worth of a gerontocracy was an accepted value in most African societies and whatever the difficulties of such an assumption in coping with the changes and stresses of modern life, it did serve African societies well for an extended period of time.

CONCLUSION

The important themes in traditional African political thought that we have examined in this chapter are not without relevance for the present situation in Africa. Despite colonial patterns superimposed on African societies and the artificial grid that resulted from the partition of the continent, the African heritage remains a significant factor influencing the course of politics today.[33] Allowing for individual leadership differences, divergent economic patterns, and the continuing intrusion of the forces of international capitalism, socialism, and communism, nevertheless, African political figures as well as academicians must examine the impact of that heritage on different countries. Without any doubt, the importance of traditional African political forms and traditional political thought for postindependent Africa is one of the most overlooked themes in African political analysis. Full exploration of such a theme lies beyond the scope of this chapter, but a number of questions readily come to mind:

[32]For a delightful account of the frustrations of the young within the confines of a gerontocracy, see Francis Bebey, *Agatha Moudio's Son* (London: Heinemann, 1967).

[33]Even the process of urbanization had begun long before the Europeans arrived. See Richard W. Hull, *African Cities and Towns Before the European Conquest* (New York: W. W. Norton, 1976).

1.   Does the single-party apparatus and the military forms that have succeeded it in so many African countries really attempt to come to grips with the basic pluralism of the African traditional societies?

2.   Is the cause of nation building most assisted if the borders of the modern state include segmented systems rather than centralized ones?

3.   Do the conflicting legacies of diffusion versus centralization of power constitute the most fundamental challenge to those who would develop a national apparatus for the integration of a variety of traditional forms?

4.   Has the intrusion of modern political forms and processes successfully overridden the age-old emphasis on the interrelationship between religion and politics?

5.   Given the widespread indication of segmented systems in traditional African life, have practitioners and theoreticians alike both missed an important, perhaps critical, variable in the process of national integration?

6.   Has the legitimacy that age and collective leadership traditionally gave to a political system been fully compensated for by the variations of African socialism and other ideologies?

7.   How much of the instability of postindependent Africa has been due to a failure to come to grips with the underlying realities of the African political heritage?

Both the inherent pluralism of African traditional forms *and* the commonality of other persistent themes would suggest that there is a great deal more to be examined and analyzed before a coherent and perspicuous holistic theory of African politics can emerge. In the chapters that follow, we hope to explore a number of ramifications that seem to have substantial bearing on the course of politics in Africa.

2

The Colonial Overlay and the African Response

Morton Schoolman

The traditional political forms outlined in the previous chapter transcended and, in many cases, outlived the colonial overlay. Yet the arrival of Europeans, with their political ideas and the ideology of colonialism, nevertheless altered and affected the ways Africans looked at both the polity and political thought. And equally important for the course of politics in Africa today, the colonial overlay spurred a series of reactions that clearly influence the conduct of the political process in the nearly fifty African states.

Many writers have stressed the differences between the various colonial patterns: the indirect rule of the British, the Cartesian wholeness of the French, the sleepy repression of the Portuguese, and so on.[1] Yet all colonial systems shared a number of characteristics and common qualities that conclusively influenced the course of politics in Africa.

By and large, all colonial systems in Africa were imposed, or at least maintained, by the use of force. The scramble for Africa that affected the European powers in the latter decades of the nineteenth century led to the imposition of colonial systems generally opposed by the indigenous peoples. While it is true that certain ethnic units, such as the Sotho and the Swazi, petitioned one colonial authority (in this case, the British) to bring a colonial pattern, this was often done out of fear of other European encroachment (in this case, the Afrikaners). In point of fact, hundreds of thousands of Africans lost their lives resisting the onset of colonialism and rebelling against it.

All colonial systems were also authoritarian; that is, undemocratic. They were authoritarian in both form and substance. Decisions were made by the colonial authority and imposed on the subject peoples. The political patterns were overwhelmingly hierarchical, and Africans were systematically excluded from decision-making roles in the colonial system. Although some systems— such as the French—provided for African access to the political process, including representation in Paris, this participation was sporadic and without undue relevance until decolonization was well advanced.

All colonial systems were likewise disruptive. Although the amount of disruption varied widely from place to place and group to group, on balance, the European penetration and subsequent imposition of economic and political structures disconcerted the indigenous societies. Some traditional systems—as in the case of the Kikuyu—were thrown out of whack by technological and medical advances (which led to overpopulation). Others were decimated by the onset of colonialism—as in the case of the Herero. New material goods, new knowledge, and above all, new political ideas stirred the essence of traditional life. As we shall see in Chapter 4, the changes wrought by colonialism remain a major theme in African thought today.

All colonial systems were essentially exploitive in character. Individual officials may well have sought to improve the life of the colonial peoples, but

[1]See, for example, D. K. Fieldhouse, *The Colonial Empires* (New York: Delacorte Press, 1965); R. Betts, *Assimilation and Association in French Colonial Theory* (New York: Columbia University Press, 1961); H. Brunschwig, *French Colonialism, 1871–1914: Myths and Realities* (London: Pall Mall, 1964); William Cohen, *Rulers of Empire* (Stanford, Calif.: Stanford University Press, 1971); M. Crowder, *West Africa Under Colonial Rule* (Evanston, Ill.: Northwestern University Press, 1968); J. Duffy, *Portugal in Africa* (Baltimore: Penguin Books, 1962); J. Duffy, *Portuguese Africa* (Cambridge, Mass.: Harvard University Press, 1959); D. Bruce Marshall, *The French Colonial Myth and Constitution-Making in the Fourth Republic* (New Haven, Conn.: Yale University Press, 1973); V. Ram, *Comparative Colonial Policy* (New York: Longmans, 1929); S. Roberts, *History of French Colonial Policy* (London: King and Company, 1929); B. S. Smith, *But Always as Friends* (Durham, N.C.: Duke University Press, 1969); Cartey Wilfred and Martin Kilson (eds.), *The African Reader* (New York: Random House, 1970).

the systems *qua* systems were overwhelmingly exploitive. Whether we are talking about forced labor, the extraction of primary products, the profits made by the captive markets for industrial and manufactured goods, or the use of African soldiers in European wars, the net balance is heavily weighted on the side of the colonizers and heavily against the colonials. The exceptions—British Somalia or Lesotho—are just that. Overall, the colonies were lucrative for the colonizer, especially if you include the total exploitive balance from the private as well as the public sector.

As many writers have noted, the very process by which the colonial powers acquired African real estate meant the colonial authorities were all arbitrary in their imposition of a structural grid over their African areas.[2] The Ewe found themselves divided in half by the British and the French. The Bakongo found themselves ruled by the French, the Belgians, and the Portuguese. The Somalis were divided between the Italians, the British, the French, and the Ethiopians. Traditional political systems were seriously affected by these impositions. In the final analysis, the structural grid and the colonial boundaries may well prove to be the most enduring of the colonial legacies.

Most important, both for the nature of colonialism as practiced in Africa and for the course of African political thought, all colonial systems were racist in the most fundamental sense of that word. All declared that European values were superior to those held by Africans. Africans were felt—by virtue of their genes *and* their cultures—to be inferior to their European counterparts.

Moreover, the colonial system, by introducing its ideology of racial and cultural superiority, had an enormous psychological impact on many African leaders; they had to decolonize themselves, their personalities, and their intellects before they could decolonize their countries. This process is today by no means complete, and even where the physical structures of colonialism are absent, many psychological remnants endure.

THE SCOPE OF COLONIALISM

With the exception of Liberia, every country now in existence in Africa came under colonial rule at one time or another. The time frames for these occupations differ greatly. Ethiopia, for example, was under Italian control for only

[2]R. Betts (ed.), *The "Scramble" for Africa* (Boston: D. C. Heath, 1966); M. E. Chamberlain, *The Scramble for Africa* (London: Longmans, 1974); J. Hargreaves, *Prelude to the Partition of West Africa* (London: Macmillan, 1963); David Killingray, *A Plague of Europeans* (Harmondsworth: Penguin Education, 1973); G. Lichtheim, *Imperialism* (New York: Praeger, 1971); G. Nadel and P. Curtis, *Imperialism and Colonialism* (New York: Macmillan, 1964); R. Rotberg and A. Mazrui (eds.), *Protest and Power in Black Africa* (London: Oxford University Press, 1970); R. Winks (ed.), *British Imperialism* (New York: Holt, Rinehart and Winston, 1965); H. M. Wright, *The New Imperialism* (Boston: D. C. Heath, 1961).

five years, while parts of Angola and Mozambique were under Portuguese rule for over four hundred years.

Spanish colonialism was introduced into Spanish Sahara, Rio Muni, and several enclave cities in Morocco. Germany came to Togo, the Cameroons, Tanganyika, and southwest Africa. Portuguese colonialism was brought to the Cape Verde Islands, Portuguese Guinea, Angola, and Mozambique. Italy occupied Eritrea, Somalia, and Ethiopia. The French controlled vast stretches of North Africa, French West Africa, and French Equatorial Africa. The Belgians took the Congo, Rwanda, and Burundi, while Great Britain occupied Gambia, Sierra Leone, Ghana, Nigeria, South Africa, Tanzania, Kenya, Uganda, British Somalia, Ethiopia, and the Sudan.

In addition to introducing new linguistic patterns, the colonial partition of Africa in the latter decades of the nineteenth century cut across existing physical, cultural, and linguistic units, as well as across economic, political, and ethnic groupings. At this point in time, it is difficult to assess objectively all the ramifications of the European occupation. Certainly, the European powers came for a variety of reasons: economic, strategic, social; for prestige, wealth, living space and, on occasion, philanthropy. The colonial countries created new administrative entities, superimposed a grid of rather artificial order across most of Africa, and introduced medical and technological advances. On one level, the colonial experience served to unify areas by providing a focal authority (though often an enemy) and, at least briefly, a common historical experience. In addition, for the 5 to 10 percent of the indigenous population who became literate, the language of the colonial authority provided a medium of communication.

Yet, the European penetrations also reinforced and, in some cases, created tribal, linguistic, and ethnic divisiveness. At the very least, the colonial experience set up new lines of division (such as Anglophone versus Francophone Africa) that may ultimately prove difficult to obliterate, and established an international economic relationship with the metropole that will have a pejorative impact on the creation of inter-African economic units.

The onset and style of British colonial rule differed from area to area.[3] It has generally been characterized as "indirect rule," referring to the widespread practice of allowing the traditional tribal authorities to remain in place and of ruling the Africans through these leaders. British rule in Northern Nigeria, Buganda, and Barotseland are classical examples of this style. In other areas, particularly those with large numbers of European settlers, a type of dual rule

[3]There is a vast literature on the British colonial impulse. Among the most useful are Ronald Robinson and John Gallagher, *Africa and the Victorians* (London: Macmillan, 1965); Robert Huttenback, *The British Imperial Experience* (New York: Harper & Row, 1966); Baron Hailey, *Native Administration in the British African Territories* (London: His Majesty's Stationary Office, 1953); and Robin W. Winks (ed.), *British Imperialism* (New York: Holt, Rinehart and Winston, 1963).

developed whereby Europeans and Africans were administrated as separate, albeit connected, entities. Irrespective of the context, however, the African authorities suffered from a loss of power and, in many cases, legitimacy.

Generally speaking, British colonial policy was designed to provide a stable framework for commerce, industry, and some settlement. There was no attempt to transform all aspects of African life. Colonies were expected to pay for their administration, and education was largely entrusted to church groups and philanthropic organizations. The British did permit some freedom of association in the form of cultural societies, labor unions, and, ultimately, political parties. At the same time, there existed firm social segregation or color bar, and most Africans were denied direct participation in the governmental process until the 1950s.

The French colonial system, at least in theory, was based on the concept that the colonies were a part of France and that, as such, they should be integrated economically and politically into a larger framework, with a small number of elite Africans being gradually absorbed into French life. Thus, there was strong emphasis on a central administration and control over the educational, economic, and political life of the territories. In reality, the policy was applied differently from place to place and time to time. On occasion, the French used a type of indirect rule *(politique des races)*.[4] The Berbers of Morocco, the Agni of the Ivory Coast, and the Tuaregs of Mauritania, Mali, and Niger were treated in this way, although most of sub-Saharan Africa was ruled more directly. The French government drew a pronounced line between its citizens (the literate, assimilated Africans) and its subjects. Individuals could attain equal status with Frenchmen, but, generally, this trend was not permitted to interfere with a view of the colonies as a source of manpower for France, an outlet for the goods of the metropole, and a source of raw materials. Forced labor (corvée) was widely practiced until 1947 and the precise degree of segregation varied from area to area, often depending upon the number of European settlers.

The Belgian colonial operation began in 1885 when the Congo Free State became the personal fief of Leopold II.[5] Even after the territory became a

[4]Stephen Roberts, *History of French Colonial Policy* (London: King and Company, 1929); Michael Crowder, *Senegal: A Study in French Assimilation Policy* (Oxford: Oxford University Press, 1962); R. Betts, *Assimilation and Association in French Colonial Theory* (New York: Columbia University Press, 1961); Francois Luchaire, *Les Institutions Politiques et Administratives des Territoires d'outremer apres La Loi-Cadre* (Paris: Librairie Generale de Droit et de Jurisprudence, 1958).

[5]For the early period see John de Courcy MacDonnell, *King Leopold II, His Rule in Belgium and the Congo* (London: Cassell and Company, 1905). The span of Belgian rule is well covered in Paul Bouvier, *L'Allession du Congo Belge a L'Independence* (Bruxelles: L'Institut de Sociologie de L'Universite Libre de Bruxelles, 1965); and Belgian Ministere des Colonies, *La Reorganisation Politique Indigene du Ruanda-Urundi* (Bruxelles: Belgian Ministere des Colonies, 1952); also, Roger Arstey, *King Leopold's Legacy* (London: Oxford University Press, 1966); and Ruth Slade, *King Leopold's Congo* (London: Oxford University Press, 1962).

Belgian colony in 1908 and Rwanda-Burundi was added as a mandate in 1924, the style remained overwhelmingly paternalistic. Control was centralized and there was a strong accent on economic development. Assimilation was not a major goal, and the distinction between European and *évolué* African was nearly as great as that between *évolué* and the mass of *indigènes.*

The Roman Catholic Church offered one of the few avenues for upward social mobility and even here, results were highly mixed. The Belgians introduced widespread medical facilities and primary and technical education but drastically limited the number of Africans attending secondary and university facilities.[6] Investment, both public and private, was extensive, and the Congo evolved a highly developed economic infrastructure. However, neither political parties nor independent African trade unions were allowed until just prior to independence, and ethnic and regional fragmentation was encouraged. Preparation for independence was minimal.

The Portuguese came to Africa in the sixteenth century and remained until 1975. For centuries, they administered their colonial areas in a haphazard and sporadic fashion.[7] The ravages of slaving and the importation of the feudal *prazzo* system did much to insure that the writ of the colonial governors seldom extended much beyond the coast. A tiny fraction of the Africans became assimilated into the *neoindigena* class (*assimilados* and Europeans), but, generally speaking, scant opportunity for education, a high incidence of forced labor, and strict enforcement of the *caderneta,* or passbook system, as well as generally harsh treatment, insured that few Africans ever crossed the cultural barrier. Although the colonial system was one of direct control, the Portuguese often encouraged tribal separatism and ethnocentricity. Color bar was less severe than in the English or Belgian territories, but was largely outweighed by a lack of civil liberties, few opportunities for African associations, and low levels of economic activity.

The Italians were among the last of the European powers to acquire colonies in Africa, arriving in the 1880s. Although of only minor consequence to most

---

[6]Dodge estimates, for example, that prior to independence, 60 percent of school-age children in the Congo were in primary school, 2.2 percent in secondary education. See Dorothy Dodge, *African Politics in Perspective* (Princeton, N.J.: Van Nostrand, 1966), p. 51. The Belgian case is given in J. Vanhove, *L'Oeuvre d'Education au Congo Belge et au Ruanda-Urundi* (Bruxelles: Encyclopedie du Congo Belge, 1953).

[7]James Duffy, *Portugal in Africa* (Cambridge, Mass.: Harvard University Press, 1962) and *Portuguese Africa* (Cambridge, Mass.: Harvard University Press, 1959), and Ronald H. Chilcote, *Portuguese Africa* (Englewood Cliffs, N.J.: Prentice-Hall, 1967) present a stern indictment of Portugal. Antonio de Figueiredo, *Portugal and its Empire: The Truth* (London: Victor Gollancz, 1961), and Adriano Moreira, *A Policy of Integration* (Lisbon: Secretariado Nacional da Informaqao, 1961) and *Portugal's Stand in Africa* (New York: University Publishers, 1962) provide a somewhat different perspective, as does Alberto Franco Nogueira, *The United Nations and Portugal* (London: Sedgwick and Jackson, 1963) and *The Third World* (London: Johnson Publications, 1967). Gilberto Freyre, although speaking about Brazil in his *New World in the Tropics* (New York: Knopf, 1959), indicates what might have been.

of the continent, they did play an important role in the Horn of Africa.[8] Libya, Ethiopia, Eritrea, and Somalia, at one time or another, were under Italian control. For the most part, Italian colonial rule was direct, although in the remote areas of Ethiopia and Somalia it was seldom much in evidence. The economic sphere was characterized by monopolies and parastatal organizations. In exchange for the development of a physical infrastructure and exposure to Italian culture, the colonies provided living space for Italian immigrants, some raw materials, and prestige. Particularly after the coming to power of the Fascists, there was a good deal of official color bar, and the Africans were denied political participation.

Nevertheless, on the local level, many Italian settlers enjoyed more or less amicable relations with the peoples of the Horn, and many stayed on after Eritrea was merged with an independent Ethiopia, and Somalia became independent. Interestingly enough, although the British conquered Somalia during 1941, the area was handed back to the Italians for administrative purposes under United Nations auspices from 1950 until 1960. Most importantly for the future of the Somali political system, Italian administration of most of the Horn gave the pan-Somali leaders a firm precedence for the idea of a Greater Somalia encompassing portions of Ethiopia and Kenya.

German colonial rule extended over Togo, the Cameroons, southwest Africa, Rwanda-Burundi, and German East Africa (which later became Tanganyika).[9] From 1884 to 1906, German rule was strongly militaristic and repressive in character. There were major revolts in southwest Africa (Hereros) and German East Africa (Maji-Maji). Exploitive German companies vied with each other for economic spoils and made little attempt to ameliorate the plight of the Africans. After the German elections of 1906, however, the style of German rule changed dramatically as a strong, vigorous policy aimed at long-range economic and political development was implemented. After military pacification, each of the colonial areas came under the direction of a governor and large numbers of developmental schemes were inaugurated.

It was expected that the colonies would provide the raw materials for an industrial Germany; therefore, physical infrastructure and plantation agriculture were developed. European settlers were never extensive and numbered

[8]See M. H. Macartney, *Italy's Foreign and Colonial Policy* (London: Oxford University Press, 1938); Tommaso Tittoni, *Italy's Foreign and Colonial Policy* (London: Smith, Elder and Company, 1914); Luigi Villari, *The Expansion of Italy* (London: Faber & Faber, 1930); F. Quaranta Di San Severino, *Development of Italian East Africa* (New York: Italian Library of Information, 1940); and R. R. DeMarco, *The Italianization of African Natives* (New York: Columbia University Press, 1943).

[9]Perhaps the best works on Gemany's colonial history are Mary E. Townsend, *The Rise and Fall of Germany's Colonial Empire 1884–1918* (New York: Howard Fertig, 1966), and Harry R. Rudin, *Germans in the Cameroons 1884–1914* (London: Jonathan Cape, 1938). Two more political works are Henrich Schnee, *German Colonization Past and Future* (New York: Knopf, 1926), and G. L. Steer, *Judgment on German Africa* (London: Hudder and Stoughton, 1939).

only 25,000 in 1914. German colonial authorities, although strict and harsh, generally enjoyed a reputation for fairness and relied on a modified form of indirect rule with some local self-government and native treasures. The German government established government schools and subsidized mission work in the area of education. It was the official policy of the government to restrict both forced labor and corporal punishment, although these undoubtedly occurred as late as World War I. With the defeat of Germany during World War I, the German colonial areas were divided among Britain, France, Belgium, and South Africa. German East Africa became Tanganyika under British control and a League of Nations mandate. Partially because of this dual authority and the small numbers of European settlers, Tanganyika developed a unique political system and emerged in 1961 as the first independent state in East Africa.

When one reads of the differing colonial policies of the European powers, the Afrikaner style is often overlooked. To be sure, the 60 percent of the European population of South Africa, whose native language is Afrikaans, is indigenous to Africa, at least to the extent that they have no European homeland to which they can return. Nevertheless, it is important to see that the blend of Dutch and French Huguenot cultures, which merged to form the Afrikaner national group, represents a colonial system in its own right. The Afrikaans-speaking settlers, arriving in South Africa in the seventeenth century, moved quickly and resolutely to establish hegemony over the indigenous peoples—the Bushmen and the Hottentots. In their migrations north, they eventually ran into another surging people, the Bantu-speaking tribes who were moving south. Both were modified pastoral cultures; both were aggressive, hardy and, to a certain extent, ethnocentric, for their world views encouraged a belief in their own primacy. The Boers, as the Afrikaans-speakers became known, had a colonial style all their own. Intensely paternalistic and committed to direct rule of individual Africans, they demanded obedience and observance of European law. Only recently has there been an attempt to move toward a more indirect type of rule with regard to the Africans, and even that seems spurious in its application.

INTELLECTUAL RESPONSES TO COLONIALISM

The colonial overlay produced a number of reactions. On the one hand, there was the push for cultural emancipation, Negritude,[10] which we shall examine in the next chapter. In addition, there was a push for political unity and the

[10]Moyibi Amoda, *Black Power and Black Vision* (Philadelphia: Westminister Press, 1972); C. A. Diop, *The African Origin of Civilization* (New York: Lawrence Hill, 1974); Woodie King and Earl Anthony (eds.), *Black Poets and Prophets* (New York: Mentor Books, 1972); I. Markovitz, *Leopold Senghor and the Politics of Negritude* (New York: Atheneum, 1969).

linking of Africans to eliminate colonialism and neocolonialism, known as Pan Africanism.[11] We shall be dealing with aspects of this when we concern ourselves with the writings of Kwame Nkrumah. Finally, there were the diverse moves for national emancipation as each African territory sought independence. This final strand remains a broad and comprehensive set of movements which, taken on a country-by-country basis, lie beyond the scope of this work, but the interested reader can consult any one of a number of standard works.[12]

In the next chapter, then, we shall be dealing with those African political authors who guided their countries to independence. What concerns us here is African intellectual response to colonialism which led to decolonization and, in the process, set the stage for postindependence politics. Too often, books dealing with contemporary patterns of African politics skirt or even overlook the importance of African political thought as both a reaction to colonialism and to the intellectual foundations of present-day politics.

In this chapter, we concentrate on two major authors—Frantz Fanon and Kwame Nkrumah. Others could have been chosen. Others will be used to examine additional African political philosophies in succeeding chapters. But Fanon and Nkrumah represent important and enduring reactions to colonialism and, more importantly, presage political efforts to create both new nations in Africa and a new Africa. Both were men of vision whose thought continues to stimulate African political debate.

FRANTZ FANON

Born in Martinique in 1925, Fanon was educated in France and eventually ended up in Algeria, where the searing experience of a civil war radicalized him and pushed him toward a number of theories about colonialism and

[11]Adekunle Ajala, *Pan-Africanism: Evolution, Progress and Prospects* (New York: St. Martin's Press, 1973); Z. Cervenka, *The Organization of African Unity* (New York: Praeger, 1969); John Henrick Clarke, *Marcus Garvey and the Vision of Africa* (New York: Random House, 1974); E. D. Cronon, *Black Moses* (Madison: University of Wisconsin Press, 1955); A. Jacques-Garvey (ed.), *Philosophy and Opinions of Marcus Garvey* (New York: Atheneum, 1969); Lilyan Kesteloot, *Intellectual Origins of the African Revolution* (Rockville, Md.: New Perspectives, 1968); C. Legum, *Pan Africanism* (New York: Praeger, 1962); George Padmore, *Pan-Africanism or Communism* (Garden City, N.Y.: Doubleday, 1971); V. B. Thompson, *Africa and Unity: The Evolution of Pan-Africanism* (New York: Humanities Press, 1969); C. Welch, *Pan Africanism: Dream of Unity* (Ithaca, N.Y.: Cornell University Press, 1967).

[12]William Foltz, *From French West Africa to the Mali Federation* (New Haven, Conn.: Yale University Press, 1969); John Hargreaves (ed.), *France and West Africa* (New York: Macmillan, 1969); J. Hatch, *Africa: The Rebirth of Self-Rule* (London: Oxford University Press, 1958); E. Mortimer, *France and the Africans 1944–1960* (New York: Walker and Company, 1969); Immanuel Wallerstein, *Africa: The Politics of Independence* (New York: Random House, 1961); John Grotpeter and Warren Weinstein, *The Pattern of African Decolonization: A New Interpretation* (Syracuse: The Maxwell School, 1973); Ken Post, *The New States of West Africa* (Baltimore: Penguin Books, 1964).

alienation. His writings also indicate the extent to which colonialism is both insidious and deeply rooted.

More than any other African political theorist whose writings we shall consider in this and the following chapter, Frantz Fanon provides us with an in-depth examination of the phenomenon of alienation under colonial rule. Fanon's psychoanalytic training in France and his clinical experience in Algeria permitted an emphasis on the psychological dimensions of alienation both on a mass and individualized level. Consequently, Fanon has made an excellent contribution to the general theory of alienation as well as to our understanding of its particular forms which result from colonial domination.

Yet, after taking the time to digest his insights, Fanon's readers pay a heavy price for this knowledge. That certain revolutionary optimism about the prospects for reducing and perhaps completely eliminating the alienation caused by colonialist socioeconomic and political institutions when they are finally overturned, is sacrificed to the despairing realization that no matter what new institutions take the place of the old, the psychological effects of oppression continue to linger, perhaps for centuries. Even after "independence" is declared, colonialism continues to reside in the minds of the native people. Fanon's work demonstrates that even more terrible than the colonization of a country is the colonization of the mind.

In Fanon's first major book, *Black Skin, White Masks,*[13] we learn that colonialist efforts to master the native population are often subtle, and for that reason can be more effective than outright methods of physical coercion. Oppression is insidious and clandestine if it is not recognized as actually being oppressive. This may seem paradoxical until we realize and fully appreciate the manner in which the beliefs, values, attitudes, goals, and aspirations of the colonial power come to be shared by the oppressed people, become part of the African's mental and thinking apparatus. The oppressed becomes like the oppressor, because the culture and politics of the foreign inhabitant have been internalized psychologically. An internal battle ensues between the authentic African cultural world views and the world views of the learned colonial culture. Eventually, this inner personal struggle gives way to the resocialization of the native. His traditional culture is abandoned and the imposed culture adopted. When this occurs a psychological victory is achieved by the colonialist which insures political victory. So long as the psychological warfare waged by colonialism is successful, domination will be bloodless.

Fanon places great stress on the political implications of language. In order to consolidate its political power, the colonial regime carries through a process of "assimilation" through "acculturation." An important first step in this process is the teaching of the colonial language to Africans. A facility with the

---

[13]Frantz Fanon, *Black Skin, White Masks* (New York: Grove Press, 1967). Although it is true that Fanon is not, strictly speaking, "an African" by birth, he is by heritage and experience; his works are clearly a part of the rich heritage of African political thought.

new language allows much more than commonplace and everyday communication with the colonialist, more than the courteous exchange of greetings and the transaction of business. The decisive point is that the learning of the colonialist language by the African opens the door to the outsider's culture and, as Fanon points out, "to speak a language is to take on a world."[14] With the new language comes a new history—that of the colonizer—and since the white man's language and history is "superior" to the Africans', so is white civilization. "Civilization" and "white" come to be inseparable. To be civilized means to be white—that is, to act and think according to the maxims of white culture. Fanon says, for example, that "in order to achieve ["civilized"] morality, it is essential that the black, the dark, the Negro vanish from the [the African's] consciousness."[15]

The equation of "white" and "civilization" in the minds of Africans implies that the opposite is also true; to be black is to be uncivilized. Colonial acculturation of the African clearly involves "racialism." The African seeks to overcome his feelings of racial inferiority through a complete identification with the white man which often far exceeds the adoption of white history, white language, and white cultural traits. For the African man and woman, overcoming this inferiority complex, a sort of racial neurosis according to Fanon, is frequently expressed through an almost compulsive desire to marry a white European. Though empirical evidence indicates that the number of such marriages are negligible, we would miss Fanon's point if we allow such data to guide our analysis.

The psychological need to marry a white European is most cruelly expressed within the marriage of two Africans. A subconscious rejection of the black partner inhibits the possibility of achieving a fulfilling conjugal relationship. As Fanon explains, because white is firmly associated with everything good, for the African marriage authentic love remains unattainable.[16] Alienation within marriage testifies to the extensiveness of colonialism and the nature of its penetration into the African's most intimate concerns. As will be seen in Chapter 4, many literary portraits of colonialism given to us by novelists, as well as the scientific studies conducted by psychologists, have examined those same social relationships which occupy Fanon's attention.

In *Black Skin, White Masks*, Fanon explores the African's personality in relation to the colonial social, economic, and political environment, as we observed in his example of the imposition of a foreign language on native inhabitants; thus, the role that colonialist domination plays in influencing attitudes and behavior is projected. Whereas a false emphasis on racial factors as determinants of personality prohibit a solution to the neurotic complexes

[14]Ibid., p. 38.
[15]Ibid., p. 194.
[16]Ibid., Ch. 2 and p. 42. Of course, Fanon himself had a white wife.

of Africans (because they come to be understood as biological givens), a proper focus on the interrelationships of psychological, social, and political factors indicts colonialism as the fundamental cause of such problems as the African's inferiority complex, and immediately suggests a solution to those problems— end colonialism!

A second example we shall mention briefly is Fanon's critique of Dominique O. Mannoni's *Prospero and Caliban: The Psychology of Colonization.* In an attempt to analyze exhaustively relations between the colonized and the colonizer, the author of this work contends that the apparent reliance of the African on the colonialist is an expression of his "dependency complex" on authority which is satisfied through colonial domination. According to this view, colonialism complements a deeply felt psychological need to be told what to do, and this view constitutes a thesis which makes colonial oppression far less punitive than it is in reality. Fanon criticizes Mannoni for arguing that the causes of the dependency complex are not located within the social relations of the colonial order, but originate in the precolonial traditional period. For Mannoni, colonialism is justified as fulfilling a natural psychological need which causes the African to assume a dependency relationship with the colonialist. Fanon's critical exposition points out Mannoni's unwitting and conservative defense of colonization.

Fanon feels that explanations that rely on racial and biological variables to account for psychological attitudes hide the true impact of colonial political and social institutions, as well as divert attention from them. The ideological pillars of colonialism are strengthened if explanations disguising political values and self-interest are accepted, as they are when biological and racial factors are substituted for the social causes of alienation. Fanon's technique of examining man in relation to his socioeconomic and political conditions allows him to tear away the nonideological facade from the "objective" explanations and to reveal a vast manipulative political structure. This method has been referred to by Marxists as the process of "demystification." Its animating principle is the concept of "totality," which always refers us to socioeconomic and political variables, fundamental to Marxist dialectics, and which has been set down with admirable clarity by a famous twentieth-century Marxist, Georg Lukacs.[17]

We have seen how acculturation leads to the alienation of black history and how the loss of such historical knowledge strengthens colonialism and alienates African political self-determination. African nations developed from the colonial period onward in accordance with priorities established by the industrialized countries. The precolonial, preindustrial period of African history is labeled "primitive" by Europeans, and is viewed as merely an unfortunate "stage" in the transition to a highly industrialized and modern "white" civili-

[17]Georg Lukacs, *History and Class Consciousness* (Cambridge, Mass.: MIT Press, 1971).

zation. Precolonial, traditional Africa is dismissed as having made no contribution to human progress as defined by western values.

Fanon, however, refuses to accept this "history that others have compiled" for the African, and insists on the highest cultural merit being accorded to the African past, just as do the writers in Chapter 4. Ironically enough, Fanon seems not to have read what Africans have said about their own cultures! Fanon says that he

> rummaged frenetically through all of antiquity of the black man. What I found there took away my breath . . . Segau, Djenne, cities of more than a hundred thousand people; accounts of learned blacks (doctors of theology who went to Mecca to interpret the Koran).
>
> All of that, exhumed from the past, spread with its insides out, made it possible for me to find a valid historic place. The white man was wrong, I was not a primitive, not a half-man, I belonged to a race that had already been working in gold and silver two thousand years ago.[18]

To recall that the African has a history filled with promise is a demand for the expulsion of those who force an alien history upon it. This demand, with its emphasis on the Africans as makers of their own history with their own politics, stresses "blackness," "black" history, and "negritude" as an end in itself, not as a transitional stage to some goal neither made by the Negro nor for the Negro.

Marxism views negritude in much the same way as the European does, making the Marxist an unwitting accomplice of colonialism. Sartre, Fanon argues, views the African struggle with colonialism as part of a much larger historical struggle of all oppressed people, black or white, working-class, peasant, or Jew, against domination. Sartre's preoccupation with "human" liberation swallows up the uniqueness of the African's struggle. The African situation becomes a "stage" in the eventual achievement of some higher human objective which sees the African only as a means to its end. Just as the colonialist destroys the African past, it seems that the Marxist neglects the African's future. Fanon asserts that "without a Negro past, without a Negro future, it was impossible for me to live my Negrohood. Not yet white, no longer wholly black, I was damned."[19] Because the colonialist exploits the African in the interest of capitalism, and the Marxist interprets the African's best interest to lie in the achievement of western-type socialism, Fanon and the African are without an ally and quite alone.

Whereas *Black Skin, White Masks* concentrates on forms of alienation that strengthened the forces of colonialist oppression, *The Wretched of the Earth*, perhaps Fanon's most famous work, focuses on the politics of decolonization,

[18] *Black Skin, White Masks,* p. 130.
[19] Ibid., p. 138.

on removing obstacles to an uncompromising liberation from colonial influence after independence has been declared, and on the very interesting and significant changes in African culture that accompany the struggle against the colonial powers. We shall briefly consider examples of each of these three major themes from Fanon's second book.

Fanon concerns himself with a question that has occupied the thinking of most serious western Marxists, often to the unfortunate exclusion of all other philosophical and political problems. This question is the task of discovering, within the social relations of capitalist domination, the forces of change that will lead to the development of a socialist society. Many western Marxists have labored to find a substitute for the revolutionary proletariat, because the rising standard of living of the working class in the industrialized countries has made it more like the nonrevolutionary middle class which views its best interest as the preservation of the socioeconomic and political *status-quo.*

Marxists who continue to argue that capitalism will eventually experience a crisis of major economic proportions that will cast the working class back into the throes of an agonizing poverty, thereby restoring its revolutionary aspirations, have had to confront rather unpalatable evidence demonstrating that past economic crises in the twentieth century have *not* inclined the proletariat to be revolutionary. Furthermore, when on occasions the proletariat has been violent, there was no apparent intention of achieving a socialist state, but rather an improved capitalist system.

According to Fanon, the African working class is as moderate as the western proletariat, content to demand and accept economic reforms and concessions. Yet, due to the very low levels of industrialization in Africa, the indigenous working class is extremely small, and even if it were not reformist in nature, its size is too inconsequential for it to constitute a genuine and effective revolutionary force. Moreover, the intellectuals, civil servants, and small businessmen comprising those studied in *Black Skin, White Masks,* have succumbed to the conservatism which results from acculturation and assimilation.

This clearly affects the process of nation building. These groups, including the workers, make up the rank and file of the nationalist parties for independence from colonialism which, with very few exceptions, have been reformist, and not revolutionary, in nature. Fanon informs us, for example, "that inside the nationalist parties, the will to break up colonialism is linked to another quite different will: that of coming to friendly agreement with it."[20] These parties "are violent in their words and reformist in their attitudes. When the nationalist political leaders *say* something, they make quite clear that they do not really think it."[21]

[20]Frantz Fanon, *The Wretched of the Earth* (New York: Grove Press, 1966).
[21]Ibid., p. 47.

Outside the geographical limits of the relatively industrialized cities and towns, the traditional feudal structure governs the attitudes and behavior of the African peasant. The anger and aggression the native feels toward the colonialist is kept in check by tribalism, which channels the African's fury at exploitation into rituals, or (encouraged by the colonizer) finds an outlet in hostilities between tribes. Ethnic anger is also directed toward the nationalist parties which attempt to destroy tribal social structure by absorbing the power of the chiefs in a highly centralized party apparatus. As Fanon explains, the autonomy of the ethnic group during the colonial period turns into a demand for regional autonomy during decolonization as tribal groups organize in an effort to decentralize the pretended power and authority of the nationalist parties.

All groups, therefore, seem to be either incapable of initiating a movement that would (in Fanon's view) produce radical social change because of strong, almost inflexible, African traditionalism, or because of an unwillingness to eliminate colonialism entirely, resulting from their liberal attitude toward the economic benefits of maintaining dependent relations with foreign powers. Clearly, the vibrancy and adaptability of the traditional forms as seen in Chapter 1 were unknown to Fanon at the time of his writing. Where, then, does Fanon discover the impetus for revolution?

Fanon's analysis of the nationalist political party structure after it consolidates its power uncovers the tensions in African society which can lead to sweeping change. The nationalist parties, after a time, cease to be ideologically cohesive and splinter groups emerge. The most significant of these groups are those which lean in a radically left-wing direction, in response to the economic and political opportunism and reformist policies of the dominant liberal centers. The radical splinter groups are banished from the party, and political harassment and persecution soon follows expulsion. The revolutionaries flee to the countryside to escape incarceration, where they begin to politically educate the peasant masses. For the first time there is an effort made to educate the people about the sober realities of colonialism, and the hierarchical distance separating the political leaders from their mass following is surmounted. The eventual result is a "revolution from below," proceeding from the exploited people as a whole, which eventually actively includes in the armed struggle all those other groups that abstained from a violent and total confrontation with colonialism.

For Fanon, the end of colonial habitation is not, however, the end of colonialism, though it is an important step in the long road to self-determination. After independence is declared, the nationalist political parties fill the power vacuum created by the colonial exodus. The African masses lack the organizational structure and knowledge that would allow them to govern themselves effectively and to develop their country economically. At this point, the educated and politically dominant middle classes are confronted with an alternative—serve the people or serve their own interests. They invariably opt for the latter choice, but it is a choice, Fanon seems to say, that satisfies the final historically necessary condition for genuine self-government.

The conservative instincts of the middle-class parties reassert themselves through a reestablishment of economic ties with the former colonial power. Thus, the phenomenon of neocolonialism is born, where the colonial power is bereft of its political power and is forced to share the spoils of economic exploitation with the newly empowered nationalists, if it intends to profit at all from the appropriation of the wealth of Africa's natural resources. All domestic opposition to this maneuver meets with increasingly dictatorial measures waged by a coalition of middle-class splinter parties that gradually consolidate their efforts into a one-party regime. Fanon explains that "the living party, which ought to make possible the free exchange of ideas which have been elaborated according to the real needs of the mass of the people, has been transformed into a trade union of individual interests."[22]

Fanon stresses the important function of African music, literature, poetry, and other forms of art during all phases of the struggle for liberation from colonialism. He offers a distinctively nonwestern concept of culture which embraces the Marxist model of historical materialism. His analysis of culture shows that all dimensions or spheres of African society, not merely social, economic, and political institutions, are radically changed because of the revolution. Fanon's analysis of African art also had the added effect of validating many of the basic principles of Marxist social science; that is, of demonstrating how culture in general and art in particular reproduces or reflects all those tensions, contradictions, and dynamics of the socioeconomic and political universe, and makes them visible even when they are as yet not apparent to the social scientist.

The western notion of the "apolitical" artist who writes or composes in a social vacuum is denied by Fanon. Before the battle for independence commences, the artist seizes upon traditional cultural and historical themes which serve to resurrect Africa's heritage aesthetically and to hold up an image of the free black to his real but exploited counterpart. Art reminds the African of another way, a freer way of life.

In *A Dying Colonialism,*[23] Fanon's last full-length work completed before his death, we are given a vivid description of the transformation of a traditional Algerian society as it occurs during the actual course of violent struggle with the French colonialists. Ironically, Fanon did not live to see the successful revolutions in Angola, Mozambique, and Guiné-Bissau, which followed his pattern. It is the people who must determine the essence of socialism for it is they who must live in the new socialist order. Socialism "from above" is authoritarian and necessarily of an alien character to the masses.

Fanon realized that the successful liberation of a single African state, a

[22]Ibid., p. 137.
[23]Frantz Fanon, *A Dying Colonialism* (New York: Grove Press, 1967).

victory won in Algeria only after years of painful and exhausting struggle, would be insufficient to maintain freedom permanently, for their economic backwardness leads them into agreements with the west that are regretted later. The logic of imperialism dictates that undeveloped nations should serve as the economic reservoir of the industrialized countries, and developing African states cannot long resist the temptation of neocolonialist imperialism unless they are economically self-sufficient.

It can only be the political and economic unification of all African states which will make economic self-sufficiency possible and which will likewise permit single African nations to fend off the threat of colonialism and neocolonialism. The equation that Fanon arrives at is that the independence of individual African countries is dependent on the independence and unification of all African countries. The passage from African nationalism to pan-African unity is clearly expressed by Fanon when he exclaims: "The future of every man today has a relation of close dependency on the rest of the universe. That is why colonial peoples must redouble their vigilance and their vigor. A new humanism can be achieved only at this price. The wolves must no longer find individual lambs to prey upon. Imperialism must be blocked in all its attempts to strengthen itself. The peoples demand this; the historic process requires it."[24]

There can be little question that Fanon rightly identified a number of critical ingredients in the African context: the conservatism of the peasantry (particularly after independence), the colonial holdovers in both the political and economic spheres, the need for African unity behind successful revolutions and, finally, the extent of "great-power" intervention in order to maintain the *status quo.*

At the same time, he clearly overlooked the revolutionary impetus which was to come from the military in such countries as Somalia, as well as the difficulties in achieving any revolutionary change once the country in question is "independent." It is difficult to judge precisely the impact of Fanon on successive African leaders but his contributions to the context of African politics are considerable.

KWAME NKRUMAH

In the years following World War II, the Gold Coast was the scene of intensive nationalistic stirrings. Renamed Ghana, it emerged as one of the first independent nations in black Africa in 1957 (in sub-Saharan Africa, only the Sudan, in 1956, preceded it). Led by the dynamic and exciting Kwame Nkrumah, Ghana became the focal point of African independence and a leader in the Third World. For nearly a decade Nkrumah ruled Ghana until he was re-

[24]Frantz Fanon, *Toward the African Revolution* (New York: Grove Press, 1967), p. 126.

placed, while on a mission to China, by a military *coup* on February 24, 1966. He subsequently went into exile in Guinea where he died.

Yet the era of Kwame Nkrumah is not completely over in present-day Ghana; he and his politics were still issues in the 1970 campaign to determine the makeup of the new National Assembly and the composition of its civilian government. Despite more than three years of military rule under the National Liberation Council (NLC)—a coalition drawn from the army and the police and headed by Brigadier A. A. Afrifa and J. W. K. Hartley, Inspector General of the Police—his memory lingered on.

This is perhaps as it should be, for Kwame Nkrumah was a towering figure, larger than life, with virtues and faults to match. History will have the final verdict, but for the moment, his image remains blurred and his contributions to Ghana and Africa highly mixed in character. There can be no question that he was a genuine hero and primary spokesman of the African struggle for independence. Kwame Nkrumah stood for the abolition of tribalism, the unity of Ghana, and the political and economic liberation of Africa. He said, with clarity and cogency, "Africa must unite" if it is to avoid economic and political serfdom. He saw in the realities of the present world market economy the enslaving forces of the past and a dark cloud hovering over the future of the continent.

He saw, most correctly, that if individual African states remained disunited, they would forever be the pawns of the great powers. In terms of liberation, Kwame Nkrumah was not simply a Ghanian or an African, for black people throughout the world looked to him as a symbol of their own political, economic, and psychological emancipation. He wore African dress with pride while most of his contemporaries were adopting western suits. He vigorously denounced the forces of neocolonialism and the European-dominated regimes in southern Africa, and spoke out against racism throughout the world.

For almost two decades, he dominated the political life of Ghana. In 1949, he broke away from the rather conservative United Gold Coast Convention to form the Convention Peoples Party (CPP), which demanded "independence now" and pressed for African majority rule. In 1956, he was elected prime minister and led his country to independence the following year. Not satisfied with the existing political system, he had Ghana adopt a new presidential system with great centralization of authority, which he maintained until his overthrow in 1966.

As leader of the country, he stressed the need for rapid industrialization and spent much of the nation's $300 million worth of foreign exchange reserves to develop a modern infrastructure of tarred roads, harbor facilities, and industrial parks at Tema and Sekondi-Takoradi. His foremost project was the Volta River dam at Akosombo, which resulted in the largest man-made lake in the world and provided Ghana with hydroelectric power for decades to come. His government also made massive strides in education, devoting nearly 30 percent of the annual budget to it and increasing the number of children enrolled by over 300 percent. Also, during his era, Ghana was the center of African diplomatic activity—a charter member of the Organization of African Unity and an exciting leader of the Third World generally—to whom many persons looked with attention out of all proportion to Ghana's size or economic might.

There was, of course, another side to Kwame Nkrumah—the one which led to his downfall. The clarity of his visions and his impatience to realize them caused him to ignore genuine opposition to his projects. For example, he alienated many of the African leaders he most needed in order to actualize the dream of African unity. In this regard, he supported some worthwhile freedom fighters, principally in southern Africa, but he also aided a host of rag-tag malcontents from neighboring countries, much to the chagrin of their leaders. He dispensed substantial sums of money to almost anyone willing to talk in favor of African unity and against neocolonialism, irrespective of the size of their followings in their own countries.

Moreover, much of his economic planning was slap-dash, an odd blend of capitalism and socialism which satisfied no one. Contrary to popular belief and his Marxist-like pronouncements concerning economic life, it was private, western firms with whom he did most of his business (in 1966, $547 million of a debt of just over $800 million consisted of short-term obligations to American, British, Dutch, and German companies).

Unlike many African countries where economic viability is a distant dream or a forlorn hope, Ghana has major deposits of gold, bauxite, manganese, and diamonds, as well as a great number of agricultural products including hardwoods and cocoa (which still provide 51 percent of all export revenues) and one of the highest per capita incomes in Africa. Yet Ghana under Nkrumah spent vast sums of money for lavish prestige projects which did nothing to aid economic development, and many state businesses ran continuously at a loss. We should also point out in this regard that while one may personally favor the long-term planning and governmental control of the essential industries and an equitable welfare program for developing countries (often referred to as "African socialism"), one can seriously doubt that Nkrumah ever took into account the petty trading impulse and long tradition of small-scale entrepreneurship indigenous to Ghana. Unlike Mali or Tanzania, for example, private ownership and widespread trading were facts of life in Ghana long before the coming of Europeans—trends not easily reversed by a few Marxist slogans.

Furthermore, Nkrumah took an essentially pluralistic society with a long history of individual freedom and personal achievement and attempted to rule it by increasingly arbitrary methods. He gradually outlawed all formal opposition, stifled dissent, and, by surrounding himself with a group of sycophants and expatriate white advisors, cut himself off from his people and ignored their increasing alienation from his regime. He did not attempt much political mobilization after independence and generally disregarded the need to engage the people of Ghana politically. As a result, the CPP, formerly a true mass party, gradually withered away. His economic schemes, whatever their ultimate worth, brought short-term chaos and an economic slump (although Nkrumah can hardly be held responsible for the drastic fall in the price of cocoa, brought about in part by the rising production in Nigeria, the Ivory Coast, and Brazil, and partly by market manipulation in London). Even then the Ghanians might have accepted these hardships had not the signs of governmental corruption and waste been so blatant and had not Nkrumah asked the people to make sacrifices which he himself was unwilling to make. In this context, Nkrumah's downfall was not widely mourned in Ghana and many Ghanians are now convinced that he was "far better for Africa than for Ghana."

But whatever the impact of Nkrumah's political activities on Ghana and Africa, there can be little question that in summarizing African response to colonialism and neocolonialism, his thoughts and philosophies will live on. To a considerable extent, these represent a definite response to the ideology of colonial repression and western political thought.

Actually, we can single out with confidence the two major influences on Nkrumah's thought. Gandhi's influence prevails at least since Nkrumah's return to the Gold Coast (independent Ghana as of 1957) in December 1947, after a total of 12 years of combined study and political organizing in America and England, until 1966, when his Ghanian regime was toppled and Nkrumah was forced to remain in exile in Guinea until his death in 1972. During the expulsion period the key influences were Marx and Engels, and we will see the dramatic changes in both his political theory and political practice in Nkrumah's Marxist writings.

The distinctive characteristic of Nkrumah's philosophy which, properly speaking, was not a philosophy at all but, rather, an organizational strategy for achieving independence and liberation through victory over British colonial rule, was the use of nonviolent methods. Immediately, therefore, Nkrumah is to be differentiated from Fanon's philosophy of violence for Algeria and Africa. If we would stretch the meaning of "philosophical," Nkrumah's methods may conceivably be called a philosophy in that he did not strategically restrict them to the Gold Coast colonial situation, but advocated their employment in all African countries victimized by colonialism regardless of whatever unique political conditions and relationships existed. Strategies are usually altered to contend with the special circumstances of a particular political system; Nkrumah, on the contrary, maintained his nonviolent methods to be *universally* applicable. Nkrumah called his political theory "positive action," and in his *Autobiography* he explicitly states that it is patterned after Gandhi's nonviolent methods of realizing self-government in India.[25]

[25]Kwame Nkrumah, *Ghana: The Autobiography of Kwame Nkrumah* (London: Thomas Nelson, 1957), p. 112.

The means defining positive action were legitimate by western democratic standards, though the British considered them illegal in the Gold Coast, where Britain was the colonial authority. Positive action included political agitation, newspaper and educational campaigns, and, if necessary, strikes, boycotts, and other forms of noncooperation. Political and economic crises during the colonial period were viewed as opportunities to rally support for these measures. There is no more substance to positive action than this, and it was used, it appears, on only one significant occasion in 1950 when the British rejected Nkrumah's demands for a general election and a referendum to permit the people of the Gold Coast to decide whether to accept the British recommendations for constitutional reform. The positive action demonstrations that followed in the wake of the British refusal to entertain Nkrumah's demands resulted in his imprisonment. Gandhi had paid a similarly heavy penalty on many occasions in India following acts of civil disobedience against the British.

Nkrumah's incarceration of 14 months ended abruptly in 1951 when a direct election gave his Convention People's Party, formed in 1949, the majority of legislative assembly seats. Nkrumah was then made the leader of government business and positive action was never again used as an instrument to achieve independence, though it always remained an alternative to his negotiations with the British for a gradual and peaceful transition to independence.

It must be said, though, that the precise value of positive action as the explanation for Nkrumah's political success is difficult to determine. There is an excellent chance that if Positive Action had never been strategically employed Nkrumah still would have successfully carried the Gold Coast to independence, for even of greater importance than his organizational skills were his personality and popular appeal. This is summed up best, perhaps, by the title of his first book, *Ghana: the Autobiography of Kwame Nkrumah,* identifying himself in an absolute sense with that nation. Though the essential core of Gandhi's philosophy was appropriated by Nkrumah, in many other important respects he and Gandhi departed. Nkrumah certainly lacked Gandhi's humility, and, though he disclaimed them, material wealth and status symbols were important to Nkrumah.[26]

Taken together, it appears to be Nkrumah's egoism and organizational skills, rather than his political theory, that accounts for his success in achieving independence for Ghana. Nkrumah had acquired years of organizational experience. While at the University of Pennsylvania, he reorganized the African Students Association of America and Canada, which under his tutelage considerably extended its work and membership. He also was associated peripherally with other radical groups and organizations in the United States and Britain, such as the Communist party, but by his own accounts he never became a member. In fact, when the authorities turned up a Communist party

[26]Ibid., p. 239.

membership card during a search of his person during the course of Nkrumah's return trip to the Gold Coast from England in 1947, he pointed out that the card was not signed! This incident reveals something about his shallow commitment to socialist ideology, but his commitment was to deepen considerably after his exile from Ghana. Nkrumah's relationship with all radical groups during his years in the United States and England was designed to teach him the techniques and principles of organization and leadership which served him quite well in the Gold Coast and Ghana.

A goal that obsessed Nkrumah was the necessary task of unifying and maintaining the unity of all factional elements in the Convention Peoples Party. The ever present danger of factional disputes escalating into civil war would have guaranteed, according to Nkrumah, the reluctance of Britain to grant independence to the Gold Coast, any civil disturbance being an indication of that country's inability to rule itself in a stable fashion.

Nkrumah relied upon this "independence-only-through-unity-of-all-political-interests" argument to bolster his own power in a highly centralized party structure. This point is not meant to suggest that factionalism was a false threat to independence. Rather that the necessary precondition of a homogeneous "team spirit" in Nkrumah's party complemented his healthy appetite for power. It simultaneously disguised undemocratic instincts which were laid bare after independence had made obsolete the need for unqualified unity at the expense of legitimately competing claims upon political and economic resources. On a few occasions before independence was realized Nkrumah dealt swiftly with political opposition by expelling members from his party, and he postponed general elections if he "perceived" any threat of open opposition through demonstration.[27]

Like Frantz Fanon, Nkrumah believed that the accomplishment of political and economic independence from colonialism rested upon the organization and education of the masses.[28] Yet, for several reasons, Nkrumah appears to be much less committed to those ideals than Fanon. To begin with, Nkrumah assumed the exclusive responsibility for defining and conceptualizing the nature and specific goals of Ghanian socialism. The articulation of the socialist principles which would come to animate the new social order was never left to the people or to the party members.

These authoritarian strains of Nkrumah's socialist practice may conceivably be excused and explained away by the form of political transition from colonial occupation to an independent state. With Fanon, it was the Algerian masses who played the dominant role in determining the social and political content of socialism because it was they who actually participated in and brought the struggle for liberation to its climax. Where collective violence was

[27]Ibid., p. 248.
[28]Cf. Ibid., pp. 47, 101, 107.

the central vehicle for achieving freedom, the input of the people could be decisive "after" the revolution because it had been most important "during" the revolution.

As we noted in our discussion of Fanon, socialist ends were lived and experienced as revolutionary means. Ends and means are born and bred at the same moment. In the Algerian struggle, political education was inseparable from political practice. Education means learning by doing. Nkrumah's vehicle of liberation, "positive action," on the other hand, emphasized peaceful methods and nonviolent struggle or, in other words, the sort of political tactics chosen strictly by Nkrumah and a handful of party leaders.

There was no mass spontaneity where socialism could emerge naturally from the ashes of burnt-out and exhausted traditions. With Nkrumah, everything was premeditated, calculated in advance by an elite core of decision makers, and the people were expected only to take orders and to follow commands. Political education for Nkrumah meant traditional classroom pedagogy—passivity, not learning through an intimate experience with socialism. Despite Nkrumah's insistence that he acted on behalf of the "will" of the people, socialism remained a distant objective, as alien to Ghana's people as colonialism. Positive action created a distinction between the knowledge of the leaders and the "ignorance" of the masses. Education was neglected and subordinated to organization.

Nkrumah's manner of speaking to large crowds and smaller groups seemed to capture the distance interposed between himself and the general population. Nkrumah took great pride in his power to persuade listeners of his point of view, regardless of whether he considered his position to be valid or not. Consider this passage from his *Autobiography,* where Nkrumah says that he enjoyed

> debates and could never resist taking the side of the minority group, whether I agreed with their view or not, because it prolonged the debate and gave me a chance to express views that I otherwise would never have thought of. I discovered that at whatever disadvantage I began, I usually ended up by winning the day, frequently converting many of my opponents to the point of view that I conveniently supported. Although this was only a kind of game with me then, it turned out to be my most valuable discovery.[29]

We observe here a need to have the final word, to overcome decisively all opposition, to dominate. Nkrumah's public speeches seemed more directed *at* the people, rather than *to* them. His oratory seemed intended to appeal to the passionate and emotional side of his followers, not to their rational and critical

[29]Ibid., p. 19.

faculties, as we would expect if education was the proposed objective.[30] His apparent lack of any real concern with his people's intelligence, and the absence of any genuine popular participation in decision making, strongly suggests that the masses were merely an instrument to accomplish party goals.

The various groups and political interests competing against Nkrumah for a federalist form of governmental structure which would decentralize the decision-making apparatus, threatened a reduction in Nkrumah's power as well as the perpetuation of colonialist ties benefiting from colonial support of tribal hierarchies. That the continuation of relations with the colonial powers meant that traditional African social structures would remain intact and unchanged often caused Nkrumah to remark that the alternative to independence would be imperialism and feudalism.[31] In times of crisis, when the traditional authorities waged political warfare against Nkrumah in a power bid rendering the society unstable, Nkrumah would not hesitate to curtail freedoms and compromise democratic principles to oppose successfully such challenges to his authority.

Totalitarian measures were introduced temporarily without hesitation to preserve democracy. This paradox is not unfamiliar to socialist leaders lacking broad-based support or, as in the example of the Gold Coast and later independent Ghana, to regime heads, such as Nkrumah, acting under the banner of socialism. After Nkrumah realized an independent Ghana, the punitive measures he directed toward any political opposition seem to demonstrate that his method of dealing with opponents at all times, whether or not in the face of imperialism and colonialism, was carried out far less on socialist and democratic principles than on the basis of an unphilosophical aggrandizement of power. It should also be noted that Nkrumah appears to have restricted his nonviolent "positive action" philosophy for use against colonialism when he was not yet in political power. When he ruled independent Ghana unfettered by the restraints of another country, however, he frequently put aside the nonviolent creed of positive action and dealt swiftly and brutally with political opponents.

Until he was deposed, Nkrumah did not share Fanon's doctrine that genuine and complete liberation from colonial domination could only become a reality by entirely breaking all economic ties with capitalist countries. In other words, Nkrumah did not view the membership of Ghana after independence in the British Commonwealth of Nations as neocolonialism.

There are several reasons that can explain Nkrumah's attitude, some of which are factual and others only speculative. As Nkrumah explains, most of the key industrial and business concerns were in the possession of colonialists. Their exodus from Ghana immediately after independence had been declared

[30]Ibid., pp. 76, 104, 269.
[31]Ibid., p. 267.

would have created an economic vacuum; this would have caused great poverty and hardship that would have taken decades to alleviate. Ghana lacked men and women properly educated to develop the industrial sector.

Second, this absence of skilled technicians extended to the public administrative sectors of Ghana. The bureaucracy was occupied predominantly by British civil servants who were asked to remain in Ghana until natives could be trained to assume administrative posts at all levels. Nkrumah, quite contrary to Max Weber's theories of the relationship between bureaucrats and political leaderships, believed that the British-trained civil servants divided their loyalties between the new Ghanian regime and the colonial power; though Britain exercised no obvious political influence after independence, British civil servants would be inclined toward a sympathetic regulation of their mother country's business enterprise in Ghana. Nkrumah knew that bureaucrats were not neutral and willing to submit generously to any political leaders regardless of ideology, as Weber had argued they would.[32]

Third, beyond its ties with the British Commonwealth, Nkrumah sought foreign aid from many other quarters, particularly the United States. Having received his undergraduate college degree from Lincoln University, he was subsequently to return to receive an honorary Doctorate of Laws, and no doubt this contributed to his initially favorable predisposition toward the United States. However, after the overthrow of his government, Nkrumah would bitterly condemn the United States as the most vicious imperialist world power.

The issue of Nkrumah's attitude toward the colonial powers is crucial because it immediately addresses the extent to which he is concerned with developing an authentic socialist society or a social order that can boast of little more than the ideological trappings and state centralized apparatus characteristic of Eastern European socialism. The postindependence relationship of Ghana to capitalism and capitalist countries will determine whether Nkrumah's socialism will permeate the very social, political, and economic relations between Ghana's people, or whether socialism will be exclusive to an authoritarian political establishment operating under the guise of socialist principles. In the example of Algeria, we have observed in Fanon's writings that African socialism emerged in the course of struggle with colonialism and could be maintained only upon a complete economic break with capitalist nations.

In Nkrumah's second important work, *I Speak of Freedom: A Statement of African Ideology,* we see a subtle and gradual shift away from an exclusive orientation toward economic ties with the west. In fact, this book is interesting in that it covers the entire span of Nkrumah's political career beginning with his return to Ghana in 1947, after completing his educational stay in America and Great Britain, up until the time in 1960 after Ghana had become a

[32]Ibid., p. 147.

Republic and an active member of the United Nations. Thus, while there is a narrative overlap between *I Speak of Freedom* and his *Autobiography,* the former work also goes further and examines those first three years after independence. Essentially, *I Speak of Freedom* reevaluates, in its initial chapters, Nkrumah's attitudes toward the colonial powers before independence, and provides readers as well, with Nkrumah's newly developed attitudes toward foreign nations after independence.

I Speak of Freedom is clearly meant to be a more authoritative statement of Nkrumah's proposed relations with foreign powers in the west—the theme that dominates each chapter of the volume—than is his *Autobiography.* Nkrumah is not just engaging in self-clarification and self-criticism of his preindependence politics, but is essentially recreating, rewriting, and reevaluating those early years in order to make his subsequent decisions seem to follow naturally and logically, and to fashion a continuity in his thought that really does not exist.

Early in *I Speak of Freedom* we find Nkrumah affirming Ghana's position as a member of the British Commonwealth.[33] Nkrumah makes it clear, at the same time, that private investment from foreign sources is desirable, and that the institutional structure of Ghana's government will deliberately accommodate a balance between a private business sector (native Ghanians), publicly owned business enterprise, and a cooperative sector emphasizing a partnership between Ghana and foreign capital.[34] Nkrumah frequently emphasized the need to attract foreign investment by virtue of the underdevelopment of Ghana's business and industry.

Yet, side by side with these plans and exhortations to engage Ghana's excolonial masters in schemes that would enrich them as they, presumably, develop Ghana, Nkrumah carefully qualifies his invitation to the west. He underscores the significance of a "common interest" between the developing west and Ghana,[35] and declares that Ghana's independence can mean only economic "interdependence" between it and foreign investors.[36] He warns that foreign investment is not to be interpreted as an open-door policy to foreign domination.[37] So, while Nkrumah, at times, seemed deferential to the assistance of the capitalist bloc, and would even go as far as ignoring the race problem in the United States so as not to seem to compromise his principles of African racial equality while asking for aid from America, he would never risk any potential threat to his authority and Ghana's freedom, which were identical.

[33]Kwame Nkrumah, *I Speak of Freedom: A Statement of African Ideology* (New York: Praeger, 1961), particularly pp. 29, 83, 204.

[34]Ibid., p. 54.

[35]Ibid., pp. 137, 139.

[36]Ibid., p. 97.

[37]Ibid., p. 104.

I Speak of Freedom is, in other words, a qualified restatement of Nkrumah's policy toward western nations first set forth in his *Autobiography.* Whereas his *Autobiography* contained such positive attitudes toward capitalist countries which justified our seeing Nkrumah as either falling prey to or collaborating with neocolonialism, Nkrumah's restrained and qualified overtures toward the west in his second book are clear indications that Nkrumah came to realize after independence that both his authority and Ghana's sovereignty would be compromised if economic ties with capitalist countries were not restricted. *I Speak of Freedom* gives the impression that Nkrumah's favorable preindependence disposition toward western aid and investment in Ghana was tempered with suspicion and caution, whereas those same attitudes are portrayed with a naive receptiveness in the earlier *Autobiography.* Nkrumah's suspicion of the economic and political intentions of western nations toward Ghana and his caution regarding the extent to which his country could pursue relations with the west without jeopardizing its autonomy, are reflected in *I Speak of Freedom* through an increasing concern with imperialism in general and its potential impact on or tendencies within Africa toward unity.

Behind sharp criticisms of United Nations' and British practices, Nkrumah is beginning to formulate a conception of a more sophisticated stage of imperialism—neocolonialism. As brief as his remarks are and as elementary as his analysis is, the flashes of understanding of neocolonialism in *I Speak of Freedom* anticipate his exhaustive study of imperialism in *Neo-Colonialism: The Last Stage of Imperialism.* In the former work, neocolonialism appears to Nkrumah as a "subtle" and "disguised" theory of domination, where colonialist powers grant a "conditional independence" which retards the economic development of newly independent African states, necessitating a dependence upon foreign aid and economic investment for survival. It is precisely these glimpses of understanding of the neocolonial phenomenon that forced Nkrumah to reconsider his own policies toward the west.

Neocolonialism becomes the focus of Nkrumah's attention to the very degree to which it thwarts his efforts to unify the nations of Africa. The three aspects of imperialism that we have mentioned—the reluctance of the United Nations to distinguish between legally and illegally constituted African governments (between the forces for independence and those seeking to preserve colonial occupation), the inclusion of colonies in the British Commonwealth, and the "conditional independence" granted to African countries by the mother country—have the combined effect of "balkanizing" (to use Nkrumah's expression) African states.

The creation of colonial and neocolonial satellites establishes political barriers between African nations and territories which prevents pan-African unification. This situation of atomized countries also weakens the resistance to neocolonialism of nonsatellite independent African states, for only the economic cooperation of all African countries, which imperialist balkanization makes impossible, could sufficiently strengthen the economies of each individual state, enabling it to eliminate its economic dependence on a foreign power. We see here that Nkrumah eventually arrives at Fanon's position. The sovereignty of one African nation depends on the sovereignty of all.

Nkrumah's estrangement from the west and his commitment to pan-Africanism, which, as we have seen, grows as much out of a concern for Ghana's continued independence as for a unified African continent, eventually leads him to a strategic policy of nonalignment with the west and the east. Although Nkrumah's policy of nonalignment is explicable on the basis of his pan-African ideological opposition to imperialism, perhaps most important and fascinating is that from the theoretical relationship between imperialist neocolonialism, pan-African unification, and nonalignment, Nkrumah proposes a theory—not just a philosophy—of world peace.

In *I Speak of Freedom,* we discover Nkrumah becoming increasingly disturbed over the impact that the cold war was beginning to have on Africa. With the testing of atomic weapons in the Sahara by France, colonialism brought escalation of the nuclear arms race dangerously close to African nations. Nkrumah's unique perspective from the African continent enabled him to see that cold-war disputes between the eastern and western blocs were far less motivated by allegiances to opposing ideologies than by economic considerations, particularly the spread of capitalism *versus* communism in the Third World. Ideological battles concealed economic conflicts. Pan-Africanism became the proposed solution to a cold war that seemed to be rapidly escalating into an international conflagration. "The whole of Africa must be free and united. Only then will we be able to exercise our full strength in the cause of peace and the welfare of mankind."[38]

The progressively radical tendencies that we detected through a comparison of Nkrumah's *Autobiography* and *I Speak of Freedom,* are fully developed in *Neo-Colonialism: The Last Stage of Imperialism.* In this latter work, we find an exhaustive analysis and critique of the dangers that accompany a close economic association of the independent African nations with western industrial powers. It is most important to underscore the intensity of the critical nature of *Neo-Colonialism,* for it was completed just a short time before the *coup d'état* deposed Nkrumah and banished him into permanent exile.

Nkrumah's theoretical orientation in *Neo-Colonialism* is a Marxist-Leninist analysis of modern capitalism. The capitalist countries promoting economic interests contrary to those of independent African states are explicitly cited as Japan, the western European nations, with the United States being the most powerful and hegemonious. These countries maintain economic footholds in the Third World in order to generate a continuous pattern of economic growth and a high standard of living at home which together insures domestic political

[38]Ibid., p. 281.

stability.[39] During the industrializing stages of capitalism, the economic system seemed to necessarily entail the exploitation and impoverisation of the working class and masses generally, and the political system was relied upon to preserve stability, with force if required. Thus, the social and political expressions of economic contradictions—which arose in all capitalist countries because of their competition for new markets and material resources—could be contained (temporarily) with the ever present possibility that revolution would occur if the competition and contradictions became too intense.

This era of competition, which lasted approximately to the end of the second world war, eventually gave way to international cooperation between capitalist nations in a mutually beneficial imperialist economic expansion to developing countries. It was assumed that imperialist exploitation of the Third World meant that economic progress and growth in the developed countries would provide a permanent solution to their socioeconomic and political crises. Nkrumah would contend that the imperial stages of capitalist development allowed for class conflict to be relocated from the capitalist countries to the newly exploited Third World economic frontiers.[40] Class war became international in its dimensions, and although imperialism may mean the end to class conflict in the western nations, it also supposes the birth of mass opposition to capitalist domination in developing countries.

At this point, Nkrumah's Marxist-Leninist analysis of modern capitalist expansion attempts to explain the struggle between Communism and democracy as the struggle between Communism and capitalism. In other words, Nkrumah sees ideological conflicts as having an economic basis, though he views the Soviet Union's opposition to the west in the Third World as motivated to the greatest extent by ideological principles, because it has sufficient material reserves and operates in accordance with a more rational set of economic principles. The possibility for capitalist and communist powers to engage in limited warfare on the African continent is very high, and this disturbed Nkrumah since the time of *I Speak of Freedom*.

Neocolonialism succeeds through generous foreign aid programs with "strings" attached. Nkrumah states, for example, that the African recipients of aid must be willing to supply raw materials to the western power, and that much of the aid must then be used to purchase goods from that nation. The western nation also has the "right" to determine how the funds should be invested, to insist that part of the aid be used to protect foreign investments in developing industry in Africa for the benefit of the capitalist entrepreneur, and to insist that trade barriers be adjusted in favor of the marketing of western goods and capital. Western powers also meddle in the internal finances of the

[39]Kwame Nkrumah, *Neo-Colonialism: The Last Stage of Imperialism* (New York: International Publishers, 1969), p. 39. The title of this work is an obvious play on Lenin's *Imperialism: The Highest Stage of Capitalism.*

[40]Ibid., p. xix.

African country in return for foreign aid. Generally, the purpose of aid is to secure an initial sphere of economic influence over African governments in order to safeguard economic holdings established during the colonial period, and to promote the further growth of new economic enterprise.

In the newly independent African states, these economic concerns disguise "their identity behind government and international agencies, whose real character is at once exposed whenever their affiliations are examined. They are the real directors of neo-colonialism."[41] The effect of foreign control and domination of African political and economic systems is to prevent the development of a strong economic sector by native Africans, the perpetuation of a low standard of living for the majority of the African people, the depletion of Africa's natural resources, and the transformation of the continent into a dumping ground for the products of the western consumer-oriented mass culture.

Nkrumah's critique of modern capitalism should not be interpreted to mean that he had either become a communist or even particularly open to establishing close relations with communist countries to the exclusion of any western cooperation. Nkrumah was sufficiently intelligent to be able to distinguish between the Marxist principles that guided his analysis of capitalist imperialism and the bogus Marxism and mock socialism of the eastern bloc. He was as careful to avoid entrapment by Soviet totalitarianism as he was opposed to the permanent exercise of economic influence in Africa by the west. Thus, Nkrumah emphasized continually in *Neo-Colonialism* that his foreign policy was based on a strategy of "non-alignment" with either power bloc, despite the fact that he considered the Soviet Union to be a far less imperialist threat "economically" to African sovereignty than were the capitalist nations.

Nkrumah's policy of nonalignment was dictated not only by his desire to protect the autonomy of African nations, but also by his concern for world peace. Nkrumah believed that the successful drive of African countries toward cooperative self-determination would force the capitalist countries to reduce, if not eliminate, their expansionist tendencies. Otherwise they would exhaust themselves economically in an international situation where they no longer had indiscriminate access to the Third World's resources, thereby falling prey to those very same economic, social, and political contradictions and crises which imperialism had enabled them to stave off for so long.

Nkrumah argued that "if the African nations were unified, those who practice neocolonialism would adjust themselves to this new balance of world forces in exactly the same way as the capitalist world has in the past adjusted itself to any other change in the balance of power."[42] World peace would be

[41]Ibid., p. 211.
[42]Ibid., p. 259.

brought about in this manner, through a planned distribution and regulation of indispensable African resources by independent and autonomous Third World countries. Nonalignment was the nonviolent means of forging international cooperation and harmony. World peace would be the result of "positive action."

Dark Days in Ghana, Nkrumah's first major work following his deposition in 1966, marks an entirely new phase of his theoretical development. There are two major themes running through this work. First, an attempt is made to explain the causes of the *coup d'état* and to justify his past policies as political ruler in Ghana in light of that explanation. Second, an entirely new approach is elaborated to confront the phenomenon of neocolonialism to the end of creating a unified and sovereign African continent.

Nkrumah contends that the neocolonial nations were responsible for precipitating the *coup* because of the threat to their power that his policy of nonalignment represented. Neocolonialism could only accomplish through a *coup d'état* what it could not achieve through the usual methods of neocolonial influence. Thus, the *coup* was both a testimony to Nkrumah's successful efforts to gain the allegiance of the masses in opposition to colonial influence, as well as to his failure to restrain effectively the challenge of those indigenous groups who stood to benefit directly and immediately from the economic appeal of neocolonial development. These latter groups included, among others, the civil servants whom Nkrumah retained after independence to meet the administrative needs of the new order; the military who stood to gain political power and prestige by cooperating with foreign powers; the middle and lower middle classes who would benefit from neocolonial economic investments; the traditional authorities (such as the Ashanti chiefs) who would negotiate directly with foreign powers interested in exchanging economic privileges; and certain sectors of the working class, which would benefit from the development of specialized productive spheres. Nkrumah draws the rather belated conclusion that, given the conservative and neocolonialist leanings of those groups who participated in the *coup d'état,* "genuine [African] independence is incompatible with capitalism,"[43] including all attempts at economic cooperation mutually beneficial to western capitalist and African countries alike.

After the *coup,* Nkrumah states that he has little regret that as political head of Ghana he had frequently resorted to strong-arm tactics in his relations with dissident elements after independence had been declared. Furthermore, he now justifies his absolute centralization of authority, and his creation of a one-party state. In retrospect, he views all authoritarian measures as instrumental to the creation of "socialism" in Ghana.[44] He declares that such tactics enabled him to expand the public sector at the expense of the private (when

[43]Kwame Nkrumah, *Dark Days in Ghana* (New York: International Publishers, 1968), p. 63.
[44]Ibid., p. 79.

previously he had stated that he was concerned with a balanced development); to control foreign investment (when in fact the only "control" exercised pertained to his rather personal and unplanned vision of what was good for Ghana); to increase the production of raw materials; to build the Volta Dam (which had taken many years longer than he had promised because of his economic procrastination); to institute an electrification program; to construct hospitals and health centers; and to increase the number of physicians, teachers, and educational facilities at all levels. Although many of these contributions, if not all, were to the benefit of Ghana's people and to Nkrumah's credit, it is far from clear that such an authoritarian regime was needed to make such progress.

Nkrumah's attitude toward the west and his theory about the most effective means to achieve and preserve independence changes radically after 1966. No longer is he predisposed to nonviolent methods of achieving social change. He now calls for a revolution with a mass base. "Imperialism and neo-colonialism must be attacked wherever they are operating throughout the world, and protracted people's wars must be fought until victory is achieved."[45] Positive action, Nkrumah's philosophy of nonviolence, is now exchanged for a philosophy of violence, and Nkrumah and Fanon find a theoretical unity in a nonunified Africa. With this agreement between Nkrumah and Fanon in mind, we can understand why many of Nkrumah's writings subsequent to *Dark Days in Ghana* bore such titles as *Handbook of Revolutionary Warfare: A Guide to the Armed Phase of the African Revolution,* and *Class Struggle in Africa.*[46] Nkrumah's only other writings were essentially lame efforts at a Marxist analysis of western philosophy for the purpose of elucidating its ideologically conservative dimensions and to salvage of it what he could for the purpose of facilitating social change and political development in a future decolonized Africa. These latter works, such as *Conscientism,*[47] are strictly philosophical and theoretical in nature, bearing no actual relationship to either peaceful or violent movements for socialism in Africa.

Thus, Kwame Nkrumah's attitudes toward colonialism and neocolonialism underwent a kind of pilgrim's progress that was similar to many other Africans' who sought to shake off the psychological and physical effects of capitalism by first seeking national independence and then by identifying with the international forces of revolutionary change. We shall be examining current efforts to use both methods simultaneously to develop national independence and reorder society in Chapters 5 and 6. The mistakes that Nkrumah made, as well as the obvious discrepancies between what he said and what he did,

---

[45]Ibid., p. 159.

[46]Kwame Nkrumah, *Handbook of Revolutionary Warfare* (New York: International Publishers, 1969); *Class Struggle in Africa* (New York: International Publishers, 1970).

[47]Kwame Nkrumah, *Conscientism* (New York: Modern Reader Paperbacks, 1970).

are not lost on the new leaders of Angola, Mozambique, and Guiné-Bissau. Nkrumah was many things, but never a consistent "Marxist modernizer."

In the next chapter, we shall identify other African statesmen who have been called "Marxist modernizers" as well as others, such as Leopold Senghor of Senegal and Julius Nyerere of Tanzania, who espouse far different responses to the dilemmas of colonialism, neocolonialism, and underdevelopment.

3

African
Political Thought

Morton Schoolman

In Chapter 2, we examined several important African responses to the problems of colonialism and neocolonialism. For Fanon, it was the catharsis of violence and liberation. For Nkrumah, it was a number of things at different stages of his development, but African unity was probably his most persistent solution.

For other Africans, there were different answers. Julius Nyerere, first president of Tanzania, felt the answer lay in the principles of Ujamaa socialism which stressed man's humanity to his fellows. Leopold Senghor, the leader of Senegal, stressed the need for individual psychic emancipation through the phenomenon of Negritude and the regional groupings of African states. Sekou Touré, the president of Guinea, saw a need for Draconian authoritarianism to wipe out the vestiges of colonialism and neocolonialism. For a number of other Africans, including Eduardo Mondlane and Samora Machel of Mozambique, Amilcar Cabral of Guiné-Bissau, and Agostino Neto of Angola, the answer lay in a modified version of orthodox Marxism, a transplanted ideology which they applied to African conditions.

But, regardless of their differences, all these leaders shared a common experience. All were theoreticians and practical leaders. All were intimately involved in the day-to-day running of independence governments. All were deeply committed to the blending of theory and practice (something which Nkrumah was not). Several, such as Cabral and Mondlane, paid the supreme sacrifice for their beliefs—they were assassinated as they sought to liberate their respective countries from colonial rule. It is to these thinker-doers we now turn.

JULIUS NYERERE

As the political leader of Tanganyika's leading party, the Tanganyika African National Union (TANU), Julius Nyerere led the drive for independence in the same decade that Algeria and Ghana also fought for their own independence. In December 1961, Tanganyika became formally independent from Britain, and Nyerere became the first prime minister. A short time later, in 1962, Tanganyika became a republic and Nyerere its first president. Then, in 1964, the leaders of Tanganyika and Zanzibar united their two countries, which subsequently became known as the United Republic of Tanzania.

The collected writings of Julius Nyerere cover to this entire period and extend to 1973. They are divided into three large volumes. *Freedom and Unity* includes writings and speeches from 1952 to 1965, the pre- and immediate post-independence periods. The political theory contained in this work is general (perhaps deliberately so), calculated, first, to rouse the feelings and interest of a politically apathetic people against colonialism and, subsequently, to harness their emotions and attention to the long and arduous task of social and economic development. The second volume of collected writings and speeches, *Freedom and Socialism,* composed between the years 1965 and 1967, contains substantial documents in political thought, and seems to mark a second phase in his theoretical development. The absence of generality, which characterized *Freedom and Unity,* can easily be explained as a concentrated effort to think clearly and originally about the great challenges associated with building a socialist society after independence and a republican government have been achieved.

Freedom and Development, the third volume of collected papers and speeches, published between 1968 and 1973, does not mark a new stage of theoretical growth, but rather a continuation of the issues and problems examined in *Freedom and Socialism.* This consistency is a virtue and not a shortcoming of Nyerere's thinking, for the project of his second work, the transition to socialism, was carried over into *Freedom and Development* because socialism had not yet been reached in Tanzania by 1967, nor by 1973. It was a distant goal which Nyerere would unwaveringly focus all his energies upon, without any distraction. The common subject matter in *Freedom and Socialism* and *Freedom and Development* is an indication and testimony to his commitment to building a socialist society.

Self-government, therefore, meant a great deal more to Nyerere than the simple transfer of power from either a highly centralized colonial government or even a centralized African government, but was intimately related to the need for political stability and an overall African character of socioeconomic development in Tanganyika. This character and the importance of self-government in promoting it will become clearly understood when we examine Nyerere's concept of African socialism.

On Nationalism

Nyerere was always a strong supporter of the concept of nationalism. In his view of nationalism, the nation is to be viewed as a whole, with its needs superseding to the needs of its individual component parts; that is, its people. This means that all disagreement must be subordinated to a single set of socioeconomic and political objectives. Sustained opposition to the establishment of national priorities could only be interpreted as factionalism and, perhaps, even as treachery.

Nyerere contended, however, that nationalism was no mere demand for solidarity that would make the country strong in the face of a common opponent, colonialism, or weak if such cooperation broke down. On the contrary, nationalism was no artificial political device, but rather had its very roots in African history and traditions. Nationalism was not alien to, but rather a natural outgrowth of, the African mind.

Nyerere, for example, points out that traditionally, despite the importance of tribal authorities, all the elders of the tribe had equal influence over decision making, and decisions were always reached, regardless of initial differences, by "talking until all agreed." Thus, African tradition maintains that unanimity is the outcome of all political process. Nationalism sees the nation and all its members in unanimous agreement on issues and proposals.

Since there is never any possibility, according to Nyerere, of a conflict between the interests of the individual and those of the community or nation, there is really no need for a political party system to represent divergent interests. Given a fundamental agreement on the importance of national interests as a whole, the conception of opposing parties loses its meaning. Indeed, a two-party system would not be recognized as representing legitimately opposing views, but only an expression of private interests. As Nyerere argues, "the politics of a country governed by the two-party system are not, and cannot be, national politics; they are the politics of groups, whose differences, more often than not, are of small concern to the majority of people."[1] In Nyerere's sense, it becomes difficult to speak of two or more "parties," at all, even if they are well-organized political groupings around certain interests. Such groups would be labeled "factions" by Nyerere, undermining their legitimacy. It must follow that only a single-party system is compatible with Africa's tradition of arriving at political decisions.

Only one party is needed to represent the overriding unanimity inherent in the African nation. Needless to say, without a two- or multiparty system, the absence of opposition to the national party, TANU, makes elections somewhat less than democratic in the western sense. Since there is a political agreement on the ends of the state, elections instead should be restricted to selecting the most technically qualified and politically astute, since all candidates have the same ideological qualifications. Nyerere does understand that opposition will arise, but he prefers to see such opponents as "harmless eccentrics," and all societies must allow for such elements if they are to be termed democratic.[2]

It is important, too, to note that Nyerere's concept of nationalism is not restricted to the single nation-state, but applies equally to all nations in the entire African continent in their struggle against colonialism. He declares that "this struggle for freedom from foreign domination is a patriotic one which necessarily leaves no room for difference. It unites all elements in the country so that, not only in Africa but in any other part of the world facing a similar challenge, these countries are led by a nationalist movement, rather than by a political party or parties."[3]

Yet, it is most certainly the case that "one-party democracy," whether it be a single party for Tanganyika or for all countries, is necessary only until independence has been achieved. He does allow for the possible development of a two-party system, of opposition to the nationalist party organization, but such a political venture could only take place when the African people are free from the influence of colonialism and can think clearly about their interests and the interests of their country. This state of purity, however, lies in the distant future.

Nyerere and Nkrumah share the strategy of nonviolence as the form of opposition to colonialism, though Nyerere apparently did not feel that nonviolence required a theoretical justification for he gives it negligible philosophical attention. This does not mean that Nyerere was less committed to nonviolence than Nkrumah. On the contrary, Nkrumah may have been preoccupied with the philosophy of "positive action" because he was extremely impressed with the outward severity of colonial oppression; he consequently believed that the choice between violence and nonviolence had to be carefully analyzed in terms of strategic as well as philosophical considerations.

[1]Julius Nyerere, *Freedom and Unity* (London: Oxford University Press, 1967), p. 197.
[2]Ibid., p. 106.
[3]Ibid., p. 106.

Nyerere, on the other hand, makes a simple, straightforward, and unqualified commitment to nonviolence. This can be explained by his understanding, unique in contrast to either Fanon or Nkrumah, that colonialism was part of a much larger socioeconomic and political system that has its origin and roots far beyond the borders of the African continent, and that could not be overcome through a defeat of its colonial representatives in African countries. Nyerere expresses this by saying that the "African can see that his quarrel is not with the non-Africans in his midst, but with the colonial system itself."[4] Violence against the colonial settlers would mistake the symptoms for the disease.

On the other hand, Nyerere found that violence was necessary if the colonial authority would not abdicate power peacefully. For example, while Nyerere constantly worked for and supported a peaceful solution to the problem of African majority rule in Rhodesia, Angola, Mozambique, Namibia, and South Africa, he gave material assistance and even sanctuary to the African nationalists from Mozambique, Rhodesia, and South Africa who were engaged in guerrilla warfare during the 1960s and 1970s.

We discover in Nyerere's *Freedom and Unity* the familiar theme that complete and permanent independence for any one African country is possible only after all African nations have pledged their unity and solidarity with one another—after pan-Africanism has become a reality. Imperialism succeeds through the method of *divide et impera,* divide and conquer. By gaining a foothold in a small number of African states, colonialism can more easily extend its influence over other African nations which could only resist through the aid of their neighboring countries—which is made impossible if the neighboring countries themselves are ruled by colonial powers.

Another difficulty associated with the "divide and conquer" influence of colonial powers over a few African nations is that there is a danger, first considered during our discussion of Nkrumah, that a disagreement between the eastern and western blocs could easily drag all of Africa into a conflict that initially would be fought in any single African country occupied by colonial power. Nyerere makes this point precisely when he states that "no one of us is safe [referring to all African nations] if any one of us gets involved in the Cold War between East and West, or in any other world conflicts which are irrelevant to our own problems."[5] Like Nkrumah, Nyerere saw pan-African unity as a means of minimizing tensions between the two great power blocs, and as a great step toward world peace and international cooperation.[6] But, unlike Nkrumah, Nyerere felt that one had to get one's own house in order first before embarking on any grand continent-wide schemes for African unity.

After independence, which Nyerere knew would be accomplished, there

[4]Ibid., p. 74.
[5]Ibid., p. 212.
[6]Ibid., p. 263.

would yet be an objective need for economic assistance from western powers. In *Freedom and Unity* he left open the possibility for neocolonial influence, although he was careful to differentiate between economic aid with "strings attached," which would not be accepted, and aid that entailed no infringements on national sovereignty. In the late 1950s, when Nyerere was leading Tanganyika to independence, he was sensitive to the backwardness of his country, and that it was afflicted with great poverty, disease, and illiteracy.

Nyerere believed that complete severing of all relations with western powers was impractical and not in the best interests of his people. He constantly underscored the importance of foreign investment to raise the standard of living in his country in the shortest possible time. Moreover, he believed that the European settler was not the enemy of the African, but rather that the larger, more insuperable opponent was the "system" of colonialism. He therefore felt that accepting some economic aid and foreign investment would at least minimize social tension and bitterness and avoid the possibility of a race war between the African and non-African who he believed had a right to remain in Tanganyika. Yet, though most of Nyerere's work seems to favor economic cooperation with the west, he is often adamant in saying that Tanganyika would accept economic loss if the political balance was upset decisively in Africa by the European settlers attempting to assert their hegemony.

One such example of Nyerere's obstinacy in refusing to enter into economic agreements with western powers, was during Britain's tacit support of colonialism in South Africa in admitting it into the Commonwealth. Like Nkrumah, Nyerere felt it was possible and desirable to do business with Tanganyika's excolonialist masters, but he threatened that no relations could be forged if it involved him in a conflict of interest—that is, a situation where he would stand for the independence of African nations, for pan-Africanism, and simultaneously belong to an international organization that engaged in trade with a colonialist country.

Nyerere declared forcefully that "in order to establish such a degree of African unity, Tanganyika would give up her Commonwealth Membership."[7] Before Nyerere had the chance to withdraw from the Commonwealth, the Commonwealth responded to Nyerere's threat by banning South Africa from the league. We will see shortly that in Nyerere's second major volume of writings, *Freedom and Socialism,* all the important issues bearing on economic relations with foreign powers are put into much sharper focus.

On Civil Service

As with Nkrumah, the recruitment of native Africans to serve in the bureaucracy was a high priority for Nyerere. In *Freedom and Unity,* Nyerere's

[7]Ibid., p. 136.

argument for an Africanized civil service was not based, as it was with Nkrumah, on the question of administrative competence and the loyalty of the bureaucracy to the dictates of the political institutions. These considerations are not even implicit in Nyerere's discussions of this issue. Nyerere was more fundamentally interested in a bureaucracy that recruited its officials according to a general quota system. All social communities are to be represented in the administrative apparatus proportional to their numbers in the society generally.

This formula comes closest to compromising Nyerere's opposition to multiracial policies, but at the same time it approximates democratic representation with the bureaucracy, though at the expense of recruiting the most qualified candidates for the administrative positions. (We shall see that Nyerere later realized this problem and altered his views on recruitment.) Because Africans comprise the majority of the population, a native African would be favored for a post over a non-African settler, even though the settler might be more qualified in terms of education and experience. This quota system of representation would succeed in giving the civil service what Nyerere referred to as a "local look" and would extend to other institutions of government. Nyerere argues, for example, that the legislature must also have a local look. It must have a "cross-section of the racial population of our country."[8] Nyerere admits, in fact, that such a system of representation is a form of discrimination.[9]

On Socialism

Nyerere's theory of African socialism is the most important dimension of his political thought. In *Freedom and Unity,* we receive an idea of its basic characteristics. Take, for example, Nyerere's attitude toward property. The most fundamental form of property is the common land, which must be used for the benefit of all people since it is a "gift from God, given to all living things." Nyerere maintains that all men have a natural right to the land and to its products, which precludes its being owned as private property to serve private interests. All those who use land should occupy it only as tenants, and their claims should be temporary and justifiable so long as the property is worked for the public good.

These conditions under which property may be used supposes other important restrictions. Since land is cultivated for the public welfare, no one can have a claim to more property than he can work himself. This means that no single individual can own a large farm, and a situation where economic distinctions between employers and wage laborers, property owners and the propertyless

[8]Ibid., p. 101.
[9]Ibid., p. 101.

prevail can never arise. These economic constraints have, in turn, a significant impact on the development of the social structure. Since an economic separation between employers and wage laborers cannot emerge, a social class structure cannot evolve from income disparities which in turn could be the result of an economic division of labor. Time and time again, Nyerere emphasized that in an independent Tanganyika he wanted to prevent a class hierarchy from taking the place of a racial hierarchy. It is certainly crucial how the logic of what appears to be a self-evident proposition, "the land is a gift from God, given to all living things," can necessarily lead to the formation of a social fabric without class distinctions.

Nyerere's "leasehold system" where no one can occupy more property than he can work or longer than he can work it, was also instrumental in his battle against colonialism, and owed much to existing patterns of land use as practiced by the many segmented societies in Tanzania. As outlined in Chapter 1, the right to the *use* of land as opposed to the ownership of land is fundamental to most African traditional systems. In the "freehold system, anyone can own land as *private* property. The rights of private ownership extend to the right to dispose of the land according to the owner's discretion. The crucial weakness of this system, as Nyerere strongly argues, is that a theory of private property does not prevent, but rather makes possible, the sale of land to wealthy non-Africans. It can easily be seen that this right of private property disposal eventually can lead to social distinctions where colonialists become powerful land owners, and Africans are reduced to dependent wage laborers. Such economic power will produce a social hierarchy which can become institutionalized as political domination. And, of course, out of a hierarchy where the economic masters become the social and political masters, the subordinate economic, social, and political class can be effectively exploited, with little chance for their successful rebellion or even an improvement in their overall societal status.

The leasehold system, where the land is nationalized for the common benefit of the nation, permits the government to oversee its distribution. This system not only guarantees that everyone who is willing to work will have land, but also provides loans to the African farmer to enable him to work the land productively. The farmer is only required to pay a yearly rent (a tax of sorts) to the government, which is then used to develop the country in important nonagricultural areas, or is invested in other farms and agricultural ventures. The leasehold system, based upon a theory of property that emphasizes common over private ownership, is closely related to the prosperity of the individual African and the country as a whole, the absence of economic and social class distinctions, and the political sovereignty and independence from colonial imposition.

Nyerere's African socialism does not exclude non-Africans from Tanganyika. He favors "integration" as we have seen, for example, in the sharing of political power in local governmental councils by white colonial settlers and African chiefs. But Nyerere would make no compromise with the colonial powers that might allow the white settler an even slightly greater influence than the native on Tanganyikan policy. Ultimately, all governmental and legislative bodies must be predominantly African; white minority interests would still be preserved and protected as long as they involved no violation of African sovereignty.[10]

Nyerere was always careful to stress that the protection of the interests of the white minorities does not involve a safeguarding of their rights as a separate racial "community," but only as "individual human" rights. Nyerere made this distinction between the rights of racial groups and the rights of individuals, to prevent any policy based on racial distinction from being formulated. A multiracial society does not mean a multiracial policy. In fact, all multiracial societies in the west that boast of being democratic have only a concept of individual rights, not racial community rights. In the latter case the danger of particularized laws turning into specialized discriminatory treatment with ethnic, racial, and geographical fragmentation and conflict was great.

Nyerere's idea that African traditions should serve as the basis for all future African development is related to a corresponding notion of "negritude," which we first encountered in Fanon's work. Nyerere is aware (although perhaps not as clearly as Fanon who was able to analyze the problem of black identity with the aid of an interesting and useful psychological framework) that continual exposure of the African to the white European settler meant that the native would adopt western values, attitudes, and aspirations. In short, he would be an African with a "black skin," wearing a "white mask."

Nyerere argues that African self-determination, following the guidelines provided by African history, would mean that "an African in Africa will never become simply a black European."[11] Nyerere was considerably more optimistic than Fanon regarding the African's ability to resist the western influence, regardless of whether the influence was felt in a colonial or noncolonial independence framework. But it is also important to understand that Nyerere had no such "pure" conception of African culture as is suggested by Fanon's (or Senghor's) "negritude." Rather he saw virtue and benefit to be derived from a synthesis of an African heritage with many of the secular and religious elements of European civilization. With Nyerere we discover a faith in the power of the African past to temper and moderate the impact of western culture. This belief of Nyerere's is fascinating, both for its originality among African political thinkers and for its open-ended and liberal tolerance toward the possible shape of the African future. This illustrated by his statement that

[10]Ibid., p. 65.
[11]Ibid., p. 116.

"no one can accurately foretell how all the different pressures will reveal themselves in the Africa of the year 2000."[12] Nyerere's philosophy appears to embrace a loyalty to the weighty traditions of Africa and, as well, a broader humanism that transcends all racial and cultural boundaries.

The power of African tradition to exercise a formative influence over the future breeding of African and European culture and civilization can be understood better by considering Nyerere's first comprehensive description, in 1962, of an African political theory, which he entitled "Ujamaa—The Basis of African Socialism."

Ujamaa means "familyhood" in a literal sense, but the family we are considering here is not related by blood ties, but rather involves a "community spirit" which sees all people as "brothers." The phrase "brotherhood of men" has become somewhat trivialized in the west owing to the violence, competitiveness, and radical individualism of modern civilization, which has made brotherhood seem either like a cliché or an unattainable ideal. In Africa, however, brotherhood had a real concrete history in familyhood, where the welfare of each individual became the direct concern of the tribal community. There, the wealth produced and acquired by the tribal members became the accumulated wealth of the community, to be then distributed equally to satisfy everyone's needs. In order to qualify for an equal share of the tribe's productivity, each was expected to contribute to the work of maintaining the material prosperity of the community. There were no distinctions based on individual wealth or on social prestige. All occupations, from the simplest farmer to the senior elder rulers of the tribe, had an equal status with equal prestige. Since all occupations had an equal standing in the eyes of the community, there could be no such distinctions as between employers and workers. All were considered to be workers. The only members of the tribe excused from work were the very young, the infirm, and the elders, who would serve the community as rulers when no longer able to work in other capacities.

These notions of equal treatment, equal standing, and equal distribution are much more than the principles of traditional African social organization. Spiritually and practically, they run much deeper. We can understand them as centuries-long practices which become a "frame of mind." Or, as Nyerere says, African socialism is an attitude. A frame of mind does not disappear under the duress of colonialism, nor is it easily exchanged for the highly competitive and self-seeking mentality associated with capitalist economic and social development.

There is no need, therefore, to speak of "converting" the African to socialism, as western socialists do when they address the possibility and necessity of "radicalizing" the westerner or "raising his consciousness" to learn and accept socialist teachings. Nor does it make sense, in the context of Ujamaa,

[12]Ibid., p. 116.

to argue that capitalism must be a fully developed system before a socialist economic basis can be produced or the social conditions for a revolution can emerge. African traditions *are* socialist traditions, and all that is required for Africa to become a socialist society is that "familyhood" be extended to the entire nation.[13]

An African country can be industrialized and modernized like a capitalist society—the decisive difference is the principles that determine the *distribution* of wealth and the principles that determine *what* will be produced, not the methods that determine its production. And, as we have seen, the extension of Ujamaa to the nation means the nationalization of land when the economy is primarily agriculture. We may add now that when the African economy becomes industrialized, "familyhood" for the entire country would also mean the nationalization of industry.

Nyerere's Later Writings

In *Freedom and Unity,* we find Nyerere to be quite general. His second volume of collected writings and speeches, *Freedom and Socialism,* was composed between 1965 and 1967, and marks a second phase in the development of his political thought. In it we find a more deliberate and conscientious effort to describe his concept of a socialist society. As Nyerere explains, to build a socialist republic after independence is a very different thing from the tasks associated with gaining independence from colonialism, for "it demands a positive understanding and positive actions, not simply a rejection of colonialism and a willingness to cooperate in non-cooperation."[14]

All the important documents which, taken together, contain Nyerere's precise statement on the nature of socialism, are included in *Freedom and Socialism.* One paper in this work holding particular historic significance— "The Arusha Declaration: Socialism and Self-Reliance"—is noteworthy because it was an explicit statement of African socialism as *the* national ideology. What was earlier a vague philosophy based on African traditions, has become transformed in 1967, the date of the public declaration, into a well-defined set of political, social, and economic goals. Since it is only remarkable for its public and not its theoretical significance, the Arusha Declaration shall be considered in the general context of an examination of *Freedom and Socialism.*

An outstanding feature of this second stage of Nyerere's socialist political theory is the open-ended character of a socialist society. A socialist order can assume any of a great variety of institutional formations. A broad spectrum

---

[13]Ibid., p. 170.

[14]Julius Nyerere, *Freedom and Socialism* (London: Oxford University Press, 1968), p. 29. Nyerere is not using the expression "positive action" in a manner after Nkrumah, but is merely speaking of activity that brings beneficial results.

of organizational patterns is possible and permissible. There may be a highly centralized or decentralized economic structure. The economy itself may be agrarian, industrial, or a combination of both types. African socialism may incorporate productive techniques from western societies. It may borrow ideas about agricultural reform used in the communes of China, or adopt the educational theories of Cuba, or the organizational patterns of the cooperative settlements of Denmark, Sweden, and Israel. Nyerere's point is that there is no single best socialist society. The universality of socialism is defined by its great diversity of methods of social construction. Each socialist order must be built in light of the character of a people, their culture and beliefs, the level of technological and scientific achievement, and a thousand other peculiarities which make them different and perhaps even unique in comparison to other peoples. A newly developing socialist order should not copy the socialism of another country. This course of action could only fail because of the radical and fundamental differences between the populations of the two countries. By the same token, experimentation must remain the rule during socialist construction, meaning that techniques, methods, and strategies for achieving socialist goals can be adopted from other nations, regardless of whether those nations are former colonial powers or communist. Nyerere summarizes this universal, experimental and creative socialist spirit by saying that there is no single "socialist road map," no "natural laws," which can guarantee a new society. There is "no 'pure' socialism."[15]

Despite the vast proliferation of shapes and contours that socialism can take, all these socialist societies hold in common certain essential characteristics. Nyerere stresses that man must be the highest value and goal of socialism. That is, the potentiality of human development is by nature limitless, and men must always be as free as possible from any political, social, or economic condition that would constrain their freedom to develop human faculties.

Thus, capitalism, which has indisputably encouraged and depended upon the development of human talents, nevertheless seems to be preoccupied with nurturing those powers which directly contribute to increasing industrial output and material productivity. Nyerere, on the other hand, would maintain that modernization should be retarded at that point at which production begins to upset the environment and destroy the beauty of nature. Man, for Nyerere, must develop as a "social consumer" as well as a "private consumer." His material appetites must be kept to that threshold at which the harmony between man and nature is not disturbed. If this necessarily means that the African socialist must be poor in comparison to his western and eastern industrialized neighbors, then poverty becomes a socialist virtue.

Socialism for the African also means an unqualified commitment to absolute equality among all people. The African socialist must be dedicated to the

[15]Ibid., p. 302.

development and preservation of a classless order, without social and economic distinctions of any kind. Second, Socialist democracy means free elections, where all equally elect candidates to, or can occupy, political office.

Third, work is a civic obligation under African socialism. For an able person not to work would be an unpatriotic act. The motivation to work, though, is very high, for the individual receives "a return in proportion to his efforts and his contribution to the well-being of the community."[16] What had been only a principle or ideal of African socialism in *Freedom and Unity,* Nyerere turns into a law with coercive sanction in *Freedom and Socialism.*

A fourth and decisive element of Nyerere's socialism is its determination to root out every form of exploitation. Since all must work, there can be no distinction between the idle and the productive member of society. No one is denied responsibility for the public good. No one can benefit from another's labor without making a comparable contribution. But, regardless of the type of occupation, there can be no disparities in the "return" for work; that is, no inequalities in income.[17]

Another crucial trait of Nyerere's socialist theory is the unqualified emphasis on the public ownership of the means of production—farms, factories, and all large apparatus and technologies of production that cannot be operated by a single person. What is particularly interesting about Nyerere's public ownership doctrine in *Freedom and Socialism,* is that there is still some discussion of private investment from foreign powers, as there had been in the preindependence and immediate postindependence writings. Although there seems to be a contradiction between the existence of private enterprise, with its accompanying attitudes of private gain, and the socialist attitudes that Nyerere wants to encourage, particularly a concern for the common good, Nyerere is oriented toward a "progressive" nationalization of the private capitalist sectors which would be completed when Tanzania is capable of economic self-sufficiency. He intends to "put a stop to any *future* large-scale exploitation of workers and peasants through the private ownership of the means of production and exchange."[18] A radical elimination of all private enterprise would upset a precarious agricultural economy and inflict intolerable hardships on his people. He prefers a gradualist approach to its removal, which is justified by the "transitional" character of Tanzania's groping toward socialism, which we shall consider shortly.

Two final aspects of Nyerere's socialism concern the sanctity of individual freedom. First, the individual's small private property holdings are untouched by the state. Homes, furniture, small tools, and so forth, which can be used

[16]Ibid., p. 5.

[17]Nyerere does admit, however, that inequality in income can sometimes be used as a serviceable device to spur the incentive to work harder.

[18]Nyerere, *Freedom and Socialism,* p. 398.

by a single person, are purchased and kept at the discretion of the citizen. More important, however, is the protection of the individual's natural and inalienable rights.

Nyerere singles out religious freedom for special attention. Unlike communist and socialist societies in eastern Europe, African socialism allows all people to practice the religion of their choice, and also refrains from making any set of beliefs into the religion of the state, which would carry the danger of religious favoritism and intolerance. Socialism must be secular. Religious freedom and all the other rights of men to be found in Nyerere's socialist society, are to be incorporated into a formal constitution and protected by the rule of law.[19] Ujamaa socialism is, therefore,

> . . . opposed to capitalism which seeks to build a happy society on the basis of the exploitation of man by man; and it is equally opposed to doctrinaire socialism which seeks to build its happy society on a philosophy of inevitable conflict between man and man.[20]

On the Transition from Neocolonialism to Socialism

Freedom and Socialism, as indicated, is devoted to a consideration of difficulties of building a socialist society, of the "transition" to socialism. Not all of the principles, ideals, socioeconomic and political goals that we have examined in this second work of Nyerere's should be understood as having been realized. On the contrary, Nyerere stresses that Tanzania will make progress toward socialism in an evolutionary manner. What we have considered thus far in *Freedom and Socialism* is an elaboration of the objectives of Nyerere's socialism, and the theory that the means to achieve those ends can be diverse and heterogeneous. But, though Nyerere does insist that the paths to socialism can be as different as peoples, histories, and cultures, he does have a specific theory about the manner in which Tanzania should make the transition to socialism.

In the transitional period, Nyerere focused much of the country's economic energies on the improvement and development of agricultural techniques. One illustration of the ambitions of Nyerere's investments in the agrarian economy is the founding of Morogaro Agricultural College in 1965. An interesting practical dimension of agricultural training at the college was the contact which the students had with the people of the surrounding districts.

Not only was there an immediate contribution made to Tanzania in agricultural production by the college's students prior to their graduation, but other skills were taught by the students, as well, to raise the literacy rate among the

---

[19]Ibid., p. 304.
[20]Nyerere, *Freedom and Unity,* p. 170.

population. This contact between students and ordinary citizens, mostly peasants, had the added effect of encouraging those who received the benefits of higher education to identify with the needs of common people. This helped to prevent the development of a status and prestige hierarchy—a socially stratified society with the tensions and inequalities which Nyerere wanted to avoid.

It was felt there was wisdom in concentrating the public's efforts in agricultural production. As all Tanzanians knew, and as Nyerere constantly pointed out, agriculture had always been the basis of the African economy and was a strong foundation to build upon. Also, since it was imperative to raise the standard of living of all Tanzanians as quickly as possible (for in many parts of the country people were surviving on less than subsistence level income), efficient agricultural production could meet the needs of the country faster than a drive towards industrialization. Agriculture, rather than industry, was given priority. Nyerere was adamant: agriculture "is the only road through which we can develop our country."[21] Yet, subsistence was the most that the majority of the population could expect, for farmers were heavily taxed by the government to pay for the rapid construction of schools, factories, roads, telephones, offices and homes.

"Ujamaa villages" would be organized as cooperatives, which the peasants and workers themselves "create and govern, and which are the basis for the productive activities of the members."[22] Eventually, several villages would combine their efforts, or become "interlocked,"[23] and together form a larger cooperative to promote an even more advanced industrial development.[24] Here we have an excellent example of Nyerere's conception of the function of national leadership, which is not to establish particular goals for Africans, but rather to set guidelines and to provide supervision.

The task of leadership is to help the people create a socioeconomic and political framework that allows for the expression of already existing socialist inclinations within the hearts and minds of the African people. We saw this same relationship between the goals of a socialist society and popular participation earlier during our examination of the idea of "socialism from below." But this democratic aspect of Nyerere's theory of the function of leadership is somewhat compromised when he points out that for the government to properly serve the interests of the people it must not *only* "propose, explain,

[21]Ibid., p. 244.
[22]Ibid., p. 405.
[23]Ibid., p. 348.
[24]For a description of Ujamaa socialism in practice, see Ibid., pp. 353-55; of the step-by-step process involved in forming an Ujamaa village, see Ibid., pp. 357-59. William Duggan and John Civille have characterized Ujamaa villages ". . . as a combination of the Israeli *kibbutz*, the Chinese-type communal farm, and the traditional African extended family." See their *Tanzania and Nyerere: A Study of Ujamaa and Nationalism* (Maryknoll, Md.: Orbis Books, 1976), p. 128.

and persuade."[25] Persuasion does not always depend on words, and may require active intervention by the government to insist that certain measures be adopted to improve the quality of life,[26] as when the government must insist that one crop be abandoned in favor of a new one. Nyerere had decided to drag Tanzania into the twentieth century through a modernization program fueled by a rather primitive economy and economic organization by any standards. But, regardless of the initially primitive character of Ujamaa socialism, Nyerere believes that it will enable Tanzania to accomplish "in decades what it took other countries centuries to build."[27]

That the Tanzanian people should forego even the most basic amenities of life beyond subsistence, was the personal cost of what Nyerere referred to as national "self-reliance."[28] Between the time of independence and 1965, nearly halfway through Nyerere's first development plan for Tanzania begun in 1964, he disclosed that many of the offers from foreign powers for economic aid and assistance had to be rejected because of the political strings attached. In addition to this problem, the benefits from many economic aid pacts that were successfully negotiated were only to be reaped years after the final agreement had been made. Since much foreign aid had to be rejected or its advantages would accrue perhaps several years after actual needs were felt, self-sacrifice for the Tanzanian was the rule. The formal public expression of this rule became self-reliance—borrowing as little from foreign sources as possible, and taxing the public to pay for all social and economic developments. This was done at the price of maintaining a subsistence-level standard of living for the great majority, who would deposit all surplus from their work into the public treasury, indefinitely postponing the smallest gratification that might be gained from such devotion.

Nyerere did not reject all economic assistance; he was not interested in self-reliance for its own sake. Such a policy would be arrogant and inconsiderate of his people. Self-reliance meant that Tanzania would be organized in such a way that there would be development even if there were no foreign investment and aid.[29] Clearly, those who would most benefit from this policy of "self-reliance" were the generations of future Tanzania. Nyerere makes great demands among his people. He argues that "there is a job to be done which will often be difficult, and often demand the renunciation of personal comfort. It will offer in return the challenge and the satisfaction of contributing to the building of a socialist society for the benefit of our children and grandchildren."[30] And Nyerere summarizes his maxim of duty and self-sacrifice for

[25]Nyerere, *Freedom and Socialism,* p. 310.
[26]Ibid., p. 386.
[27]Ibid., p. 317.
[28]Ibid., p. 171.
[29]Ibid., p. 388.
[30]Ibid., p. 326.

posterity by saying that "the more we buy goods to enjoy [in the present], the less we can buy of the goods [e.g., machines] which will produce wealth in the future."[31] Self-reliance, it must be understood, is the sacrifice that Nyerere determined must accompany independence from neocolonialism.

Within this context we can get a clearer picture of Nyerere's attitude toward pan-African unity. The sacrifices that the Tanzanian people make on behalf of their nation's drive toward self-reliance, could easily become impossible to bear if they were increased by efforts to relieve some of the economic hardships in Tanzania's neighboring African countries. Yet, the need to make a common pact between the nations of Africa, to provide economic supports in order to promote unity, is necessary to eliminate the vulnerability of *some* African states to colonial or neocolonial influence. Such cooperation makes it all the more likely that *all* African countries can more effectively oppose colonialism in all its forms by opposing its "divide and conquer" strategy.

There is a conflict, then, between the African political leader's dedication to his own nation, his people's self-sacrifice and contribution to the nation, and the "inter"-national need for unity and cooperation to prevent colonialism from acquiring a permanent foothold in any part of Africa. If the head of state exacts greater public sacrifice for the cause of unity, he stands the chance of losing the support of his people; instability being the consequence. If he does not promote African unity, he runs the risk that the weaker African states will fall to colonialism, thereby weakening collective resistance to foreign domination and placing other single African countries in jeopardy of losing their independence! Nyerere refers to this situation as the "dilemma of the Pan-Africanist," and is expressed simply as the conflict between African nationalism and internationalism, something Nkrumah failed to understand. Nyerere articulates the dimensions of this conflict and the implications of a premature solution:

> Those who would like to advocate complete concentration on national interests, and those who would demand the sacrifice of all national interests to the cause of African freedom and unity, both have an easy road to tread. The one can appeal to "realism" and "pragmatism," and can appear to be devoted to the practical interests of the people. The other can appeal to the hearts of men, and can appear courageous, self-sacrificing, and revolutionary. Both would lead Africa to disaster.[32]

Nyerere's own solution to the "dilemma" is cautious, or at least somewhat conservative, but involves the same spirit associated with the "transitional" stage to Tanzanian socialism. Nyerere suggests that the problem should not be defined in either-or terms, but that all African states should encourage the

[31]Ibid., p. 168.
[32]Ibid., p. 216.

growth of nationalism to make all states strong economically and politically, but such national growth should always be equally for promoting international cooperation. Thus, an economically developing African nation can offer some assistance to other African states on particular and manageable problems. Unity can begin with the movement "toward" integration, until all African states are sufficiently strong—as a result of efforts of each nation's people, and the aid extended in limited areas by other African countries—that a "merger of international African sovereignties" can occur. As Nyerere declares, "African unity does not have to be a dream; it can be a vision which inspires us."[33]

Nyerere's belief in the importance of self-reliance also entails a compromise of an earlier position found in *Freedom and Unity*. It will be recalled that before independence had been achieved, Nyerere favored the Africanization of the Tanganyikan civil service. Administrative personnel recruitment would be primarily among native Africans, though it would also be representative of other non-African groups. This was Nyerere's "cross-section" proposal, which would staff the bureaucracy according to general racial quotas, rather than on the basis of merit.

In *Freedom and Socialism,* Nyerere does an about face, and argues that civil servants should be recruited strictly according to ability, regardless of whether they are native or non-African. "When members of our family are sick," points out Nyerere, "what we want is a competent doctor, not necessarily a citizen."[34] What is said here about the doctor applies equally to bureaucrats.

But the most important qualification is the recruit's political beliefs, and if a native Tanzanian and non-African of equal competence were being considered for a civil-service post, the decision would rest on their respective ideologies. Nyerere makes this very clear when he says that in Tanzania "we also have a second thing which we really desire of people working for us. Ideally, we also need socialists in every job—which is not necessarily the same thing as wanting a citizen, because not all Tanzanians are socialists."[35] The lesson here, which Nkrumah learned too late, is that to have a socialist nation one must first have socialists.

It can be expected that building a socialist order required that Nyerere do some serious thinking, if not comprehensive planning, about the nature of education during the transitional stage. The most important goal of the educational system in Tanzania, Nyerere contended, was the task of overcoming deeply implanted antisocialist attitudes inherited from the colonial experience. In this regard, Nyerere and Fanon are in complete agreement that capitalist values remain long after independence has been achieved. This comment by Nyerere could have been composed by Fanon:

[33]Ibid., p. 216.
[34]Ibid., p. 386.
[35]Ibid., p. 387.

There has been a general acceptance of the social attitudes and ideas of our colonial masters. We have got rid of the foreign government, but we have not rid ourselves of the individualistic social attitudes which they represented and taught. For it was through these overseas contacts that we developed the idea that the way to comfort and prosperity, which everyone wants, is through selfishness and individual advancement.[36]

In addition to the individualism and private gain attitude promoted by colonialism, the lures of the supposed advantages of urban life in a modernizing society prevailed. If Africans continue to prefer the questionable comforts and security of urban living, popular support for a transitional economy to socialism based on Ujamaa would receive little support. Where there was agricultural production, it often was contrary to the spirit of African socialism. Thus, Nyerere urged in 1967 that Tanzania should be turned against the dominant trend—agricultural production on capitalist principles—which turned cooperatives for the public good into cooperatives to serve the private interests of individual farmers.

To overcome the colonial heritage, education must do more than teach skills, facts, and basic curriculum. It must provide a "social" education. There must be a conscientious effort to restore the temporarily misplaced traditions by rediscovering African history and language in the classrooms. In this way, education would teach cooperation and other values of African socialism; such as equality and hard work, by recovering the African past. The practical side to such education is decisive. The traditions of Africa are learned as they are "experienced." The student works in the villages, on the farms, with the people, as he is being educated. The wisdom of the past is joined with the methods of the present. These ideals associated with Ujamaa are not, therefore, abstract; they are not being imposed from above or imported from a foreign country. They are located in the memories of the African people. For Nyerere, socialism is a remembering.

In Nyerere's most recent collection of writing and speeches, *Freedom and Development,* composed between 1968 and 1973, we find a continuation of the same themes discussed in *Freedom and Socialism.* Nyerere is preoccupied with further elaborating the importance of self-government and administrative decentralization, the supremacy of the people, and the task of the party in maintaining constant contact with the people. In addition, he discusses the significance of the rule of law, the conviction that a healthy democracy depends upon the public exercising its right to vote by responsibly choosing the candidate best qualified for office, his strong determination to overcome nationalism in order to engage in greater economic cooperation to promote pan-Africanism, and the many other topics considered in the previous works.

[36]Ibid., p. 340.

Freedom and Development also charts the progress Tanzania has made toward socialism. The nationalization of the private sector has proceeded according to plan; although the rural areas are frequently bedrocks of conservative peasant farmers who resist change, Ujamaa villages have expanded their numbers greatly. Some progress has been made toward industrial development, and production targets have been established in both industry and agriculture as part of a more efficient comprehensive planning program guiding the construction of a socialist order.

Yet, while little is new in *Freedom and Development* in the way of domestic project proposals (beyond Nyerere's steady commitment to pan-Africanism), there are a few new and important developments in the international arena. In particular, he called for moral and economic support from the industrialized eastern European socialist regimes to aid the developing countries in the battle against colonialism and in their efforts to become economically self-sufficient. Perhaps the most dramatic change in his thinking has occurred in his attitude toward the west. In *Freedom and Development,* he unabashedly declares that capitalism and socialism are incompatible because the former *must* resort to imperialist exploitation to survive. This tendency of modern capitalism is clearly a threat to the security and sovereignty of developing socialist countries.

We should remember, however, that, regardless of Nyerere's increasing attention to the domestic technical problems and the international political problems which retard the transition of Tanzania to socialism, he never lost sight of the highest value in his political thought. This goal is man.

LEOPOLD SENGHOR

If Julius Nyerere advocated a nonracial, humanistic form of African socialism (socialism with a small "s"), Leopold Senghor can be thought of as proposing an elite-oriented (even elitest) form of African socialism. This is due, in part, to his background. Born to a family of considerable wealth, Senghor spent his early childhood in Djilor, but quickly became noticed as a brilliant student. He won a number of scholarships, attending the Lycée Louis-le-Grand and the most prestigious of French schools, the Ecole Normale Supérieur.

Reacting to the tenets of French colonialism, particularly its denigration of African civilizations, Senghor joined with a number of other black students from the West Indies to form a library group that published a cultural magazine featuring works by black people. *L'Edudian Noir* was designed specifically to resist the French system of assimilation. These alienated, lonely students began to say that western, European values should be rejected. They argued the African culture was rich, beautiful, and worthy of emulation. In fact, they went further, asserting that black was truly something special:

> The white will never be negro
> for beauty is negro
> and negro is wisdom
> for endurance is negro
> and negro is courage
> for patience is negro
> and negro is irony. . . . [37]

This assertion of the worth of blackness became known as "Negritude." Although the term originated in a 1939 poem by Aime Cesaire, then a student from Martinique, it became most clearly associated with Senghor. For Senghor, Negritude was the essence of blackness, the African gift for mythmaking, rhythm. The Negro personality relied on intuition, on emotion, on going to the heart of things. It was antimaterialistic, "antirational," against the dehumanization of modern life as practiced in Europe. Viewed 30 years later, Negritude seems vain, puffed up, and almost silly. But in the context of colonialism, it served a poignant and real need for those who expressed it. As a movement, it grew following World War II. In 1947, Alioune Diop founded Presence Africaine, which published the works of black authors, even where Senghor himself published his *Anthologie de la Nouvelle Poésie Nègre Et Malgache de Langue Francais.* To those African students struggling against the suffocating embrace of colonialism, Negritude was an expression of revolt.

Senghor himself quickly turned from the "antiracism racism" of the early Negritude to a fuller and richer meaning whereby Negritude was a broader, more all-encompassing assembly of African contribution to world civilization. Yet, for all its poignancy and shifting concepts, Negritude as a movement never caught on in Africa. Its strength and heartwrenching power for black men in Europe or America was its weakness in Africa. As we shall see in Chapter 4, Negritude never became an African literary attitude, but, rather, one which Africans living in Europe or the United States expressed. The black writer living in Africa, embedded in his own society, did not need to claim his blackness; it was his to begin with. It was, rather, the black intellectuals abroad, cut off from their spiritual and actual homeland whose alientation was the real source of the movement. Negritude remained a psychological, cultural, and intellectual movement, with only minimal political impact in Africa.

Indeed, Negritude was attacked by a host of political thinkers from Fanon to Soyinke. Wole Soyinke, for example, wrote, "Negritude is rather silly. After all, a tiger does not spend his time going around expressing his tigertude." Ezekiel Mphalele put it another way:

Must the educated African from abroad come back to recolonize us? Must he walk about with his mouth open, startled by the beauty of African

---

[37]From the poem, "Negritude," by Leon Damas.

women, by the black man's "heightened sensuality"? Its all so embarras-
ing.[38]

Marcien Towa goes even further, terming Negritude a servant of colonialism
and claiming that it has done more harm than good for the cause of African
liberation.[39]

But these criticisms may go too far, for Negritude certainly played a valid
role in liberating some African minds from the cloying embrace of colonialism.
At the very least, it represents an expression of cultural rebellion that enables
an African to assert his humanity and strength in the face of the colonial
overlay. And although it may not have much relevance for independent Africa,
it certainly had meaning for individual Africans who were seeking to decolonize themselves before decolonizing their countries.

On Socialism

We would probably not spend much time discussing Senghor if his only
contribution to African political thought had been Negritude, however. But
Senghor did not stop there, he urged African unity (particularly in the form
of the Mali Federation) and evolved a set of theories supporting African
socialism; a socialism far more elitest than that of Nyerere or Kaunda. For
Senghor, emerging as the leader of decolonialization in Senegal and its first
president, African socialism was not the socialism of the west or of the east.
For him African socialism combined two key elements—economic democracy
and spiritual freedom. Because African traditional communities were classless,
he argued, there was no need to use Marxian methods to eliminate class
exploitation.

In Senghor's mind, African society is "community based," " . . . in which
the hierarchy—and, therefore, power—is founded on spiritual and democratic
values; on the law of primogeniture and election, in which decisions of all kinds
are deliberated in a palaver, after the ancestral gods have been consulted; in
which, work is shared out among the sexes and among *bechnico*—professional
groups based on religion."[40]

For Senghor, then, " . . . the problem is not how to put an end to the
exploitation of man by his fellow, but to prevent it ever happening, by bringing
political and economic democracy back to life."[41] There is no need to eliminate

---

[38]Ezekiel Mphalele, *The African Image* (New York: Praeger, 1962), p. 23. For an even more
devastating attack on the entire concept of Negritude, see Taban lo Liyong, *The Last Word*
(Nairobi: East African Publishing House, 1969).

[39]Marcien Towa, *Léopold Sédar Sénghor: Negritude ou Servitude* (Yaounde: Editions CLE, 1971).

[40]Leopold Senghor, "African-Style Socialism," in William H. Friedland and Carl G. Rosberg
(eds.), *African Socialism* (Stanford, Calif.: Hoover Institution Publications, 1964), pp. 264–66.

[41]Ibid., p. 265.

capitalism from African society by governmental decree. According to Seng-hor, it will naturally fall away as Senegal develops, although during the development phase, capital must be gotten from the private overseas sector. Much of what Senghor rebels against is what we would call industrialization. His socialism would help the peasant enrich his life without being a servant to a machine. Since he argues that an ethical society already exists in Senegal—that is, one with no antagonistic and exploitive classes—one has only to prevent its decay. One must use machines; in order to enrich people's lives, one must not allow machines to disrupt the ethnic society.

Socialism, then, became the rational organization of human society considered in its totality. It means that people should be paid according to their work, but without forgetting those who cannot work. It means providing the opportunity to work. It means proving intellectual and moral rigor in the face of hardship and problems. It means planning, not just in terms of the day-to-day production of this item or that, but of the whole range of human needs as spun out over time:

It is evident that the plan is not only a sum of objectives to attain. The plan is also, perhaps especially, a mystique, a spirit. To be faithful to the plan is to introduce into national life at all levels, in the fields, in the offices, in the workshops, this spirit of rigor, of continuity in effort without which one would have to speak not merely of delays, but of the nonexistence of a plan.[42]

But, unlike Ujamaa socialism, all do not participate in the formulation of the plan—or of the goals. The new technocrats are about as far away from the traditional villagers as it is possible to be. In fact, some critics have abused Senghor mightily for "the politics of technicity."[43]

We shall be examining the actual course of politics in Senghor's Senegal in Chapter 5. For the moment, it will suffice to indicate the extent to which there are major paradoxes in Senghor's philosophy. On the one hand, his Negritude statements support emotion and feeling and deep-seated stirrings. On the other hand, his preoccupation with socialism and development places an incredible importance on the activities of those who work from opposite perspectives. Then, too, his persistent attempts to avoid the Marxian implications of a class society make him obscure the extent to which Senegal's society is very much based on definite socioeconomic differentials. These may not coincide with racial groups but they exist, nevertheless.

[42]Leopold Senghor, "Discours à L'Assemblée National," April 19, 1967.

[43]See, especially, Irving Markovitz, *Leopold Sedar Senghor and the Politics of Negritude* (New York: Atheneum, 1969). See also John Reed and Clive Wake (eds.) *Sengor: Prose and Poetry* (London: Oxford University Press, 1965).

AMILCAR CABRAL

No such set of ambiguities exists for Amilcar Cabral, one of the foremost theoreticians of the "Marxist modernizers," whom we shall be examining in Chapter 7. Cabral accepts the primacy of Marxian thought, although he reapplies it to the African context.

Amilcar Cabral was the founder and leader of the *Partido Africano da Independencia da Guinè e Caso Verde* (PAIGC) until his assassination in 1973. The PAIGC became a revolutionary organization dedicated to carrying out armed struggle in Guiné-Bissau for the purpose of eliminating Portuguese colonialism from its homeland. Guineans were not originally committed to violence and, in fact, both before and after the PAIGC became engaged in guerrilla warfare, efforts were made to promote peaceful negotiations with Portugal. Though the party had its birth in 1956, it was not until 1961 that Cabral and the PAIGC had the necessary experience and theoretical and practical training to initiate an effective national liberation movement.

Though by Cabral's own admission the most seminal influences on his thinking were (the presumably post-exile) Nkrumah (for whom Cabral expressed his highest regard by saying that he was the African head of state he most admired in his life), Mao Tse Tung, and Che Guevara. In the two collections of Cabral's writings and speeches we shall examine, *Return to the Source* and *Revolution in Guinea,* [44] it will become apparent that not only are the historical situations of Guinea and Algeria comparable, but the responses by Cabral and Fanon are also similar.

According to Cabral, colonial domination in Guinea differed from colonialism in other parts of Africa. The colonial power, Portugal, was itself a developing country in that it had not achieved the level of industrialization and modernization that characterized France and England during the last remaining years of their hold on Algeria and Tanganyika.

Consequently, as little as France and England had contributed to the development of their colonial provinces, Portugal could contribute even less to the welfare of Guinea. Guiné-Bissau therefore, not only remained underdeveloped socioeconomically, but was virtually stagnated in all areas of growth during Portuguese rule. Portugal could not afford capital investment in the industrial development of Guinea and could not be concerned with furnishing the material resources to construct the institutions necessary, such as educational facilities, to teach and train the population in the basic skills required for modernization. At the time of Guinea's initial struggle against colonialism in the late 1950s, 99 percent of the people were illiterate.

The backwardness of Guiné-Bissau all during colonial domination meant

---

[44] Amilcar Cabral, *Revolution in Guinea* (London: Stage 1, 1969); and *Return to the Source: Selected Speeches of Amilcar Cabral* (New York: Monthly Review Press, 1973).

that the Guineans were more susceptible to the measures adopted by the Portuguese to maintain their dominant status. With such widespread illiteracy, the very great majority of the people were completely unequipped to evaluate the promises of increased prosperity made by the Portuguese government.

Laws, rules, and regulations were brutally discriminatory, and the system of taxation left the Guineans no means of improving their standard of living. Ignorance permits easy manipulation and a gullibility to the explanations and excuses for the postponement of implementing economic reforms. The extreme poverty and otherwise backward conditions in which the Guineans lived denied them a standard for evaluating to what extent they should be making progress and reaping material rewards for their labors which, in fact, were serving only to accelerate the progress and raise the living standard of a country they had never seen and could not begin to comprehend. A civilization whose history had unfolded by means of the most rudimentary economy could hardly understand the western concept of wealth and progress, or that there was widespread exploitation in light of violation of those standards. The Guineans were deprived easily of human rights because they had little idea what were those rights. Colonial domination could be efficiently maintained by lies, propaganda, and false promises, or at the first sign of resistance, by crude and ruthless violence.

The relative backwardness of Guiné-Bissau only served to reinforce the ideological pillars of Portuguese colonialism. Portugal could justify to itself (and to much of the rest of the "developed" world) the immaturity of the Guinean people and their unpreparedness for self-government.

Portugal, like many other western colonialist countries, viewed the African as inferior to the white European, as almost subhuman in the sense that humanity is equated with the accomplishments of western civilization. The inferior status of the African exposed him to a variety of forms of suppression. Entire villages and crops would be completely destroyed by bombs and napalm, and other centers of resistance to colonialism would be systematically deprived of foodstuffs and basic supplies. In the Cape Verde Islands, thousands of workers were cast out of work and the general population was subjected to artificially induced "agricultural crises" which produced widespread famine.

There was little impetus for the Portuguese to settle their differences with the PAIGC, according to the usual pattern by which a neocolonial compromise is substituted for outright colonial domination. Despite overtures by Cabral for a peaceful settlement to hostilities and his promise to "consider ways of taking into account the interests of Portugal in Guinea," Portugal's stage of development was such that it could not offer a neocolonial Guinean government much in the way of economic investments in exchange for a favored economic position in the "liberated" country. The impossibility of this more advanced form of imperialist exploitation by Portugal meant that it could only continue to prosper at Guinea's expense by securing traditional colonial domination. In its struggle with the anticolonialist movement in Guinea, Portugal either had to win an all-out victory through suppression of the PAIGC, or lose all influence and control over Guinea and be completely driven out.

On National Liberation

The essential core of Cabral's political theory is the complex development of political strategies for achieving national liberation. In this respect, his work comes closest to the thinking of Fanon, though the obvious difference between the two is that Fanon participated in the Algerian struggle actively as a hospital physician and as a theoretical analyst of the psychological and political dimensions of an anticolonialist national liberation movement. Cabral participated in the Guinean struggle as the leader of the PAIGC.

Cabral combines, to a far greater extent than Fanon, a theoretical and a practical perspective. Yet, it is important to note that in spite of the responsibility placed upon Cabral's shoulders for the results of his strategies, and regardless of the degree of his personal commitment and practical involvement in Guinea's struggle, it would not be valid to say that his theory is, for that reason, necessarily "better" than Fanon's.

Cabral's concern for theory first began with his recognition that the strategies borrowed from the experiences of other national liberation movements in Africa and elsewhere, such as Cuba, China, and South Vietnam, were not necessarily relevant to the situation in Guinea. The socioeconomic, political, and general historical conditions of Guinea differed to some extent from those same types of conditions in other countries. Cabral's first theoretical principle, then, which is fundamentally Marxist in nature, is that all practice must be based upon a careful theoretical analysis of the material conditions to be found in the particular country in question.

Theory must be formulated prior to political practice, and must serve as a *guide* for practice. Theory and practice will differ from country to country precisely to that extent to which the conditions of those countries are different. Furthermore, the empirical experience of revolutionary practice should serve as a constant check upon the continuing relevance of a theory and, if a practice or strategy fails, the theory must be altered. Cabral not only argues that theory must guide practice, but acknowledges that theory can be incorrect. A crisis in revolution does not reflect the political immaturity of the movement for liberation—he refuses to pass off political failure that conveniently—but rather a "crisis in knowledge." Cabral's attitude toward theory is an illustration of his disdain for orthodoxy, a trait we considered in Nyerere's discussion of the principles which should guide a nation's transition to socialism.

Cabral's first concerns in organizing the struggle against Portuguese colonialism are *who* can be organized and the question of nonviolent opposition.

Cabral indicates that he was compelled to pass from a nonviolent "purely political phase" to the violent "phase of direct action" because Portugal refused his offers to negotiate a settlement. The problem of defining the agent of revolutionary change, however, was considerably less straightforward. Cabral boasts that all social strata of Guinea participated in the struggle, but such a generalization obscures the identity of the authentic revolutionary class.

The revolution can be *based* on the masses, but the masses cannot themselves lead the struggle, nor develop its strategies. The majority of popular support came from the peasants in the rural areas of Guinea, not so much because the peasant classes were more radical than the urban working and middle classes, but, rather, because the armed revolutionary struggle could be most effectively waged in the vast rural areas where it was possible to liberate sectors abandoned by Portuguese soldiers as they were forced to concentrate their efforts to defend other locations. When the Portuguese would thin out their troop detachments to defend great stretches of rural territory, Cabral's forces could easily overcome them through sweeping guerrilla assaults. Though guerrilla tactics meant a protracted struggle, as occurred in Vietnam, for example, in less than a decade Cabral and the PAIGC had succeeded in liberating 75 percent of Guinea's land area and perhaps 60 percent of its population.

A political strategy based on a belief in the revolutionary potential of the working class was the orthodox Marxist basis of a party strategy that led to abysmal failure in Guinea. The workers, though quite radical, were naturally centered in the cities, where industry was located. Cabral's party first attempted to attack colonialism by organizing strikes and worker demonstrations. This tactic failed, however, because the Portuguese police and military were densely concentrated in the cities and could be quickly mobilized to deal swiftly with a marginal working class in an industrially underdeveloped country. Consequently, the Marxist allegiance to the working class had to be discarded in favor of Lenin's theoretically and practically significant reliance on the peasants.

It would be an oversimplification, however, to stress the "objective" factors contributing to revolution—that is, the problem of the relative dispersion of Portuguese soldiers in the urban and rural areas of Guinea and the extent to which such dispersion led Cabral to focus his political energies on the peasants. Another set of conditions with which he was preoccupied were the so-called subjective factors or the real attitudes and dispositions of the various classes toward revolutionary activity.

The working classes were *consciously* the most radical, but physically least able to combat the Portuguese. The peasant classes were the *least* radical (because of their conservative tribal traditions) but geographically the group best situated to wage effective armed struggle against the colonialists. Since Cabral could neither enlarge the size of the working class nor alter its geographical location, his task was to bring the subjective attitudes of the peasant classes into harmony with their objective conditions or, in other words, to radicalize, or politically educate, the peasant masses who were the key element in the liberation of Guinea.

We arrive, therefore, at the importance of the revolutionary "vanguard," the educated lower middle classes, or petty *bourgeoisie.* Cabral declares that it is only this educated class of people who are capable of understanding the nature of imperialism and colonialism and thus able to initiate a revolutionary struggle by educating and radicalizing the political consciousness of the peasant masses. Cabral points out that it is not the entire petty bourgeoisie that seizes the opportunity to effect a revolution against the colonial power, but only a small number who are no longer able to tolerate the abuse of the colonialists and are then driven to identify with the needs and aspirations of the underlying population. From the petty bourgeois class emerge the intellectuals and leaders—in which Cabral himself must be included—and the bulk of party members who are charged with the function of organizing and educating the peasant rank and file.

Cabral insists on the distinction between a national liberation struggle and the continuation of the revolution after independence has been achieved. He insists on this all-important distinction because he perceives the great danger of the establishment of Guinea as a neocolonial state after independence has been won. He declares, for example, that the general cultural underdevelopment of the peasant and working classes do not allow them to be able to "distinguish true national independence from fictitious political independence," and that "the liberation struggle is a revolution which is not completed at the moment when the national flag is raised and the national anthem played."

His fears of national liberation leading into a neocolonial compromise of real (social, political, *and* economic) independence for a limited political sovereignty originate in his analysis of the ambivalence of the vanguard revolutionary class, the petty bourgeoisie. The lower middle class, by virtue of its leadership role in the struggle against colonialism, stands to inherit the state apparatus after the struggle for independence. This tremendous power can either be used to promote the development of a socialist nation, or it can serve as the foundation for a self-serving and self-aggrandizing neocolonial tie with the former colonial power and, most likely, particularly in light of Portugal's inadequately developed economy, with other imperialist countries. Cabral believes that the petty bourgeoisie has an almost overpowering temptation to betray the liberation struggle as a result of its experience with exclusive political power during the national liberation movement.

It is the natural class disposition of the petty bourgeoisie to be reluctant to relinquish power, so much so, in fact, that Cabral suggests that to ask or to expect the petty bourgeoisie to promote a popular socialist regime is to "ask it to commit suicide"; that is, for it to go against everything associated with its class interests. Cabral concludes that after independence the leaders of the national liberation movement "must struggle against our own weaknesses." As we shall see in Chapter 7, these types of problems did not disappear with the attainment of independence.

Yet, while Cabral often speaks as though he fully expects that the stage that naturally and necessarily follows the struggle against colonialism is neocolonialism, his analysis goes beyond this premise in an attempt to discover contradictions within a fully developed neocolonial regime which lead to socialism. The politically dominant petty bourgeoisie endeavors to become a fully developed middle class along western lines. This means that the newly independent neocolonial African state must become industrialized. With rapid industrialization comes a complex modern system of social stratification which breeds a large and powerful working class. Within this proletariat lies the seeds for a new revolutionary upsurge and the creation of a socialist state.

Cabral's conception of a socialist society, therefore, differs substantially from Nyerere's. He envisions a fully industrialized and modernized society with a socialist political organization and social and economic structures that parallel the socialism of eastern Europe. Nevertheless, critical questions should be raised about certain elements of Cabral's "socialism" For example, why is it necessary, as Cabral indicates, to have trade unions in a socialist society? Cabral explicitly lists, under the PAIGC program for an independent Guinea, "trade union freedoms and guarantees for their effective exercise."

He also promises that in an independent nation not only will personal property be permitted without state regulation, but "private property" will be one of the four types of property allowed to flourish. It seems here as though Cabral is overly flexible in precisely the manner that Nkrumah was permissive; that is, in his willingness to promote institutions such as trade unions and private property, which are to be found in a capitalist society. Does this mean that Cabral was ultimately sympathetic to neocolonialism and was, in fact, one of those members of the petty bourgeoisie, who Cabral felt was incapable of fostering a socialist regime contrary to that class's economic interests?

There can be no decisive answer to this important question, but one answer is suggested by Cabral's constant overtures to bring the struggle against colonialism in Guinea to a speedy culmination by entering into a cooperative agreement with Portugal. On more than one occasion Cabral expressed a desire to establish "with Portugal itself the most excellent relations of collaboration and cooperation on the basis of equality, on the basis of absolute reciprocity of advantage, taking into account the interests of Portugal in Guinea," though he adds also, "on the basis of the highest regard for our sovereignty."[45] At the very least, these considerations and his statement that "we must guard against weaknesses in ourselves" indicate that his own attitudes toward neocolonialism were uncertain and ambivalent.

[45]This degree of compromise has been criticized: see Ronald H. Chilcote, "The Political Thought of Amilcar Cabral," *Journal of Modern African S udies,* vol. 6, no. 3 (1968), pp. 373–88.

Cabral's attitude toward the unity of all African nations was quite similar to that of Nyerere, though at least one of his views is unique. Cabral clearly favored pan-Africanism, though he recognized the necessity for the emergence and development of strong nationalist sentiments to further nationalist political movements and parties. Although he was never as explicit or as articulate as Nyerere on this matter, he clearly understood the contradictions between the commitments to pan-Africanism and to a nationalist opposition to colonial domination, which we have examined in Nyerere's political theory.

One notion of Cabral's that does stand out, however, from those views toward African unity we have considered previously, is his willingness to forge cooperative relations with those African countries that have established neocolonial regimes after gaining their national independence. This is an important point and should not necessarily be understood as sympathy with neocolonialism. On the contrary, Cabral seems to believe that all African nations, even those that have neocolonial arrangements with a former colonial power after national liberation, have an equal interest in eventually achieving complete autonomy from imperialism in all its forms.

According to Cabral's thinking, a politically independent, but economically dependent, neocolonial African nation could honestly pursue conflicting aims; that is, could be under neocolonial influence while simultaneously cooperating with nonneocolonial African countries for the purposes of helping them to remain free and with an end to gaining their own economic liberation. It is difficult to determine if Cabral's idea contains real merit or is naive, but on the surface it appears as though Cabral may just have been interested in preserving his alliances with African countries to benefit from their economic aid, despite the fact that these countries had neocolonial regimes.

Also pertinent to explaining why Cabral was willing to cooperate with neocolonial African nations, is his belief that neocolonialism was a passing phase on the way to a genuinely socialist political and economic system. In those countries, such as Ghana, where a violent transition by way of revolution was not in the making, it is no doubt true that Cabral believed that Nkrumah would lead that nation to socialism and that neocolonialism was merely a temporary concession which would quickly be passed over as soon as Ghana became sufficiently industrialized to have a modern socialist economy along the lines of eastern European models.

Cabral always expressed the highest respect for the ideals which the United Nations represented. But his regard had a more practical dimension to it than a simple moral attachment to the United Nations' normative commitments. Cabral found in the UN declarations against colonial domination a legal justification for his party's armed struggle against the Portuguese. He would often remark that the activities engaged in by his national liberation movement were on behalf of the United Nations' anticolonialist proclamations—regardless of the fact that the UN had not commissioned Cabral and the PAIGC to undertake its armed struggle—and that the members of the PAIGC were actually "anonymous soldiers for the United Nations."

On two occasions Cabral addressed the United Nations, requesting material and moral support. But although many members of the United Nations enthusiastically provided moral encouragement, few provided material support. Many member states of the United Nations, such as Italy, France, Germany, England, and the United States, had been furnishing weapons and other aid to the Portuguese, through NATO, and could hardly be expected to support a UN resolution to intervene in the conflict on behalf of Guinea. Cabral and the PAIGC had relied primarily upon USSR, socialist countries of eastern Europe, and from Sweden, Norway, Denmark, and Finland.

Unfortunately, Cabral provides us with too infrequent glimpses into the improvements made in Guinea during the armed struggle, as the movement gradually eliminated colonialism from large parts of Guinea. Cabral's speeches to the United Nations, however, include descriptions of the strides which the PAIGC made—Cabral had to demonstrate to the United Nations that what he intended to offer Guinea was far superior to the colonial situation. In the rural sectors, schools were begun as a result of the party's efforts at political education. In addition, the peasants acquired experience with the political process through the village committees which were established as an integral part of the PAIGC's program of decentralization aimed at involving the masses at all levels of party activity. Following in the wake of these democratic measures came local self-government, where the PAIGC trained civil servants to occupy administrative posts vacated by the Portuguese.

On a national scale, Cabral introduced an executive branch of government to be chosen through popular election, an elected national assembly, and the adoption of an entirely new constitution. The changes in Guinea during the movement for national liberation did not only proceed from the highest levels of party officialdom, but the goals of the future Guinea were also forming *during* the actual struggle in a manner very similar to that described by Fanon in *A Dying Colonialism.*

On this matter, Cabral is not as clear or as rigorously analytical as Fanon. He summarizes his thesis (that the goals of the new Guinean society are articulated during the anticolonial struggle) by saying that it has "created a new man and a new woman, people possessing an awareness of their rights and duties, on the soil of the African fatherland. Indeed, the most important result of the struggle, which is at the same time its greatest strength, is the new awareness of the country's men, women and children."

On African Culture

Of all of Cabral's political theses, perhaps the most interesting and original contribution to African political thought is his conception of "cultural resistance." It is here that we discover a significant theoretical departure from the views expressed by Fanon on the relationship of the African to the culture of the colonialist. We also find a perspective on culture which supplements Nyerere's thought on the importance of African cultural traditions to the construction of a socialist society.

Cabral argues that physical forms of political and social oppression are, in themselves, insufficient to guarantee the unchallenged hegemony of the colonial power. Unless the violence perpetuated by the colonialist is so sweeping that every member of the indigenous population is eliminated, the cultural values and aspirations of the native population, will still remain after the colonial power has successfully dominated the political and economic institutions of the African country.

Colonialism may break the body, but never the spirit. To the extent that the cultural norms of the African are different from those of the colonialist, the African culture presents an obstacle to the acceptance of the life style and objectives of the colonialist. And as long as the cultures are opposed, there can be no question of a peaceful coexistence between the African and the colonizer. Physical coercion and perhaps violence must remain permanent means of insuring the continued domination by the colonialist.

Cabral contends, and herein lies the difference between his views and those of Fanon, that the colonialist was unsuccessful in his attempts to assimilate the African into the European culture, with the result that the native African culture stands as a potentially insurmountable barrier to unqualified colonial domination. This is true primarily of the African mass culture; that is, for the culture of the peasant and working classes.

The petty bourgeoisie, however, is the class *most* susceptible to European cultural influences by virtue of the western character of their education during colonial rule. This is the class, as we have seen, that is sympathetically inclined to the establishment of a neocolonial regime after liberation has been declared, and for this reason must, according to Cabral, be reconverted to the cultural view of the masses, the group to which they belonged prior to colonialization.

At this point we confront a paradox. For Cabral, the masses are culturally backward. They are not in possession of the education that would allow them to articulate competently the oppositional elements to colonialism deeply embedded in their cultural tradition, although objectively it is *their* culture which is potentially the most radical anticolonial weapon. The petty bourgeoisie, on the other hand, has the intellectual training to express a cultural opposition, but it is precisely this class that has the most conservative cultural attitudes. The dilemma is solved if the petty bourgeoisie is somehow persuaded to voluntarily adopt the culture of the masses in order to enable the working and peasant classes to articulate their own cultural values against the threats of colonial cultural domination.

Cabral contends that the petty bourgeoisie will, in fact, eventually perform this task as the vanguard of the revolutionary movement. The lower middle classes are most frequently humiliated by the colonialist, owing to the intimate nature of contact between the colonizer and the petty bourgeoisie as a result of the latter's strategic importance in carrying out the political and administrative aims of the colonialist.

It is the task of the petty bourgeoisie to oppose colonialism by educating the masses about the wealth of their African traditions, much in the same way as Nyerere had attempted to recapture those popular historical traditions of Tanzania which would contribute to the construction of Ujamaa socialism. Yet, as Nyerere had discovered in Tanzania, the culture of any African country can be extremely heterogeneous, and many of the traditions may be conservative and less apt to serve in the struggle against colonialism than others. Cabral points out that the petty bourgeoisie must labor to uncover the most progressive dimensions of all the indigenous cultures and combine these radical elements into a single popular culture. The great diversity of the ethnic and tribal popular cultures, in other words, must be synthesized into a homogeneous national cultural outlook. After this has been accomplished, and Cabral provides no set guideline to deliver this outcome, Guinea can be developed and modernized under a coherent national cultural and ideological vision, which will eventually permit its integration into a worldwide and universal cultural synthesis.

KENNETH KAUNDA

Kenneth Kaunda, like Nkrumah, began his professional career as a teacher. As an intellectual, he was particularly sensitive to the abuses which the Zambian people suffered under the colonial government in Northern Rhodesia. He seems to have first become incensed at colonialism as a result of his personal experiences with apartheid racial discrimination in Zambia. In his autobiography, *Zambia Shall Be Free,* [46] he describes frequent humiliations where he was refused admittance to shops to purchase basic commodities, and where he was refused service in restaurants. His anger at these petty, but universally discriminatory, practices in Northern Rhodesia is reminiscent of the response by black civil rights leaders in the United States during the first years of their civil rights movement. He complains that Rhodesian Africans had fought together with the British against the National Socialists in World War II and as a result of their sacrifices had been promised that their basic human rights would be reinstated and that their standard of living would be improved after the war came to a close. The contributions that the Zambians made to keep Britain free

[46]Kenneth Kaunda, *Zambia Shall Be Free* (London: Heinemann, 1962).

and independent proved, however, to be gratuitous, for the promises made by the British government were never kept.

Kaunda's first major political engagement began with his association with the Northern Rhodesian African Congress (NRAC), later renamed the African National Congress (ANC). This organization's first task in promoting the cause of Zambia's opposition to colonialism was to ensure that Britain would keep its word in permitting a gradual increase in African territorial local self-government in Northern Rhodesia.

In 1953, the British violated this commitment by encouraging the formation of a Federation of Northern Rhodesia and Nyasaland, which would expose Zambians to the danger of complete political domination by white European settlers in Southern Rhodesia. The Federation meant the indefinite postponement of any possibility of Zambians eventually controlling their own national affairs, and would reduce their autonomy to the merest local governmental responsibilities.

Despite the great success of the African National Congress in mobilizing popular opposition to the Federation, the Federation became a hard political reality in 1953. The Northern Rhodesian government did not impose the federated union without first attempting to subvert the popular basis of support for the African National Congress by turning the Zambian tribal chiefs against the leaders of the ANC. The colonial government tried to persuade the chieftains that the ANC was only interested in taking away their power and privileges, and that financial support that the chiefs contributed to the African National Congress was being squandered on luxury items, such as automobiles. Kaunda points out that these colonial practices of divide and conquer were familiar tactics used to destroy any semblance of a national liberation movement.

Kaunda rose quickly through the hierarchy of the ANC. He was first appointed as Organizing-Secretary for the northern province, and his responsibilities consisted primarily of riding around the country on a bicycle organizing party support. His success as an organizer enabled him, subsequently, to become Secretary-General of the ANC. Kaunda frequently referred to his experience as a political organizer as the finest teacher for developing skills which served him in his contact with all social strata in Zambia. Later these skills aided him in effectively galvanizing popular support for the United National Independence Party of Zambia, of which he became leader in 1960. Like Cabral, Kaunda's background as an organizer and his status as an intellectual provided him with the necessary political credentials to work equally competently with chiefs, village headmen, teachers, traders, farmers, ordinary clerks, and with all other groupings in the peasant, working, and middle classes.

As Kaunda explains, the problem of having an effective impact on the policy of the colonial government of Northern Rhodesia was severely complicated by the fact that since the majority of Africans in Zambia were not voters, the African National Congress could not be considered a political party. Consequently, the tactics used by the ANC were not "democratic" in the strict sense of influencing governmental decision making through the ballot box. Kaunda and the African National Congress, instead, resorted to "positive action," meaning nonviolent demonstrations and boycotts. Kaunda, in fact, often mentions that Nkrumah was the major influence on his thinking, though it is clear from Kaunda's *Zambia Shall Be Free* that his commitment to nonviolence originates in the early years of his childhood and therefore greatly precedes his first exposure to the leader and head of state of Ghana.

Kaunda, like Nkrumah, spent time in prison for his political activities. During his incarceration in a rural province, Kaunda first became associated with the peasant classes. Contrary to the attitudes of Cabral toward the masses, Kaunda seems to be most impressed with the decay of their moral character and the poverty of their cultural traditions. These experiences prompted Kaunda to express the need for a massive social welfare program in Northern Rhodesia; his recognition of such a need for governmental intervention foreshadows many of the policies he introduced after Zambia became independent.

In his autobiography, Kaunda indicates that ANC tactics from 1953 to 1956 did not reflect the aspirations of an organization geared to seeking independence but, rather, one which performed much like a third political party. In the absence of the real possibility of winning an election, third parties resort to attracting some popular support through the issues they define, in full knowledge that if their issues do become sufficiently popular, one of the major parties will adopt them for its own in order to regain the lost political support. Kaunda declares, for example, that his "advice to Government is this: that the best way of destroying the African National Congress is not by damaging it violently, but by removing as much of what forms Congress' platform as they can possibly manage." Kaunda points out that the real purpose of the African National Congress was not to achieve political power, but merely to improve the living conditions of the Zambians and to eliminate all forms of discrimination and exploitation. It is clear, therefore, that the original aspirations of the African National Congress were considerably more modest than any of the national liberation and revolutionary movements we have examined.

The African National Congress, however, was content to moderate its demands only as long as the British and the Northern Rhodesian government intended to honor their pledges to Zambia for gradual self-government. After the federation was imposed, the ANC regretfully discovered that no constitutional reforms would be forthcoming from the colonialists which would at all threaten the hegemony of the federation by relinquishing constitutionally sanctioned political powers. For the African National Congress, the demands for constitutional reform and its opposition to the federation became inseparably linked, for unless the federation was dissolved, Zambia could never achieve its constitutional rights and national self-government.

During 1957, when violence was becoming the central issue in debates among the leaders of the ANC, the President-General of the African National Congress, Harry Nkumbula, had begun to lose the confidence of the rank and file of the ANC. He was charged with incompetent leadership, poorly representing the ANC in negotiations with the British, and becoming increasingly sympathetic to the Northern Rhodesian government, as evidenced by his invitation to members of the colonial power to attend ANC executive meetings. In response to Nkumbula's compromises with colonialism, and in view of the extreme danger of the ANC embracing the tactics of violence, Kaunda broke with the African National Congress and began the Zambia National Congress. Kaunda had been particularly critical of Nkumbula for the latter's denunciation of the methods of positive action, particularly boycotts and demonstrations.

From the very beginning, Kaunda intended that the Zambia African National Congress (ZANC) should become a full-fledged political party with the aim of achieving national independence for Zambia. In 1959, the ZANC demanded a new constitution which would include, among many other things, universal one-man one-vote suffrage; an elected national assembly; a national council of chiefs; and ministers and an executive chosen from the majority party *in consultation with the colonial governor.* Most interesting, perhaps, is that this constitution would obligate the highest Zambian government official to allegiance to the British crown, and that, despite this decisive concession to colonialism, the constitutional proposal by the Zambia African National Congress was refused. Ironically, the constitution eventually installed in 1962 by the British after the possibility of violence had emerged in Zambia, was almost identical to the ZANC constitution proposed in 1959.

In the late 1950s, after Kaunda had spent his second term in prison, the Zambia African National Congress was outlawed by the colonial government. Shortly after that, in 1960, Kaunda began the United National Independence Party (UNIP). The slogans adopted by the UNIP give insight into the tactics of Kaunda's new political party. "Freedom Now," "Self-Government Now," and "Service, Sacrifice, and Suffering" of course mirror Nkrumah's party politics in Ghana. With the UNIP, we once again find Kaunda's uncompromising commitment to nonviolence. And, like Nkrumah, Kaunda emphasized the decisiveness of party organization and discipline, for only with sound management and control of the activity of the UNIP's rank and file could violence be averted.

Yet, regardless of Kaunda's and the UNIP's attempt to restrain the increasingly aggressive response of Zambia's people to the government of Northern Rhodesia, the Zambians lost all patience with the broken promises and breaches of contracts of the colonialists and violence became a grim reality.

In 1962, Britain and the Northern Rhodesian government dissolved the Federation and instituted constitutional reforms along the lines requested earlier by the Zambia National Congress. In 1963, Zambia became fully independent and in 1964, it became a republic with membership in the British Commonwealth. Kaunda remarked, in the closing lines of *Zambia Shall Be Free,* that he could not be certain whether it was the political tactics of the UNIP or the violence of the Zambian people which eventually forced the British and the Northern Rhodesian government to restore their independence.

Whereas *Zambia Shall Be Free* is a biographical and historical work devoted to a description and analysis of Kaunda's political career up to the time of Zambia's independence, *A Humanist in Africa*[47] is a collection of letters, indeed, essays, of a genuinely philosophical nature. In these writings we are engaged by a different Kaunda, often speculative and profound, always incisive and instructive.

Many of the thoughts contained in this anthology are valuable reflections on the differences between African and western culture as seen by Kaunda; and in fact, many echo the complaints and observations of Senghor. Whereas the west is primarily occupied with industry and the development of sophisticated technologies, African culture's contribution lies in its emphasis on the importance of man. The industrialist uses and exploits man to produce wealth, and "makes him fit into the system." A technological society appears oriented toward the domination of nature and human nature to satisfy the apparently insatiable appetites of man. Africa, on the other hand, claims traditions which place a higher value on nature and insists on preserving its beauty and pristine character.

The African emphasizes a spiritual relationship with nature and between men, and disregards the western philosophy of transforming nature within a social and economic framework that celebrates productivity for its own sake. Social harmony is stressed over social competitiveness, and individual merit is not determined by economic success. Although the west places greatest value on material consumption, African traditions place community needs over private wants and discourage individualism. Failure is not evaluated according to the western unidimensional criteria of prestige, power, and material worth, but these values are subordinated in favor of a normative system which maintains that all members of society can be useful in their contributions to the good of the community, regardless of their talents or abilities.

Moreover, the African family differs from the western family precisely in that all people are viewed as "family" responsibilities, and no distinction is made between the social obligations of the family and those of the state. The

[47]Kenneth Kaunda and Colin Morris, *A Humanist in Africa* (New York: Abingdon Press, 1966). An interesting overview of Kaunda and Zambia is provided by Fergus Macpherson, *Kenneth Kaunda of Zambia: The Times and the Man* (London: Oxford University Press, 1974).

entirety of society is, according to Kaunda, an extended family system "which constitutes a social security scheme which has the advantage of following the natural pattern of personal relationships rather than being the responsibility of an institution."

These views contain rather definite implications for the type of society Kaunda believes to be most appropriate for Zambia and all of Africa. "Moderation" is certainly the most appropriately descriptive term. Technology brings great benefits, but these would be abused and carried to an extreme with their inherent dangers, as they have already begun to unfold in western nations, unless there exists in Africa some cultural padding, or underpinning, which would temper the growth of technology.

Kaunda argues that African culture does provide a basis upon which a sound, but unextravagant, modern civilization can be founded. Technology and science will become the servant of the African on his own terms. Through these thoughts we can see the image of a gradually developing Zambian nation, and one in which definite limits to growth will obtain. Kaunda seems to be in no rush to modernize—the blessings of a fully modernized society being questionable—and such restraint would most likely inhibit any impulsive agreements for a neocolonial regime. As Kaunda reminds us, the Africans "are a patient people."

Along with the African's patience is an unshakeable optimism, both in the future and in the nature of man. Consequently, Kaunda asserts that the African has little time for a religion that underscores sinfulness and depravity as the essence of humanity. Kaunda subscribes to a Christianity that opposes such a dark and gloomy view of man's nature, and embraces a Christian doctrine emphasizing the possibilities for the growth and maturation of human nature. Only such a positive religion could successfully address the real possibilities for the future which the African has at his disposal. And there are other oppressive religions that Kaunda rejects. Marxism and Communism are related, according to Kaunda, in their disillusionment with man and their focus on his quest for power and domination. Perhaps Kaunda's interpretation of Marxism and his critical attitude toward western science and technology partially explain his insistence on a policy of nonalignment.

Kaunda's philosophical speculations extend to a consideration of the *benefits* to be derived from the colonial experience in Africa, and in this regard his work is truly unique among those we have discussed. Kaunda argues that in certain important respects colonialism brought greater freedom to Africa. He states that "the peoples of Africa were freed from certain enemies—disease, ignorance, superstition, and slavery—the horizons of their lives were lifted, offering new areas of choice and fresh possibilities of material and spiritual development." After the perspective we have acquired on colonialism, we are inclined to be skeptical at hearing these words, yet there is substance to

Kaunda's implicit claim that Britain was a considerably less harsh colonial master than either Portugal or France.

Nevertheless, a few of the contributions made by the colonialists pertain to colonial situations in addition to that of Northern Rhodesia, and to that extent Kaunda is quite correct in alleging that there were rewards from colonialism to all African countries. Kaunda points to the "application of a uniform system of law," which freed the ordinary African from the fear of arbitrary expressions of power by tribal chieftains. The universality of a single code of law delivered the African into a new security. Colonialism also bred the destruction of the tribal system, Kaunda argues, breaking down traditional forms of African association. The newly atomized African sought substitute types of association and discovered "political parties, trade unions, social clubs and churches." Ironically, the methods of overcoming the isolation that resulted from the colonial erosion of African feudal and semifeudal social structures became instrumental in the elimination of colonialism.

Kaunda also focuses on the benefits of industrialism in Africa. He argues that the skills and technology required to develop and operate an industrializing society established new and higher standards of attainment for the African. Individual achievement and social mobility that follow from industrial development helped to create a fluid social structure in Africa far less biased and discriminatory than the traditional practices of assigning economic and social status on the basis of blood relations.

Most important of all of the consequences of colonialism, perhaps, is the birth of African nationalism! Colonialism presented the African with a common opponent, forcing the African to overcome tribal, linguistic and regional divisions. Kaunda clearly understands that colonialism can be viewed as a necessary stage in accelerating the growth of the African nation-state.

Kaunda is seriously concerned with the problems of a new African state after the national liberation movement is successful. He complains that immediately following the declaration of independence, new goals must be quickly introduced to fill the vacuum created by the accomplishments of the nationalist party.

The colonialist power is no longer present to unify the African and "unless new, exciting and worthwhile goals can be proposed for nationalism, there is a danger of the movement of protest turning inward upon itself and becoming destructive of the national good." Naturally, this problem places a weighty burden on the shoulders of Kaunda and leaders of other newly independent African nations, for, in addition to the usual responsibilities of statesmanship, the African chief of state must discover a means to rechannel the enormous popular energies that swell during the drive for liberation.

Kaunda is afraid that these energies will be dissipated in anarchy or in other behavior that would threaten, not only the future of the new African state, but independence itself, for colonial powers had always justified their domination by reminding the African of his immaturity and lack of preparedness for self-government. The question of rechanneling energy bottled up during the liberation movement was not problematic for Fanon, for he argued that through a violent transition to independence the victims of colonialism become freed of aggressive energy through a psychological catharsis. This difference between Kaunda and Fanon provides insight into the basis for differences in the problems confronting newly independent African nations.

Although Kaunda does not oppose a multiparty democratic system of government, he contends that a one-party state is most appropriate for a new African nation. Only a single party, with a single leader, can unify the people and prevent the new nation from redissolving into the many tribal and ethnic cleavages which a multiparty system would accentuate and aggravate. As we shall see in Chapter 5, this view has never been shared by all Zambians. Moreover, the problem of succession of leadership is of paramount importance for Kaunda—the nation's first leader has won the confidence and respect of his people because of his role in the independence movement. Subsequent leaders cannot expect that they will acquire the same popularity, and if ever strong leadership fails, the dangers of conflicts and factionalism emerging are great.

A solution to the problem of succession of leadership is for the head of state to stress the importance of the newly founded *institutions* and the newly instituted constitution. This would separate the legitimacy of the leader from the legitimacy of the institutions, for, when the former would pass away, the latter would prevail. The task of legitimating institutions is compounded by conflicts between the role of the military and the role of the intellectual in the independent state, each trying to make his skills and technical knowledge most salient and indispensable to the functioning of the state. Reconciling these two groups to each other and to the power of the executive is one of the greatest challenges to a leader bent on creating a just and stable regime.

Internal problems, however, are not the exclusive obstacles to maintaining a free and strong nation-state. Kaunda is also concerned about international intrusions. He states unequivocally that neocolonialism is the greatest threat to African unity. Pan-African cooperation is for Kaunda the most effective means of staving off neocolonial influence. In pan-Africanism is contained the promise for the solution to debilitating economic problems which make African nations vulnerable and receptive to overtures of foreign investment and control. It is quite clear from Kaunda's writings that he, more than any of the African political thinkers we have examined thus far, is concerned with evolving a philosophy of statecraft and joining together political science with the exercise of political power.

Nyerere, Senghor, Cabral, and Kaunda thus emerge as political figures with definite responses to the problems of colonialism and underdevelopment. How they were able to actualize their philosophies after independence will be treated in Part 2. Before we move from the theory of African politics to its practice, however, it remains for us to examine the "mind set" of current Africa; that is, how Africans themselves view colonialism, decolonization, independence, *and* the philosophies of the African thinkers outlined in Chapters 2 and 3.

4

Political Themes in Recent African Literature

In Chapter 1, we examined the themes and patterns in traditional African political systems. In Chapters 2 and 3, we looked at the important strands of indigenous political thought and the imported political philosophies with an eye toward determining their impact on contemporary politics in Africa. In this chapter, we seek to expose the reader to both the diversity and the commonality of political themes in recent African literature.[1]

Because of the intertwined nature of literature, politics, and society, African literature remains a legitimate expression of political ideas and valid descriptions of both society and politics. This is true, in part, because, as Nadine Gordimer has written, "Black writers choose their plots, characters and literary styles; their themes choose them."[2] By that, she means themes as " . . . statements or questions arising from the nature of the society in which the writer finds himself immersed, and the quality of the life around him."

[1]An earlier draft of this chapter was prepared for delivery at the African Studies Association Annual Meeting in Boston, Massachusetts, November 1976.
[2]Nadine Gordimer, *The Black Interpreters* (Johannesburg: SPRO-CAS/RAVAN, 1973), p. 1.

As a reflection of the human condition in Africa, works of literature provide valuable insights into both the past and the present by sketching the African reaction to colonialism, racism, and independence. They can help us understand the workings of African society at the village level, as well as enhance our understanding of the national political systems. As a mirror for changing societies, literature can help us to come to grips with the underlying realities of all political systems on the continent. And it can indicate the extent to which changing social and economic conditions affect the political systems that have evolved.

Henry Holland, Jr. has indicated that literature may enable the reader to see through to the "heart of the matter"—to get the sense of political realities more directly than from conventional political descriptions.[3] Particularly in the African context, literature has proven a useful vehicle for understanding both politics and society. This is due, in part, to the fact that "The African writer himself has almost always been a microcosm of the accumulated expressions of his society."[4]

It is also the result of the paucity of political analysis by African scholars over the past twenty-five years. Although this situation is now changing, the significant outpouring of African literature during the same period has meant that much of our understanding of African society—as seen by Africans—comes to us from literature.[5]

In fact, there is such a body of useful literature that a primary task is reducing the material to manageable proportions. Since the 1950s, there have been hundreds of poems, plays, short stories, and novels. In addition, much of the rich oral traditions of precolonial Africa have also appeared in print. Our emphasis in this chapter on recent major works, primarily novels and plays, should not suggest that these other expressions are unimportant. Indeed, in some instances, the very translation of some oral traditions may be acts of considerable political importance.[6] It is simply that much of this rich and variegated material lies beyond the scope of this chapter. Here, we are primarily interested in what Africans have to say about society and politics and we have, therefore, concentrated on the longer expressions of those views as found in novels and plays. We have also avoided the extensive literature created by

[3]Henry Holland, Jr. (ed.), *Politics Through Literature* (Englewood Cliffs, N.J.: Prentice-Hall, 1968).

[4]Charles R. Larson, *The Emergence of African Fiction* (Bloomington, Ind.: Indiana University Press, 1971), p. 280.

[5]In over a decade of teaching African politics, I have found students at Vassar, Dartmouth, and Bowdoin very responsive to this approach and would like to acknowledge their important interaction with the themes of this chapter. In particular, I would like to thank Kenneth Slutsky, Gail Hines, and Holi Rafkin for their observations and comments.

[6]For example, the appearance of Shona and Amatabole materials can be treated either as an expression of pride in traditional African culture or as a neotribal assist in perpetuating racial domination. See E. W. Korg, *African Literature in Rhodesia* (Gwelo, Rhodesia: Mambao Press, 1966) or the oft criticized *Indaba My Children* by Vusamazulu Credo Mutwa (London: Kahn and Averill, 1966).

Europeans,[7] not because these expressions do not tell us something about man in Africa, but because our central concern is looking at African society and politics through African eyes.

We also leave literary criticisms to others. Whether a novel or short story is "good literature" or not is irrelevant for our purposes, since we are primarily interested in what African educated elites, writing in the context of their society and heritage, have been concerned with, and what themes reoccur in their observations about the nature of society and politics. For those interested in literary criticism, there are a number of recent books which not only examine African writing in terms of itself, but also in relation to fiction more generally.[8]

We have limited the focus of this chapter in other ways as well. By and large, we are relatively uninterested in the rites of passage which individual writers have undergone (although we are concerned in the obvious cases where their location and exile are directly related to the society which they represent). Thus, we are concerned with the fact that Wole Soyinka or Ezekiel Mphahlele or Kofi Awoonor cannot write with impunity in the countries of their birth. We are concerned with the fact that "In many cases the new nations of Africa have not accommodated their poets and intellectuals very successfully and the treatment individuals have received has been severe."[9] We are not concerned if an author toils abroad simply because it is more lucrative.

What is paramount for our purposes is the understanding of the Africa

---

[7]The interested reader should look at the various works of such writers as Stuart Cloete, Alan Paton, Nadine Gordimer, Robert Ruark, and Paul Theroux.

[8]In addition to Larson, *The Emergence of African Fiction,* there are James Olney, *Tell Me Africa* (Princeton, N.J.: Princeton University Press, 1973); Ulli Beier, *Introduction to African Literature* (Evanston, Ill.: Northwestern University Press, 1967); Claude Wauthier, *The Literature and Thought of Modern Africa* (New York: Praeger, 1967); Adrian Roscoe, *Mother is Gold* (Cambridge, England: Cambridge University Press, 1971); Wilfred Cartey, *Whispers from a Continent* (New York: Random House, 1969); Eustace Palmer, *Introduction to the African Novel* (New York: Africana Publishers, 1972); Pio Zirimu and Andrew Gurr (eds.), *Black Aesthetics* (Nairobi: East African Publishing House, 1973); Kofi Awoonor, *The Breast of the Earth* (Garden City, N.Y.: Doubleday, 1976); A. C. Brench, *The Novelist's Inheritance in French Africa* (New York: Oxford University Press, 1967), and *Writing in French from Senegal to Cameroon* (New York: Oxford University Press, 1967); Cosmo Pieterse and Donald Munro (eds.), *Protest and Conflict in African Literature* (New York: Africana Publishing, 1969); Eldred Jones (ed.), *African Literature Today* (New York: Africana Publishing, 1972); Mercer Cook and Stephen E. Henderson, *The Militant Black Writer* (Madison: University of Wisconsin Press, 1969); Taban Lo Liyong, *The Last Word* (Nairobi: East African Publishing House, 1969); Ammanuel Obiechina, *Culture, Tradition and Society in the West African Novel* (Cambridge, England: Cambridge University Press, 1975); Gerald Moore, *Seven African Writers* (London: Oxford University Press, 1970); and Adrian Roscoe, *Uhuru's Fire* (Cambridge, England: Cambridge University Press, 1977). Among the best-known literary journals are *Transition, Black Orpheus, The Journal of the New African Literature and the Arts,* and *Presence Africaine.*

[9]Thomas Knipp, "Poets and Politics: Speculation on Political Roles and Attitudes in West African Poetry," *African Studies Review,* vol. 18, no. 1 (April 1975), p. 48.

which the various authors portray. What do they tell us about the nature of society? What can they tell us about the impact of modernization? What can they tell us about the impact of colonialism? Or decolonization? How do they view the workings of the contemporary political system they are describing? Why have the twin themes of African socialism and pan-Africanism, which are so important to the formal body of African political thought, been so absent in its literature? What are the similarities and differences among the various political systems operative throughout the continent?

For analytical purposes, we have divided the main themes of contemporary African literature into six categories. To a certain extent, these are both artificial and arbitrary, and the reader should be aware that these typologies are not exclusive. A writer may, for example, be describing the process of social and political decay as well as indicating a pattern of military intervention in politics. These categories are intended to focus on the major recurring themes in African literature today. In terms of our consideration, these themes are: (1) traditional society; (2) the sacred and the profane, African metaphysics; (3) colonialism (including its onset, impact and the struggles against it); (4) the clash of cultures or societal change; (5) the European shadow or continued racism; and (6) contemporary political patterns.

TRADITIONAL SOCIETY

As we indicated in Chapter 1, the multiplicity of traditional African political systems and their concomitant economic and social structures made for a great variety of forms. Contemporary literature is filled with attempts to depict the African past in terms of those forms.

Elechi Amadi, for example, in *The Great Ponds* and *The Concubine,* depicts life in segmented societies.[10] *The Great Ponds* is a simple, but moving, depiction of the struggle between the villages of Chiolu and Alaikoro for control over fishing rights, especially in the very productive pond of Wagaba. A band of Aliakoro poachers is ambushed; then the men of Alaikoro kidnap several Chiolu women. Full-scale war erupts and the struggle goes on and on. Both villages are decimated and exhausted, but only the arrival of *wonjo,* an influenza epidemic, brings the fighting to a close.

Amadi skillfully takes this tiny war between two small villages and turns it into an heroic clash. In addition, his portrayal of traditional segmented societies indicates the extent to which the very nature of those societies abetted fratricidal warfare. Without a meaningful central authority to mitigate conflict between the segments, the struggles between them could go unchecked.

The theme of the tension between centrifugal and centripetal forces in society is one which occurs over and over in African literature. In Sahle

[10]Elechi Amadi, *The Great Ponds* (London: Heinemann, 1969), and *The Concubine* (London: Heinemann, 1966).

Sellassie's *Warrior King,* for example, we see the struggle between a central authority and the various subordinate units which need to be subdued.[11] Seen through the eyes of a peasant boy, Begreya, *Warrior King* is the story of the rise of Kassa Hailu, who was to become the Ethiopian Emperor Teowodros II. It is the saga of a forceful and dynamic leader who, through conquest and intrigue, subdues those who resist his authority.

In D. T. Niane's *Sundiata: An Epic of Old Mali,* there is the sweep and grandeur of the rise of the empire of Mali.[12] There is turmoil here, captains and kings, the struggle between centralization and the tug of anarchy. There is a need for unity, stability, and control, but there is rebellion against them. Thomas Mofolo's classic, *Chaka,* one of the few African novels written in the vernacular, likewise depicts the warrior-hero who unites his people and asserts his power over them, and their power over others.[13] It depicts cruelty, the savagery and treachery of life and death politics—the strong central authority is able to stay in power only as long as he can suppress others. And there are always others.

As we shall see in the section on colonialism, a number of African authors see tragedy in the disruption of traditional society by the Europeans. Yet others see traditional society as stifling or ineffective or both. For Sahle Sellassie, the classic Amharic institution for conflict resolution, the *Afersata* cannot do the job in the face of changed realities.[14] A peasant's house burns down while the 30 villagers of Wudma sleep. The *Afersata* is convened by the village headmen. Every adult male is expected to attend, with the hope that the truth will come out and the problem solved.

Although Sahle Sellassie portrays some of the beneficial aspects of traditional life—Namaga's hut is rebuilt by the villagers working together—the *Afersata* is held to be ineffectual. Various sessions are convened. Many witnesses are called. But, in the end, no one is found guilty and there are strong arguments for other solutions to conflict resolution, such as the creation of a modern police force.

For a number of writers, traditional society is rigid, cloying, and oppressive to the individual. Flora Nwapa, for example, although not antitraditional, nevertheless indicates the extent to which the individual is bound up with the total community and its mores; this can often lead to unhappiness and tragedy. In *Efuru,* the heroine flaunts convention and it costs her dearly.[15] In *Idu,* the

[11]Sahle Sellassie, *Warrior King* (London: Heinemann, 1968).

[12]D. T. Niane, *Sundiata: An Epic of Old Mali* (London: Longmans, 1965). Other important epics include Jordan Ngubane, *Ushaba* (Washington, D.C.: Three Continents Press, 1974); *The Mwindo Epic,* edited and translated by Daniel Biebuyck and Kahombo Mateene (Los Angeles: University of California Press, 1969); and Yambo Ouolognem's controversial *Bound to Violence* (New York: Harcourt Brace Jovanovich, 1971).

[13]Thomas Mofolo, *Chaka* (London: Oxford University Press, 1931).

[14]Sahle Sellassie, *The Afersata* (London: Heinemann, 1968).

[15]Flora Nwapa, *Efuru* (London: Heinemann, 1966).

central character spends a good part of her life trying to have children and thus fulfill the role into which she is cast by traditional society.[16]

Idu is unable to have children for a long time, so her husband, Adiewere, finally takes a second wife. Idu then gives him a child but before she delivers a second, Adiewere dies. Through the terrible trauma of his death, Idu gains the strength to go against tradition. She refuses to marry his brother according to tradition and even fails to mourn his death according to custom. Instead, she follows him to the grave.

Two other authors also successfully depict the relationship between the individual and society in the traditional setting. Bonnie Lubega writes in *The Outcasts* of social stratification and the weight of tradition.[17] Karekyezi, the hired herdsman from a different tribe, is looked down upon by those who own the cattle. Eventually, he is fired and driven away. Lubega gives Karekyezi some revenge in that he has systematically been stealing from the cattle owners and can go away laughing. At the same time, he has been driven out of the human collectivity, and condemned to remain an outcast forever.

For his part, Bediako Asare depicts an allegorical political system situated on an island off Africa. Ngurumo is the *Rebel* who seeks to break the tyrannical hold of tradition.[18] Although faced with starvation and disaster, the people of his village refuse to leave. The conservative priest and ruler, Mzee Matata, not only insists on the following of tradition, he tries to have Ngurumo killed. Ultimately, Ngurumo and many of the others escaped from the controlled gerontocracy to begin a new life.

Perhaps the most scathing indictment of traditional society remains Yambo Ouolognem's *Bound to Violence.* Reacting to both the assimilation of European values and the excessive romanticism of the neotraditionalists, Ouolognem celebrates not the glorious African past, but its squalor, its treachery, its inhumanity to man. Sweeping across a 700-year canvas, his figures portray centuries of violence and the suppression of Africans, first by other Africans, then by Arabs, and then by Europeans. He asserts that only the endurance and the suffering is worthy of eulogy.

THE SACRED AND THE PROFANE

We have seen that descriptions of life in traditional society abound in recent African literature. But the hold of tradition in the form of interaction between the natural world and the supernatural is an even more widespread theme. In

[16]Flora Nwapa, *Idu* (London: Heinemann, 1970). For a happier portrayal of a woman caught in the dilemma of childlessness, see Asare Konadu, *A Woman in Her Prime* (London: Heinemann, 1967). Konadu has also created a moving portrayal of the efficacy of tradition in *Ordained by the Oracle* (London: Heinemann, 1969).

[17]Bonnie Lubega, *The Outcasts* (London: Heinemann, 1971).

[18]Bediako Asare, *Rebel* (London: Heinemann, 1969).

fact, a majority of the novels written in the last two decades contain this theme. As we indicated in Chapter 1, the sociopolitical systems of traditional Africa cannot be separated from the African views of metaphysics, for both society and the traditional political systems are upheld by them.

There is no space here for a full examination of African religions and their sociopolitical role, but certain broad patterns of beliefs can be sketched.[19] In the traditional view, there is a unity of the world—the sacred and the profane, the natural and the supernatural are integrated along a space-time continuum. The here and now, the there and then, are related in what Solomon Iyasere has termed the "eternal present"[20] and what John Mbiti calls the "indefinite past."[21]

Not only is there a space-time continuum, but the living and the dead, the human and the spirit world, live side by side. Generally speaking, whatever their views of an ultimate, all-creating god behind everything, most African cultures accepted the notions of lesser gods and spirits intervening and interacting with human affairs.

In *The Great Ponds,* for example, although one battle takes place between the two villages, a second rages within the context of man and the gods. Olumba, champion of Chiolu, swears by the gods that the pond of Wagaba belongs to Chiolu and that if this is not true, "let me die within six months." When he is stung by a swarm of bees and nearly dies, many of the villagers assume the gods' intervention. He struggles not to die as the great pressures from the supernatural build and are accepted. Although he survives, the arrival of *wonjo* (influenza) is seen as the wrath of the gods. The intermingling of the gods and men is perceived as perfectly commonplace.

In fact, a number of observers have commented on the extent to which religion is an integral part of African life and politics.[22] As Amadi himself put it in *The Concubine;*

> The Thunder-god feasts in his grove,
> Then naps 'twist rainbows up above;
> But justice suffers here below,
> And we know not which way to go.[23]

[19]For a review of African religious and belief systems, see John Mbiti, *African Religions and Philosophy* (Garden City, N.Y.: Doubleday, 1970), and *Concepts of God in Africa* (New York: Praeger, 1970); Benjamin Ray, *African Religions* (Englewood Cliffs, N.J.: Prentice-Hall, 1976); and Geoffrey Parrinder, *Religions in Africa* (Baltimore: Penguin Books, 1969).

[20]Solomon Iyasere, "Oral Tradition in the Criticism of African Literature," *Journal of Modern African Studies,* vol. 13, no. 1 (1975), p. 115.

[21]Mbiti, *African Religions and Philosophy,* p. 17.

[22]For an analysis of this phenomenon in several different settings, see V. W. Turner, *The Drums of Affliction: A Study of Religious Processes Among the Ndembu of Zambia* (London: Oxford University Press, 1967); and M. J. Field, *The Search for Security* (New York: Norton, 1970).

[23]Amadi, *The Concubine,* foreword.

Thus, it is the intermingling of the sacred and the profane, the interaction of the living and the dead, the mortal and the immortal which, at base, provides so much of the fabric of life. The actions of the gods cannot always be understood, but their intervention is accepted. Ihuoma brings, with her bad luck, suffering and death to her lovers. At the conclusion of *The Concubine,* her son accidently shoots her husband, Ekwueme. "The Spirit of Death was known to take away people's souls shortly after midnight. That was when Ekwueme died."[24]

Perhaps the most outstanding examples of the intermingling of the real world and the world beyond have been produced by the Yoruba writer, Amos Tutuola. His *The Brave African Huntress* and *The Palm-Wine Drinkard,* portray the constant interaction between the living and the dead.[25] The theme of *The Palm-Wine Drinkard* is the specific search for the Drinkard's dead tapster in Deads' Town. But it is in *My Life in the Bush of Ghosts* that Tutuola describes the space-time continuum in its most vibrant aspects.[26] In the confusion of a slave raid, a small boy is left alone to face the bush, a dense jungle inhabited by ghosts and demons. Although the story can be read at a variety of levels (including as allegory in a kind of pilgrim's progress), one gets the overwhelming sense that the coexistence of the worlds of the living and the dead makes traditional society a place where man is not at liberty to act out his individual fate independent of the gods.

Clearly, this world view and the unity of the natural and the supernatural influence the course of individual behavior, even among Africans who have become "westernized." In Onuora Nzekwu's *Wand of Noble Wood,* Peter Obiesie, an educated journalist, is torn between the new life in Lagos and the old traditional life he left behind in Iboland.[27] He decides to follow his parents' wishes and marry the girl of their choice. But Nneka is under a curse and takes her own life. The reason? Peter would die if the marriage were ever consummated. In *Ordained By the Oracle,* the prosperous trader, Boateng, disbelieves in the old customs and ignores the old way.[28] As a result, his wife dies and he is catapulted back into a state of mind where the old gods and their rituals again have meaning.

Even when there is an occasional work in which traditional society is not depicted as being under the steady influence of the gods, the protests seem half-hearted. For example, Ola Rotimi's play, *The Gods are Not to Blame,* is

[24]Ibid., p. 280.

[25]Amos Tutuola, *The Brave African Huntress* (New York: Grove Press, 1958), and *The Palm-Wine Drinkard* (New York: Grove Press, 1953).

[26]Amos Tutuola, *My Life in the Bush of Ghosts* (New York: Grove Press, 1954). Although Tutuola is often dismissed as "primitive," this same theme occurs in the writings of the sophisticated Wole Soyinka. See especially his *A Dance of the Forests* (London: Oxford University Press, 1963).

[27]Onuora Nzekwu, *Wand of Noble Wood* (London: Heinemann, 1961).

[28]Asare Konadu, *Ordained by the Oracle* (London: Heinemann, 1969).

a translation of the Oedipus tale into a Ghanian setting.[29] It ends on an unreal
and unconvincing note when King Odewale says:

> No, no! Do not blame the Gods. Let no one blame the powers. My people,
> learn from my fall. The power would have failed if I did not let them use
> me.[30]

But clearly that is asking one to rip oneself free from the total context of life
and to ignore what is occurring. The powers still intervene.

This world-view is not without important political ramifications. In *Rebel,*
Mzee Matata calls on the gods, citing them as the reason the village cannot
be moved. In Chinua Achebe's *Arrow of God,* Ezeulu fights on behalf of his
gods.[31] And, in a thinly veiled description of present day Malawi, Legson
Kayira etches a sharp portrait of Dr. Banda and his dictatorship by stressing
the "supernatural" power behind his rule. *The Detainee* is incarcerated by the
forces of Sir Zaddock.[32] The simple peasant, Napolo, finds his way blocked
by youth brigades and party hooligans and, only narrowly escaping death, ends
up in a detention camp. Revolt against Sir Zaddock is stifled because of his
supernatural powers:

> It's been said where I come from that Sir Zaddock can turn himself into
> a bird or a snake and that he can make himself invisible at will. I have heard
> from people who say they have seen him turn into a thunderbolt. Isn't that
> how he was able to outwit the white man and become ruler of this country?
> They say he is descended from the great Mlozi himself.[33]

The persistent theme of the intertwined nature of the sacred and the profane
is echoed in the "real" world of politics. Colonel Micombero does not attempt
his *coup* in Burundi until the Mwami is out of the country and the sacred
drums which are the spiritual link to ruling can be captured. In the civil war
in the (then) Congo in 1964, both sides made extensive use of ritual specialists,
magic to ward off bullets and other paraphernalia designed to take political
advantage of this particular mind set. Kwame Nkrumah took the title of
Osagyefo, the Blessed Redeemer, in part because of its symbolic connotation;
later, however, he came to believe in the use of ritual specialists to ward off
his domestic enemies. Likewise, the current presidents of Malawi and

---

[29]Ola Rotimi, *The Gods are Not To Blame* (London: Oxford Univeristy Press, 1971).
[30]Ibid., p. 71.
[31]Chinua Achebe, *Arrow of God* (Garden City, N.Y.: Doubleday, 1969). See also T. C. Echewa,
    The Land's Lord (Westport: Lawrence Hill, 1976).
[32]Legson Kayira, *The Detainee* (London: Heinemann, 1974).
[33]Ibid., p. 22.

Equatorial Guinea have gone to great lengths to project images of supernatural power.

This is not to suggest that African politics is, in and of itself, necessarily bound up with the sacred and profane continuum at all times and in all places. But there are enough instances to suggest that the prevalent theme so richly developed by contemporary authors has a firm basis in the reality of African society. This basis must be dealt with by those who would lead the political kingdom.

COLONIALISM

The theme of African metaphysics and the theme of the colonial experience are often related; the arrival of the Europeans brought new ideas and new gods. The clash between the colonialists and the African peoples was also the struggle between gods and technologies. Thus, it is not surprising that many Africans saw the power of the colonizer as being related to the power of their gods.

Colonialism itself, especially the concomitant clash of social, economic, and political values, stimulated many writers. Some dealt with the onset of colonialism and African resistance to it. Some dealt with what it was like to endure the colonial experience. Still others concerned themselves with the struggle for independence and the decline of colonialism. In all cases, colonialism proved to be a wellspring of creativity and some critics, such as Ihechukwu Madubuike, have gone so far as to assert that modern African literature arose primarily as a reaction to colonialism, oppression, and racism.[34]

As we stated in Chapter 2, all colonial systems shared a number of characteristics. All were authoritarian, exploitive, disruptive, undemocratic and fundamentally racist. There is widespread agreement among African writers concerning these characteristics, although some treat the experience with humor, others with bitterness. In the section that follows, we outline several novels that most effectively capture the flavor of the colonial experience from the African perspective. Bear in mind that the earlier themes—life in traditional settings and African metaphysics—appear and reappear in these works, even though their primary subject is the colonial experience.

The Onset of Colonialism

Some of the best descriptions of the onset of colonialism have been done by Chinua Achebe. His *Arrow of God* and *Things Fall Apart* have received wide critical acclaim and are extremely useful portraits of the impact of the exoge-

[34]Ihechukwu Madubuike, "The African Novel in the 1970's," *Issue,* vol. 4, no. 4 (Winter 1974), pp. 15–18.

nous intrusion called colonialism.[35] In *Arrow of God,* the village priest, Ezeulu, uses the traditional religion to resist the encroachment of European ways. Ezeulu, who sees himself as "an arrow in the bow of his god," refuses to sanction the New Yam feasts and harvest.

The people of Umuaro, the Igbo village in eastern Nigeria, are torn between the new god of Christianity and the older gods so intimately bound up with the traditional. By refusing to name the day of the New Yam feasts, Ezeulu is destroyed along with his god even if the fabric of traditional society is not completely rent.

Things Fall Apart also depicts the onset of colonialism. Okonkwo is an important and respected man in the nine villages of Obi. The story takes place just as the Europeans are arriving, bringing with them roads, taxes, and missionaries. The old gods (Amadiora, Idemili, Otakagu, and Ekwensu) are abandoned as more and more people become Christians. Within seven years (while Okonkwo is in exile) the traditional nature of society is continually undercut and he returns to see the clans breaking up and the prisons full of "men who had offended against the white man's law."[36]

In desperation, Okonkwo leads some men in the burning of the Christian church. They are seized and held until a fine of 250 bags of cowries are paid. The District Commissioner sternly tells the people:

> We shall not do you any harm . . . if only you agree to cooperate with us. We have brought a peaceful administration to you and your people so that you may be happy.[37]

Finally released, the men call a meeting of the entire village. They are ashamed for themselves and for the entire population because even "all our gods are weeping."[38] The men call for further resistance. The District Commissioner sends messengers to disperse the crowd and, in a fit of frustration, Okonkwo kills one with his machete. Then, realizing that the villagers will not fight, he commits suicide.

In the microcosm of Okonkwo's frustration and tragedy is a recurring theme in the works dealing with the arrival of the Europeans. Stanlake Samkange, in *On Trial for My Country,* describes the similar onset of colonialism in a different part of Africa.[39] Lobengula, king of the Amatabele, and Cecil Rhodes, the British imperialist, are on trial by their peers. Lobengula's defense is that the Europeans lied, stole land, and never lived up to their treaty. He plaintively describes trying to repudiate the Rudd concession and the en-

---

[35]Chinua Achebe, *Arrow of God,* and *Things Fall Apart* (London: Heinemann, 1958).
[36]Achebe, *Things Fall Apart,* p. 158.
[37]Ibid., p. 175.
[38]Ibid., p. 182.
[39]Stanlake Samkange, *On Trial for My Country* (London: Heinemann, 1966).

croaching march of colonial rule. But, inexorably, the Europeans march north, establishing Fort Salisbury, and then intervening in the 1893 struggle between the Vashona and the Amatabele. The Africans are subjugated and the colony of Rhodesia comes into being.

Southern Africa, which witnessed the largest number of European settlers, is also the scene for Peter Abrahams' *Wild Conquest.* [40] Book One accurately underscores the dual impact of European ideology and technology: "Bible and Rifle." Book Two, *"Bayete!"* depicts Mzlikazi, the former commander in Shaka's army, and the exhaustion the Africans feel at the continual struggle. Book Three, ironically entitled "New Day," describes the defeat of the Africans by the Europeans and their flight across the Limpopo river (which merely prolongs the struggle, for, soon enough, the Europeans follow).

Life Under Colonial Rule

To a certain extent, there is an overlap between the onset of colonialism and its eventual impact on the traditional African societies. Many works clearly deal with both facets of the African experience. For this section, one could use literally dozens of different works.

There are the sardonically humorous works, such as T. M. Aluko's *One Man, One Wife,* which describes the alien rule in western Nigeria. [41] The village of Isolo is not only subjected to the imposition of colonial authority, it is also afflicted with strange, imported notions, such as the idea that a man is entitled to only one wife.

There are the almost tender recollections of the rites of passage under colonialism in William Conton's *The African.* [42] The author's progress to obtain education and study overseas also underlines the tremendous impact of the colonials' mystique on individual Africans. For example, Conton describes the incredible sensations he felt when he first encountered a white sweeping the streets in England, a sight which helped to destroy

> ... the illusion created by the role the white man plays in Africa: that is, a kind of demigod whose hands must never get dirty, who must not be allowed to carry anything heavier than a portfolio or wield any implement heavier than a pen. Without realizing it we had come to think of the white man only in the role of missionary, civil servant, or senior business executive, one who was always behind the desk, never in front of it. [43]

[40]Peter Abrahams, *Wild Conquest* (Garden City, N.Y.: Doubleday, 1971).

[41]T. M. Aluko, *One Man, One Wife* (London: Heinemann, 1959).

[42]William Conton, *The African* (New York: Signet Books, 1960). See also Abioseh Nicol, *Two African Tales* (Cambridge, England: Cambridge University Press, 1965), and Bernard Dadie, *Climbié* (London: Heinemann, 1971).

[43]Conton, *The African,* p. 45.

Or, there are the sardonic views of such as Dominic Mulaisho, whose *The Tongue of the Dumb* is set in what is now Zambia.[44] Two leaders struggle. Lubinda opposes the new rulers and their crazy ideas about lepers, floods, and taxes. Chief Mpona is allied with the Europeans and the subject of great abuse. He is accused of being a witch and of selling a child, Mwape, to the white men. Tortured and threatened with death, Mpona is saved by the return of the child, who had simply wandered off. He is reinstated and it is Lubinda who is driven off into the woods to die. Symbolically, the new order has triumphed over the old.

And there are a number of African writers who take a more realistic view of colonialism. The same authoritarian racist imposition of new values also brought health benefits, new products, and creative ideas. Some, like James Ngugi (now using his Gikuyu name, Ngugi Wa Thiong'o), accurately depict the dilemma of being caught between two worlds, at home in neither, yet realizing the drawbacks and benefits of both. In *The River Between,* Waiyaki acquires the education which he needs to get ahead, but realizes that it separates him from his people:

> For Waiyaki knew that not all the ways of the white man were bad. Even his religion was not essentially bad. Some good, some truth shone through it. But the religion, the faith needed washing, cleaning away all the dirt, leaving only the eternal. And that eternal that was the truth had to be reconciled to the traditions of the people. A people's traditions could not be swept away overnight.[45]

Others, like Mongo Beti, enhance our appreciation of the contradictions in colonialism simply by not glorifying traditional society. In both *Mission to Kala* and *King Lazarus* he satirizes colonialism, but he also indicates the failures of traditional society and the extent to which Africans accepted many of the assumptions of colonialism without question.[46] For him, as Oolougum, the Africans who were conquered were neither saints nor lacking in faults.

But, for a number of writers colonialism could not be justified. Ferdinand Oyono, for example, writing of French rule in the Cameroons, is uncompromising and devastating. *The Old Man and the Medal* is probably the finest description of colonial rule we are likely to have.[47] Meka, the old man of the village, has made many sacrifices on behalf of the colonizer. He divorced his other wives and gave his land to the mission for the use of the church. He sent his two sons off to war for France. Both were killed. Finally, belatedly, the

---

[44]Dominic Mulaisho, *The Tongue of the Dumb* (London: Heinemann, 1971).

[45]James Ngugi, *The River Between* (London: Heinemann, 1965), p. 162.

[46]Mongo Beti, *Mission to Kala* (London: Heinemann, 1964), and *King Lazarus* (New York: Collier Books, 1971). Mongo Beti is the pen name of Alexandre Biyidi.

[47]Ferdinand Oyono, *The Old Man and the Medal* (London: Heinemann, 1969).

French authorities decide to give him a medal. Meka's wife says simply that it is a poor bargain. At the airport, Meka cannot keep his mind on the medal of the honor. His shoes hurt and he must urinate. At the banquet that follows, Meka and the other Africans sit apart and on the way home, Meka is arrested, jailed, and beaten for being out of the African area after dark. Bitterly, he declares:

> What have we got in this country? Nothing! Nothing! Not even the liberty to refuse their gifts.[48] Tell him I am a very great fool, who yesterday still believed in the white man's friendship . . . I am very tired. They can do what they will with me.[49]

In *Houseboy,* Oyono etches his entire portrait with acid.[50] Toundi, the mission boy, is well trained and well recommended. He is brought into the house of the local commandant. Unfortunately, Toundi sees the weakness of the commandant and the unfaithfulness of his wife. The colonial myth must be upheld at any cost, so Toundi is arrested and beaten. He watches other Africans whipped and tortured to death. The book closes with Toundi seeking to escape at all costs.

The gradual awareness that Europeans were only human, that they were fallible and even fragile, was often slow to dawn on Africans who had been subjugated during the struggle for Africa. But, as it came, slowly and hesitantly at first, then inexorably, it set in motion the struggle for independence and the eventual departure of the colonial authority. Sembene Ousmane's *God's Bits of Wood* serves as a useful transition between colonial rule and the movement for independence.[51] Set in the Senegal of the late 1940s, the novel outlines the colonials' dimensions in French West Africa and the gradual movement toward opposition on the part of the Africans. With skill and control, Ousmane describes the railroad strike of 1947–48 and the beginnings of African nationalism as a vehicle of individual and societal liberation.

The Struggle Against Colonialism

With the rise of nationalism in Africa following World War II, the struggle against colonialism intensified. As such countries as India obtained independence, more and more Africans called for the end to colonial rule. A number of novels depict this, many set in Kenya, where the so-called Mau Mau revolt became a favorite topic.

[48]Ibid., p. 165.
[49]Ibid., pp. 134–35.
[50]Ferdinand Oyono, *Houseboy* (London: Heinemann, 1966).
[51]Sembene Ousmane, *God's Bits of Wood* (Garden City, N.Y.: Doubleday, 1970).

There is the hauntingly pessimistic account of Meja Mwangi, *Carcase for Hounds.*[52] Set in the beautiful Laikipia district of Kenya, it is the story of the fight between the colonial authority in the person of Captain Kingsley (a former District Commissioner, now under pressure from the army to deal with insurgents in his region) and his opponent, General Haraka (who used to work for the government, but now is the leader of a band of freedom fighters). After leading a number of successful raids, General Haraka is finally wounded and dies in agony as his band is wiped out.

Mwangi's description of the struggle is often heavy-handed, but he does succeed in outlining the pressures on Africans to decide for or against not only independence, but the most likely way to obtain that independence. Chief Simba, for example, the former friend of Haraka, becomes a government-sponsored chief and, like so many other Kenyans, sides with the government in the suppression of the insurgents.

This ambiguity toward the decolonization struggle is also the subject of James Ngugi's gripping *Weep Not Child.*[53] Njoroge, the Gikuku boy, is caught in the middle of the Mau Mau insurgency and its repression. The evils of colonialism spawn the rebellion. The rebellion, in its turn, leads to brutality and terror. Terror results in counter-terror in a spiral of violence and hatred. Njoroge is educated and a Christian, but he sees his father tortured in prison and Isaka, his Christian teacher, killed by white soldiers because he does not have his papers. Yet, he cannot join wholeheartedly in the struggle and witnesses the loss of faith in the movement's early goals. His brother, Boro, is asked:

> Don't you believe in anything? No, nothing. Except revenge. Return of the lands? The lost land will come back to us maybe. But I've lost too many of those whom I loved for land to mean much to me.[54]

For Ngugi, "Hope of a better day is the only comfort he can give a weeping child."[55]

Ngugi's third novel, *A Grain of Wheat,* continues this theme up to the eve of independence.[56] The insurgency has been crushed, but the colonial authority is leaving anyway. The stalwarts of the Kenyan African National Union come forward to receive the spoils. The ex-freedom fighters get little. Heroes of the revolution turn out to be traitors.

Karanja, who betrayed his people, becomes an assistant at an agricultural research station and many others who worked with the government get high

[52]Meja Mwangi, *Carcase for Hounds* (London: Heinemann, 1974).
[53]James Ngugi, *Weep Not Child* (New York: Macmillan, 1969).
[54]Ibid., p. 145.
[55]Ibid., p. 1.
[56]James Ngugi, *A Grain of Wheat* (London: Heinemann, 1968).

positions. Living with his guilt becomes intolerable for Mugo. A Gikuyu detainee, Mugo is regarded as a leader of the revolution. In reality, he betrayed Kihika, the true leader: "Kihika came to me by night. He put his life into my hands and I sold it to the white man. And this thing has eaten into my life all these years."[57] Mugo is killed during the independence celebrations and the reader is left to puzzle about what Uhuru will bring.

Even in those territories where there was not open warfare, the nationalist movements often met governmental repression and individual Africans found themselves forced to take sides. Aubrey Kachingwe traces the evolution in *No Easy Task.*[58] Set in Nyasaland, it is the story of Joe Jozeni, the son of a rural pastor, who becomes a newspaperman and is gradually drawn into politics. Through his eyes, Kachingwe sketches the growth of the nationalist movement, the emergence of the new politicians, the attempts of the police to harass them, and the succession of constitutions that heralds the coming of independence.

The concern with the struggle for independence continues and we shall be dealing with it in the context of the liberation of southern Africa under the heading, "Racism and Racial Domination." In the next section, however, we wish to concentrate on the theme of social change engendered by the colonial experience and the intrusion of modernity.

SOCIAL CHANGE

Related to many of the issues previously discussed, but also subsuming virtually all of the African novels, is the subject of social change. It is connnected to the colonial experience, but is also related to the broader impact of modernization. In many instances, it is modern life which intrudes into the African context and produces social, economic, and cultural changes. In fact, the clash of cultures—African and European—is also the clash of societies—traditional and modern.

Many African writers have focused on the clash of cultures as it relates to colonialism and to the broader issues of social change, in both pre- and postindependence situations. For example, the process of rural-to-city migration, although obviously stimulated by colonialism, took place prior to its onset and continued, often at an accelerated pace, after decolonization. As Africans moved from villages to the urban centers of Lagos, Accra, Dakar, Brazzaville, Nairobi, and Lusaka, a host of changes occurred, not only in the lives of the individuals involved, but in the urban centers and in the communities that were left behind.

[57]Ibid., p. 252.
[58]Aubrey Kachingwe, *No Easy Task* (London: Heinemann, 1966).

Scholarly studies have accented the most important of the trends that accompanied these changes, including the unusual pattern of target workers. Coming from their villages to the city for specific purposes and often definite time periods, these individuals linked the cities to the countryside.[59]

Three African writers—one from the Sudan, one from Senegal, and one from Nigeria—capture the essence of urban life and its impact on individuals and their societies. Tayeb Salih, in *Season of Migration to the North,* writes of the pejorative impact on the individual, who ends up at home neither in the east nor the west nor in the village of Khartoum.[60] Sembene Ousmane also deftly sketches the individual faced with modernity and bureaucratic difficulty as Dieng tries to cope with *The Money Order.*[61]

But the real flavor of the urban experience is captured by Cyprian Ekwensi. His stories pulsate with the excitement and heartbreak of city life, the hopes and dreams and often depressing outcomes which accompany its vitality. His *People of the City, Lokotown and Other Stories,* even *Jagua Nana*[62] all portray a society in transition—the "high life" and fast pace of the city, the liberation it provides those fleeing the confines of traditional society, and its often bewildering costs for those who do not adapt. In "The Glittering City," for example, he describes the allure for Essi, the young girl from the provinces:

> She had forsaken her mother, her fiancé and everything she had ever learnt at school. The magic of the glittering city had confused her. It was unlike her to be awake so long after midnight. To tell herself the truth she was enjoying it. The experience was so new, it fascinated her. The lights—blue, green, orange—were whirling round and round in her head. Surely, this was a dream. She would soon wake up and find herself in the late train from Kano, covered with coal particles and smoke.[63]

But when her newly found friend, Fussy Joe, is killed in an accident, the hard fast life of the city turns sour and she returns to the north, forever changed.

The intrusion of modern life, in the form of technology and bureaucracy, is satirized by T. M. Aluko in his *One Man, One Matchet.*[64] In a classic example of a clash of cultures, the book depicts Yorubaland in the 1950s— the time of the swollen shoot disease, which threatened the entire cocoa crop. The agricultural agent, Mr. Gregory, backed by the District Officer, Mr.

---

[59]See, for example, the works of Abner Cohen, *Custom and Politics in Urban Africa* (Los Angeles: University of California Press, 1969); and Herbert Werlin, *Governing an African City: A Study of Nairobi* (New York: Africana Publishing Company, 1974).

[60]Tayeb Salih, *Season of Migration to the North* (London: Heinemann, 1969).

[61]Sembene Ousmane, *The Money Order* (London: Heinemann, 1965).

[62]Cyprian Ekwensi, *People of the City* (London: Heinemann, 1963), *Lokotown and Other Stories* (London: Heinemann, 1966), and *Jagua Nana* (New York: Fawcett Books, 1961).

[63]Ekwensi, *People of the City,* p. 114.

[64]T. M. Aluko, *One Man, One Matchet* (London: Heinemann, 1964).

Stanfield, insists that the Africans cut down the diseased trees. Chief Momo and the elders oppose this, and Chief Momo is not surprised by the European's approach:

> He had at no time expected anything sane from the White Man, and was therefore not surprised at his outrageous suggestions.[65]

Although the book goes on to depict the decolonization struggle and the dilemma of moderates caught in the middle, it remains a sturdy portrait of the clash of cultures and the tensions such a clash brings to all levels of society.

As a variation on this theme, some African writers have stressed the problems of reentry, whereby the educated African returns to a more traditional society and finds that he or she does not fit in at all, or that the clash of cultures makes integration very difficult. For Gabriel Okara, in *The Voice,* it is clear that there is no compromise in the struggle between the old and the new.[66] The clash must end in the destruction of one or the other. Okolo returns from his studies to question the traditional authorities, especially the chief, Ozongo. When threatened by the tribal leaders, both Okolo and Tuere, the girl who helps him, retaliate and are put to death.

Likewise, Cheikh Hamidou Kane outlines the destructiveness of the clash in the appropriately entitled *Ambiguous Adventure.* [67] Samba Diallo is anxious for independence but he becomes enmeshed in the struggle of the old and the new, torn between two cultures. As if to underscore the futility of trying to deal with this dual heritage, he is killed by a demented religious figure. The demented fool symbolizes the clash of cultures, for he wears both a traditional boubou and a tattered European coat.

For John Munonye, the matter is less drastic, but the clash of cultures is clearly depicted. In *Obi,* he sketches the return of Joe and Anna to their native village.[68] Although Christianized and westernized, they seek to live where they were born, to build their house, or *obi,* and settle down. But pressures mount when Anna does not conceive and the village elders insist that Joe take a second wife. Joe tries traditional religion, witch doctors, and the modern hospital in an effort to get Anna pregnant. In the end, she does have a child, but they decide to leave the village of Umudiobia, "on the first stage of their journey back into a bigger world."[69]

The disruptive aspects of colonialism and modernization, as well as their lingering effects, are well portrayed in the Ghanian writer Ama Ata Aidoo's

[65]Ibid., p. 4.
[66]Gabriel Okara, *The Voice* (London: Heinemann, 1964).
[67]Cheikh Hamidou Kane, *Ambiguous Adventure* (New York: Collier Books, 1963).
[68]John Munonye, *Obi* (London: Heinemann, 1969).
[69]Ibid., p. 210.

works, *No Sweetness Here* and *Dilemma of a Ghost.*[70] In *No Sweetness Here* there are no brutal white colonizers. Independence has come. But colonialism has left behind a tortured legacy—the clash between city life and the rural areas, between the old values and the new, and the very real human sufferings in the context of social change are described.

For some writers, the answer is clear and direct, there must be a retention of the traditional values. The disintegration of society must be halted by reaffirming the best of the old values. This neotraditionalist position is upheld by two of Africa's better writers, Okot p'Bitek, from Uganda, and Kofi Awoonor, from Ghana. Okot p'Bitek's biting *Song of Lawino* is a vitriolic attack on those Africans who have sold out their heritage.[71] In a moving allegory, the traditional wife, symbolizing Africa, mourns the husband's interest in western women but takes pride in her ignorance of foreign customs:

> It is true
> I am ignorant of the dances of foreigners
> And how they dress
> I do not know.
> Their games
> I cannot play
> I only know the dances of our people.[72]

"Let no one uproot the pumpkin" is the refrain—do not abandon your traditional heritage for the false gods of modern life.

Awoonor's works are softer and more compassionate, yet as fiercely determined to hold the traditional values ahead of the modern ones. *This Earth, My Brother* is a collection of poems lamenting the neglect of the ancestral shrines and the failure of modern Africa to maintain its continuity with the past.[73] He sees tradition as a stabilizing agent in the time of turmoil and advocates a return to the past instead of the "huge senseless cathedral of doom" embodied in western values.[74]

In *Night of My Blood,* Awoonor depicts the plight of the new, educated African.[75] The lawyer, Amamu, suffers a nervous breakdown and dies, as Africa is dying in imitating the worst aspects of colonialism. His is not a simple-minded condemnation of colonialism *per se,* for he blames the Africans themselves for being "liars" and "fools" for trading their precious heritage for

[70]Ama Ata Aidoo, *No Sweetness Here* (Garden City, N.Y.: Doubleday, 1972), and *The Dilemma of a Ghost* (Accra: Longmans, 1965).

[71]Okot p'Bitek, *Song of Lawino* (Nairobi: East African Publishing House, 1965).

[72]Ibid., p. 31.

[73]Kofi Awoonor, *This Earth, My Brother* (Garden City, N.Y.: Doubleday, 1971).

[74]Ibid., p. 25.

[75]Kofi Awoonor, *Night of My Blood* (Garden City, N.Y.: Doubleday, 1971).

the dross of modern life. For him, art can lead the way to a rejuvenation of the African spirit:

> Above all, the literature, like the music, art and sculpture, must return to the traditional sources for inspiration. . . . It is only when this line of continuity is forged that the continent that has been harassed for centuries will recover the personality of her true self and in so doing cease to be a bad caricature and copy of her external mentors.[76]

Finally, there are the writers who recognize the ambiguity that results from the imposition of alien values. Isidore Okpewho talks against colonialism and the fast life in *The Victims,* but does not idealize traditional life.[77] In fact, he speaks out against polygamy and some of the romantic attachment to it. For Okpewho, the old and the new, the good and the bad, the African and the western will have to live side by side, with intelligent people choosing neither one nor the other, but the best features of both.

In fact, the contiguous existence of both sets of values may simply be a fact of life for Africans and their societies. In Daniachew Worku's moving *The Thirteenth Sun,* the conjure woman exists side by side with the neon lights announcing "Ethiopian Airlines."[78] For those seeking to shape the political and economic destinies of the African countries, a frank recognition of the existing duality of life may well be a prerequisite for solving the problems of the past, the present, and the future.

THE EUROPEAN SHADOW: CONTINUED RACISM

If Africans differ among themselves concerning the clash between tradition and modernity on the one hand, and the proper response to social change on the other, they are, nevertheless, united in opposing continued racism in the African context. Whether it is a vestige of the colonial system, as in the French Territory of the Afars and Issas (until 1977), or the maintenance of white oligarchies in Zimbabwe, Namibia, and South Africa, there is strong African opposition.

This opposition is keenly expressed in a number of contemporary novels. Both the oppression itself and the struggle to end that oppression have spawned dozens of works, many of which are powerful expressions of anguish and suffering, mirroring the difficulties of life under alien rule and racial suppression.

[76]Kofi Awoonor, *The Breast of the Earth* (Garden City, N.Y.: Doubleday, 1976), p. 356.
[77]Isidore Okpewho, *The Victims* (Garden City, N.Y.: Doubleday, 1971).
[78]Daniachew Worku, *The Thirteenth Sun* (London: Heinemann, 1973).

There are, for example, the works of Peter Abrahams, *Mine Boy* and *Tell Freedom,* which detail life in South Africa.[79] *Mine Boy* is the simply told tale of Xuma, who comes from his village to work in Johannesburg. It is a vivid portrayal of life in the mines, the danger of the work, the harassment of the police, the destruction of the African family as a result of pass laws, and residential segregation. In that society a white can never fully understand the black experience:

> "You say you understand," Xuma said, "but how can you? You are a white man. You do not carry a pass. You do not know how it feels to be stopped by a policeman in the street. You go where you like. You do not know how it feels when they say, 'Get Out! White people only.' "[80]

For Abrahams, the only escape from oppression was exile as the pressures and injustices mounted, and life itself became suffocating and terrifying:

> Perhaps life had a meaning that transcended race and colour. If it had, I could not find it in South Africa. Also there was the need to write, to tell freedom, and for this I needed to be personally free.[81]

For Can Themba, who died in exile in nearby Swaziland, it is the day-by-day buildup of oppression from apartheid which twists and warps the individual's ability to cope. Not just the brutality and the discrimination, but the sense of impotence, the mingled fear and rage, the overwhelming need to survive in a landscape littered with broken hopes:

> As I brood over these things, I, with my insouciant attitude toward matters of weight, I feel a sticky despair, which the most potent bottle of brandy cannot wash away. What can I do?[82]

For his part, Richard Rive has contributed a sweeping novel, *Emergency* (about the 1960 Sharpseville massacre in South Africa) and a number of short stories.[83] African frustrations with apartheid culminated in the organized campaign to turn in passbooks, the internal passports all South African non-whites are required to carry. The shooting of unarmed Africans and the subsequent police crackdown that resulted in the arrest of thousands was

---

[79]Peter Abrahams, *Mine Boy* (London: Heinemann, 1946), and *Tell Freedom* (New York: Macmillan, 1970).

[80]Abrahams, *Mine Boy,* p. 236.

[81]Abrahams, *Tell Freedom,* p. 394.

[82]Can Themba, *The Will to Die* (London: Heinemann, 1972), p. 115. Other writers who mirror the frustrations are Enver Carim, *The Golden City* (New York: Grove Press, 1969); and Dugmore Boetie, *Familiarity is the Kingdom of the Lost* (New York: Fawcett Books, 1970).

[83]Richard Rive, *Emergency* (New York: Collier Books, 1965), and Rive (ed.), *Quartet* (London: Heinemann, 1963).

recently repeated in the urban riots of 1976 in Soweto, so Rive's descriptions have both a freshness and an aura of *déjà vu*.

The tragic sense of futility and degradation, the inability of the African to rise above the system of political and economic discrimination has also resulted in a number of works which are set in the nation's prisons. Alex La Guma, in particular, has used the prison setting to starkly portray life in South Africa. In *The Stone Country* and *In the Fog of the Season's End,* he looks at the gulf separating white and black, and the horrifying torture and maltreatment reserved for South Africa's political prisoners.[84] As Nadine Gordimer puts it, Alex La Guma's protagonists ". . . do not talk about inequality; they bear its weals."[85]

Perhaps the starkest vision of South Africa is D. M. Zwelonke's *Robben Island,* an account of life on South Africa's maximum security island prison. Bekimpi is an African who, despite being in jail, refuses to go along with the system and resists it. For his efforts, he is hung upside down, tortured, and eventually taken away to die:

The one playing with the testicle squeezed harder. Bekimpi emitted a long, painful moan. Mucus and saliva came out of his nostrils and mouth and oiled the floor. The colonel came and stood at the door, an angry, frightened man. "Do you want to kill this man? Then don't do it here. Take him to Cape Town."[86]

The alternative to prisons and death is represented as exile. To leave apartheid and oppression is also to cast oneself adrift, to undergo severe stresses and frustrations once the euphoria of escape has worn off. In fact, there is a solid body of material, done by both Africans and non-Africans, outlining the exile condition and its impact on individuals.[87] The subculture of exile life has spawned its own literature and there are a number of fine works which indicate its particular problems.

Dennis Brutus, who has been on Robben Island as well, suggests that the exile can never totally leave behind the world he has escaped and that the agony of exile is unrelenting:

[84]Alex La Guma, *The Stone Country* (London: Heinemann, 1967), and *In the Fog of the Season's End* (New York: The Third Press, 1973). *The Stone Country* is "dedicated to daily average of 70,351 prisoners in South African gaols in 1964." See also his earlier *A Walk in the Night* (Evanston, Ill.: Northwestern University Press, 1967).

[85]Gordimer, *The Black Interpreters,* p. 29.

[86]D. M. Zwelonke, *Robben Island* (London: Heinemann, 1973), p. 146.

[87]For nonfiction, see John Marcum, "The Exile Condition and Revolutionary Activeness," in C. P. Potholm and Richard Dale (eds.), *Southern Africa in Transition: Essays in Regional Politics* (New York: Free Press, 1972), pp. 262–75; C. P. Potholm, "Wanderers on the Face of Africa," *The Round Table,* no. 261 (January 1976), pp. 85–92; and C. P. Potholm, "Refugees: Africa's Persistent Problem," *Africa Report,* vol. 21, no. 2 (March-April 1976), pp. 12–14, 54.

> I am the exile
> am the wanderer
> (whatever they say)
> gentle I am, and calm
> and with abstracted pace
> absorbed in planning;
> courteous to servility
> but wailings fill the chambers of my heart
> and in my head
> behind my quiet eyes
> I hear the cries and sirens.[88]

Ezekiel Mphahlele, who has written extensively on South Africa, also gives us valuable insights into the exile condition, as a refugee becomes "baffled" with freedom. In *The Wanderers,* Timi Tabane has fled South Africa with his family and spends years wandering to Nigeria and Kenya.[89] Rootless, he tries to make life meaningful; purposeless, he tries to justify his existence. He is at home nowhere and sensitive to his situation. His son, Felang, cannot cope either and he goes off to die in the struggle to liberate Zimbabwe.

For Bessie Head, another South African exile now living in Botswana, there is a cycle of exile—excitement and exhilaration; subsequent frustration and depression; enormous pressures, even madness; and a constant gnawing doubt that you will ever belong again. Her three works echo the call that love, not revolutionary violence, is the answer, even when her assistance to the host country is resisted:

> She had fallen from the very beginning into the warm embrace of the brotherhood of man, because when a people wanted everyone to be ordinary it was just another way of saying man loved man. As she fell asleep, she placed one soft hand over her land. It was a gesture of belonging.[90]

Yet, for others, there is frustration and criticism of those (be they from east or west) who would stand in the way of total liberation of Africa, and great concern for what the liberation will mean to those who have been exiles.[91]

---

[88]Dennis Brutus, *A Simple Lust* (New York: Hill & Wang, 1963), p. 137.

[89]Ezekiel Mphahlele, *Down Second Avenue* (Garden City, N.Y.: Doubleday, 1971), and *The Wanderers* (New York: Macmillan, 1971).

[90]Bessie Head, *A Question of Power* (New York: Random House, 1973), p. 206. See also her previous works, *When Rain Clouds Gather* (New York: Simon & Schuster, 1968), and *Maru* (New York: McCall Publishing Company, 1971).

[91]See, for example, Ayi Kewi Armah's angry *Why Are We So Blest?* (Garden City, N.Y.: Doubleday, 1972); and Peter Abrahams, *A Wreath for Udomo* (New York: Collier Books, 1971). In *A Wreath for Udomo,* the exile waits for the return, only to be killed by those who take power after independence.

The dislocation and suffering of exile and the impotence of the individual often overshadow concern for the future of an entire nation.

CONTEMPORARY POLITICAL PATTERNS

Such prominent writers as Achebe, Laye, Soyinka, Mazrui, Armah, and Kayira have focused on the postindependence period and have analyzed the course of politics under African rule. Their observations are both harsh and disturbing. They see corruption, repression, political decay, and violence as the predominant features of the new political landscape. In *No Longer At Ease,* for example, Chinua Achebe highlights the corruption within the civil service of Nigeria.[92] Although actually set in the preindependence period, the book foresees the strains and pressures which eventually proved so detrimental to the functioning of the Nigerian political system. Obi Okonkwo is the grandson of the central figure of *Things Fall Apart,* but he lacks the old man's dignity and strength of character, and succumbs to the lure of ill-gotten gains.

Corruption is also the central theme of T. M. Aluko's *Chief the Honourable Minister* and Cameron Duodu's *The Gab Boys.*[93] In the former work, Africans come to power and Alade Moses, the headmaster of a small school, is suddenly informed that he has been made Minister of Works. Although he initially tries to prevent government waste and inefficiency, he is eventually swept up in the tide of corruption, election scandals, political violence, and repression. He and many of the other ministers are killed in a *coup* when the army intervenes:

To prevent a future deterioration of this very bad situation the National Army has decided to take over the administration of the country till such time as it considers the situation justifies a return to civilian government.[94]

The Gab Boys, set in Nkrumah's Ghana, provides a worm's-eye view of the corruption, nepotism, and venality of a regime which promised a great deal and delivered very little as party hacks came to power and used it for their own selfish purposes.

Perhaps the most scathing denunciation of corruption and political decay is Ayi Kwei Armah's powerful *The Beautyful Ones Are Not Yet Born.*[95] Although ostensibly set in Ghana as well, *The Beautyful Ones Are Not Yet Born* offers a far wider perspective. It represents a political system which has

[92]Chinua Achebe, *No Longer at Ease* (New York: Astor-Honor, 1961).

[93]T. M. Aluko, *Chief the Honourable Minister* (London: Heinemann, 1970); and Cameron Duodu, *The Gab Boys* (London: Fontana Books, 1969).

[94]Aluko, *Chief the Honourable Minister,* p. 213.

[95]Ayi Kwei Armah, *The Beautyful Ones Are Not Yet Born* (Boston: Houghton Mifflin, 1968).

lost sight of the common man, where the politicians and their friends grab power, wealth, and luxury while the poor are given slogans. The narrator, who stands outside the quicksand of corruption (despite his wife's urging) takes the reader through a landscape covered with filth and degradation. The matches don't work, the buses are falling apart, there is physical decay to match the political decay.

Koomson, the big man, who enriched himself at the expense of the people, and the other ministers are forced to flee for their lives when the army intervenes. In fact, Koomson ends up hiding in the bottom of a latrine, forced to lie in his own vomit. But for Armah, there is no joy that the new leaders will be better than the old:

> "They say they have seized power."
> "Who?," the man asked.
> "Army men and police."
> "Oh, I see. I thought they always had power. Together with Nkrumah and his fat men."[96]

The alteration of elites, the coming to power of a new group of leaders, does not change anything, declares Armah:

> But for the nation itself there would only be a change of embezzlers and a change of the hunters and the hunted. . . . A pitiful shrinking, to days when all the powerful could think of was to use the power of a whole people to fill their own paunches. Endless days, same days, stretching into the future with no end anywhere in sight.[97]

For Achebe, there is much the same cynicism about the ability of the military to wipe out corruption and reverse the spiral of political decay. In his *A Man of the People,* the young and naive Odili challenges the power of Chief Nanga, who has risen to become Minister of Culture.[98] For his trouble, Odili is assaulted and ends up in the hospital. Weapons are planted in his car and the police join with the thugs to make sure the government is returned with a big majority:

> But the Army obliged us by staging a coup at that point and locking up every member of the government. The rampaging bands of election thugs had caused so much unrest and dislocation that our young armed forces seized the opportunity to take over. We were told Nanga was arrested trying to escape by canoe dressed like a fisherman.[99]

[96]Ibid., p. 184.
[97]Ibid., p. 191.
[98]Chinua Achebe, *A Man of the People* (Garden City, N.Y.: Doubleday, 1966).
[99]Ibid., p. 139.

Achebe is critical of the cynicism which prompted so many to change sides immediately:

> Overnight everyone began to shake their heads at the excesses of the last regime, at its graft, oppression and corrupt government: newspapers, the radio, the hitherto silent intellectuals and civil servants—everyone said what a terrible lot; and it became public opinion on the next morning.[100]

But he has little hope that the mere change in leadership will fundamentally alter the way in which the country is run.

Disillusion is also the theme of a number of other writers. Pete Palangyo has written a searingly powerful account of the story of Ntanya, who lives in a remote village in Tanzania. The government is far away and uninterested in the plight of the people. The people are wretchedly poor and life is hard. For them, the government exists only for itself while they are *Dying in the Sun:*

> Why, even new-born babies are government officers. We shall soon be a country of government officers, money and propaganda. All these half-truths being dished out on the radio, all those things directed at making one believe that there's nothing left but money and guns and the police.[101]

For Meja Mwangi, the problem is not simply poverty and hard times, it is the government's lack of concern for the maldistribution of wealth. In Kenya there is opulence and wealth and a new elite with several homes and big cars. By way of contrast, the urban poor are forced to live hand to mouth, raiding garbage cans and sleeping in the gutter. Even worse, there is not chance for improvement, no opportunity for upward mobility. Maina is a street person, unable to get steady work. He and his dustbin partner, Meja, go from odd jobs to stealing and killing. The end is cell number nine and the plea is *Kill Me Quick:*

> On the highway half a mile away from cell Number Nine and its sorrow, a car honked and sped towards the sleeping city, with its tall buildings, blinking neon lights, and its unfathomable back streets and their mysteries.[102]

If Mwangi and his characters have no hope, Camara Laye's vision of independent Guinea is one of rage and despair. For him, independence was a hope dashed. In *A Dream of Africa,* he tells the tale of the return of a native son to the land of his birth.[103] The colonists are gone, but neocolonial forces

---

[100]Ibid., p. 141.
[101]Peter Palangyo, *Dying in the Sun* (London: Heinemann, 1968), p. 68.
[102]Meja Mwangi, *Kill Me Quick* (London: Heinemann, 1973).
[103]Camara Laye, *A Dream of Africa* (New York: Collier Books, 1971).

are still at work. A new black upper class has sprung up. The revolution has been betrayed. No one cares for the masses. Dissent is not tolerated. Political repression is everywhere and the future is bleak indeed:

> I don't know. All I know is that one day someone must attack all those lies. Someone must say that though colonialism, villified by that committee, was an evil thing for our country, the regime you are now introducing will be a catastrophe whose evil consequences will be felt for decades. Someone must speak out and say that a regime built on spilt blood through the activities of incendiarism of huts and houses is nothing but a regime of anarchy and dictatorship, a regime based on violence.[104]

Then there are the works of Wole Soyinka. His plays and novels echo and reecho the themes of political repression, the betrayal of hopes and dreams, and the corruption and madness that has afflicted Nigeria since independence.[105] The spreading cancer of political corruption and decay which brought the most populous country in Africa to civil war and the brink of destruction has not, to his mind, been eradicated by successive regimes.[106] In each of his major works he reiterated that the new times have brought with them a political sickness that eats away at the heart of the entire nation. For his trouble, various regimes have incarcerated Wole Soyinka.

In fact, judging from the number of authors who have written on the theme, it is almost as if, as Charles Larson has written in the *New Republic*, "The prison has become a metaphor for the modern African state."[107] Although this may be an overstatement, enough African writers have commented, both on the situation itself and by their own imprisonment or exile, to suggest that by and large the hopes and dreams of independence have not been actualized and the political authorities have generally been uninterested in the problems of the masses.

As Ali Mazrui has suggested, for the African intellectual, the writer, the social critic, there is the often overwhelming "tyranny of the domestic scene."[108] It involves the threat and actuality of prison, exile or death, all

---

[104]Ibid., p. 146.

[105]See his *Madmen and Specialists* (New York: Hill & Wang, 1971), *Kongi's Harvest* (London: Oxford University Press, 1967), *The Interpreters* (New York: Macmillan, 1965), and *The Man Who Died* (New York: Harper & Row, 1973).

[106]Space limitations prevent us from examining the rich literature which arose out of the Nigerian civil war, especially on the Biafran side. The interested reader should consult Chinua Achebe, *Christmas in Biafra and Other Poems* (Garden City, N.Y.: Doubleday, 1973), and *Girls at War and Other Stories* (New York: Fawcett Books, 1972); Ali Mazrui, *The Trial of Christopher Okingbo* (London: Heinemann, 1971); S. O. Mezu, *Behind the Rising Sun* (London: Heinemann, 1971); and I. N. Aniebo, *The Anonymity of Sacrifice* (London: Heinemann, 1974).

[107]Charles Larson, "The African Writer," *The New Republic,* April 20, 1975.

[108]Ali Mazrui, as quoted in *Issue,* vol. 6, no. 1 (Spring 1976), p. 39.

designed to suppress the unfavorable descriptions of African political systems. In this regard, Legson Kayira's deceptively simple tale of *The Detainee* stands as the archetypal outline of the repressive government. Its head, Sir Zaddock, is remote and powerful, ruthless to his opponents, and willing to use whatever means are necessary to stay in power. While Kayira obviously had Malawi in mind, the description is not inappropriate for a variety of other systems, such as Equatorial Guinea or the Central African Republic or Zaire.

With few exceptions, those writers who have dealt with the postindependence political system have had to pay a significant price, whether exile, prison, or arbitrary segregation. Few African writers have been allowed the luxury of following the calling of their craft as described by John F. Kennedy:

> The highest duty of the writer, the composer, the artist is to remain true to himself and to let the chips fall where they may. In serving his vision of the truth the artist best serves his nation.[109]

THE MISSING THEMES

African preoccupation with such themes as colonialism, modernization, and contemporary politics seems both understandable and explicable, but there are a number of themes which have been ignored until now. Why this is so is not completely clear, but it does suggest a divergence in attention between the politicians and their rhetoric and the writers and their activities.

For example, with several notable exceptions,[110] few African writers have dealt with the postindependence aspects of Great Power rivalry in Africa. There may be occasional references to "neocolonialism" and the like, but there is precious little in the literature dealing with the exogenous intrusions of the United States, the Soviet Union, the People's Republic of China, and now Cuba.

Surprisingly absent, as well, is a recognizable body of work dealing with the aspects of nation building. Despite the multitude of references to the task of nation building put forth by the new political authorities, and despite the obvious importance of its success or failure to the future of African nations, no writer has dealt with this theme, except in instances where the process failed.

Likewise, there is very little about the military in power. As we have seen, a number of prominent writers have dealt with the seizure of power by the military, either from a promilitary ("they brought stability and peace") or an antimilitary ("they are just as corrupt as the civilians they replaced") point of

---

[109]John F. Kennedy, speech at Amherst College, October 1963.

[110]See, for example, Aime Cesaire, *A Season in the Congo* (New York: Grove Press, 1968); and Taban lo Liyong, *Fixions* (London: Heinemann, 1969).

view. But there is almost nothing in the literature which portrays life under military rule. Although one can see the obvious difficulties of writing such an account if one is under such a rule, the exile condition of so many contemporary African writers would seem to obviate this reason. Certainly, the military themselves, the way in which they conduct themselves in power, their goals, hopes, and processes, to say nothing of their situational ethics, would all seem to be interesting, even vital, subject areas.

Finally, although, as we saw in Chapters 2 and 3, there has been considerable African attention devoted to the notions of African socialism and the pan-African movement, none of it has surfaced in the works of African writers. Nor has there been much in the way of emphasis on Marxism in the literature. This may appear as the regimes in Benin, Somalia, Angola, Mozambique, and Guinea-Bissau develop. But to the present there is very little in the way of overt ideological content to the works of most African writers. Tradition and societal change seem far more important than the debate over which ideologies presumably can influence the course of that change.

African writers are clearly concerned over what happened in the past. They are anxious to lay out the colonial experience and its aftermath, they are generally disturbed with the collection of values we term modernization. And most, if not all, seem genuinely upset with the progress of politics since independence. Yet, few offer models for the future course of politics. There is an ongoing concern for social justice, for the eradication of the vestiges of racism and for more openness and tolerance on the part of the new governments and their transitional societies. But, few writers seem to be driven by a vision of how all of this is to take place.

In this book, we have used Part One to set the stage for our analysis of contemporary political patterns. We have examined the traditional historical context. We have looked at the overarching themes of African political thought and their relationship to the ideas and philosophies from abroad, particularly as a result of the colonial overlay. Finally, we have probed the mind set of African writers and intellectuals to see which concerns occupy their interests and energies.

It is to the actual workings of the contemporary political systems that we now turn. Part One has provided the background and the multiplicity of contexts that influence the course of politics in Africa. Part Two deals with the actual course of contemporary politics.

two

THE PROCESS OF AFRICAN POLITICS

5

The Polyarchal Spectrum

THE ONSET OF INDEPENDENCE

As we outlined in Chapter 2, the colonial experience was, by and large, authoritarian and undemocratic. Many African political leaders stressed the need for independence and democracy so that the African peoples themselves could shape their own destinies. Although the colonial authorities initially resisted the notion of independence, competitive democratic elections were held in most states once decolonization began. This was due, in part, to African desires for democratic politics and, in part, to the colonial authorities' desire to transplant their political systems in the colonies.

This exporting of the metropole political systems to the African colonies took place over time and generally meant that at the time of independence, the African territory inherited—more or less intact—a European form of government. Thus, most areas under British control went (after a series of constitutions that gradually increased African participation) to a Westminster form of government; that is, a system with competing political parties and a prime minister as the head of government.

Usually, the prime minister was simply the head of the majority party or the leader of a coalition of parties if none obtained a majority of seats in parliament. The prime minister was supposed to call new elections every five years, or sooner if he lost his majority in the parliament. Kenya, Nigeria, and Ghana, for example, inherited this system.[1]

In the formerly French areas, a somewhat different system was generally adopted. Having seen and experienced the vagaries of the Fourth French Republic with its rapidly changing governments and parties, most African states under colonial rule ended up with a presidential form of government modeled on the French Fifth Republic.[2] Such states as the Ivory Coast, Niger, and the Cameroons had electoral and party competition, but with the head of the government a president chosen by the people for a fixed term, usually five years. This more highly centralized form was supposed to reduce the frictions and centrifugal forces in the new nations.

The Belgian and Italian areas inherited political frameworks modeled after the parliamentary forms of government in existence in both countries. The Congo, Rwanda, Burundi, and Somalia would be examples of this process, although in the first three, the decolonization period did not feature much familiarity with elections, since some were held only a month prior to independence.

In addition to receiving the European forms more or less intact, the sub-Saharan states also had a smooth and relatively bloodless transition to independence. Thus, Fanon and the Algerian experience, although very important for the theory of decolonization, actually did not have much relevance for the process in, say, Nigeria or Upper Volta. Further, the national unity surrounding the attainment of independence tended to obscure the inappropriateness of some of the European forms for Africa.

Only in the Portuguese colonies, where the colonial authority held on for 15 years longer, was there widespread revolutionary violence and only there did the emerging national leaders adopt entirely new forms of their own choosing. We shall examine this phenomenon in Chapter 7, although the outline of Cabral's thought in Chapter 3 was not inappropriate. At this juncture, it is important to note that, unlike other African states, independence did

---

[1]Those interested in the process of decolonization in Anglophone Africa should consult pages 257–258 of the Bibliography. An earlier draft of this paper was presented at the United States Foreign Service Institute, January 1977. The author is grateful for the many helpful comments of John Collier.

[2]In fact, many Africans from French West Africa played active and often major roles in the formation of both the French governments and those of the new states. See, for example, the pivotal role of the African delegates to the French National Assembly in the critical elections of 1956: William Foltz, *From French West Africa to the Mali Federation* (New Haven: Yale University Press, 1969), and the other works listed on page 257 of the Bibliography.

not come easily to Angola, Mozambique, or Guine-Bissau. In the 10- to 15-year struggle, the nationalists had to create their own governments in exile as the wars dragged on. This undoubtedly accounts for their adoption of strikingly different forms than those inherited from the metropole by other African countries.

As we indicated in Chapter 1, the vibrancy and multiplicity of the traditional African political systems made for a serious problem concerning the smooth adaptation of the metropole models. In the case of Uganda, for example, there was a highly centralized monarchy—the Baganda—in a complicated federal system with federated monarchies such as the Ankole, and many segmented societies such as the Karamojong, the Acholi, and the Nuer. In Nigeria, there was a most delicate balance between the hierarchical forms of the northern areas, such as the Hausa, the segmented forms of the east, such as the Ibo and Ibibio, and the federated monarchies of the west, such as the Yoruba.

Moreover, in addition to problems of differing traditional political forms, there was the matter of ethnicity. Only in a very few instances, such as Somalia or Swaziland, did the political system roughly correspond to the prevailing ethnic unit. The king of the Swazis was also the king of Swaziland, something that could not be said for the king of the Baganda in Uganda or the king of the Lozi in Zambia.

The failure of the colonial authorities and many of the new leaders of the African states to take into consideration the existing traditional forms or overlapping ethnic units, undoubtedly added to the instability of the postindependence period. Many African writers felt that the clash between tradition and modernity—whether between African and African or between African and European—was the central feature of Africa in transition. They were not wrong.

On the political level, this meant that the problem had to be dealt with, and not simply ignored. This is not to say that the new African leaders had to give in to the local traditional authorities at the expense of the national political system. Nor is it to say that these new leaders had to capitulate to each ethnic unit's whim. But it is to state that those leaders who ignored the continuing realities of the situation did so at their own peril. Thus, Julius Nyerere in Tanzania, while reducing the power of the local chiefs, also made a major effort to integrate them into the new political party, TANU. By taking the traditional ideology, Ujamaa, for the country, he undoubtedly made a better "fit" between modern form and traditional process.

Likewise, President Felix Houphouet-Boigny in the Ivory Coast, although a doctor and a skilled modern political figure in his own right, was careful to create a council of chiefs at the national level in order to coopt the traditional authorities. Houphouet-Boigny was also careful to make sure that he was elected head of that council as "chief of chiefs." In contrast, Nkrumah in Ghana completely underestimated the primordial attachments of the Asante and others to the traditional authorities and their own sense of importance to the new nation. Many of his theories concerning a nontribal polity, while laudatory in the abstract, simply ignored the realities of the Ghanian situation. Not surprisingly, when Nkrumah was overthrown by the military in 1966, Asante officers in the military and the police were at the heart of the effort.

THE COLONIAL LEGACY

Most sub-Saharan territories came to independence during the late 1950s and the 1960s with institutional holdovers from the colonial era. Most had political frameworks which called for participatory democracy based on nonracial criteria for membership. Most had a period of electoral competition just prior to independence. This electoral competition and the widening of political participation usually resulted in the development of different political parties. Although there were some territories—such as Guinea or Mauritania—where a single party emerged totally victorious prior to independence, most parties came to power with one or more competitors.

In Kenya, the Kenyan African National Union (KANU) formed the independence government while the Kenya African Democratic Union (KADU) was in opposition. In Nigeria, there were the Action Group (AG), the National Congress of Nigerian Citizens (NCNC), and the Northern People's Party (NPC). In Ghana, Nkrumah's Convention People's Party (CPP) was confronted by opposition including the National Front (NF). In Sierra Leone, the Sierra Leone People's Party (SLPP) formed the government with the All People's Congress (APC) in opposition. In Zambia it was the United National Independence Party (UNIP) of Kenneth Kaunda which formed the independence government with the African National Congress (ANC) of Harry Nkumbula in opposition.

Leaving aside, for the moment, the makeup and motivation of the opposition parties, for these differed from country to country, it is safe to say that a majority of African countries came to independence with three colonial legacies. One was the colonially inspired political framework. A second was a period of electoral competition, generally by opposing parties. The third was a sense of competitiveness over the leadership positions in the new nation.

The degree of electoral competition and the colonial frameworks have been suppressed in most African countries following independence. In fact, after nearly 20 years, it is hard to remember that this competition was such an intrinsic part of the decolonization period. But it was. In fact, while most, if not all, Africans in most countries were united on the question of independence (that is, they wanted it), most did not agree as to what should happen after independence and who should make it happen. As matters turned out, the combination of electoral competition and ethnic and personal rivalries with an alien imported political system and conflicting traditional political forms proved to be an explosive mixture.

But, at independence, things looked much brighter. Regardless of the colonial legacy, independence was to bring Africans control over their own destinies (although some, like Fanon and Nkrumah, obviously challenged this view). Independence would bring economic development. Independence would bring national integration. Independence would restore African dignity and sense of purpose. Life would improve. To those in power, there was also the expectation that they would share in these good things. To those out of power, there would be ample opportunity to get into power (few in the opposition foresaw the rapid closure of the political system and the lack of opportunity for those on the outside of government to get on the inside through the mechanism of fair and open elections).

Curiously enough, the artificial grid which the colonial powers had imposed during the scramble for Africa, while opposed during decolonization, was generally accepted by the African leaders themselves after independence. It seems possible that African leaders could have gotten together to redraw those lines, whether by recombining their territories into meaningful federations, or in an exchange of territories and populations to more accurately reflect the ethnic realities of Africa. But no meaningful attempt was made and the diplomacy of independence turned to other matters.[3]

As was noted in Chapter 4, those prominent African writers, such as Achebe, Laye, Soyinka, Mazrui, Armah, and Kayira, who have analyzed the course of politics under African rule, have, by and large, taken a very critical view of how African leaders and their political systems reacted to the stresses of the postindependence period. For them, corruption, repression, civil violence, and ethnic slaughter became widespread. Instead of independence bringing with it political development and democracy, it brought with it political decay and authoritarianism. Neocolonialism, a new black elite, and political repression all combined to thwart the true independence of the masses. Why did this happen? Why did the bright dawning of independence turn so swiftly into the twilight of democracy and the long night of political repression? It is to these subjects that we now turn.

POLITICAL DECAY AND THE EROSION OF DEMOCRACY

There is no single cause of the massive erosion of democracy which occurred after independence in black Africa. Instead, the stifling of electoral competition and the forced entrenchment of a ruling elite was due to a number of

[3]The conduct of intra-African relations and the development of the Organization of African Unity (OAU) lies beyond the scope of this book, but the interested reader should consult "the diplomacy of independence" outlined in Chapter 8 for relevant works.

factors. These often influenced and complemented one another, adding to the process of political decay. Although we shall be listing them in discrete categories, it should be remembered that although all factors were not present in all situations, there was a complex interplay of most in many African countries.

The Inappropriateness of Colonial Transplanted Systems

We have already commented on the extent to which the colonial powers simply transferred to Africa the political systems of the mother country. These were not always suited to the multiplicity of ethnic groups and the traditional political heritages that flourished before the coming of the Europeans. At the same time, the frameworks themselves were not, *ipso facto,* overwhelmingly inappropriate. It is just that the colonial power often allowed the preindependence electoral competition to be conducted along tribal lines and, indeed, often created opposition parties in order to perpetuate a neocolonial domination following independence.

In addition, as the events happened too quickly during decolonization, there was often an insufficient interlude for the process of *national* electoral politics to take hold. Following independence, some states, such as Tanzania, moved rapidly and effectively to tailor their existing political systems to the societal ingredients. But most did not. Many governmental elites simply let the old forms continue while competition faded and the political systems stagnated.

Exogenous Intrusions

When analyzing the causes for the erosion of democratic politics in Africa and the process of political decay (which became such prominent features of Africa's first decade of independence), the extent of foreign involvement is either drastically over- or underestimated. Certainly, it is extremely simplistic to argue that all African governments fell because of outside intrusions. Indeed, it is insulting to Africans to assert that in and of themselves they could not plan and execute *coups* and governmental seizures. And the mind boggles at the assumption that the American CIA or the Russian KGB really cares which of the factions triumphed in Dahomey in any of the five or six *coups* that took place during the period following independence.

Still, one cannot overlook the numerous examples of foreign intrusions in the domestic affairs of African states. Often, these intrusions took the form of backing one group or another in the domestic political situation. For example, the Belgians, the Americans, and the Russians all backed different factions in the Congo during the period 1960–64, and this backing included material support, cash, and weapons. Likewise, Cubans, Russians, South Africans, Chinese, and Americans took sides during the Angolan struggle for independence and in the civil war that followed. Portugal and France conducted well documented intrigues with separatist Biafra. Israeli intervention in the Sudanese civil war, by funneling arms and ammunition to the southern forces via Uganda, at the very least, prolonged that conflict.

France used its not inconsiderable power to maintain the regime of Fulbert Youlou of Congo-Brazzaville when it was threatened during the early 1960s, but eventually acquiesced in his overthrow. In February 1964, French forces moved directly to reinstate Leon M'Ba after his government was overthrown. When President David Dako of the Central African Republic was the victim of a *coup* in January 1966, the French did nothing to reinstate him, although in November 1967, French troops were used to protect his successor, Colonel/President (now Emperor) Jean Bokassa.

South Africa has been linked to the secessionist forces in Barotseland. Portugal supported dissidents against Sekou Toure in Guinea and helped to carry out several armed invasions of the country. Soviet intelligence officers are said to have been actively involved in the Somali *coup* of 1970; they clearly assisted Kwame Nkrumah in holding on to power as long as he did. On the other hand, American support for General Mobutu enabled him to come to power in the Congo, not once, but twice. Undoubtedly, there are other cases of exogenous intrusions into the political life of individual countries, although it would appear that in a number of cases (such as Burundi) the internal political situation was so fractious as to obviate any central role for those external forces seeking to determine the course of politics.

Separatist Tendencies and Heightened Ethnicity

Closely linked to the exacerbating factor of exogenous intrusions is the phenomenon of separatism. This was often geographical, almost always ethnic, as one group or another felt itself short-changed by either the ruling government, the outcome of independence, or both. Heightened ethnicity and separatist tendencies enervated polyarchal politics in a number of African states.

The artificiality of the colonial frontiers and the ethnic mosaic of Africa often continued to produce severe tensions within individual African states. The Ewe in Ghana and Togo, the Sanwi in the Ivory Coast, and the Lozi in Zambia all tended to engage in politics from an ethnic point of view. The Asante in Ghana, the Baganda in Uganda, and a number of other groups tended to place their particular goals over and above those of the entire nation.

Even without foreign intrigue, heightened ethnicity remained a persistent problem for the new states. Often, there was communal violence on a grand scale. In Rwanda, tens of thousands of Tutsis died in massacres and tribal violence. In Burundi, more than 100,000 Hutus lost their lives. In Nigeria, ethnic massacres led to a bloody civil war.

So, many African leaders cannot be faulted for seeking to curtail ethnically inspired opposition, particularly where it seemed bent on tearing the country apart. Given the kind of linguistic, ethnic, and socioeconomic fragmentation inherent in most African countries, one can well sympathize with the political leadership's accent on unity. At the same time, the very different points of view that sprang from this diversity should not have been ignored. The African adage of "talking until they agree" was of no functional utility when those who didn't agree weren't allowed to talk. Papering over ethnic differences, ignoring entirely different perceptions of who was a threat to whom, and stressing unity at the expense of a rational examination of reality all worked to further the process of political decay.

The Illusion of Unity

As we indicated above, there was a lack of unity among the various groups (both ethnic and socioeconomic) about the goals of the new states. This diversity of opinion was always there, although it had been masked during the decolonization struggle. The existence of a common adversary, the colonial authority, and the widespread agreement on the goal, if not always the tactics, of independence, engendered a sense of "national" unity. This sense of unity, real enough during the decolonization period, was illusionary following independence.

Coupled with the substantial participation by the masses in political activity, the previous unity gave many national leaders a false sense of power. Although much of the political analysis of the decolonization struggle in Africa has stressed the elite aspects of the process by focusing on such leaders as Jomo Kenyatta, Kwame Nkrumah, or Sékou Touré, it now appears that there was widespread participation by large numbers of Africans. Even where the masses did not participate in the decision-making aspects of the party— as was the case in the PDCI of the Ivory Coast or the Parti Progressiste du Tchad (PPT) of Chad—they did engage in political activities and were successfully mobilized. Leaders across Africa assumed that with independence, unity would continue without continuing mobilization.

The Decline of Mass Participation

Such mass involvement in politics and the general agreement on the goal of independence undoubtedly gave many political leaders of independent Africa an exaggerated estimate of their ability to mobilize the people after independence. This helps to explain why there were so few attempts to stimulate popular participation after independence through electoral competition and party politics, even when the groundswell of identification with the leaders and the parties ebbed. Government officials often turned their attention from the process of political socialization and became absorbed in the day-to-day affairs of running a country. Scarce resources—whether trained manpower, money, or time—were recommitted to the new governmental bureaucracies or allocated to the struggle for economic development.

This might have made sense if the leaders had created alternative linkages with the population. As it was, however, the decline often coincided with the formulation of single-party regimes, whether this process was undertaken *de facto* (by absorbing the counter-elites and giving them jobs) or *de jure* (by simply outlawing their political organizations).

With the political opposition momentarily bought off, harassed, or outlawed, many of the new political leaders lost interest in electoral politics and the mass parties themselves. Multiparty states became single-party states. Soon, the single-party states became, in effect, "no party" as the parties became hollow shells. Many of the new political leaders lost interest in the generation of public enthusiasm through (and *for*) politics.

Elections, which had engendered both excitement and commitment and which had resulted in political mobilization, were curtailed. In fact, independence often meant less mass participation in politics than in the period prior to it. Polyarchal politics, the choice of leaders by nonleaders, became incidental to the new leaders! Democratic politics simply slowed down and, in many cases, stopped.

For example, from 1957 until 1963, there were three national elections in Kenya. From 1963 until 1970, there was only one. In Chad, from 1956 until independence, there were three national elections, but only one after it. In Uganda, there were four elections just prior to independence, none afterwards. In a number of other systems, elections continued to be held, but they were often rigged. In November 1965, for example, President Maurice Yaméogo of Upper Volta was credited with receiving 99.7 percent of the popular vote. Two months later, he was overthrown by one of the most welcomed *coups* in postindependence Africa.

Elections were either not held (as in Congo-Brazzaville) or held in such a way as to deny any opportunity for leadership alternation (as in Upper Volta). In many instances, political demobilization took place. The political parties that had been major agents of political socialization faded away. Without electoral competition (either within or among political parties), politics became merely a symbolic exercise. As a symbolic exercise, it lost value in the eyes of masses, who increasingly took a very cynical view of it.

The Failure to Create Alternative Linkages

This is not to say that it was crucial for a multiparty institutional arrangement to continue after independence. Such a political system could have been superseded by some suitable alternative. Nor is it to suggest that the activities of a mass party were the *sine qua non* for maintaining true contact between the people and their government. The fact is, the decline in party activity might have been compensated for—as it was in the case of the Ivory Coast—had alternative national institutions developed to maintain linkage between the central government and the mass of the population.

But, as so many African writers suggested in Chapter 4, with few exceptions, local political structures, national assemblies, and participatory institutions on all levels declined in efficacy right along with the parties. Further, in many instances, the political center lost whatever power it still possessed to mobilize the population. Channels of information became clogged as well and, in purely systemic terms, many African governments began to suffer from a progressive hardening of their political arteries.

Thus, even when the political leaders subsequently realized the extent of the political decay and the growing danger to the system and made the "right" (that is, functional) decisions, they were unable to carry them out. Moreover, the failure to develop an alternative set of effective institutional buffers meant that when the euphoria of independence wore off, and society pressures for economic progress, education, and the like built up, there was no way to channel them away from the political center. Lacking a functional political net to absorb, or at least moderate, these demands, the system itself became the target. Without electoral competition, the stresses that developed had no outlet and the target of the concomitant anger and rage became the political center itself.

The Buildup of Demand Pressures

For build up the pressures did. During the decolonization period, the political leaders had raised the expectations of various interest and pressure groups as well as the mass of the population. This heightening of expectations had been due to a number of factors: the leaders wanted to galvanize public support behind them and the end of colonialism, they felt that after independence a great deal could be accomplished, and they were frankly often unaware of the magnitude of the difficulties which they faced.

In any case, despite the promises of the new political elite, the end of colonial rule did not mean the radical transformation of the existing socioeconomic system. With few exceptions—such as Zanzibar—independence merely meant an alteration of elites, from white to black, and very little meaningful economic change in the lives of the average citizen. After independence, various indigenous groups, such as the military, the students, the bureaucracies, and the labor unions, increased the scope and intensity of their demands for opportunity, rewards, and security.

When these were not forthcoming, these groups often went into active opposition to the government. Without competitive elections, the government could not pit the demands of one or more of the special interest groups against those of the general population. To the specific demands of the interest groups were added the not inconsiderable demands of the general population for welfare, education, and meaningful change in their life situations.[4]

Although the political elite in the new countries made an effort to meet some of these demands, the means to achieve them were often lacking. Foreign aid was undependable and steadily diminished during the first decade of African independence. Capital was scarce, regardless of the source or the intention. There was widespread disagreement over the means of meeting the demands. Should a political system, as in the case of Nkrumah's Ghana, seek international prestige and continental unity at the expense of domestic concerns? Should it, as in the case of Gabon, seek the perpetuation of the existing socioeconomic system in order to gain foreign investment and capital? And, in candor, many African leaders simply made no effort to meet the demands of the people beyond the small circle of their intimates and other members of the elite.

When the system did not deliver what its leaders had promised and the political elites continued to ask the masses to make sacrifices that the elites themselves were unwilling to make, much of the aura of legitimacy gained during the decolonization period was dissipated. The symbolic strength of the various regimes eroded.

Corruption and the Ineffectiveness of National Leadership

Unable to satisfy the demands pressing in upon them, and having done away with such homeostatic mechanisms as periodic electoral competition, many African political systems lost their ability to cope with the situation and drifted from crisis to crisis. In such circumstances, the loss of symbolic credibility often tipped the scales. As the African authors in Chapter 4 pointed out, the inability to meet the people's demands was coupled with conspicuous consumption on the part of the new elite. This conflict made it difficult for the average citizen to relate to his or her government.

Only a handful of regimes—as those in Tanzania, Botswana, and Gambia —managed to keep their images as governments of the people, struggling against odds to make life better. By dealing with the problems in a self-effacing and nonconsumptive way, these leaders simply said: "Yes, things are rough,

---

[4]"Meaningful change" obviously had different connotations for different people. For the Asante woman I interviewed in Ghana, it was a village well and tap so she did not have to walk six miles a day for water. For the Kikuyu, it meant a small plot of land to work. For the Nigerian man, it was a scholarship for his eldest son.

but we are sharing in your suffering." For other postindependence governments, such as Somalia, Nigeria, Upper Volta, and Mali, there was widespread
corruption, highly visible and highly demoralizing. *The Beautyful Ones Are
Not Yet Born* was written about Ghana, but it could have been written about
any number of African states after independence.

Although virtually every military *coup* which took place in Africa during
the last 15 years has claimed the motivation of wiping out corruption, many
military men actually did act because they were genuinely appalled at the level
of corruption in their societies. The first and second Ghanaian *coups*, the
Somalia *coup* of 1970, and the first Nigerian *coup* would all be clear-cut
examples of instances in which anticorruption, together with other factors,
motivated military intervention.

The Refusal to Play the Game

There were a number of countries in which democratic politics were not
done in by exogenous intrusions, or widespread corruption, or a failure to hold
open and free elections. The regime in power did not declare the opposition
illegal, at least not until the opposition won the elections. This refusal to play
by the rules of competitive electoral politics was, therefore, quite different from
changing the rules through an executive fiat establishing a single-party state
or a military rule. Here we are concerned with functioning political systems
in which the voters were allowed to choose their leaders. They chose new
leaders in national elections only to have the government in power refuse to
accept their choice.

In Sierra Leone, for example, during the elections of 1967, the government
of Albert Margai and his Sierra Leone People's Party (SLPP) was defeated by
the opposition All People's Party (APC) led by Siaka Stevens. The Force
Commander, Brigadier Lansanna, refused to accept the outcome, and the
military then brought a swift end to the Sierra Leone experiment in polyarchal
politics.

In Lesotho, during the elections of 1970, Ntsu Mokhehle and his Basutoland Congress Party (BCP) emerged victorious, only to have the government
of Chief Leabua Johnathan and his Basutoland National Party (BNP) suspend
the constitution, declare a state of emergency, and remain in power. Chief
Johnathan continued to rule Lesotho through 1977 without regard to the
previous election.

Even in Swaziland, long held as a serious example of polyarchal politics,
the government refused to play the game even when the opposition, far from
winning the election, simply managed to elect three members to the House of
Assembly. The ruling party, Imbokodvo, led by the Swazi King, Sobhuza II,
won a huge majority in the elections of 1964 and all seats in 1967. When

however, in 1973, the Ngwane National Liberatory Congress (NNLC) won three seats, the King singly declared on April 12 that the constitution was "un-Swazi." He suspended it, abolished political parties, and took personal command of the government and the civil service in order to "preserve order." A 60-day detention act was soon announced and the leader of the NNLC, Dr. Ambrose Zwane, was jailed. By 1978 the constitution had not been replaced and the King's personal choice, Colonel Maphavu, remained as Prime Minister.

The Inherent Weakness of the Independence Governments

A final factor in the continent-wide erosion of political systems is undoubtedly the inherent weakness of many of the independence states. We have already alluded to two sources of that weakness—the "thinness" of support for particular regimes and goals, as opposed to independence *per se,* and the low extractive and distributive capabilities of the new states in meeting demands.

Here, we are considering another dimension, the regulative capability. Once the symbolic favor of the government disappeared (for whatever reason) and once the homeostatic feature of periodic elections was lost, many systems lacked the strength to resist the new forces impinging on it.

Particularly vulnerable were those systems where the regime in power had itself ignored, or arbitrarily altered, the rule in law. Civil disorder, communal strife, and political violence spilled out; force, whether employed by labor unions, students, mobs, or the military, became the ultimate source of authority. In this situation, many African governments proved to be almost defenseless. Often the amount of force necessary to overthrow the system was minimal —a few hundred striking civil servants or a couple of dozen military. It was in this Hobbesian situation that the military (or, more accurately, portions of the military) found it could easily overthrow the regime and indeed the entire political system.

In Chapter 6 we shall be discussing the praetorian impulse and the subsequent imposition of military rule in a majority of African countries. At this juncture we should simply indicate that, given the ingredients listed in this chapter, it is not surprising that within a decade of independence there were dozens of *coups,* attempted *coups,* and army mutinies. As we shall see, motivation for intervention differed and there was undoubtedly a factor of contagion as army officers in one country saw their counterparts moving against their regimes. But whatever else this widespread intervention signaled, the wholesale involvement of the military in Africa and the ease with which it surplanted the political authority in power indicated the fragility of many systems and the extent to which political decay and the erosion of polyarchal politics had already occurred. Despite the many dissimilarities among the various systems and the motivations behind the army's intervention, the systems in question all shared severe enervation and political decay.

THE REMNANTS OF POLYARCHAL POLITICS

Considering the weakness of most African political systems at the time of independence and taking into account the various forces working against the maintenance of democratic multiparty politics, it is not surprising that so many systems experienced severe birth pains and eventual political decay. At the same time, the extent to which democratic politics declined across the continent may be thought of as quite astonishing. By 1978, only a half dozen African political systems could be accurately termed polyarchal; that is, with nonleaders choosing leaders. Out of nearly 50 African states, a very low figure and indeed, as will be seen by the analysis that follows, there can be serious questions raised as to just how "polyarchal" some of the polyarchal states (such as Zambia) really are. In fact, it may be that some of these states can be considered "polyarchal" only in direct comparison to the degree of authoritarianism displayed by other political systems on the continent.

Of the states we have placed on the polyarchal spectrum, there are two major groups. In the first, there are those states, such as Botswana and Gambia, that have multiparty competitive elections which are held openly and fairly. In the second, there are those states, such as Tanzania and Kenya, that have single-party arrangements but that also retain considerable electoral competition within such a framework.

ELECTORAL COMPETITION: THE MULTIPARTY STATES

The only two African states that have had a continuously functioning, polyarchal, multiparty system since independence are Botswana and Gambia. Several other states, including Senegal and Sierra Leone, have recently moved toward multiparty elections after extensive periods of either single-party hierarchical rule or military intervention in politics.

Botswana

In the case of Botswana, multiparty politics have flourished since before independence. The basic traditional underpinnings have undoubtedly played a role. The population is, by African standards, quite homogeneous, with the vast majority of its 672,000 people belonging to the Batswana ethnic group. The Batswana are divided into a number of clan families, such as the Bamangwato, Bakwena, the Batawana, the Bangwaketse, the Bakgatla, the Bamalete, the Barolong, and the Batlokwa which have interacted over a long period of time. Moreover, the traditional leadership has been partially absorbed by the process of modern politics (the president, Sir Seretse Khama, was himself a paramount chief of the largest clan family, the Bamangwato) and partially integrated through an important advisory body, the House of Chiefs.

Since independence, the Batswana have demonstrated a respect for, and interest in, multiparty competition and electoral opportunity. There are four principal parties, the Botswana Democratic Party (BDP), the Botswana National Front (BNF), the Botswana People's Party (BPP), and the Botswana Independence Party (BIP).

The basic political framework revolves around a division of power between the executive and the legislature. The president is the chief executive officer and he is elected by the majority vote of the National Assembly for a five-year term. This is basically the Westminster model which Botswana inherited from Great Britain, with the major qualification that the president does not have to be a member of Parliament. The president chooses his cabinet and the vice president from the membership of the National Assembly.

There are 37 members of the National Assembly, plus a speaker. Thirty-two members are chosen from single member districts and serve for a period of five years. There are 4 additional members elected by the National Assembly and an Attorney General, who may speak but not vote. There is also a House of Chiefs which serves as an advisory body with reference to matters dealing with tribal concern. There is also a fairly extensive local government net including nine District Councils and four Town Councils.

In the elections prior to independence in 1966 and in the two elections following independence, the Botswana Democratic Party has emerged as the strongest political force, forming all the governments since the constitutional arrangement was initiated. In the 1969 elections, the BDP held 24 seats, the BNF and BPP each held 3, and the BIP 1. In the 1974 elections, the BDP picked up a number of seats so that at the present time, it holds 27 out of the 32 elected seats.

Yet the leaders of all three opposition parties are in Parliament: Gaseitswe Bathoen of the BNF, Philip Matante of the BPP, and Motsamai Mpho of the BIP. Bathoen has strong support among the Bangwaketsi, Mpho is felt to have a secure base among the Okavango and the other non-Batswana, and Matante draws from a wide spectrum of groups.

Why does the Botswana polyarchal system operate so well? A number of observers have stressed the following points.[5] First, there is the relatively

---

[5]For the more important works on Botswana, see pages 271–272 of the Bibliography.

homogeneous nature of the polity. Second, there is the very important traditional political system which encourages the free and open interaction so important to a truly democratic system. Third, there is the very important variable of leadership. Seretse Khama is a dedicated leader who is truly concerned with the democratic aspects of the political system. He would be uncomfortable with a single-party system. He treats the opposition with respect and they in turn show respect for the system and play the role of a loyal, not disloyal, opposition. Both sides play by the rules. Fourth, there has been (until 1978) a national army, so the system enjoys a certain amount of breathing space from the praetorian impulse. Fifth, the leaders, both executive and Parliamentary, have not exaggerated their ability to meet the demands of the population and have not engaged in conspicuous consumption (although the president is by no means poor).

Questions undoubtedly remain. The political system which has functioned so well during adversity may face different problems as new mineral wealth begins to accumulate and greater socioeconomic differentiation takes place. Also, Sir Seretse's health is not good. He is badly overworked and in 1976 had a pacemaker implanted for a heart condition. As in so many other African political systems, Botswana's time of testing will come when the father of independence leaves the scene, although there are signs that the system is strong enough to withstand the transition. Indeed, the transition may serve to revitalize the opposition parties who are currently hurt by voter apathy and their sense that things are going as well as could be expected.

Gambia

In the case of Gambia, a number of the variables in the Botswana situation are not reproduced. The Gambia is a small country of only 4,003 square miles (Botswana is the size of France). It also lacks Botswana's ethnic homogeneity, with a large number of ethnic groups such as the Mandingo, the Fula, Wolof, Jola, and Serahuli.

What the Gambia shares with Botswana is the same dedication to polyarchal politics. Independent in 1965, the Gambians moved away from the prime minister form of government which it inherited from the British and adopted a presidential system. As of April 1970, the government consists of a president who is elected to a five-year term by the general public and a vice president who is elected in the same manner. The president, as chief executive officer, appoints the cabinet.

The legislature is composed of 37 members, 32 of whom are elected by universal adult suffrage for five-year terms. Four additional members are appointed by the traditional chiefs and there is an attorney general who is appointed by the president and who serves ex-officio.

The Gambia has a genuine multiparty system. Although the Progressive

People's Party (PPP) of the president, Sir Dawda Kairaba Jawara, has won a majority of seats in each of the pre- and postindependence elections, there is electoral competition. The United Party (UP) has been the principal opposition for many years, although there are a number of independent candidates who run in each election; one is presently a member of Parliament.

The UP won 13 seats in 1962, 8 in 1966, 4 in 1972. The 1972 elections saw 103,000 out of 130,000 voters go to the polls, a very high 79 percent turnout and hardly the "stagnation some have called it.[6] The PPP took 28 seats and there was 1 independent candidate elected. In all, 19 independents and 14 UP members ran, and the independents received more votes (20,747) than did the UP (17,167). In fact, in the future, the independents may prove to be a more important political force than the UP led by its aging P. S. N'Jie and its parliamentary chieftain, John Foster.

In April 1977 the PPP received 70 percent of the vote and 27 of 35 seats in the National Assembly, while the New National Convention Party won 5 seats and the United Party 2. A fourth party, the New National Liberation Party (NCP) also vigorously contested the election.

There were some complaints that a number of traditional authorities put pressure on voters to support the PPP, but such efforts probably had very little to do with the outcome. Certainly, many of the traditional authorities have been integrated into the civil service and the PPP. Other complaints that the government is "dull" help to give a measure of the present situation in Gambia.

As Alan Hutchison has written, Gambia's "sins" are really sins of omission. There is no army. There is no political violence. The government, although poor, has a balanced budget. There are no grand projects, no repression of opposition parties. The press is as free and open as any on the continent. There is freedom to dissent and if the PPP's slogan, "Peace, progress and prosperity," does not seize the imagination that, too, may be a good thing in light of the heightened demand pressures in other parts of the continent.

Senegal

Although Gambia and Botswana are the only two African states to have a continuous operation of their multiparty system, several other states have returned to such an arrangement after experiencing other forms of government since independence.[7] In the case of Senegal, the return to a multiparty situation follows more than a decade of single-party rule.

[6]For an interesting analysis of the 1972 elections, see Alan Hutchinson, "Gambia, the First Ten Years," *Africa Report* (July-August 1975), pp. 11–14. Further background material can be found on page 276 of the Bibliography and in the recent book by Walter Barrows, *Grassroots Politics in an African State* (New York: Africana Publishing Co., 1976).

[7]Although we shall be considering Sierra Leone and Senegal in this section, Mauritania also has a fledgling opposition party and several other states may join in this movement.

With a population of over four million and an area of more than 76,000 square miles, Senegal has been led by Leopold Senghor since independence.[8] As we saw in Chapter 3, Leopold Senghor led one of the earliest reactions to colonialism and established the philosophical underpinnings of Negritude. But Senghor has been far more than a theoretician or visionary. He has survived and prospered in the rough-and-tumble politics of western Africa for over 30 years. His recent adoption of a multiparty system would seem to be one more twist in his remarkably successful political career.

Senghor founded the old *Bloc Démocratique Sénégalais* (BDS) in 1948, later changing the name to *Bloc Populaire Sénégalais* (BPS) in 1956, and again to the *Union Progressiste Sénégalaise* (UPS) in 1958 as the party absorbed other splinter groups, including the *Parti de Regroupement Africain* (PRA). He was also one of the founding fathers of the Mali Federation which became independent in June of 1960.

Within a short time, tensions developed between Senegal and the former French Sudan and by September, 1960, the federation had fallen apart. All during the preindependence period and immediately thereafter, multiparty politics were the order of the day in Senegal, although the UPS was clearly dominant. Under the independence constitution, Senghor was president and he, together with his prime minister, Mamaduo Dia, governed a parliamentary democracy.

However, in December of 1962, Mamadou Dia attempted a *coup* and was arrested. Senghor, seeing the office of prime minister as a potential training ground for overmighty vassals, got the UPS to push for a new constitutional arrangement which eliminated that office. The National Assembly did so and also outlawed all parties save the UPS. In fact, all parties were actually given the choice of merging with the UPS or going underground. All "joined" except the pro-Communist *Parti Africain de l'Indépendence* (PAI).

In February 1970, the constitution was amended in order to restore the office of prime minister although the office was greatly reduced in power. No longer was the prime minister chosen by the National Assembly (as Dia had been). Instead, the prime minister was appointed by the president for a period of three years. Since the president serves for five years and was elected directly by the people, the new office simply gave the president a tame interface with the National Assembly.

Under the single-party constitution, the UPS enjoyed a monopoly of political power. All members of the 100-person National Assembly were members and the population was simply given a slate of UPS candidates to approve. Not

[8]In addition to the works listed in Chapter 3, the interested reader should consult pages 285–286 of the Bibliography. A recent article by Lucy Creevey Behrman suggests that the stability of the system is due in part to the wise use the central government has made of the traditional *Marabouts:* L. C. Behrman, "Muslim Politics and Development in Senegal," *Journal of Modern African Studies,* vol. 15, no. 2 (1977), pp. 261–277.

surprisingly, politics stagnated under the single-party arrangement. Dissent was stifled and there was little interest in the elections of 1973 which saw the UPS slate "victorious." The single-party arrangement simply papered over opposition to Senghor and UPS as well as the real divisions over the future of the country. Students remained one source of opposition; so, too, did the trade unions, as well as some intellectuals. The army, which might have energized this discontent into political action, was carefully watched by Senghor and stiffened by the presence of French troops in Dakar, the capital for much of the time. Faced with continuing opposition, Senghor could have continued on with the single-party arrangement and simply suppressed, by force if necessary, those who had a different view of the government.

Instead, in 1974, Senghor moved to have the country declared a multiparty state again. The *Parti Démocratique Sénégalais* (PDS) was the first to spring up. Led by a French-educated lawyer and economist, Abdoulaye Wade, the PDS stressed the nationalization of foreign-owned industries and greater economic and political independence from France. At the same time, the party's assistant secretary general, Fara N'Diaye, stressed that the party was not in any sense Marxist. A second opposition party, the *Rallé Démocratique National* (RDN), was formed the following year. During 1976 it changed its name to the *Parti Africain Independent,* (PAI).

However, the multiparty situation is by no means identical to that in Botswana or Gambia. During 1976, the government passed an election law which required each of the parties to declare for one of three "ideologies." As the oldest party, the UPS got its choice, "democratic socialism," and changed its name (again) to *Parti Socialiste* in December 1976. "Democratic socialism" stands for a modified version of "African socialism" as outlined in Chapter 3. This left the PDS with an unpleasant choice concerning the remaining two "ideologies." On the one hand, it could adopt "Marxist-Leninism" which probably would have little appeal in a country where approximately 85 percent of the population are devout Moslems. On the other, it could take the third typology, "liberal democratic," which is roughly equated with capitalism; that is, the ideology of the former colonizer, France!

The PDS complained bitterly about the choice but finally settled for "liberal democratic," leaving the PAI with the "Marxist-Leninism" label. Clearly, Senghor and the ruling UPS did not want to give their opponents free reign in the electoral competition next scheduled for the presidential elections in 1978. The idea of each party having a "monopoly" over a particular ideology may well be a novelty, but it certainly would seem to put limits on the opposition's ability to generate support. That, of course, was probably the idea behind it. In any case, Senghor was reelected with 80 percent of the vote and the PS won a big majority in Parliament.

Much clearly remains to be seen. The PDS and PAI complained during 1977 that they had had difficulty in getting access to the state-owned media and in acquiring permits to hold local rallies. Yet, although Senegal is not now Botswana or the Gambia, it has moved away from a single-party state with no electoral competition.

At the same time, Senghor is clearly taking few chances. The PS-controlled legislature recently passed a further constitutional amendment enabling the prime minister to fill out the unexpired term of the president should he resign. This would clearly give Senghor the opportunity to win the 1978 election and then handpick his own successor regardless of how many seats the opposition captures in the next election.

Sierra Leone

The situation in Sierra Leone is likewise clouded. The country had moved back to civilian rule with multiparty competition after a long and convoluted period of military control.[9] Although there are some forces at work seeking to develop a true multiparty arrangement, it approaches authoritarianism. At the present time, although the country is technically a multiparty state, the opposition's refusal to participate in the May 1973 elections because of alleged "irregularities" makes any judgment about its polyarchal character highly qualified, especially after the APC won 76 seats (50 unopposed) in the 1977 elections amid widespread charges of intimidation, arrests, and voter fraud.

Sir Milton Margai and the Sierra Leone People's Party (SLPP) led the country to independence in 1962 following a series of hotly contested elections with the opposition All People's Congress (APC). Upon the death of Sir Milton, he was succeeded as prime minister by his half brother, Sir Albert Margai. Once in office, Albert Margai and his close associates within the SLPP felt that Sierra Leone should move from the Westminster model toward a single-party state. This view was vigorously contested by the APC and the elections in March 1967 were fought in part over this issue. Shaka Stevens, as leader of the APC, was to become prime minister when the APC narrowly won those elections.

However, Brigadier David Lansanna, egged on by some members of the SLPP, refused to accept the results and arrested both Stevens and Margai. This action began a dismal series of *coups* and counter *coups,* finally ending in a 1968 *coup* to restore civilian rule! Shaka Stevens was installed as prime minister and the APC became the ruling party. Subsequent *coup* attempts were foiled and a new constitution was approved in 1971.

Presently, therefore, Sierra Leone is a *de jure* multiparty state. There is a

[9]The course of Sierra Leonean politics under the military lies beyond the scope of this chapter. See Thomas S. Cox's excellent *Civil-Military Relations in Sierra Leone* (Cambridge, Mass.: Harvard University Press, 1976). Further background material is listed on page 286 of the Bibliography.

presidential system like that of Botswana in that the president is chosen by the National Assembly. He in turn appoints the prime minister. The members of the House of Representatives normally serve for five years but elections can be held earlier. The Parliament consists of 100 representatives, 85 of whom are elected by popular suffrage from single member districts, 12 paramount chiefs chosen by tribal council, and 3 members appointed by the president.

Shaka Stevens was appointed president by the House in April 1970, although he appeared close to retirement in 1976. He was eventually persuaded to stay on and was eventually chosen for another five-year period. The next general elections are scheduled for 1982 and any final judgment on the efficacy of Sierra Leone's quasi polyarchal arrangement will have to await them. Politics in Sierra Leone continue to bear the stamp of ethnicity, with the northern tribes and the Euro-Africans generally siding with the APC, and the southern tribes, especially the Mende, traditionally supporting the SLPP.

ELECTORAL COMPETITION: THE SINGLE-PARTY STATES

In addition to those African states where multiparty electoral competition exists, there are also states that have a single-party apparatus, but permit electoral competition *within* that framework. Given the large number of African states that have a single-party arrangement, this type of political system may well have more efficacy than that of a multiparty system which is rejected by many African leaders as too devisive.

Tanzania

Perhaps the best known of the single-party states which permit electoral competition is Tanzania. We shall be describing the working of that system in some detail for a variety of reasons. In the first place, as we saw in Chapter 3, the president of Tanzania, Julius Nyerere, is one of the major African political thinkers and his expression of African socialism is highly regarded. In addition, the fact that many of the tenets of African socialism have actually been embodied in the process of politics in Tanzania makes it a very interesting case. Also, the Tanzanian experience beyond that of Kenya and Zambia may well serve as a model for other states that have already adopted similar arrangements in terms of electoral competition within the boundaries of a single-party state. Finally, unlike political descriptions of many African states, the current literature on Tanzania is extensive and well documented.[10]

---

[10]See, for example, the large number of books listed on pages 293–294 of the Bibliography. Tanzania has probably been the most closely studied of all the African states since independence.

With an area of over 362,000 square miles and a population of slightly more than 14 million persons, Tanzania is one of the most sparsely settled countries in Africa. It also has one of the lowest *per capita* incomes on the continent. It has very little mineral wealth and very little opportunity for economic advancement. At the same time, it is one of the most intriguing political experiments in all of Africa.

In Chapter 3, we outlined the political views of Julius Nyerere. A teacher educated at Makerere College and Edinburgh University, he transformed the cultural Tanganyika African Association into the Tanganyikan African National Union (TANU) in 1954 and led the party to a series of electoral victories in the late 1950s. Defeating all other parties by a wide margin, TANU emerged as a major political force in Tanzania, and Nyerere was asked to form the first African government. Independence followed in December 1961.

Tanganyika, like so many other former British territories, inherited a political framework based on the Westminster model. But early in 1962, Nyerere resigned as prime minister to revitalize the party, to draw the rural population into political participation, and to work for the establishment of a republic. A new constitution was drawn up which retained the ministerial system but which also included a strong presidential chief executive and vice president who acted as a prime minister. Tanganyika became a republic in December 1962, and Nyerere, as the TANU candidate, was overwhelmingly elected as president. Rashidi Kawawa, who had served as prime minister in Nyerere's absence, became vice president.

Yet, the Tanganyikan political system did not function as its leaders had hoped. The merger of the miniscule African National Congress (ANC) into TANU and the disbanding of the last splinter party, the People's Democratic Party (PDP) in 1963, created a *de facto* single-party state. Because of a lack of opposition, it was felt that TANU, as an effective institution, might well wither away, and that the heretofore representative function of the government would be undercut by meaningless elections. Therefore, the president appointed a commission to examine the ways in which a blend of direction and democratic participation might be achieved within the framework of a single-party system. The formation of the commission and the subsequent implementation of its unusual proposals were acts of great import and political courage, particularly in the context of an army mutiny, labor unrest, and a hasty merger with the islands of Zanzibar and Pemba, which underwent a bloody revolution in 1964.

The recommendations of the president's Commission became the basis of the Interim Constitution of July 1965, and the *de jure* formation of a single-party state, the United Republic of Tanganyika and Zanzibar, later called Tanzania. We shall examine in turn the political framework which resulted, the process of decision making which occurred within it, and the environmental factors which encouraged its operation.

By way of introduction, it is necessary to qualify the description of the Tanzanian political system. It was not, until 1977, a single-party regime. The Afro-Shirazi Party on Zanzibar and TANU on the mainland retained their individual identities until their merger in 1977, although they participated jointly in major political decisions affecting both areas. Also, for most of the intervening period, Tanzania was not actually a "united" republic. Although the Zanzibaris were initially overrepresented in the national government (7 of 22 ministries and 40 seats in the National Assembly), the system remained a federation, since the Revolutionary Council on Zanzibar retained *de facto* control over its own defense, internal security, public service, and immigration operations. For these reasons and because the polyarchal decision-making features found within the mainland system have not yet been duplicated on the offshore islands, our analysis will essentially deal with the mainland portion of the political system of Tanzania.

The president of the United Republic stands at the head of the political structure. He is both head of state and commander-in-chief of the armed forces. Elected by universal adult suffrage after being nominated by an electoral conference of TANU and the Afro-Shirazi Party, the president is the repository of all executive power; he appoints the Cabinet and the important regional commissioners. He serves for a period of five years or until Parliament is dissolved (he may dissolve it, but must then stand for reelection along with its members). There are two vice presidents. The first is the chief executive for Zanzibar and the head of the Afro-Shirazi Party. The second is the leader of the National Assembly. Julius Nyerere is currently the president; Aboud Jumbe is the first vice president; Rashidi Kawawa was the second vice president and prime minister until February 1977 when he was replaced as prime minister by Edward Sokoine, former defense minister.

The National Assembly is the chief legislative organ. Its membership reflects a blend of direct and indirect representation. In 1974, there were 120 members from single-member constituencies (which average 30,000 persons in size, but which range from a 5,000-member district on Mafia Island to a 60,000-member district in Dar es Salaam, the capital). An additional 15 members are selected by the executive committee of TANU to represent the "national institutions," such as the National Union of Tanganyikan Workers (NUTA), the Union of Women of Tanzania, and the Cooperative Union of Tanganyika (CUT). The 17 regional commissioners of Tanganyika and the 3 from Zanzibar are also members, as are up to 32 persons from the Revolutionary Council of Zanzibar. In addition, the president may appoint up to 10 members from Tanganyika and up to 20 from Zanzibar.

Thus, the total membership of the Assembly may legally reach 204, but has generally fluctuated between 180 and 190. The Assembly is charged with making laws of the land, and may override a presidential veto by a two-thirds vote (although the president may then dissolve the Assembly and take the issue to the people).

The judiciary consists of a chief justice and a High Court appointed by the president "after consultation with the Chief Justice," as well as subordinate and local courts. Judges serve until age 62 (65 with presidential approval) and can be removed "only for inability to perform the functions of his office . . . or for misbehavior," as stipulated by a tribunal of fellow judges. There is no Bill of Rights, although the Preamble to the TANU Constitution embodies most of the basic individual freedoms normally found in a Bill of Rights. There is also a Permanent Commission of Inquiry to investigate any abuse of authority by state officials. The legal fabric of present-day Tanzania has been woven from a variety of threads—African customary law, British common law, and Islamic law—and is in the process of being coordinated and updated.

Local government within the Tanzanian political system is a vital part of the political process; it focuses on political and economic development and provides a two-way channel of access from the center to the people. There are some 7,000 village-development committees, 13 town councils, and 58 district councils. Members of the government bureaucracy, the party, and the people meet at all levels. Representatives of the Ministries of Regional Administration and Economic Affairs and Development Planning, TANU, and the local community are involved. As mentioned earlier, the 17 regional and 60 area commissioners appointed by the president are critical links between the government and the people; they serve as members of the government bureaucracy, act as party secretaries, and chair the elected councils. They are, thus, in a position to pass information and decisions both upward and downward within a variety of political institutions.

In addition the local assemblies, which are open to all, are parallel structures for TANU members. There are some 1,500 local party cells, as well as district and regional conferences (each with a standing executive committee) leading up to the biennial National Conference and the National Executive Committee. The party structure, thus, acts to augment local governmental bodies and is itself, likewise, a blend of direct and indirect representation. It helps to make Tanzanian local government a complex and multidimensional operation, characterized by extensive participation and a pattern of leadership choice.

There is a blending and harmonizing of the party and government through interaction and cross-membership; civil servants are encouraged to become members of TANU. The president and vice president of TANU are the president and second vice president of the Republic. The party membership, first through its district conferences and finally through the National Executive Committee, preselects the candidates for the National Assembly and screens the nominees of the national institutions. Members of the National Assembly are likewise members of the TANU National Conference, so that, at all levels, the party feeds its members into the representative bodies (whose membership, particularly at the village and district levels, may include non-TANU personnel).

The party maintains a national Central Committee, which used to consist of the president of TANU, the vice president, secretary general, and treasurer, as well as nine persons appointed by the president. It is somewhat smaller now, the posts of secretary general and treasurer having been abolished in 1967. The Central Committee meets weekly and acts as a sounding board for the government's proposals. Of more importance is the larger National Executive Committee, made up of the Central Committee, 17 regional chairmen and their secretaries, 17 delegates chosen by the National Conference to represent the districts, and 1 representative each from the national institutions and 2 from the TANU Youth League. Although the proceedings of the NEC (as well as those of the Central Committee) are not public, it seems clear that the National Executive Committee plays an important role in policy formation as well as in the selection of National Assembly candidates. It often causes a reassessment of the executive proposals. On occasion, the debate within its membership is vigorous and the criticisms hostile although, by the time a policy decision has been made public or presented to the National Conference, most difficulties have been resolved.

The National Conference, now held every two years, is of less importance in the process of decision making, although it selects the party and national presidential nominees. It consists of 400 delegates, including 300 voting members, and is made up of the members of the National Assembly, the Central Committee, 17 at-large members of the National Executive Committee, 1 representative from each of the national institutions, and 60 district party secretaries. Its primary function is to serve as a public forum and to provide contact between the national personnel and their local counterparts. Because of the difficulties of communication, the dispersed nature of the population, and the free-floating character of the national offices (which lack ethnic or regional bases of support), this function is of considerable importance in stimulating a feeling of solidarity, in making opinions and policies known, and in linking the national center with its political, as well as its geographic, periphery.

In addition to providing political representation, TANU and the government also direct national institutions, such as the army and the bureaucracy, and, hence, mute the centrifugal forces which have proven so divisive to other political systems. The techniques and strategies adopted by the leaders of the Tanzanian political system are worth noting, for they aim to utilize these institutions both as instruments of political power and national politics as well as channels of information. Subgroup autonomy is reasonably well established in Tanzania, and the political center seems inclined to interfere with their operation only if the institutions or groups in question threaten the system or jeopardize its primary goals.

The presidential Commission and the TANU persistently stressed the "channel" functions of the various party and governmental institutions and indicated that participation lies at the heart of the political process:

> There shall be the maximum possible participation by the people in their own government and ultimate control by them over all the organs of State on the basis of universal suffrage.[11]

From its inception, TANU stressed that this participation was to be meaningful and not of the fleeting type often associated with plebiscites:

> It is also necessary to have a strong political organization active in every village which acts like a toll way, all-weather road, along which the purposes, plans and problems of the Government can travel to the people, at the same time as the ideas, desires and misunderstandings of the people can travel direct to the Government.[12]

Leaders within the party and the system are chosen from a broad spectrum of socioeconomic groups, and recruitment patterns are achievement-oriented. Ascription is not a critical factor. During the elections of 1965, for example, few constituencies were decided on tribal grounds. Non-Africans, such as the Asian Minister of Finance, Amir Jamal, and the European Minister of Agriculture and Cooperatives, Derek Bryceson, have been freely chosen by the population over African opponents. Indeed, in the 1975 elections, the biggest majority obtained in the contested-seat area was attained by Derek Bryceson. And there is a greater percentage of non-Africans elected to the National Assembly than exists in the society as a whole.[13] Nor is age a limiting factor —59 out of 101 elected members of the National Assembly of 1965 were under 35.

The achievement orientation of politics in Tanzania and the population's realization of this are reflected in the operation of the system. According to what surveys we have, there are high levels of involvement on the part of individual citizens and a strong belief in the efficacy of political activity.[14] Voters seem to feel that their votes count and that the government is responsive

---

[11]J. K. Nyerere, *Freedom and Unity: Uhuru na Umoja* (London: Oxford University Press, 1967), p. 262.

[12]Lionel Cliffe (ed.), *One Party Democracy: The 1965 Tanzania General Elections* (Nairobi: East African Publishing House, 1967).

[13]Several writers have, however, pointed out the apolitical character of the Indians in East Africa and their generally low levels of political efficacy: Barton M. Schwartz (ed.), *Caste in Overseas Indian Communities* (San Francisco: Chandler, 1967), pp. 267–320; and Yash Tandon, "A Political Survey," in Dharam P. Ghai (ed.), *Portrait of a Minority: Asians in East Africa* (Nairobi: Oxford University Press, 1965), pp. 65–89.

[14]Kenneth Prewitt and Goran Hyden, "Voters Look at the Elections," in Cliffe (ed.), *One Party Democracy,* p. 277.

to their interests and desires. Participation has increased steadily. During 1962, only 20 percent of the eligible voters registered and voted, while in 1965, 50 percent of the population registered and 76 percent of those registered voted. In addition, over 3,500 political meetings involving over 2.25 million people were held. A brief examination of the general elections will illustrate the kinds and levels of participation. By 1975, a total of 5,577,569 Tanzanians registered to vote, an increase of more than half a million over the previous record total of 1970.

After the election dates (September 21 for president, September 25 for the National Assembly) were announced, nominations began. There was to be a single presidential nominee, selected by the electoral conference of the party, but, if in the general elections he did not receive a majority of "yes" votes, another candidate would be chosen until one received a majority. For the National Assembly, any 18-year-old citizen who was a member of TANU could, after accumulating 25 signatures of qualified voters, apply for nomination. It was decided that each constituency would have two candidates wherever possible to insure voter choice, but the number was held at two in order to insure that no minority candidate would be elected. If there were more than two petitioners, the respective candidates were questioned by the TANU regional conference, which then ranked the candidates in order of preference and sent their names to the National Executive Committee, which selected the final contestants. Six candidates ran unopposed, so that the committee chose 202 candidates out of the 803 aspirants to contest the 101 seats. TANU's selection of candidates did not favor the party stalwarts. Cliffe estimates, for example, that 74 percent of those chosen were "merely card-holding members with no special status in TANU," although the percentage has increased since then.[15]

By the Election (Amendment) Act of 1965, the two candidates in each constituency campaigned as one, sharing transportation and expenses. Oration had to be conducted in Swahili, with each candidate given the same opportunity to speak. "Private" competition was discouraged and candidates were not allowed to claim special TANU support. There were also restrictions on the use of racial or ethnic competition and the discussion of foreign policy issues. The basic nonracial socialist character of the system and its foreign policy objectives were not open to debate. Because perhaps 90 percent of the electorate is illiterate, each of the candidates was given a symbol, either a hoe (jembe) or a house (nyumba), in their constituency.

Julius Nyerere was elected president on September 21, with a majority of 97 percent, doing slightly better on Zanzibar (which participated in the presidential elections, but not the National Assembly elections) than on the mainland. Five days later, the elections for the National Assembly were held and

[15]Cliffe (ed.), *One Party Democracy,* p. 267.

the results were surprising. Not only were the elections free and indicative of polyarchal decision making, but the voters defeated so many incumbents—including 2 ministers, 6 junior ministers, 13 district chairmen, and 16 of 31 former MPs who ran—that the election could quite properly be classified as a "sweeping turnover" which few political systems anywhere could match.[16] It seems clear that members of the National Assembly had lost touch with their constituents and that, since most races were decided on the basis of local issues, the leadership alteration did not reflect a rejection of the system. If that were the case, it seems likely that the vote for Nyerere would have reflected that rejection.

Subsequent elections under the single-party electoral competition system resulted in a continuation of the above pattern. People participated in large numbers. There were significant levels of competition within the single-party framework, although the turnovers were not as sweeping in subsequent elections because, by and large, MPs tended to pay more attention to their districts.

In 1970, three ministers were defeated and fairly large numbers of MPs either lost, failed to obtain nomination, or chose not to stand for reelection. All but 6 of the 120 elective constituencies for the new enlarged National Assembly had competing candidates and over one-third of the 71 incumbents were defeated. Polyarchal decision making clearly occurred on the mainland and, once again, Julius Nyerere was elected by a resounding margin, receiving 3,450,000 "yes" votes against just over 109,000 "no's" for a 97 percent approval rating.

In 1975, results were similar. Of the Parliamentary seats at stake, 92 were contested. There was vigorous campaigning on the local level and, once again, important political figures were defeated, including two ministers and one junior minister. Nyerere was again returned by an overwhelming mandate although he turned aside suggestions that he become president for life, claiming that periodic approval by the voters was essential for any political leader.

The Tanzanian political system continues to change and adapt to new circumstances. We indicated earlier that although the citizens of Zanzibar and Pemba participated in the presidential elections of 1965, 1970, and 1975, there was no electoral competition within the Afro-Shirazi Party. In an attempt to stimulate such competition and to complete the merger between the mainland and the islands, a joint commission headed by Afro-Shirazi Secretary General Thabit Kombo called for the merger of TANU and ASP to form one totally integrated party.

Early in 1977, TANU and ASP were officially merged into *CHAMA Cha Mapinduzi* (CCM), the revolutionary party of Tanzania, and a new constitu-

---

[16]Ruth Schacter Morgenthau, "African Elections: Tanzania's Contribution," *Africa Report* (December 1965), p. 16. For an in-depth view of one such surprise, see Bismark Muansasu and Norman N. Miller, "Rungwe: Defeat of a Minister," in Cliffe (ed.), *One Party Democracy,* pp. 128–54.

tion was adopted in April. Under its provisions, Zanzibaris will vote on 10 representatives to the Tanzanian Parliament, while 96 will be elected from the mainland. In addition there are a variety of appointed positions. The post of the second vice president was abolished and the first vice president will come from Zanzibar. The new party, which was in fact a true blend of the original two parties, took up its headquarters in the new capital, Dodoma, and had overarching responsibility for several mass organizations, including the old TANU Youth League, the Workers' Organization, the Union of Co-operative Societies, and the United Women of Tanzania. Membership in either TANU or ASP was considered grounds for admission to CHAMA, although members had to reregister.

It remains to be seen, of course, whether CHAMA will continue to function as TANU had in the past. Certainly, the more hierarchical bent of some ASP members may have some influence on joint policy, but to date, there is little to indicate that the pattern of politics outlined above will be seriously affected by these changes. Likewise, plans to reduce the size of the National Assembly so that there is one electoral district for each district of CHAMA may alter the course of representation, particularly in the most sparsely populated rural areas.

How to categorize the Tanzanian political system? Certainly, on a number of levels it is markedly polyarchal, even though there is a great deal of direction from the political center and electoral competition takes place within carefully proscribed limits. Representatives of the people in TANU choose the party conference, which in turn chooses the presidential candidate, and final authority rests with the population as a whole. Representatives of the people in TANU choose among the petitioning applicants, but the population ultimately decides between the final two candidates selected. The elected members of the National Assembly form a majority of that body. There is also evidence that the National Assembly is playing a more important role in policy formation than it did when there was a well organized TANU parliamentary party in 1964 to mute public debate. Even in the process of nomination to the National Assembly, the public is considered. For example, in October 1965 the National Executive Committee of TANU rejected the nominees of the national institutions on the grounds that they were members of those institutions (TANU wanted less parochial representation) and because many of the nominees had previously been defeated in the September elections.

Thus, a characterization of the Tanzanian political system as both democratic and egalitarian does not seem unwarranted. The National Ethic and the Creed of TANU calling for individual freedom as well as social solidarity seem operative. Observers commended the antiauthoritarian style of the leadership and have described the operation of the system as "exceptionally honest."[17]

---

[17]Cliffe (ed.), *One Party Democracy,* p. 229.

Information and decision making seem to flow both upward and downward along both the government and the party structures.

There seems little reason to suppose that an organized, formal opposition, which proved so meaningless during the 1961–65 period, would more effectively insure the democratic functioning of the system. Generalized support for TANU has always been so overwhelming (far more so than that enjoyed by the Convention People's Party in Ghana or the *Parti Democratique de Guinée* in Guinea), that *de jure* recognition of a *de facto* situation and subsequent democratization of the political process within a single-party framework may well have, as its proponents claim, opened up the decision-making process to more meaningful levels of participation.

Not that the system is without flaws. One may well wish for a more widespread appreciation of, and participation in, the major foreign policy decisions which Tanzania makes, as well as a more formal institutionalization of a Bill of Rights and other safeguards which could not be overridden by some capricious future leader. But, in light of the erosion of democratic politics which has been such a persistent phenomenon throughout the Third World, the accomplishment of Tanzania seems well worth noting. It seems to have evolved, in a few short years, a system designed to prevent political fragmentation and to curb the centrifugal forces which threaten so many other regimes, while at the same time preserving a democratic core which ensures, indeed encourages, meaningful and widespread participation. The Tanzanian system may well serve as a model for other single-party regimes seeking controlled democratization of their political culture and an increase in the representative function of the central government. Clearly, it could have a good deal of relevance for existing regimes of this type in Europe, Latin America, and Asia, as well as in Africa.

There are, of course, some factors in the social, economic, and political context which have aided this experiment in basic democracy. There are few Europeans within the system and little land alienation, so that the colonial overlay was not significant. There is also a marked lack of "tribal" tension. The largest political community is that of the Sukuma, which has over a million members, but there are a dozen groups with hundreds of thousands of persons (such as the Nyamwezi, Makonde, Haya, Chagga, Gogo, Ha, and Hehe), so that there is little danger of numerical domination.

Also, as was suggested in Chapter 1, the traditional African political systems which now fall under the jurisdiction of the Tanzanian government, generally speaking, lacked strong, centralized authority, and this has had a salutary effect on the growth of nontribal politics. One has only to compare the role played by the powerful centralized kingdom of Buganda in the postwar history of Uganda (relatively the same size as the Sukuma), or that of the Asante in Ghana with those of the Tanganyikan groups to see the importance of the traditional political structures. Many traditional systems in Tanzania are either acephalous lineage segments (such as the Kutu or Luguru), independent village systems (Zaramo, Kwere, and the Swahili groups of the coastal region), or age-set segments (Masai). Other groups had chieftains before 1963, but these were divided into multiple, often small, units (Nyamwezi, Nyakyusa, Sumbwa, Kimbu, Konongo). Even if there were paramount chiefs over these small groups (as are found among the Vidunda, Zigula and Shambala), they enjoyed little political power over their subordinates. There were some peoples with ruling dynasties and identifiable class stratification, as the Haya and Ha, but these groups were confined to the northwest corner of the country near Lake Victoria and were politically unimportant.

In short, judging from the data we now have, the traditional political systems of Tanzania were characterized by diffused political power and authority fragmentation. The existing situation was, no doubt, enhanced by the German predilection to use Arab intermediators. Even when the British tried to institute a process of indirect rule, they found over 120 units (which by 1950 had 435 recognized native authorities). TANU and the independent government of Tanganyika did nothing to create or enhance tribal authority, and, in fact, abolished it in 1963 with the African Chief Ordinance (Repeal) Act. The political leadership has been able to move ahead with its proposals for a modern system without major blockages from the traditional authorities. Because of the lack of sufficient manpower resources, TANU has used some of these former authorities as individuals within the party and the bureaucracy, but this was done on a selective basis.

There seems little question that the traditional African systems provided a suitable environment for the present system and that long traditions of internal democracy and opposition to arbitrary rule facilitated the development of the present system. The formation of a Tanzanian political system has also been aided by the existence of a national language, Kiswahili, and a quasi-national culture (which, at the very least, contributed a few central reference points, such as communal cooperation, welfare concerns, and a social obligation to work).

There is the matter of national poverty. Henry Bienen has made an excellent point in recognizing that the very low levels of wealth, which inhibit the formation of a strong central party and, hence, rapid economic development, also mean that the system qua system is not faced with many entrenched socioeconomic oppositions.[18] The low levels of income, the dependence upon subsistence agriculture, and the scattered rural nature of the population mean that a stage-three "modern" government has been superimposed on a stage-one socioeconomic context. The lack of socioeconomic differentiation and the relative classlessness of Tanzanian society do seem to facilitate the formation of an egalitarian democratic political system.

[18]Henry Bienen, *Tanzania: Party Transformation and Economic Development* (Princeton, N.J.: Princeton University Press, 1967).

The astute leadership of Tanzania is also a factor. We have deliberately downplayed the role of Julius Nyerere in reaction to many of the highly personalized political accounts of other African political systems, but, also, in order to indicate the historical and societal underpinnings of the present system. Nevertheless, his vision and foresight, his commitment to a nonracial democratic government, and his rational guidance may well have provided the necessary impetus to ensure the present accomplishment of at least a modified polyarchal political system. In fact, it may well be that the single most important variable in the success of a polyarchal system is the leadership itself. Does it *want* such an arrangement to work?

Ironically enough, most of the strains and tensions within Tanzania have not come from the actual workings of the electoral aspects of the political system; that is, most people who participate in the elections, either as candidates or as voters, support the system because they perceive it to be fairly and honestly run. The major difficulties in Tanzania have come with the implementation of the ideals of Ujamaa.

Ujamaa socialism is not debatable. As was indicated in Chapter 3, many of the goals of that philosophy may be laudatory. Indeed, they may be highly desirable for poverty-stricken people engaged in subsistence agriculture. But the government efforts to prod and move the country toward Ujamaa has resulted in a number of unpleasant side effects.

For one thing, the nationalization of all foreign firms quickly dried up investment capital and Tanzania has had to pay a severe price for that action. In 1974, for example, the country failed to produce enough food to feed the population. Maize, wheat, rice, and sugar had to be imported. A good bit of the blame can be placed on a series of droughts as well as on sharply higher prices for petroleum and fertilizer. But certainly to blame is the severe loss of production which resulted on the nationalized "capitalist" farms. In fact, the government has had to revive an old colonial law which required each peasant farming family to grow a minimum amount of food.

More importantly for our overall judgment of the system, the forced relocation schemes which resulted from the implementation of Ujamaa socialism have not taken place without harmful side effects. In 1969, the government decided that the only way to increase agricultural production and move toward true Ujamaa socialism was to embark on a nationwide program to move peasants from isolated locations and extremely fragmented farming arrangements into new villages where they could interact with each other, form more viable economic units, and have their agricultural activities more easily coordinated.

Whatever the economic thinking behind the move, or its ultimate wisdom (for it is too early to determine the long-term outcome), the implementation has not gone smoothly. Many people were forced to move rather than simply encouraged to move. TANU stalwarts were often accused of ordering peasants about rather than convincing them. Nyerere himself admitted that there were a number of abuses.

Many of the moves were also ill-timed, coming during the growing season or taking place too late in the year to allow for planting at the new location. By 1974, some 7 million people had been relocated. Three million were in Ujamaa villages, 2 million in other new villages, 1.5 million remained in old non-Ujamaa villages, and 3.5 million still existed in scattered homesteads.[19] Many of those transplanted were moved against their will. Clearly, one has to break eggs to make an omelet, but this method is more often associated with authoritarian regimes than polyarchal ones.

Kenya

Kenya stands in marked contrast to Tanzania. It is a veritable tribal mosaic with strong tribal undercurrents to its politics. The Kikuyu, representing approximately 20 percent of the population, are clearly dominant. There are several hundred thousand non-Africans who play major roles in the economy. With an area of 224,960 square miles and a population of over 12 million, there are over 400 people per square mile and there is intense competition for land. It is one of the most beautiful countries in the world.

Kenya is a booming, bustling country with a modified free enterprise economy, strong socioeconomic differentials which make it a class society. Corruption is noticeable at the higher levels of government. There has been considerable political violence, including the assassination of two major political figures, Tom Mboya and J. M. Kariuki. Certain ethnic units, particularly the Kikuyu, have taken hold of the distributive capability of the system to the detriment of others, particularly the Luo, who make up 14 percent of the total.

Yet, in spite of all this, Kenya has a modified polyarchal system, with electoral competition within its single-party framework. Its history is vibrant with multiparty competition and a struggle for political position. During the period from 1952 until 1959, Kenya was in a state of emergency as the so-called Mau Mau revolt among the Kikuyu divided that ethnic group and caused considerable violence. Ironically, it was an alleged leader of the movement, Jomo Kenyatta, who emerged from prison to lead the Kenyan African National Union (KANU) to victory over its rival, the Kenyan African Democratic Union (KADU). The electoral competition was reflected in the struggle over constitutional form as well. The smaller tribes feared the Kikuyu-Luo domination of KANU and sought a federal system which would preserve their rights.

The constitution was not agreed upon until March 1963 and independence

[19]Colin Legum (ed.), *Africa Contemporary Record: 1974–1975* (New York: Africana Publishing, 1977), p. 297.

followed in December, with KANU forming the first government. The independence constitution called for an executive president to be elected by the National Assembly. The president chose the vice president, the Cabinet ministers and vice ministers from the National Assembly.

The National Assembly consisted of 158 elected members (chosen from single member constituencies), plus 12 who were chosen by the elected members. There is also an attorney general who is an *ex officio* member of that body. The National Assembly serves a period of five years unless dissolved earlier.

Following independence, Kenya went to a republican form of government and a presidential system calling for the direct and popular election of the president. In 1964, Kenya became a single-party state as KADU members in the Parliament crossed the aisle and joined KANU. In 1965, the remnants of the federal system were eliminated and Kenya became a unitary state.

However, during the next year, Oginga Odinga, vice president of Kenya and the most prominent Luo, split with the rest of KANU's leaders over a number of issues, including land reform, social and economic inequality, and the rising tide of Kikuyu domination. He then formed a new party, the Kenya People's Union (KPU). Those MPs who joined the new party were forced to stand for reelection and some were defeated. A period of some tension followed, exacerbated by the assassination of Tom Mboya, Minister of Economic Planning and Development in July 1969, and shooting by police into a crowd of people at Kisumu in October of that year. Citing the political violence, the government banned KPU and went ahead with the planned KANU primary election in December.

It was in this backhanded way that Kenya became a single-party state with electoral competition, for in the primary, 600 persons contested for the nomination to 158 seats (since the general elections which followed allowed only KANU nominees to stand). The results were similar to those experienced in Tanzania during the 1965 elections. Two-thirds of the KANU incumbents, including 5 ministers and 14 assistant ministers, were defeated and there was a wholesale turnover of leadership. Even within the confines of this modified polyarchal system, the voters exercised a wide range of choice (although many in Luo areas boycotted the elections).

In 1974, President Jomo Kenyatta was elected unopposed and in the general elections of October there was significant electoral competition. No fewer than 4 cabinet ministers (including Foreign Minister Dr. Njoroge Mungai), 13 assistant ministers, and 71 MPs were defeated as a total of 737 candidates vied for 158 seats. Secret ballots were used for the first time and fully 80 percent of the eligible population registered to vote.

President Kenyatta continues to dominate the political life of Kenya despite his advanced age. He has used arbitrary rule on occasion to implement policies and to muzzle critics. For example, in 1974 he announced that Swahili would become the national language, despite constitutional qualifications to the contrary. He also moved to restrict debate following a Parliamentary inquiry into the assassination of MP J.M. Kariuki in 1975. Kariuki, who was a harsh critic of corruption, felt that the president himself was linked to illegal amassment of wealth through the actions of his wife, Mama Ngina.

There are conflicting views of just how polyarchal Kenya is. Some observers have cited Kikiyu domination and the government's willingness to crack down on and muzzle opponents. Other, including Henry Bienen, the highly respected political scientist who studied Tanzania as well, have concluded that Kenya, despite its faults, is a "participant society" in many important respects. If one looks beyond the cult of Mzee Kenyatta and governmental corruption, there is significant citizen participation in decision making, a fair civil service, and an allocation of resources that is not overly inequitable.[20]

Be that as it may, there is significant opposition to the government along ethnic, socioeconomic, even linguistic lines. It may well be that the modified polyarchal system currently serves as a safety valve and that, coupled with Kenyatta's attention to controlling the military (through the use of Kikuyu officers and an elite General Service Unit), accounts for the system's ability to survive the considerable stresses at work. There may also be the "golden goose" factor. Kenya is highly dependent on foreign investment for its economic growth and on the tourist industry to provide much needed foreign exchange. Even those who oppose the present regime would not like to jeopardize this lucrative—even necessary—stimulation to the economy.

Yet Kenya continues to flirt with authoritarianism. In May 1977, President Kenyatta announced that the KANU party elections were to be postponed indefinitely. Disorganization of the party structure and concern over electoral chaos were cited but an additional factor was undoubtedly the strong showing Oginga Odinga was apparently making for the vice presidency against KANU regulars Daniel Arap Moi and Taitta Arap Toweett. The prominent writer Ngugi Wa Thiongo was detained without trial early in 1978.

Zambia

A third example of a modified polyarchal political system within a single-party arrangement is Zambia. With a population of five million and an area of 290,724 square miles, it is a landlocked country, highly dependent on its single major export, copper.

As we saw in Chapter 3, Kenneth Kaunda has evolved a political philosophy which is somewhat similar, although by no means identical, to Ujamaa

---

[20]Henry Bienen, *Kenya: The Politics of Participation and Control* (Princeton, N.J.: Princeton University Press, 1974). See, also, John Harbeson, "Land Reforms and Politics in Kenya 1954–1970," *Journal of Modern African Studies,* vol. 9, no. 2 (1971), pp. 231–51. See also the variety of opinions contained in the literature on pages 279–280 of the Bibliography.

socialism. For Kaunda, "humanism" is a broad-gauge program for human betterment. In addition, it has a number of practical ramifications for, as one sees signs everywhere in the country, "Humanism is Safe Driving."

Unlike Tanzania, but rather like Kenya, there is no universal agreement that a single-party state is ideal for the country. There is simply far less consensus within the polity concerning its advisibility. For one thing, the present ruling party, the United National Independence Party (UNIP) has generally had serious organized opposition since it was founded in 1959 as an offshoot of the African National Congress (ANC), formed in 1948 by Harry Nkumbula. Although UNIP quickly came to be the majority party, its base among the northern Bemba meant that the southern tribes, such as the Lozi and Tonga, have tended to back the opposition, first ANC and then the United Progressive Party (UPP), which was formed by Simon Kapwepwe in 1971, notwithstanding the fact that Kapwepwe was a close friend of Kaunda and vice president of Zambia.

Claiming a threat to the security of Zambia and charging that the opposition had links to a foreign power (presumably South Africa), Kaunda banned the opposition in February 1972 and declared Zambia a single-party state. Observers of the Zambian scene have argued that his move was unnecessary and basically unwelcome by large segments of the population. In fact, it has been asserted that the 1972 decrees froze the power position ". . . in an artificial and unrealistic way."[21]

Clearly, Humanism as a philosophy cannot simplify all the intricacies of modern political life. In moving to a single-party state, the Zambian government developed a new constitution, which was promulgated in August 1973. It has a strong president chosen by the general population, but there can only be a single candidate, the president of UNIP, as chosen by the general party conference. The vice president is the secretary general of UNIP (rather than the head of the National Assembly).

In an imitation of Tanzania, the National Assembly has 136 members, of whom 125 are elected. The president may appoint 10 others and the speaker of the House is chosen by that body from outside its ranks. The prime minister is appointed by the president and serves as the liaison between the executive and the legislature.

As in Tanzania, the elected members are nominated by UNIP after considerable consultation at the local and district level. All candidates must be members of UNIP and approved by the party through a primary election in

[21]Jan Pettman, "Zambia's Second Republic—The Establishment of a One-Party State," *Journal of Modern African Studies,* vol. 12, no. 2 (1974), p. 243. For further background on the Zambian situation, see the works on pages 296–297 of the Bibliography. Algeria, which lies outside the scope of this study also has modified electoral competition for parliament. For example, in February, 1977 over 780 candidates vied for 261 seats although all were members of the ruling National Liberation Front.

which only party officials may vote. Up to three candidates may be nominated for each district.

The only election held thus far under the new arrangement took place in December 1973. There were some interesting crosscurrents. Kaunda received 80 percent of the vote for president, but in a number of southern districts his candidacy was rejected. In Nkumbula's home district, for example, there were 2,837 "no" votes and only 727 "yes" votes. Moreover, the turnout was quite light nationwide, averaging 32 percent and going to a low of 18 percent in some of the hostile districts.

Still, the pattern of voter choice was similar to that seen in Kenya and Tanzania. The voters went to the polls and took advantage of the electoral competition to defeat a large number of incumbents, including 3 cabinet ministers and 11 ministers of state. Although existing in circumscribed form, polyarchal politics within a single-party state had made a modest beginning. As one of only three such experiments in Africa, it remains well worth watching, and, should the complex racial situation in southern Africa be resolved and Zambia's former routes to the sea through Rhodesia (Zimbabwe) and Angola be reopened, some of the international and economic pressures could be reduced and the government could turn further attention to the considerable task of making humanism work in a country of 73 tribes and half a dozen major language groups.

6

The Authoritarian Spectrum

In Chapter 5, we discussed the onset of independence and the widespread erosion of democratic politics in the newly emergent African states, and described the workings of those polyarchal and modified polyarchal systems which remain in operation. In this chapter, we shall examine a number of governments which, in their current operation, are more authoritarian in character. We say "more authoritarian in character" because some of the governments described in Chapter 5, such as Sierra Leone, were clearly not totally polyarchal and the differences between some of them and some of the forms to be covered here, while discernible, may not be completely clear-cut.

In point of fact, just as it is difficult to say at precisely what point on a color spectrum yellow becomes orange, so too it is not a simple matter to indicate precisely at what point a particular system crosses the boundary from a modified polyarchal situation to a modified authoritarian one. Take, for example, the government of Kenya. We have chosen to call it a modified polyarchal system, even though there are a number of strands of authoritarianism present in the political structure. Likewise, we have termed the government of Swaziland modified authoritarian even though it shares some characteristics with modified polyarchal systems.

For our part, however, what is involved is a cluster of characteristics such as electoral competition, basic political civil liberties, and dissent protection. Taken together, these place a given political system at a given location on the political spectrum. It is our view that in the aggregate, these characteristics enable us to draw a portrait which can indicate one system's status at a given moment in time. But the reader should be aware that many political systems are in a state of constant change and that some countries can exhibit polyarchal characteristics at a given moment in time, only to be distinguished by authoritarian features six months later. Therefore, when the political snapshot was taken is a matter of considerable importance.

There is also the matter of individual choice. We have selected a number of countries and designated some of them polyarchal and some authoritarian. Different observers might well choose to categorize them differently. They might use other criteria or weigh the ones we have selected in a different fashion. They might, for example, regard the Cameroons or Liberia as modified polyarchal when we have called them modified authoritarian. Or they might consider Kenya a modified authoritarian system instead of a modified polyarchal one.

THE AUTHORITARIAN CRITERIA

There are certain characteristics which, taken together, add up to a condition of political authoritarianism. If a political system exhibits a majority of the criteria, we have labeled it authoritarian. In other words, it is not necessary that every system under review in this chapter exhibit every single characteristic we have outlined in order to be considered authoritarian. A certain amount of common sense is involved in these judgments and even then, disagreements may rightly occur. But we feel that the political systems outlined in this chapter do, in their current operations at least, exhibit a cluster of characteristics we have labeled authoritarian. For the most part, they conduct politics on a discernibly different basis than those in Chapter 5, even though some political systems in both chapters may well have *some* characteristics in common. What are the chief features of authoritarian political systems?

Lack of Electoral Competition

As we suggested in Chapter 5, the most critical ingredient in the polyarchal classification is electoral competition, irrespective of whether or not such competition takes place within a multiparty or single-party framework. In a polyarchal system, as a result of this electoral competition, nonleaders have the opportunity to select leaders. This does not mean that all nonleaders have the opportunity to select all leaders, but there are significant amounts of competition at high enough levels of politics to enable nonleaders to influence decision makers and cause leadership alteration.

Therefore, a primary characteristic of an authoritarian regime is the lack of electoral competition, especially at the national level. In the regimes we have chosen to cover in this chapter, the nonleaders simply do not choose their leaders. Nonleaders may participate in elections and/or plebiscites, but they have no choice in terms of that participation nor do they have an opportunity to choose among candidates for election.

Pattern of Hierarchical Decision Making

Another characteristic of authoritarian government is found in the pattern of decision making. In the case of authoritarian regimes, that pattern is essentially hierarchical; that is, decisions are made at the top of the political system and flow downward relatively unchecked. Now, in some sense, all political systems use their centers to make basic decisions but in polyarchal systems those decisions are subject to interaction with, and ongoing checks and balances by, interest groups, voters, and a variety of other citizen influences. This is not the case in authoritarian regimes.

In authoritarian regimes, decisions are made by a small number of non-elected elites (often by individuals) and forced upon nonleaders, irrespective of their preference. Again, this does not mean that all decisions taken at all times are always forced on nonleaders against their wills, or that all such decisions run counter to the will of the population. It does mean that over time, there is a definite pattern of decision making made at the very top of the political system and forced upon the nonelites without their generally having the opportunity to influence the ultimate pattern of decision making, either by impinging on the decision makers or having the opportunity to select new leaders at discernible points of time. In short, in authoritarian regimes there is no direct (and often little indirect) accountability to the population.

Lack of Civil Liberties

Authoritarian regimes are also characterized by a basic lack of civil liberties. Individuals cannot go where they want, say what they want, or express opposition to the existing regime or its politics without fear of substantial retribution. Individuals and groups lack access to media outlets (which are usually controlled by the government). Indeed, individuals are generally denied the right to form groups not sanctioned or controlled by the government.

Overall, authoritarian regimes exhibit a marked disinclination to allow individuals to speak out in opposition, not only to the policies of the government but to the government itself. This is not to suggest that African governments must be "perfect" in terms of civil liberties in order to avoid the title "authoritarian." Nor is it to assert that non-African governments are any better or worse on the average in setting the limits of dissent. But it is to suggest that there are definite differences within the African context as to the extent to which citizens of various countries are able to exhibit their political sentiments and to express dissent. In Gambia or Botswana, a citizen can speak out on issues, the press is free, and there are guaranteed and enforced rights for individual political behavior. No one would confuse the situations in these countries with those in Uganda, Zaire, or Malawi. There are, of course, verifiable differences among authoritarian regimes as well. For example, in Swaziland or Nigeria, the press is—by world standards—free and individuals can express their political viewpoints through it (even though citizens in these countries lack the right or even the opportunity to form political parties or to participate in electoral competition). In Malawi, on the other hand, in addition to having no opportunity to exhibit legal opposition by political means, citizens have absolutely no access to the government press, which is completely controlled by the president, Dr. Hastings Kamuzu Banda.

Arbitrary Arrest and Imprisonment

Authoritarian regimes also make a fundamental political assumption which true polyarchal states do not, and that is that political dissenters can and should be punished and imprisoned. This accent on arbitrary imprisonment as a right of the government stems from the assumption that dissent is unlawful and wrong, and that it is the right of the state to treat dissent in any fashion in order to eliminate it. Citizens who have spoken out against the government, or who are suspected of having spoken out against the government, are arrested, imprisoned, beaten, and killed as a matter of course.

Many observers of the African political scene have been reluctant to criticize this type of behavior when they encounter it in black Africa. Some excuse it as a sign of Africa's political "immaturity." Others suggest that it is a necessary reaction to outside interference or tribalism. Still others condemn similar patterns of behavior in South Africa or Zimbabwe/Rhodesia, but go to considerable lengths to distinguish this "bad" repression from the necessary or "good" repression in the black states.

These reactions seem both misguided and patronizing. The denial of civil liberties, patterns of arbitrary arrest and imprisonment, indeed all forms of political repression are no less repugnant to those affected whether practiced by rulers of one's own color or not. Advocates of the reverse, such as E. J. M. Zvobgo, are singularly unpersuasive in arguing that there are "intensity" or "infra-structural" differences between black repression and torture and white repression and torture.[1] The horrible treatment of South Africa's political prisoners should not make the brutality and staggering excesses of Micombero's Burundi or Amin's Uganda any less repugnant to men of good will.[2] Certainly, the origin of the terror can make little difference to the maimed and the dead.

The Existence of Bona Fide Refugees

Although not all authoritarian regimes have large numbers of political refugees who have fled the system, many do. At the present time, there are over one million refugees in Africa currently living outside the country of their birth or national origin.

We have indicated elsewhere that all persons who have left their home countries are not necessarily *bona fide* refugees.[3] Some people classified as refugees are simply looking for employment opportunities which may not be present in their own country. Some are seeking educational opportunities which may be more forthcoming for "refugees" than for a country's own nationals. Some are interested primarily in travel and adventure, while others are actually immigrants who have kinship or marriage ties to their adopted country. There are even some who are actually spying on real refugees for the governments of their countries.

But the vast majority of Africa's one million refugees have fled their country of origin because they feared for their safety and their lives. The cause of this fear could be drought and starvation. It could be a civil war. Or, in the cases which are of the greatest concern to us, it could be political repression. Individuals who cross international boundaries because of political, ethnic, and cultural persecution are indicators of authoritarian and repressive regimes and are thus aids in identifying the governments in question.

As indicated above, not all authoritarian regimes produce large numbers of

---

[1] E. J. M. Zvobgo, "The Abuse of Executive Prerogative: A Purposive Difference Between Detention in Black Africa and Detention in White Racist Africa," *Issue*, vol. 6, no. 4 (Winter 1976), pp. 38–43. The entire winter 1977 issue is devoted to the question of human rights in Africa.

[2] Although the course of politics under the remaining white minority governments lies outside the scope of this book, pages 260–261, 287–291, and 297–298 of the Bibliography contain numerous works the interested reader can consult.

[3] These themes, as well as the difficulties in telling a refugee he or she is not a refugee, are amplified in C. P. Potholm, "Wanderers on the Face of Africa," *The Round Table*, no. 261 (January 1976), pp. 85–92, and "Refugees: Africa's Persistent Problem," *Africa Report*, vol. 21, no. 2 (March-April 1976), pp. 12–14, 54.

political refugees. In the countries under review, Ghana has not, nor has the Ivory Coast. Yet, many others have in the past and still do generate significant numbers of refugees who flee repressive regimes and political repression. Rwanda, Burundi, Uganda, Guinea—to name but the most obvious—have spawned tens of thousands of refugees who cross state borders to avoid political repression. Under different regimes or political systems, most would return home.

The characteristics outlined above are exhibited by many governments in Africa today. Indeed, whereas in Chapter 5 we found ourselves hard pressed to find many examples of true polyarchal governments currently in power in sub-Saharan Africa, here the problem is the reverse. There are simply too many authentically authoritarian regimes for us to go into all of them. Rather than cover them all superficially, we shall try to give the reader (1) some generalized portraits of some of the most important *types* of authoritarian rule (such as civilian versus military), (2) some in-depth analysis of several important examples of each type, and (3) examples of other political systems correspond to our illustrations. In this way it is hoped that the reader will be able to gain an appreciation for the broad and encompassing spectrum of authoritarian politics in Africa.

One note of caution. Many African leaders, particularly those in authoritarian governments, and some analysts of African politics, have suggested that authoritarian rule is not only a fact of African political life, but a necessary one. They have suggested that the multiplicity of people and traditional forms outlined in Chapter 1, the artificial boundaries and foreign domination described in Chapter 2, the failure of pluralistic philosophies and political systems analyzed in Chapters 3 and 5, and the continuing interference in African national life by outside forces all *require* authoritarian rule for unity, stability, and independence.

Suffice it to say that we are not totally persuaded by these arguments. Certainly, it has yet to be proven, even in a statistical sense, that authoritarian-ruled countries are "more stable," "more unified," or "more impervious to outside forces." In fact, the reverse may well be true. At the same time, it is not the point of this chapter or, indeed this work, to argue for either the polyarchal or Marxist modernizer alternatives. Rather, it is our intention simply to indicate what we believe the types are and how they operate. The political systems described in Chapters 5, 6, and 7 all suggest political trade-offs, all have goals (some of which are attainable and some of which are not), and all have costs that go with the pursuit of those goals. As Aldous Huxley put it so well with regard to alternative political futures, "You pays your money and you takes your choice."[4]

[4]Aldous Huxley, *Brave New World* (New York: Bantam Books, 1966), p. xiv.

BASIC TYPOLOGIES

The authoritarian spectrum contains two basic typologies (which can be further subdivided)—the civilian-run oligarchies and the military-run governments—although there are a number of regimes that can be thought of as fusions of the two. In the cases we shall be examining, the differences are not as simplistic as they might first appear. The civilian oligarchies are currently headed by people who came to power prior to independence and simply kept it ever since. Most often, these civilian authoritarian patterns exhibit the trappings of their nonauthoritarian past—constitutions, political parties, "elections," and often some continuing legitimacy as the bringer of independence.

The military typology, however, involves elites who came to power since independence by a *coup d'état.* In fact, many of the current military regimes represent second and third "generation" *coups* which have had to create their own legitimacy (beyond their control of weapons) as rulers, not simply as overthrowers. This had led to a much wider variation in the style and role of military rule, ranging from caretaker governments of short duration, to mixed civilian-military cooperation governments, to regimes in which the military figures have created the same trappings as civilian regimes.

Although the regimes described below differ one from the other in a great variety of ways, all share the authoritarian characteristics outlined at the beginning of this chapter and are distinguishable from the governments described in Chapter 5. Moreover, the regimes treated here also lack the ideological basis as well as the holistic societal goals of the political systems described in Chapter 7.

THE CIVILIAN OLIGARCHIES

Malawi

A classic example of the authoritarian pattern is found in the present government of Malawi.[5] It is virtually a textbook version of the "ideal" authoritarian type outlined in the beginning of this chapter and rules five million people in this 36,000 square mile south central African country.

The president, Dr. Hastings Kamuzu Banda, is president for life. He rules despotically and virtually on personal whim. As the father of independence, Dr. Banda encouraged the breakup of the Central African Federation and the creation of Malawi in 1964. At independence, Malawi had a prime minister form of government and a modified version of polyarchal rule.

---

[5]For portraits of Malawi's past and present, see pages 281–282 of the Bibliography.

A new constitution was passed in 1966 which set a presidential form of government, with the chief executive chosen by the country's only party, the Malawi Congress Party (MCP), and called for the election of the president every five years. In 1970, this arrangement was abandoned and Dr. Banda was made life president.

The life president currently enjoys a number of political prerogatives which are worth mentioning. He appoints the Cabinet, the National Assembly, and the Judiciary. Although technically the National Assembly is chosen by the people, the most recent "elections" in 1976 produced few surprises. In fact, the results were published in the *Malawi News* in advance. The fact that the nation's only newspaper was totally owned by the life president undoubtedly lent the "election" announcement some credibility. The life president feels that actual polling is required only as the need arises. In 1976 the need did not arise.

The life president also holds the portfolios of External Affairs, Defense, Public Works, and Supplies, as well as Agriculture and Natural Resources. He is the head of the MCP, to which all adults must belong, and will brook no rivals. There is no position of vice president under the new constitution, and any government officials who appear to become popular are relieved of their duties (as was the former Minister of Tourism, Aleke Banda). In addition, Banda appoints all the traditional authorities, having evolved the doctrine that the chiefs lost all their power during the colonial period and were only reinstated through his efforts.

Dr. Banda runs the country with an iron hand. Dissent is not permitted. Internal censorship is extremely harsh and few outside journalists are permitted access to the society. Youth Brigades of the MCP operate all over the country and in conjunction with the 1,600-man army severely curtail internal movement. Harassment of the population, arbitrary arrests and executions are widespread, and thousands of citizens have fled to neighboring Zambia and Mozambique.

Banda, who was 71 years old in 1978, has steadily consolidated his power until his domination of the country is complete. Freedom of speech and association are unknown, and Malawians in exile have compared the country to one gigantic concentration camp.[6] Certainly, although other African dictators, such as Idi Amin, Jean Bokassa, and Macias Nguema, are more flamboyant, Banda certainly merits attention as a strong-willed despot whose word is law and whose country is tightly controlled.

Nevertheless, Banda's regime is not without support. His decade-long emphasis on agricultural development has been meaningful to the 85 percent of the population who live off the land. And he has elevated the status of women in Malawian society. Also, his confiscation of some Asians' property in 1975 and 1976 was not widely opposed. How long Banda remains in power is a

[6]Legson Kayira, *The Detainee* (London: Heinemann, 1974).

matter of conjecture, but it seems clear that for the moment his place in the civilian oligarchies of Africa is secure.

The Ivory Coast

Across the continent, on the west coast of Africa, is another authoritarian system, which is much less despotic than Malawi and enjoys much greater economic success. In Chapters 2 and 3, we outlined a variety of African political ideas and discussed the considerable variations contained under the title "African socialism."

In that context, we did not accent the Ivorian concept of what amounts to state capitalism. We did not go into the Ivorian concept in any detail because it remains almost idiosyncratic to the Ivory Coast and Gabon (and perhaps the "humanistic capitalism" of Liberia) and, more importantly, because there is little in the way of a formal body of writing about the philosophy *per se*. But in the sections that follow, it will be clear that the Ivory Coast remains a most interesting political system, not simply as a modified authoritarian typology, but for its almost unique accent on individual and corporate enterprise in modern Africa.

The Ivory Coast, which is approximately the same size as Great Britain, has nearly 7 million people.[7] Of these, 10,000 are Syrian or Lebanese in origin, and nearly 50,000 are Europeans (over half of whom have come since independence in 1960). The rest are Africans representing some 60 ethnic groups, ranging from traditionally segmented societies in the north to highly developed kingdoms in the south. The Ivory Coast came under French domination late in the nineteenth century, and it was not until after World War II that the forces seeking greater autonomy, and later, independence, began to stir.[8]

Following the failure of the French government to implement the colonial reforms suggested at the Brazzaville conference in 1944, Africans from the francophone territories met in 1946 at Bamako, then in the French Sudan, to form a transterritorial party, the *Rassemblement Démocratique Africain* (RDA). Each territory was to have its own branch under local leadership to promote political socialization and to galvanize popular support for the RDA.

---

[7] Further background can be found in the books listed on pages 278–279 of the Bibliography.

[8] For an in-depth analysis of decolonization in French West Africa, see Immanuel Wallerstein, *The Road to Independence: Ghana and the Ivory Coast* (Paris: Mouton, 1964); Virginia Thompson, "The Ivory Coast," in Gwendolen Carter (ed.), *African One Party States* (Ithaca: Cornell University Press, 1962), pp. 237–324; Ruth Schacter Morgenthau, *Political Parties in French-Speaking West Africa* (Oxford, England: Clarendon Press, 1964), pp. 166–219; Felix Houphouet-Boigny, "Black Africa and the French Union," *Foreign Affairs,* vol. 25, no. 4 (July 1957), pp. 593–99; Aristide Zolberg, "The Ivory Coast," in J. S. Coleman and C. G. Rusberg (eds.), *Political Parties and National Integration* (Berkeley: University of California Press, 1966), pp. 65–89, and "Mass Parties and National Integration," *Journal of Politics,* vol. 25, no. 1 (February 1963), pp. 36–48.

In the Ivory Coast, the RDA branch, the *Parti Démocratique de la Cote d'Ivoire* (PDCI) was led by Felix Houphouet-Boigny, one of the founders of the RDA, who was also a chief of the Baoule people and a medical doctor.

Because the RDA was initially supported by African and metropolitan communists and because it took an increasingly radical stance toward France, it was harassed by the French colonial administration and opposed by those Africans who were allied with the more moderate French Socialist Party (SFIO). Nevertheless, it soon emerged as the dominant political force in French West Africa. Then, in one of those antic situations so characteristic of French politics, it was the RDA which provided the votes necessary for the formation of a socialist government under Guy Mollet in 1956, after the Africans previously loyal to the SFIO broke with them to form a new transterritorial party, the *Independents d'Outre Mer.*

Yet, this success was to be the high water mark of the RDA, for it became increasingly subject to centrifugal forces; by the second Bamako Conference in 1957 it was in a state of internal disarray. The chief cause of the RDA's decline was a set of conflicting views held by its members concerning the future of French-speaking West Africa. While some of the territories, such as Senegal and the Sudan, favored the formation of a large, powerful federation, others, such as the Ivory Coast and Mauritania, demanded that the territories be linked individually to France.

The position of the antifederation forces was strengthened by the passage of the *loi cadre* of 1956. Written largely by Houphouet-Boigny, who was a minister without portfolio in the Mollet cabinet, the *loi cadre,* or enabling act, provided for universal African suffrage and, perhaps more importantly, extended greater authority to the individual territories, decentralizing power away from the federal structure. The coming to power of General de Gaulle in 1958 and the subsequent decision by Guinea not to remain in the French Community, also undercut those who favored a federation of French West Africa.

The leaders of Senegal and the French Sudan continued to push for the formation of a smaller union, however, subsequently named the Mali Federation, and they were initially joined by Upper Volta and Dahomey. The leaders of the Ivory Coast, encouraged by many French officials, opposed the federation on personal, political, and economic grounds and succeeded in applying sufficient pressure to force Dahomey and Upper Volta to drop out of the Mali Federation.[9] The Ivory Coast, again with French support, then formed a looser, primarily economic union with Niger, Upper Volta and Dahomey, the *Conseil de l'Entente.*

In sharp contrast to their counterparts elsewhere in Africa, the leadership

[9]William Foltz has written an excellent study of this subject: *From French West Africa to the Mali Federation* (New Haven: Yale University Press, 1965).

of the Ivory Coast resisted the lure of independence. Only after France granted independence to the Mali Federation did the Ivory Coast and the *Entente* states drift reluctantly to independence even while maintaining the closest of ties with France. When the Mali Federation broke up soon after independence in June 1960, the *Conseil de l'Entente* remained primarily an economic grouping.

The present institutional framework of the Ivorian political system was initially set in the constitution of 1960. Centered around a strong executive branch, the new constitution replaced the earlier parliamentary system which the Ivory Coast had inherited from the French Fourth Republic. The president of the Republic remains the exclusive repository of executive authority and there is no vice president or prime minister. Chosen by universal suffrage for a period of five years, the president is commander-in-chief of the armed forces. He makes all civil and military appointments and the Council of Ministers, or cabinet, is directly responsible to him.

The National Assembly of the Ivory Coast consists of 120 members chosen by universal adult suffrage from a single list prepared by the only recognized political party in the country, the *Parti Démocratique de la Côte d'Ivoire.* Members do not represent geographical constituencies, but are chosen by universal suffrage as part of a national slate. They serve for five-year terms and are supposed to represent the country as a whole and to be concerned with national issues.

Felix Houphouet-Boigny, who served as prime minister from 1959 until 1960, has been president of the Ivory Coast since independence. Elected in 1960, he was reelected in 1965, in 1970 (when he received 99.19 percent of the vote), and in 1975 (with 99.8 percent of the vote). There was no opposition. All members of the National Assembly since independence have been members of the *Parti Démocratique de la Côte d'Ivoire.* As there was no opposition, those elected in 1965, 1970, and 1975 received over 99 percent of the votes. In order to analyze the present course of decision making in the Ivory Coast, it is necessary to examine the rise to power of the PDCI and its leader, Houphouet-Boigny, and the gradual elimination of all organized opposition. For in the case of the Ivory Coast, authoritarianism came steadily and discernibly during both decolonization and the early years of independence.

During and after the 1944 local elections, several parties sprang up in the Ivory Coast, based on one or more of the 60 ethnic groups in the country. We have already mentioned how the PDCI became the territorial branch of the RDA. It was, from its inception, essentially a coalition open to a variety of occupational and ethnic groups. Despite the radical stance of the RDA, the bulk of its early support came from the African bourgeoisie, primarily those in the planter class and their major interest group, the *Syndicat Agricole Africain.*

Organized structurally along the lines of the communist party, the PDCI sought to create a "cell" in every village and every urban ward. Each cell was to have a central committee or *bureau* and a secretary general. The various secretary generals then met at the regional level in approximately 55 *sous-sections*, each of which had a *bureau* and a secretary general of its own. These, in turn, represented their districts at the national executive committee, the *Comité Directeur*, which was linked to the inner core of the party, the 15- to 25-member *Bureau Politique*, and the national secretary general. Since then, the *Bureau Politique* has gradually been expanded until it now totals over 100 persons.

Aristide Zolberg, whose *One Party Government in the Ivory Coast*[10] was a pioneering study of politics in Africa, indicates, however, that despite its modern orientation, the PDCI stressed primordial ties and that linkage within the party was actually based on ethnic groups, thus relating much of the political development to the existing traditional patterns outlined in Chapter 1. In many situations, the village and rural committees corresponded to existing ethnic groups. Where they did not, as in portions of the capital, Abidjan, they were created. Thus, during stages of its existence, the PDCI resembled the federative systems outlined in Chapter 1 in that members often belonged to the PDCI through their membership in those ethnic groups rather than as individuals, although many also belonged as individuals.

The use of these ethnic "building blocks" enabled the PDCI to mobilize large numbers of persons rather quickly and to galvanize popular support for its programs and personnel. It should be pointed out, however, that the PDCI was not simply a neotribal organization, one bent on preserving the status quo. Although it utilized the ethnic groups and encouraged traditional authorities to join it, only those who held "modern" views were allowed to participate in the decision-making process within the party. It was, and is, the ethnic groups, not individual tribal leaders, who are considered important in the Ivory Coast. This was true in the party itself, and later in the national government as well. Moreover, as economic development spurred the formation of associations and interest groups, these in turn were also both absorbed and represented, eventually forming a counterweight to the ethnic groups.

As the party with the greatest organization and the most prominent national figure, the PDCI jumped off to an early electoral lead, winning all 15 seats in the Ivory Coast Territorial Assembly and 94 percent of the vote in 1946. However, the militant stand taken by the RDA at the federal level and the formation of a series of smaller parties weakened the PDCI's power base. This, coupled with the jailing of many PDCI leaders by the French, led the

[10]Aristide Zolberg, *One Party Government in the Ivory Coast* (Princeton, N.J.: Princeton University Press, 1964).

party to what was to be its nadir in 1951–52, when it won but 1 of the 2 seats in the French National Assembly and 28 out of 32 seats in that of the Ivory Coast on the strength of 74 percent of the vote.

Reacting to this decline, Houphouet-Boigny and the PDCI leadership insisted that the RDA drop its Communist affiliations and expel the secretary general, Gabriel D'Arboussier. When the RDA did this in 1951, the PDCI set about rejuvenating itself—making its peace with the conservative elements in the political culture of the Ivory Coast by absorbing the smaller parties and their ethnic groups. By the elections of 1956 and 1957, the PDCI had regained its momentum and was again in a position of overriding strength as it won both seats in the French Assembly and 58 out of 60 seats in the Ivory Coast. Opposition within the country faded and in 1960, the PDCI presented the only list of candidates for election for the 100 seats in the enlarged assembly and 160 local offices. Its candidate for president, Houphouet-Boigny, received 1,586,518 out of 1,641,352 votes cast.

On the surface, there would seem to be a parallel between the rise of the PDCI in the Ivory Coast and that of TANU in Tanzania. Although there are basic similarities in the all-encompassing nature of their successes in the national arena, there are significant differences in their central goals, their relation to society, and their process of internal decision making. Whereas TANU's history has been a search for mass involvement in the politics of the party and the nation, as well as a drive toward polyarchal participation in both, the reverse has been true in the case of the PDCI. Decision making and leadership selection within the PDCI have always been hierarchal.

In theory, elections for party representatives are supposed to take place at regular intervals. In point of fact, such elections have seldom been held and most officials have, during the history of the PDCI, been appointed by the *Comite Directeur* and the *Bureau Politique.* On the national level, moreover, there have been but six party congresses since the PDCI was founded, none during the period 1950–59, and only two since independence. Even when these were held, their principal role seems to have been symbolic. Particularly during the formative years from 1949–57, all major decisions were made at the top by a small number of leaders, and at no time did the rank and file directly choose either their leaders or the goals of the party. The elaborate cell system and network of ethnic committees were used primarily as a set of communication channels to carry party decisions to the population at large, rather than as a method of leadership selection or policy formation. As opposition to the PDCI withered away or was absorbed, the process of hierarchical decision making within the party became intensified so that, by the time of independence the PDCI had become, in Zolberg's terms, a patronage regime—one we would label authoritarian.

In addition to a lack of democratic decision making within the party structure, the PDCI exhibited a drift toward a similar espousal of authoritarian decision making vis-à-vis the society. The PDCI, beginning as a patron party, took on mass party characteristics in the 1950s and then evolved into a party which could be classified as one for the masses. In short, rather than encouraging mass participation in the party and the decision-making process of the political system, the PDCI by independence regarded itself as "the only valid embodiment of mass will." The PDCI in effect ruled out democracy for the party and for the society. Held by the organization which was to enjoy a political monopoly, these views were to have profound implications for the kind of decision making which would evolve within the political systems as a whole.

> Democracy is a system of government for virtuous people. It seldom works even in very mature countries. Why should we expect it to work here? We must be realistic. Our people are ignorant of the problems we face. They cannot be left to choose the solutions to our overwhelming problems but must approve the alternative debated by an elite.[11]

This view of the people and the society, when coupled with the hierarchical tendencies within the party structure, transformed the nature of the PDCI. After independence, the PDCI as a party lost some of its *raison d'être*. It has attained independence and secured the president of the National Assembly. Reinforced by the 1960 constitution (which they themselves wrote), a small group of PDCI and government officials make the basic policy decisions for the entire system and tightly control access to the decision-making apparatus.

Great power is in the hands of Houphouet-Boigny. His trusted lieutenants hold the other positions of authority, not only within the various regulative agencies such as the police and the army, but within the government and the PDCI as well. The secretary general of the PDCI and president of the National Assembly, Philip Yacé, is his handpicked second in command. The president appoints the administrative heads of the 6 departments and 107 subprefectures which make up the central administration of the Ivory Coast. He selects the 35 members of the important advisory body, the *Conseil Economique et Social,* and with the *Bureau Politique,* chooses the members of the National Assembly. In point of fact, his power is as great as that of Banda in Malawi or Touré in Guinea, although he has seldom exercised it as arbitrarily as either of them.

The National Assembly of the Ivory Coast merits a closer examination because it is an interesting example of an institution which could have decision-making power in the system, but which does not. The tight control over the nomination procedure enjoyed by the PDCI center and the president, and the fact that the deputies do not represent regional power bases, but are selected

---

[11]For the results of this philosophy, see Martin Kilson, "Authoritarian and Single Party Tendencies in African Politics," *World Politics,* vol. 15, no. 2 (1963), p. 266. The quote is from Zolberg, *One Party Government,* pp. 253–54.

as part of a single slate by the entire country, militates against the National Assembly playing an independent (let alone opposition) role in the process of decision making. The process of rule formation is illustrative: the government generally proposes laws and submits them to a committee of the National Assembly, which examines them in the presence of a government official. The bills may be slightly modified before the government submits them to the National Assembly, but this is not always the case. In theory, the National Assembly may reject any proposed law. In reality, it has never done so. It has the slight power to delay passage of a particular bill by talking about it at length, but observers have pointed out that even here its power is minimal and it is not even a debating society.[12]

The National Assembly does fulfill some necessary functions in the Ivorian system, however. In the first place, its very existence helps to legitimize the system's democratic pretensions by giving "popular" approval to the laws of the land. Even though the National Assembly exercises virtually no decision-making power, the ritual of bill passage probably serves to aid the symbolic capacity of the regime.

Most important, the National Assembly serves as a patronage mechanism to coopt would be counter-elites and insure loyalty to the leaders of the system. The salaries, privileges, housing, and transportation allowances which accrue to members of the National Assembly are powerful inducements to loyalty. The president and the *Bureau Politique* are quite willing to shift membership to suit the changing political and social configurations within the system and to utilize its patronage to best advantage. The National Assembly also acts as a channel of communication whereby the major decisions of the government are passed on to the ethnic and interest groups which its members "represent." As pointed out above, this representation is more symbolic than real, but it does provide for a flow of information outward from the party-government center, and serves to legitimize the action of the government. These functions of the National Assembly are of importance, and aid in maintenance of order and stability, but they should not be construed to mean that the National Assembly is in any way instrumental in making the decisions for the political system.

The status of the National Assembly is illustrative of the attitude held by the political center toward groups and institutions whose personnel might seek access to the decision-making process, for subgroup authority in the Ivory Coast is limited. This is true of labor unions, students, and traditional authorities.

The political center in the Ivory Coast has been successful thus far in containing potential counter-elites and fragmenting their force. The position

---

[12]Robert Tice, "Administrative Structure, Ethnicity and Nation-Building in the Ivory Coast," *Journal of Modern African Studies,* vol. 12, no. 2 (June 1974), pp. 211–29.

of this small number of decision makers is reinforced, not only by the regulative and distributive capabilities of the system, but also by the prevailing ethos
of the society which they govern. The government has always stressed the need
for national unity in the following fashion: unity is essential for equality, for
national integration and for economic development. Unity keeps 60 or more
ethnic groups pulling together. Unity alone can prevent the tragedy of the
Congo or Nigeria. The Ivorian government, however elitist and authoritarian
it may be, provides that unity; it has been successful in appealing to this felt
need for unity and has often found it useful to regard any antigovernment
groups as posing threats to the unity of the nation and its not inconsiderable
economic progress. The PDCI government is able to appeal to what seems to
be a considerable fear within the society and to rally support on the basis of
that fear.

Yet, the power of the government is not complete.[13] As the situation with
regard to the labor and student movement indicates, there is some dissatisfaction in the political culture. The political structure, while authoritarian, is not
totalitarian. There are societal values that cannot, at least at this stage, be
tampered with.[14] For example, the PDCI government could not eliminate
"tribalism" in 1959, and during 1966, widespread opposition to the status of
"foreigners"'forced the government to drop its plans for extending dual citi-
zenship to the population of the *Conseil* states.

The government remains willing to bargain with individuals and groups
that are anxious to acquire a share of the spoils of the system. But the leadership of the PDCI government continue to see politics as a zero-sum game of
the greatest magnitude, and groups, whether ethnic or interest, will not be
tolerated if they seek control of the system. There are no ongoing, organized,
institutional, countervailing influences to PDCI governmental control; without any system of leadership selection or goal choice, such systems are not
likely to be forthcoming. In short, then, the decision-making process in the
Ivorian political system is limited to a small number of participants, mostly
handpicked by the president and his closest advisers. This elite prefers buying
off dissidents to regulating them, rewards to punishment, and economic largess
to force. It even forgives those who make mistakes and recant—if they will
rejoin on the government's terms. For example, Jean-Baptiste Mockey, who
was sentenced to death for his part in a 1963 "plot," was eventually reinstated
in 1975 as Minister of State for Health and Population.

At the same time, the government will brook no opposition of the type likely
to supplant its preeminent position, and is disinclined to loosen control over

---

[13] *West Africa,* June 26, 1965, p. 707. See also, Elliot J. Berg, "The Economic Basis of Political
Choice in French West Africa," *American Political Science Review,* vol. 54, no. 2 (June 1960),
pp. 391–405.

[14] Michael A. Cohen, "The Myth of the Expanding Centre—Politics in the Ivory Coast," *Journal
of Modern African Studies,* vol. 11, no. 2 (June 1973), pp. 227–246.

the decision-making apparatus of the system. The Ivory Coast has seen a number of antigovernment plots, most noticeably in 1963, 1970, and 1974. There remain pockets of dissatisfaction among some students, some intellectuals, and those in the northern region. But, overall, the Ivory Coast has few political prisoners (less than 100 in 1977) and very few political refugees. In fact, there are over one million non-Ivorians (from such places as Upper Volta, Guinea, and Mali) currently in the Ivory Coast.

How to explain the stability in the Ivory Coast? For one thing, the military has been kept under close control, both by the political authorities and by the presence of French troops. Fully 18 years after independence, the French fourth *Regiment Interarmée d'Outremer* is stationed at Fort Bouet, near the capital, and the Ivorian army of 3,100 men is simply not allowed continuous access to weapons.

In addition, the economy of the Ivory Coast is booming and its successes have undoubtedly prompted widespread satisfaction with the current regime. Since 1960, the growth rate has averaged an impressive six to seven percent a year and the per capita income is well over $600 a year, one of the highest in Africa. (Indeed, the Ivorian per capita figure is even higher since the million migrant workers from outside the country tend to fill the less desirable and lower-paying jobs.) The new five-year development plan which runs through 1980 calls for nearly $5 billion in new investments to spur agriculture, industry, and the country's infrastructure. The economy remains one of the most balanced in all of Africa, producing a wide variety of products such as sugar, cocoa, coffee, iron, palm oil, wood products, and various fruits as well as a broad range of manufactured goods. The economic philosophy of the Ivory Coast has also encouraged economic development. Deciding that major amounts of foreign investment, both private and public, were necessary if the Ivory Coast was to develop, the leaders set out to create a climate where investment would feel secure:

> We have no factories to nationalize, only to create; we have no commerce to take over, only to organize better; no land to distribute, only to bring into production.[15]

In the process, they developed an ideology which has been variously called "state capitalism" or "economic liberalism." Strictly speaking, it is not pure state capitalism for, in the Ivory Coast, the state does not take over any businesses or industries. In fact, the government goes out of its way not to compete with private enterprise and, although it insists on a share of the industry, it will not seek to replace the private interest at some future date. The government has seen its role as one of mediating between foreign investment

[15]William Derman, *Serfs, Peasants and Socialists: A Former Serf Village in the Republic of Guinea* (Berkeley: University of California Press, 1973).

and the domestic environment, and insuring that investment is suitably rewarded.

Toward this end, the government passed an extremely liberal investment code, *the Statut de la Fonction Publique,* in 1959, which provides for tax exemptions for from 5 to 25 years and virtually eliminates all restriction on the expatriation of profits. When coupled with the government's regulation of organized labor, the strong well-managed monetary policy, and the lure of substantial profits, this has made for a very healthy investment climate. Its pragmatic, *laissez faire* attitude toward foreign investment has, despite its political implications, been an outstanding economic success.

Gabon

Another authoritarian regime which is similar to both Malawi (in terms of the degree of despotism) and the Ivory Coast (in terms of economic development and philosophy) is Gabon. Located on the west coast of central Africa between the Congo and the Cameroons, it has a population of slightly more than 550,000 and an area of 102,000 square miles.

Its autocratic, one-party regime is headed by El Haj Omar Bongo. President Bongo, like Dr. Banda, does not believe in spreading his power around to subordinates. He is currently president of the Republic and head of the country's only political party, the *Bloc Démocratique Gabonais* (BDG). In addition, he holds the ministerial portfolios for National Defense; Information; Posts and Telecommunications; Plan, Development, and National Guidance; Civil Service; Popular Education; and Women's Advancement. He appoints the central committee of the party and the entire National Assembly of 70 people. His handpicked slate won 99.6 percent of the vote during the last elections in February 1973, and none is scheduled again until 1980. He presides over a strong presidential system, having taken the precaution of eliminating the post of vice president in 1975.

The economic growth of the country has been steady and impressive. Gabon is rich in timber, iron, manganese, uranium, and oil. Under Bongo's "directed and planned liberalism," or what he often calls "democratic and concerted progressism," there is state planning, but the bulk of development is left up to private (often foreign) firms. Gabon, like the Ivory Coast, has provided a very positive investment climate. Per capita income is currently the highest in Africa.

The Republic of Guinea

Compared to the three countries discussed above, the Republic of Guinea stands as revolutionary, socialist-oriented dictatorship. With the process of decolonization hesitantly underway in French Africa during the 1950s, Sekou

Toure of Guinea emerged as a leader in the fight for independence, first as the leader of Guinea's most militant trade union within the *Confederation Generale du Travail* (CGT) and later the *Parti Democratique de Guinee* (PDG), a militant branch of the RDA. Unlike the situation in the Ivory Coast, the RDA branch was opposed by two other groups, the Guinean sector of the *Mouvement Socialiste Africain* (MSA), led by Barry Ibrahima, and *Bloc Africain de Guinée* of Barry Diawadoe.

Touré's more militant approach and his early call for complete independence made the PDG the most popular party and led to Guinea's resounding "no" vote in 1958 on a referendum concerning whether or not the country should remain under French tutelage. France cut all ties with the fledgling nation and Guinea, alone of all the francophone countries, was cast adrift. At the time, there was great excitement and hope that an independent Guinea could develop a just society, more equitably distribute the wealth, and become a true democracy.

Certainly, Touré's initial emphasis on a "non-exploitive socialist regime" and his concern for the peasants and masses, as well as his firm anticolonialism, seemed to suggest that a more decent and equitable society would develop. Indeed, his political thought, ". . . an amalgam of Marxism, Africanity, populism and ideals,"[16] seemed to suggest his concern for a fairer and more just human collectivity.

But embedded in Touré's many published works,[17] and certainly in his actions, there is a strong totalitarian bent and he has consistently opposed any expression of individual or group interests.[18] For Touré, society is to be organized, directed, and controlled, so that only through the principle of democratic centralism can the individual find the opportunity to assert his views.

This basic political philosophy, coupled with the internal machinations of Guinean politics and the intrusion of exogenous forces,[19] quickly led Touré to adopt a radical form of authoritarianism—one which has steadily increased in terms of its intense dictatorship and capricious application. At the present time, it remains a powerful and cogent example of a personal authoritarian regime exemplifying Marxist slogans, an economy in ruins and a hollow shell of political favoritism.

[16]Lansine Kaba, "Guinean Politics: A Critical Overview," *Journal of Modern African Studies,* vol. 15, no. 1 (March 1977), pp. 25–45.

[17]Sékou Touré, *La Guinee et L'Emancipation Africaine* (Paris: Présence Africaine, 1959); *L' Afrique et la Revolution* (Paris: Présence Africaine, 1966); *Guinean Revolution and Social Progress* (Cairo: Société Orientale de Publicité, 1963); and *Guinee: Prélude à l'Indépéndance* (Paris: Présence Africaine, 1958).

[18]Charles Andrain, "The Political Thought of Sékou Touré," in W. A. E. Skurnik (ed.), *African Political Thought* (Denver: University of Denver, 1968).

[19]See pages 263 and 278 of the Bibliography. Also, Margaret Dobert, "Who Invaded Guinea?" *Africa Report* (March 1971), pp. 16–18.

Over the years, Touré has taken for himself a wide variety of titles designed to enhance his own personality cult. He is the "Faithful and Supreme Servant of the People," the "Doctor of Revolutionary Sciences," and the "Liberator of Oppressed Peoples." He is the supreme political authority and his opinions become laws "as they are uttered."[20] He hand picks the special *Conseil National de la Révolution* and the *Bureau Politique National* of the PDG as well as the 150-member National Assembly.

Even by African authoritarian standards, elections are in a class by themselves. Not content with the "normal" 90 percent turnouts and 99 percent approval votes associated with most authoritarian regimes, Touré insists on unanimity. For example, in 1974, of the 2,436,487 Guineans registered to vote, no less than 2,432,129, or an astonishing 99.89 percent turned out, and 100 percent of those turning out voted for Touré and his candidates for the National Assembly.

In addition to choosing the National Assembly and the inner circle of the PDG, Touré also appoints the regional governors for each of Guinea's 33 districts. He is commander in chief of the 5,550-person army and the 8,000-person people's militia. In addition, he presides over one of the most extensive security systems in sub-Saharan Africa.

What have been some of the results of Touré's approach to politics? Certainly, widespread discontent is well documented. His 16 years of brutality and Draconian measures have led to over 100,000 exiles in Senegal, the Ivory Coast, and France. This represents a substantial number of people out of a total population of less than 5 million. Rigid censorship, rigid control over internal and external travel, and the constant use of security personnel increase his dominance over the people who remain.

The economy is in a shambles. Although Guinea had over 25 percent of the world's bauxite as well as diamonds, gold, and iron, its economy is on the verge of bankruptcy. And although much of its land is fertile and its people industrious, agricultural production has declined markedly since independence. Food production has fallen since independence and Guinea is now an importer of 60,000 tons of rice a year. Strange and contradictory state planning, capricious administrative decisions, and constant meddling by party functionaries are all debilitating factors.

There is also the matter of widespread corruption:

> The members of the governing elite, as the beneficiaries of the system do not experience shortages, and can buy all items at official prices. They can even afford late car models and beauty frills. This group's life and prosperity contrast with the hardship and poverty of the population, and are inconsistent with the P.D.G. ideals of equality and justice.[21]

[20]Kaba, "Guinean Politics," p. 34.
[21]Ibid., p. 40.

Indeed, it is not the authoritarian bent of Touré which seems so tragic, nor the abuses of power. It is precisely the contrast between the realities of the present situation and what was promised and sought prior to independence. Guinea was not a neocolonial creation, nor a political puppet. Rather, it is a revolution betrayed. The bright and shining hope of a better society and a new world of equality and justice submerged under the weight of a personal dictatorship: "The magnitude of autocracy contradictory to all democratic ideals has destroyed individual initiatives and rights, and has produced a Kafkaesque world generally unknown to outsiders."[22]

The Guinean revolution, spawned in hope and exhilaration, is betrayed by the very people who promised to bring it about, and to substitute political repression for democracy is galling, particularly to those Guineans who hoped for so much and who received so little. To have the hopes crushed and replaced by brutality, even toward the children, is what makes the Guinean case so sad to people: "No, no," my father cried, with a gesture of protest. "Our regime puts our children before a firing squad for the slightest thing."[23]

But Guinea is not unique. In fact, perhaps the most capricious and violent of the civilian dictatorships is to be found in Equatorial Guinea, between Gabon and the Cameroons, where Life President Macias Nguema (now Masie Nguema Biyogo Ndong) stands astride a regime of terror. Soon after independence, he abolished parliament, the courts, political parties, and elections and set himself up as the sole arbitrator of human activity in the country. Mass arrests, wanton killings, incredible brutality, and ongoing public executions have led to a situation where fully one quarter to one third of the population has already fled the country. There are currently 60,000 refugees in Gabon, 5,000 in Nigeria, 6,000 in Spain, and 30,000 in the Cameroons, out of a total population of 300,000 people. Without a doubt, this is one of the highest ratios of refugees to total population in the entire world.

THE PRAETORIAN IMPULSE: THE MILITARY TAKES POWER

It is 2 A.M. in the capital city of one of Africa's new nations. The streets are almost deserted as two jeeploads of soldiers arrive at the presidential residence. Several dozen armed men go through the gates and into the residence. They seize the president and capture his bodyguard. At the same time, other soldiers have seized the radio station and an armed squad has taken over the airfield, closing it to incoming traffic.

[22]Ibid., p. 32.

[23]Camara Laye, *A Dream of Africa* (New York: Collier Books, 1971), p. 188. In 1977, the International League for Human Rights charged that terror and torture had become "commonplace" in Guinea.

When the citizens of the new nation wake up, they will learn that the previous government has been overthrown and that a new Revolutionary Council, headed by military personnel, has been formed "to wipe out corruption and get the country moving again." By noon, the airfield will be open again and shops and market stalls will be doing business. Another African government has been overthrown by the military.

This hypothetical description could depict any of the dozens and dozens of military *coups* which have been such an intrinsic part of the African scene since the mid-1960s. In fact, next to attaining independence itself, military takeovers have been the most widely experienced political phenomenon in the last 20 years of African history.

Ironically enough, few observers of independence in Africa either studied the military or predicted their massive involvement in the political life of the new states. Most observers of the African scene concentrated on the political leaders who had emerged as the founding fathers. These "new men," the Nkrumahs, the Tourés, the Senghors, and the Nyereres were virtually all civilians with no military backgrounds. These political figures and the mass parties which they founded or led seemed to presage electoral politics, competition by ballot, and civilian rule into the indefinite future. Considerable academic debate swirled around whether one-party or multiparty rule would be the most effective, or whether mass parties could be used to stimulate economic or political development. Few bothered to do more than dismiss the future role of the armed forces, citing their small numbers, the lack of external threats, and their apparent docility.

But in the decade from 1966 to 1976, there were more than 100 *coups* and *coup* attempts in sub-Saharan Africa. In fact, by 1978, more than half the countries on the continent were controlled by the military or had been for substantial periods of time. Mali, Niger, Upper Volta, Benin, Togo, Nigeria, Chad, the Central African Republic (now Empire), the Congo, Zaire, Uganda, Rwanda, Burundi, Somalia, Ethiopia, Mozambique, the Sudan, and Guinea-Bissau. Even Angola, nominally headed by a civilian, could be classified as a "military in power" state,[24] and Sierra Leone, now under civilian government, had spent a number of years under military control. In a number of instances —such as Ghana, Nigeria, or Congo—the military had been in power longer than had civilians since independence.

The military in Africa quickly went from being understudied to being overstudied. In fact, the long list of books outlined in the Bibliography on the "Praetorian Impulse" clearly indicates the extent to which the military has

---

[24]The problems of classifying Guinea-Bissau, Angola, and Mozambique will be covered in Chapter 7 but in all three the military elements were responsible in large part for the political movements coming to power. The armed forces' continuing dedication to the revolution remains one of the key variables in those new states.

become a growth industry in academic circles.[25] Although most of these studies are somewhat deficient in analyzing just how the military ruled once it seized power, many are very helpful in putting the rash of *coups, coup* attempts and counter-*coups* in perspective.

Why did the military intervene in so many African states and why have military regimes proved to be so long-lived? Part of the answer is to be found in the analysis at the beginning of Chapter 5, where we outlined the extent to which political decay had enervated the existing civilian regimes. For whatever else the widespread military intervention signalled, the wholesale involvement of the military in the political life of Africa and the ease with which it supplanted the political authority in a majority of independent African states indicated the fragility of most of these systems and the extent to which political decay and the erosion of democracy and polyarchal politics had already occurred. Despite the dissimilarities among the various political systems and the motivation behind individual army officer's intervention, the systems in question had all been enervated by considerable political decay and devolution.

In a context where the civilian authorities lost control of the situation, allowed no safety valve elections, permitted widespread corruption, and were unable to deliver on their promises, the military emerged as a powerful counterweight. Also, as the introduction to this section suggests, small numbers of armed men were all that it took to overthrow most of the political systems, and with the exception of such situations as Nigeria, most *coups* were relatively bloodless.

In the section that follows, we shall examine the course of military intervention. Before we begin, however, a word of caution is necessary. It should be remembered that in any political situation, whether civilian or military dominated, the military does play a role in politics. This may be an indirect role, but at the very least, all societies that have standing armies have political situations in which the military competes with other groups in the society for scarce resources such as manpower, capital, or equipment. Thus, as Claude Welch and A. K. Smith have written, ". . . the military's political role is a question, not of whether, but of *how much* and what kind."[26] In the next section, we analyze why the military chose, in so many African situations, to intervene more directly and to replace the civilian authorities.

Motives for Intervention

Why did the military intervene in so many situations? It is almost impossible to tell if one relies on the statements of the military themselves. No matter what the real motivation for a particular *coup*, virtually all claimed that a

[25]See page 260 of the Bibliography.

[26]Claude Welch, Jr. and A. K. Smith, *Military Role and Rule* (North Scituate: Duxbury Press, 1974), p. 6.

desire to stop "widespread corruption" motivated them. And almost all claimed to be "revolutionary" even if they were, in fact, reactionary! But, looking beyond the rhetoric of the *coup* makers, it is possible to see a number of factors which induced the military to intervene. It should be remembered that the motives listed below are not mutually exclusive and often the particular military officers moved for several reasons (or different officers within the same group moved for different reasons). In any case, there are at least a dozen reasons why the African military decided to replace the civilian authorities.

1. Although we have indicated how virtually all *coup* perpetrators cited the corruption of the previous regime as a decisive factor in their intervention, in a number of cases there is no doubt that the military officers were genuinely upset about corruption and saw themselves as societal instruments to change that situation. Many officers who participated in the 1966 Ghanaian *coup* against Nkrumah, as well as those who moved in Somalia's 1969 *coup,* did so because they felt the civilian regimes in question has gone beyond a point of no return in terms of corruption.

2. Sometimes the military intervened because the political system had completely broken down and was unable to function. Again, we have stressed how some degree of political decay had already occurred in most systems prior to the military involvement. But in several instances the political devolution went beyond inefficiency and corruption to a state bordering on paralyzed anarchy. The military intervened in order to hold the system together. Concern over the total collapse of the system was a considerable factor in the 1966 Nigerian *coup,* the *coups* in Congo-Kinshasa in 1960 and again in 1964, and in Ethiopia in 1974.

3. On the other hand, at times the military seems to have moved for no other reason than that the army itself was getting short shrift. This took the form of a military fear that they were being replaced by another institution (most often a people's militia) or that they were not getting proper equipment or uniforms. In fact, several key officers in the Ghanaian *coup* of 1966 expressly cited specific grievances (such as "worn-out boots") as reason.

4. But if some army personnel moved against the civilian authorities because they felt they had legitimate grievances in terms of protecting the army as an institution, still others intervened because the civilian authority was about to discipline them—about to move against inefficiency or corruption in the army itself. Certainly the 1971 *coup* in Uganda sprang in part from fear on the part of some officers, particularly General Amin, that their malfeasance was about to be punished.

5. Sometimes the military intervened because the existing civilian regime seemed to be pursuing an ideology which was either alien to, or unwanted by, the officers in question. Civilian regimes that swung to the "left" were replaced (as in Ghana, 1966; Mali, 1966; or the Central African Republic, 1966). So were civilian governments that either swung to the "right" or failed to move

to the "left" (as in Dahomey, 1972; Togo, 1963; and Upper Volta, 1966). And
there were instances in which the military moved against "feudal" systems (as
in Burundi, 1966; and Ethiopia, 1974). Regardless of whether accurate or
inaccurate, the officers' appraisal of "right" or "left" or "feudal," their ideological perceptions were a substantial factor in their actions.

6. The military men often intervened, however, simply because of internal
rivalries. As Thomas S. Cox has suggested, cleavage within the military themselves ". . . probably forms the basis for most *coups* in Sub-Saharan Africa."[27]
This is something of an overstatement, but it does indicate the extent to which
military men have been capable of acting for internal motivation (such as why
brigadier X was promoted over officer Y) and was undoubtedly an ongoing
factor in those countries where there were a series of *coups,* with military men
replacing military men.

Military rivalries can be pinpointed as the major motivation in a number
of cases, such as the second Nigerian *coup* in July 1966, the successful Nigerian
coup in 1975 (and the unsuccessful attempt in 1976), as well as others in
Dahomey, Togo, and Sierra Leone. Perhaps the classic example occurred in
February 1975 when the Malagasy Head of State, Colonel Richard Ratsiman-
drava, who had just replaced General Gabriel Ramanantsoa (whose own *coup*
succeeded in 1972), was assassinated by the Malagasy Mobile Police Group,
who then put other officers in power.

7. In addition to individual rivalry within the military, there is also motivation which springs from ethnic sources. Thus, officers from one tribe will try
to seize power, not simply on personal or societal motivation, but for ethnic
reasons. The July 1966 *coup* in Nigeria was an anti-Ibo movement within the
officer corps. Several of the *coups* in Dahomey's tortured history have been
ethnically inspired and various *coup* attempts (and successes) in Ethiopia have
been inspired by ethnic opposition to the long-dominant Amhara.

8. Sometimes the military has intervened, not simply to replace a civilian
regime or to change the direction of domestic or foreign policy but, in fact,
to make major societal changes—in fact, to make a revolution. In Chapter 7,
we shall be dealing with Somalia, which is a classic example of where the
military reacting to corruption of the civilian authorities, also had in mind a
grand design for society and wanted to revolutionize it. Military officers in
Ethiopia have, since 1974, also shown this motivation.

At the same time, one should be wary of revolutionary rhetoric by the
military. Certainly, the current regimes in Benin and the Congo sound like
revolutionaries, but their militaries have been quite conservative in terms of
domestic societal transformation. Ali Mazrui and others have pointed out that,
despite their assertions, many military men aim, not at modernization, but at

---

[27]Thomas S. Cox, *Civil-Military Relations in Sierra Leone* (Cambridge, Mass.: Harvard University
    Press, 1976), p. 12.

retribalization, or "retraditionalization," of society (as in the Uganda *coup* of 1971).[28]

9. There is also the element of exogenous intrusions. In a number of situations in the African context, outside forces have been a factor in *coup* motivation. It seems less important whether country X went out and recruited officers a, b, and c in order to make a *coup,* or whether officers a, b, and c came to the representatives of country X and asked for either (1) help in planning or carrying out the *coup* or, more likely, (2) recognition once the *coup* had been carried out.

Soviet support for the 1969 Somalia *coup* is well known, as is American involvement in the 1960 and 1965 *coups* in the Congo-Kinshasa. Colonel Ngoubi did not move in Congo-Brazzaville without assurances of French support, and General Amin sought and received Israeli assistance in planning his *coup* against Milton Obote. This is not to say, of course, that all African *coups* (or even a major portion of them) are the result of outside interference. In fact, it is somewhat belittling to Africans to assert that they cannot plan and carry out their own *coups* without foreign assistance. But there can be little question that different countries prefer, for a variety of reasons, to see different elements in various societies control the government, and exogenous intrusions have been a factor in enough instances to warrant close scrutiny.

10. There is also the military motivation to be an "arbiter" in society. That is, military officers have intervened in African countries, not to seize power or to transform society or, even, to strike out at corruption; but rather, merely to arbitrate among feuding factions within the civilian sector. In Sierra Leone, for example, the army moved in 1967 because the results of the election seemed to result in possible instability. In Dahomey and in Togo, for the better part of a decade, the army has slid in and out of power as civilian factionalism has increased or decreased.

11. The military has also intervened because individual army officers have wanted to make personal power grabs. Although these individuals have always clothed their actions in terms of improving society or reducing factionalism, in point of fact, the real motivation has been personal aggrandizement. The *coups* in 1967 and 1970 in Dahomey, Uganda in 1971, Togo in 1963 and 1967, and Congo-Brazzaville in 1968 all had substantial elements of personal power grabs whatever else they may have involved and whatever the diverse motivations of some of the figures in the *coup.*

12. Finally, there is the matter of *coups* stimulating other *coups,* not just within a country (although that seems to be an influence as well), but from

---

[28]Ali A. Mazrui, "The Lumpen Proletariat and the Lumpen Militariat: African Soldiers as a New Political Class," *Political Studies,* vol. 21, no. 1 (March 1973), pp. 1–12. For an interesting view of the role of African armies in traditional situations, see David Chanaiwa, "The Army and Politics in Pre-Industrial Africa: The Ndebele Nation, 1827 to 1893," *African Studies Review,* vol. 19, no. 2 (September 1976), pp. 49–67.

country to country. What Ruth First has called "the contagion of the *coup,*"[29] where the occurrence of a *coup* in country X stimulates the military in country Y to think about staging their own *coup.*

This has certainly been a factor in the spread of *coups* throughout tropical Africa. Nor is it surprising when one considers that most contemporary officers who staged the first round of *coups* in the 1960s had similar backgrounds and often trained together in Britain or France. They knew each other as individuals and by example even when they returned to their own countries to begin by serving the very civilian authorities they eventually overthrew.

These various motivations, then, provide much of the thrust for the involvement of the military in overt seizures of government. Taken together, they provide a host of variables and, as Henry Bienen has indicated, the widespread incidence of military *coups* and the tremendous variation in motivation make it very difficult to generalize about what caused African *coups.*[30] As he points out, military *coups* have come from little armies and big armies;[31] armies that

[29]Ruth First, *Power in Africa* (Baltimore: Penguin Books, 1972), p. 20.

[30]Henry Bienen, "Outline of Military Rule in Africa," unpublished paper.

[31]As of 1977, the size of Africa's armed forces, according to the International Institute for Strategic Studies, ran from zero to over 208,000:

State	No. of troops
Congo (Peoples Republic)	5,500
Ethiopia	44,800
Ghana	15,450
Kenya	7,550
Nigeria	208,000
Rhodesia	5,700
Somalia	23,000
South Africa	50,500
Tanzania	14,600
Uganda	21,000
Zaire	43,400
Zambia	5,800
Cameroon	5,600
Chad	4,200
Dahomey	1,650
Guinea	5,650
Ivory Coast	4,100
Liberia	5,220
Malagasy	4,760
Malawi	1,600
Mali	4,200
Mauritania	1,250
Niger	2,100
Rwanda	3,750
Senegal	5,900
Sierra Leone	2,125
Togo	1,750
Upper Volta	2,050
Gambia, Botswana, Lesotho	no armed forces

were well organized and those that were not; army leaders who were trained in the United States, the Soviet Union, China, Great Britain, Belgium, and France; and societies where there was widespread instability and where there was little instability. Interstingly enough, the fact that we cannot generalize about the causes of military intervention indicates how widespread they are and how diverse their motivation, and it is to the role of the military in power that we now turn.

The Military in Power

There are many works that investigate how the military came to power, but there have been few books dealing with the military *in* power. This is the case even though some countries, such as Ghana and Nigeria, have been under military rule for longer periods of time than they have been under civilian authorities. Part of the problem deals with access. Many military regimes simply do not foster the kind of research climate in which an investigator can operate, and many of the decisions made by the military authorities are made behind closed doors (and in some cases, with principal decision makers unknown). Consequently, our portrait of military rule in Africa is far from complete. At the same time, enough work has taken place concerning the outcome of military rule to enable us to make some generalizations about what the military has—or has not—done as opposed to how the decisions were made.

First, military regimes have been, on the average, no more stable (or unstable) than the civilian regimes they replace. In a number of instances, such as Sierra Leone, Togo, Dahomey, Ghana, and Nigeria, the initial military *coup* in turn sparked a number of additional *coup* attempts, civil disorders, and even successful counter-*coups*. The military, once having undermined the authority of the civilian political system, found that its own sources of legitimacy were often quite weak, especially within the armed forces themselves.

Second, although virtually all military rule in sub-Saharan Africa was at least ostensibly established to eliminate corruption, in point of fact, the military rulers of sub-Saharan Africa have proven no less corrupt than the civilian regimes they replaced. There have been exceptions, such as the 1969 *coup* in Somalia, which brought to power almost puritanical officers who sharply reduced corruption. But, for the most part, the military regimes differed only in the matter of degree, as witnessed by the two military regimes in Ghana which succeeded "corrupt" governments under Nkrumah and Busia. And, if one looks at the levels of corruption in military Nigeria, Zaire, or Congo-Brazzaville, one can conclude that at least some military regimes have made it virtually an art form.

Third, although most military *coups* have been justified by a need to "get the country moving again" in terms of economic development, military regimes have simply not proven very successful in promoting economic development. No military regime in Africa can match the economic growth rate of, say, the Ivory Coast or Gabon; and Zaire, potentially one of the richest countries in Africa, has, after more than 12 years of military rule, come to the brink of bankruptcy. In fact, *per capita* income has actually declined under military rule. Likewise, the economic picture in Uganda and Dahomey (Benin) has darkened since the military came to power.

All in all, as Samuel Decalo has concluded, ". . . military rule has not proved to be significantly different from civilian rule."[32] What distinguishes military rule from civilian rule, then, is the origin and style of the ruling elite, not its outputs. In this context, it is interesting to note that there is a great deal of structural variety among the more than 20 military governments in Africa, and it is necessary to get below the surface of their statements (and even their outputs) in order to see how they operate, to check on the workings of military rule in Africa.

The Modalities of Military Rule

In what is probably the most important work to date dealing with the differences and similarities of military rule in Africa, Decalo has developed a set of given categories, or "modalities" of military rule.[33] Although we have considerable problems with the classification of a number of African states into the precise category suggested by Decalo, this may be in large part the result of the particular time cut, for military regimes, like their civilian counterparts, evolve over time. And, as will be developed in the conclusion of this chapter, by adding additional categories, it is possible to refine the typologies to include virtually all military governments in sub-Saharan Africa.

Decalo's first category is the *praetorian*. In a praetorian system, the military's rule is hierarchical and authoritarian, but the central core of authority is weakened by "acute societal and military factionalism."[34] That is to say, whichever military men currently hold power, they must spend most of their time worrying about and preventing plots against their continued rule.

In the praetorian type of system there is little societal consensus. Within the ruling military elite there are factions, cliques, and rival groups. Instability is widespread. There is a mixture of civilian and military actors in the political sphere since the military makes no attempt to replace all civilians, but the cleavages within the government and society militate against any meaningful societal program, economic development, or the creation of a stable political system.

---

[32]Samuel Decalo, *Coups and Army Rule in Africa: Studies in Military Style* (New Haven: Yale University Press, 1976), p. 240.

[33]Ibid., p. 240.

[34]Ibid., p. 243.

This typology very clearly describes the political systems of Congo-Brazza-ville, Dahomey (Benin), and the Malagasy Republic. All have exhibited over the last 15 years consistent signs of insecure authoritarianism; that is, a politi-cal situation devoid of civil liberties, no choice of leaders by nonleaders, and no political competition *except by rival cliques.* Likewise, in Mali, in November 1968, a group of young Malian officers overthrew the government of Modibo Keita, who had led Mali since its independence eight years before. Lieutenant Moussa Traoré soon became the head of the military junta called the Military Committee of National Liberation. Despite fragmented opposition from some students, younger civil servants and former members of the ruling party, the regime ruled until the present although there were a number of attempted *coups,* most noticeably in 1972. Decalo quite rightly suggests that this type of system simply cannot be expected to produce meaningful change as long as the factionalism continues. Return to civilian rule is tentatively set for 1979.

A second group of African systems clearly falls into the category of *personal dictatorship.* Here, the system is highly authoritarian, highly personal. The military takes power as it does in the praetorian system, but the rule is not collegial. Rather, a single strong man emerges and ends up completely domi-nating the original junta.

In this personalist type, the cleavages within the armed forces are eradicated by the leader and the boundaries between civilian and military sectors are blurred. The dictator purges dissenters from both groups and uses whatever means are necessary "to coerce, punish, purge or liquidate officer cliques or even entire army strata."[35] As a result of these purges, the army as an institu-tion is not as highly regarded as it is under the praetorian typology because it is subject to the same tyranny as the civilian sector. The basic structure and routine of the army is upset and personal favoritism helps individuals just as liquidation hurts others.

This type of army rule is inherently unstable, even though it may last a long time, for the individual leader is not able to institute his rule beyond his moment-to-moment decision making. There is a lack of economic or political development as the military dictatorship overshadows all activities.

The personal dictatorship typology is very useful for it enables us to see that such diverse regimes as Uganda under General Amin, the Central African Republic (Empire) under Colonel Jean Bokassa, Burundi under Colonel Michel Micombero, and Zaire under General Mobutu Sese Seko are markedly similar in terms of the modalities of rule.

Uganda under General Amin is a classic case in point. In the first place, there was substantial decay in the political system prior to the army *coup* as a direct result of what Nelson Kasfir has called the "pervasive spread of departication."[36] The government of Milton Obote had undermined its legit-

[35]Ibid., p. 245.
[36] Nelson Kasfir, *The Shrinking Political Arena* (Los Angeles: University of California Press, 1976), p. 227.

imacy by adopting a number of ideological positions which alienated many citizens and by crushing the Kabaka of Buganda, Sir Edward Mutesa. Most importantly, Obote went off to a Commonwealth conference after giving the army clear signals that General Amin was guilty of a number of crimes and was likely to be punished upon his return.[37]

Once in power, General Amin proceeded to develop almost a caricature of the personalist dictatorship outlined by Decalo. Holding all power to himself, he brutally subjugated this 91,000-square-mile country of over 12 million people. First, he liquidated all Acholi and Langi members of the armed forces and police, and replaced them with members of his own tribe, the Kakwa, and The Nubians (Nubi) from the southern Sudan.

In a well-documented reign of terror, Amin unleashed various groups and caused a country-wide blood bath until "There is no area in Uganda where people have not been killed. There is no clan in Uganda where blood has not been shed."[38] Upwards of 100,000 people were killed by 1978 and tens of thousands fled the country. The economy was devastated and Amin continued to use torture and massacres to stay in power. He escaped a variety of assassination attempts and plots.

In Zaire, the regime of Mobutu Sese Seko is a variation on this theme. Although the levels of political violence subsided since the 1960s, Mobutu has ruled this huge, sprawling country (two-thirds the size of western Europe with 25 million people) since 1964 by regularly purging the army and destroying his civilian and military enemies although seldom executing his opponents. In the process, he has amassed a huge fortune and runs the government on a day-to-day basis. For added amusement, he has formed the only political party in the country, the Popular Revolutionary Movement (MPR) which can accurately be described as neither popular, nor revolutionary, nor a movement.

In Burundi, 10 years of horror were at last punctuated by a *coup* in December 1976 when Colonel Jean-Baptiste Bagaza overthrew Michel Micombero. Micombero took over this 10,000-square-mile country with 3.5 million people in 1966, after assisting Natare, the son of the Mwami Mwambutsa IV, in taking over the government from his father. Micombero moved to establish himself, purged the army, and, in a bloodbath of epidemic proportions, encouraged the slaughter of 200,000 Hutus and drove another 100,000 into exile. While Micombero cannot be held totally responsible for the ethnic hatred between the 84 percent of the population who are Hutus and the 14 percent who are the ruling Tutsis, he actively encouraged the massacre of all "educated" Hutu in an operation bordering on genocide.

[37]David Martin, *General Amin* (London: Faber & Faber, 1974).

[38]Ibid., p. 231. In 1977 the Commonwealth heads of government, led by many African states condemned Uganda for "excesses so gross as to warrant the world's concern and to evoke condemnation by heads of governments in strong and unequivocal terms." The International Commission of Jurists said the death toll in 1971–72 was over 80,000.

In the Central African Republic (Empire), the personalist dictatorship of Colonel, then President, then President for Life, then Field Marshal, then Emperor Jean Bokassa likewise continues to hold sway over a population of 3 million in this 236,000-square-mile country in north central Africa. Emperor Bokassa currently holds 14 out of the 16 ministries in the CAR and his repeated purges of the army, as well as the arbitrary arrest, torture, and killing of civilians are well established.

Decalo's third military modality is that of the *managerial brokerage system.* In it, the military comes to power in order to arbitrate disputes among various sectors of society, such as the politicians, the civil servants, and the labor unions. Once in power, the military continues to see its primary function as moderating or managing conflict and, by doing so, promoting stability and economic development.

In this type of system, the status of the army is far higher than that of the personal dictatorship. Moreover, the boundaries between the civilian and military sectors are firm. Military personnel are there to keep society on an even keel and to prevent one group or another from upsetting the system, but they are not interested in running the entire society. Thus, the civil service is often left intact, even if some of its overall demands are curtailed. The military is not anxious to turn power back to civilians, but neither does it see itself taking over the workings of the entire government and society. The military continues to function properly as an institution—promotions are routinized and there are military-performance criteria for commands. In the managerial typology, there is considerable stress on economic development so that the competing groups can each get additional material satisfaction.

Decalo argues that military regimes of this type, such as that of General Eyadema in Togo and the present military government in Chad, can be quite stable and can actually promote a degree of economic development even as they leave the society more or less intact.

Decalo's praetorian, personal dictatorship, and the managerial brokerage systems are useful in helping us to distinguish the various kinds of military rule in Africa. His final two categories, the *bureaucratic modality* and the *holding operation system,* are less helpful. Indeed, the differences between them are small, and are based in large part on the author's perception of what the military ultimately plans to do. For Decalo, the holding operation category is simply that, the military intervenes to prevent bloodshed, anarchy, chaos, or even the disruption of essential services, but it has no long-term interest in running society. In fact, the military says—and means—that it wants to return government to civilian control when conditions have changed.

The holding operation model certainly describes a number of situations in tropical Africa. In Ghana, following the 1966 *coup,* there was never any real idea that the military government of General Ankrah would remain indefinitely in power and it moved relatively quickly to restore civilian rule (even though it made sure that the forces of the previous Nkrumah government did not emerge victorious in that transition). In Upper Volta, the government of General Lamizana also fits this pattern.

In the bureaucratic modality, the army has less well defined plans to retire from the political scene. Even though individual officers may articulate the desire to return to the barracks, or even though the military government seems to be saying that it will eventually turn power back to the civilians, there is a real question as to whether or not it will actually do so (unless forced to).

In any case, in the bureaucratic modality, the army becomes more highly enmeshed in the actual running of the government and military personnel assume a variety of roles, becoming, in the words of Ed Feit, "armed bureaucrats."[39] Other writers have accurately noted the difficulties faced by the military in this situation; Anton Bebler suggests that "The military lacks the political instruments to shoulder the task at which the civil leaders with political parties at their disposal failed."[40] J. M. Lee sees the problem, in part, a problem of legitimacy, "The successful *coup* may be either a corporate act or a group action. Neither form of intervention need oblige all sections of society to recognize a common system of politics."[41]

These problems become exacerbated when the military tries to take over the running of the country for an indefinite period of time. The army may attempt to rule directly through military officers, it may attempt to coopt some civilian to assist and add legitimacy, or the military men may try to create new political parties and structures in order to develop the legitimacy lacking from the regimes.

The difficulties with the Decalo models at this end of the military spectrum is that some regimes are very difficult to place precisely. Take the case of Nigeria, Africa's most populous nation with over 70 million people, it has been under a variety of military regimes since 1966 and, despite many claims to the contrary, the military has still not relinquished control.[42] Let us look into the operation of the Nigerian government to see its operational style and to suggest some of the difficulties in labeling it simply a "holding operation."

In 1960, Nigeria began independence with an apparently firm polyarchal tradition with a variety of competing parties, the Action Group (AG), the National Council of Nigerian Citizens (NCNC), the Northern Peoples Congress (NPC), and a variety of others. Yet regional and ethnic divisions soon undermined the unity of the country. The NPC dominated the government of Federal Prime Minister Abubakar Tafawa Balewa and corruption became

[39]Edward Feit, *The Armed Bureaucrats* (New York: Houghton Mifflin, 1973).

[40]Anton Bebler, *Military Rule in Africa* (New York: Praeger, 1973), p. 211.

[41]J. M. Lee, *African Armies and Civil Order* (New York: Praeger, 1969), p. 185.

[42]The Nigerian situation has been widely reviewed. See pages 284–285 of the Bibliography. Guy Arnold has written as late as 1977 that the failure to return to civilian government was a major issue in Gowon's fall: Guy Arnold, *Modern Nigeria* (London: Longmans, 1977), p. 17.

widespread. A key census in 1963 (on which the next parliament was to be based) was widely rigged and the elections in 1964 and 1965 became a farce. Many Yoruba-speaking people in the western region and Edo-speaking peoples in the eastern region felt left out of the political process and there was widespread political violence.

In January 1966, a group of young Ibo officers from the northern region staged a *coup,* led by Major Chukwuma Nzeogwu. Clearly, the plotters had a variety of motives. Some were genuinely appalled at the incompetence and corruption of the civilian authorities. Others wanted to see the Ibos play a greater role in the affairs of state, and still others simply wanted to establish a new regime which included themselves.

Whatever the mix of their intentions, the fact that the *coup* leaders killed Prime Minister Balewa, the Sardauna of Sokoto (the important Hausa leader of the north), and Chief Akintola (the prime minister of the western region), but no Ibos, gave the *coup* very strong ethnic overtones. Intra-army struggles led to the leadership of General Johnson Aguiui-Ironsi, who had not been part of the original *coup,* and who reasserted army control over the young Ibo officers. General Ironsi might have been able to hold the country together but, as an Ibo, he was highly suspect, especially when he took no action against the original perpetrators of the *coup.*

In July 1966, a group of northern officers staged a second *coup,* killing General Ironsi and unleashing a savage series of pogroms in the northern region. Thousands of Ibos were massacred, including all those Ibo soldiers who were not able to flee to the eastern region. The new head of state, Lt. Colonel Yakabu Gowon, although a Christian and from a minority tribe in the north, attempted to carry on negotiations concerning a new governmental structure. But the Ibos in the east, led by Colonel Odemegwu Ojukwu, declared the independence of the region in May 1967, calling it Biafra.

A bloody civil war ensued as a number of great powers scrambled to intervene. Egypt, the USSR, and Great Britain supported the federal forces, while France and Portugal assisted Biafra. African states were themselves divided over the war. Most countries favored the federal position, with such notable exceptions as Tanzania, Zambia, the Ivory Coast, and Gabon recognizing Biafra. Gradually, the federal forces crushed the eastern region and in January 1970 the war ended.

Despite widespread fears of massacres, the federal government fairly administered the captured region, and General Gowon is largely credited with insisting on a just peace. But he was unable to solve the problem of corruption, army malfeasance, and tremendous disparities in wealth spurred by Nigeria's vast oil revenues, and despite many promises to do so, made no real attempt to turn the government back to civilian control. In 1975, he was overthrown while attending an Organization of African Unity conference in Kampala.

The new military government was headed by Brigadier General Murtala

Mohammed, a 37-year-old Hausa, who embarked on a vigorous anticorruption campaign. Within a year, he was assassinated, so it is impossible to know whether his efforts would have succeeded or whether he would have returned the country to civilian rule by 1979, as he had promised. His death aroused a backlash within the army and those responsible for his assassination were captured and killed. A Supreme Military Council, led by General Olusegun Obasanjo (a Yoruba) pledged to follow Murtala's policy and return the government to civilian rule.

Claude Welch and Arthur Smith have quite rightly pointed to the "problem of withdrawal" in the Nigerian context.[43] The military has stated that it wants to return the country to civilian rule, but considerable problems remain. Corruption is virtually a national way of life. A new census conducted in 1973 suggests that the inflated results of 1963 are not a thing of the past, for many districts, especially in the north, claimed population increases of 80 to 90 percent. The number of states in the federal system has been increased to 19, but there is a controversy over whether or not this is too few or too many.[44] The army, still swollen at over a quarter of a million men, may be difficult to bring under civilian control.

A constitutional commission, formed in 1976, recommended a presidential system as the most likely to solve Nigeria's problems. It called for universal suffrage at 18, a president and vice president elected directly by popular vote, and a two-house legislature—a 350-person House of Representatives and a 95-person Senate. At the time of this writing, it remains to be seen whether the military will actually move toward civilian rule and, if so, what form that civilian rule will ultimately take. For the moment, skeptics may well want to reserve judgment based on the military's inability or unwillingness to return the reins of government to civilians, or to move from what is currently a bureaucratic modality to what would have been a true "holding action."

Another interesting variation on the bureaucratic modality is to be found in neighboring Ghana. Ghana, which came to independence in 1957, had civilian government until 1966, and again from 1970 to 1972. When the current leader, General I. K. Acheampong, overthrew the elected government of Dr. Kofi Busia and his majority Progress Party, he claimed to have done so because of corruption and mismanagement. Since then, Acheampong's government has oscillated between the holding operation modality and the bureaucratic model. It claims, on the one hand, to want to return to civilian control and, on the other, insists that civilian rule must not take any of the "previous forms."

[43]Claude Welch, Jr. and Arthur Smith, "Nigeria: Moderate Reform and the Problem of Withdrawal," in their *Military Role and Rule* (North Scituate: Duxbury Press, 1974), pp. 112–41.

[44]Omolade Adejuyigbe, "The Size of States and Political Stability in Nigeria," *African Studies Review*, vol. 16, no. 2 (September 1973), pp. 157–82.

Most recently, Acheampong seems to have favored a further entrenchment of the military in power (as suggested by the bureaucratic model), but with the inclusion of the civilian sector on at least some decision-making roles. This "union government," as currently proposed, would be a melding of civilian and military rule in order to produce a regime with wider support and greater efficiency. Although many Ghanians appear to favor a return to a straight civilian government, a union arrangement might have the advantage of at least giving the civilians some standing with the military authorities, who have previously not held civilian regimes in high regard.

Acheampong's willingness to consider a sharing of power may in fact be due to nothing more than a realization that the solutions produced by the military thus far have simply not solved Ghana's problems. Although the country gained in food self-sufficiency early during the Acheampong regime, inflation is very high (currently approximately 50 percent a year), the staggering foreign debt from the Nkrumah era still stands at over $500 million, and corruption and smuggling are widespread. A union government might well give the military an opportunity to more widely spread the blame for the failure to solve these problems although in July 1977, General Acheampong announced that July 1979 would see the end of military rule under some new political system as yet undecided.

Although the Decalo typologies are a useful point of departure in helping us understand the various types of military regimes and the differences among them, much more work needs to be done in terms of research into existing military regimes and in terms of the development of new typologies to cover the rich diversity of existing military forms. Certainly, one additional category is already required: a situation where the military comes to power, not simply to wipe out corruption or to gain control over the government or to enrich the members of the ruling junta, but, rather, to completely revolutionize society and, once in power, proceeds to act accordingly. In these systems, the military works to reduce the boundaries between the military and civilian sectors by pursuing revolutionary goals by radical means. Society is to be transformed, not simply governed. The military and their quasi-political cadres are to take society completely apart and put it back together again.

Unlike the military in Decalo's typologies, the military has concrete ideas about how to transform society and, in most cases, a definite ideology, usually with Marxist principles. Thus, they differ from other military regimes, both in the thrust of their goals and in the existence of a concrete ideology to guide their actions and, more importantly, justify and legitimize them. In the next chapter, we will be dealing with these military revolutionaries in Somalia, Ethiopia, Mozambique, Guinea-Bissau, and Angola.

7

The Marxist Modernizers and the Future

When the first generation of texts dealing with politics in independent black Africa appeared, most political forms then in existence were those inherited directly from the colonial power. As we have seen, in the course of the next 20 years, African leaders evolved a number of political patterns which by and large replaced the colonial legacies. The considerable diversity of forms was examined in Chapters 5 and 6. Here, however, we are interested in the relatively recent development of African governments based on Marxism. This phenomenon was simply not present when the earlier works were published. Now there are a variety of Marxist-inspired governments in a number of contexts and these have sparked a great deal of interest, not only in and of themselves, but as "models" for Africa's future.

The existing diversity and multiplicity of alternative political patterns would seem to obviate any single form becoming a model for the 50 or so countries on the continent but, historically, there has been a series of rolling patterns which has dominated the political life of Africa at various stages.

212

Often, these different patterns have been heralded as "models" so it is not surprising that the latest of these, the Marxist modernizers, would also attract considerable attention.

During decolonization, the prevailing political pattern was one of multiparty electoral competition with generally polyarchal characteristics. After independence, as a general rule, the multiparty arrangement was superseded in most countries by the development of a single-party form which dominated the early 1960s. As we indicated earlier, for the most part, these single-party forms were characterized by authoritarian decision making and often resulted in the withering away of political activity and the ironic corollary of a "no-party" state.

If the first wave of political forms was multiparty in character, and the second single-party in focus, the third wave can quite properly be called the praetorian impulse. Over much of the continent, military men intervened directly in national politics, overthrowing single-party, multiparty, and no-party states throughout the late 1960s and early 1970s. The ubiquitous nature of the African *coup* and the multiplicity of political forms which it spawned suggested to many observers that the military was in fact the model for African statecraft.

But just as the civilian-run, single-party state was widely regarded as the model for African political life in the 1960s only to be overtaken by the praetorian model, so in its turn, the traditional military regime was supplanted by the advent of various avowedly Marxist regimes. First Congo-Brazzaville, then Dahomey, then Somalia, then the Malagasy Republic and the three former Portuguese territories of Guinea-Bissau, Mozambique, and Angola declared themselves to be Marxist states. A new wave of political forms had arrived and soon these in their turn were heralded as "models" for African political life.

In this chapter, we seek to examine the Marxist phenomenon and to assess its relevance for the future of Africa. The task is not a simple one. In the first place, there is considerable confusion in separating governments that use Marxist jargon but that are not revolutionary in any real sense of that word. Secondly, there is the problem of becoming. For the most part, even those governments that are actually bent on a Marxist revolution of their societies have not accomplished this as yet. The observer is faced with the difficult assignment of making guesses as to the likely outcome of the Marxist governments' attempts to alter society. Finally, and perhaps most difficult of all, is the determining delicate balance of how much of a particular effort is Marxian and how much is mere modernization.

On the face of it, the Marxist modernizers could be regarded as a mere variation on the authoritarian patterns outlined in Chapter 6. But we would argue that the existence of the Marxist blueprint for the radical transformation of society and the philosophical underpinnings which it provides for the regime in question (especially in terms of legitimacy) makes it qualitatively different from the other authoritarian patterns. In addition, there is the accent on political development—that is, on the generation of a political party which is to serve as the vanguard of the revolution. This clearly runs counter to several of the trends noted in most authoritarian contexts, where political development is not regarded as a principal goal and where the mere survival of the ruling clique is most likely to be the central political motivation.[1]

The Marxist modernizers are also characterized by a strong attachment to uncompromising, one-party rule, in keeping with Stalin's strategy of "revolution from above." The party acts on *behalf* of the people and the ruling elite is arranged in overlapping fashion in terms of parallel organization of both the party and the state. They believe in the notion of democratic centrism, the inevitability of class conflict, and the ultimate triumph of the communist system.

In terms of the revolution, the Marxist modernizers are committed to the nationalization of industry, media, communications, educational and medical institutions, as well as to the "harmonization" of society through the creation of a large public sector in which the state centralizes all economic decisions. Critical to their theory of the revolution is the additional nationalization of all land and the leveling of the differences between one class and another. In practice, this also implies the collectivization of farms and the integration of individual farmers into state cooperatives. In addition, it involves massive involvement in the process of political socialization in which the educational system is used to infuse new values and to create a new type of citizen dedicated to the ongoing revolution.

Because of the newness of the phenomenon and the present inchoate nature of the revolutions themselves, it is important to distinguish among those governments claiming to be Marxist and those using Marxist terminology to describe political occurrences. In our judgment, such countries as Benin, the Malagasy Republic, and the Congo People's Republic are not now true Marxist governments. This is not to say that they could not become so in the future, but for the present all three seem to conform far more to the praetorian typology outlined in the last chapter than to the pattern of Marxist-inspired modernization depicted here. Therefore, we have not included detailed studies of these three governments in this chapter.

Nevertheless, there are at least five African states which fit the pattern of Marxist modernizers in that their leadership is committed to, and is actually attempting, vast societal and economic reorganization in accordance with the ideology of Marxism-Leninism. Three of the countries, Guinea-Bissau,

---

[1]This is not to say that Marxist leaders are any less concerned about holding onto power. Rather, it is to suggest that operationally the formation of a functioning political party suggests a fundamental difference in approach from the more traditional authoritarian patterns.

Mozambique, and Angola, have governments which came to power during the decolonization period through armed struggle. This not only gave the leadership its quasi-military quality, it also meant that the leadership itself emerged during the period of actual warfare. For the leaders of these three countries, independence was not (as it was for most African countries) "given"; instead, it was fought for during a decade-long struggle. As a corollary, the leadership in these three countries thus had a long period of trial and testing, during which the revolutionary principles were tried and in the liberated zones, the revolution was in some real sense, actualized.

In the other two countries, Ethiopia and Somalia, the leadership (which now seeks to implement a Marxist revolution) did not emerge during the decolonization struggle. Instead, both groups came to power by more or less conventional military *coups* and only after being in power did the leaders adopt Marxism as a philosophical and political guide. In one sense, Ethiopia offers somewhat analagous conditions to those which pertained in the former Portuguese territories (although the ruling class was indigenous) in that a privileged class dominated the economy and society as well as the polity. Furthermore, the emergence of Marxism as a viable political strategy occurred in the context of a vast and continuing civil war.

SOMALIA

In the sections that follow, we shall examine the present course of politics in Somalia, Ethiopia, Guinea-Bissau, and Mozambique.[2] We begin with Somalia because it seems to be the most unusual of the five. For one thing, it would seem to lack many of the critical ingredients that sparked revolutionary activity elsewhere: there is no indigenous land-holding class to be overthrown. Society was traditionally egalitarian and, for males at least, strongly polyarchal. The consuming poverty of the country means there is little to nationalize. In addition, the Somali political system was the most intensely polyarchal of any on the continent prior to the military *coup* of 1969. Yet, the Somali system is currently undergoing the most thorough of revolutions.

To understand the Somalia experience, it is necessary to have a good deal of background. The present Somali Republic currently encompasses 246,000 square miles and has a population within its internationally recognized borders estimated at 3.2 million people. Unlike most African countries, the Somali Republic's population is virtually homogeneous, with the vast majority of its people ethnic Somalis.

---

[2]We do not deal with Angola except in passing, in large part because the presence of some 12,000 Cuban troops suggests that the government there is currently struggling to maintain itself and that considerable portions of the country are under the sway of the forces of UNITA, who continue to challenge the legitimacy of the present regime. This is, of course, not to say that the Marxist modernizers in that country may not ultimately triumph.

In addition to those Somalis who live in the Republic, there are over a million other Somalis who are under the jurisdiction of Ethiopia (over 500,000), Kenya (over 250,000), and the newly independent Djibuti (over 60,000). These Somalis occupy another 125,000 square miles of territory. Linguistically, ethnically, culturally, and psychologically, these Somalis consider themselves part of a great Somali nation and the present leadership of the Somali is dedicated to their eventual incorporation. In fact, the Somali flag contains a star with five points to symbolize the five centers of the Somali people (two of which, British Somaliland and Solia, have already merged).

The Somalis, a pastoral nomadic people with a long and proud warrior tradition, moved into the Horn of Africa over a long period of time. Their traditional political system was a classical segmented one and the far-flung Somali clans seldom combined against their myriad foes. Their nomadic life, their relatively small numbers, and their segmented political structure and internecine warfare militated against a common front.

Following the opening of the Suez Canal in 1869, European interest in the strategic possibilities of the area increased. European involvement in the Horn coincided with Ethiopian expansion under Menelik II; protection treaties with local chiefs, the establishment of refueling rights, and the gaining of concessions led, rather inexorably, to physical occupation. By the turn of the century, there was a French Somaliland, a British Somaliland, an Italian Somaliland, and an Ethiopian Ogaden. Although individual Somali leaders were parties to many of the protection treaties, the formal occupation of the Horn was actualized in the various treaties between the French and the Ethiopians (1887), the British and the Ethiopians (1887, 1897), the British and the French (1888), the Italians and the Ethiopians (1889, 1891, 1897), and the Italians and the British (1894, 1905, 1924).

Somali opposition to colonial rule flared into open rebellion on various occasions, the most famous and long-lived instance being the jihad of Sayid Mohammed Abdullah Hassan. From 1900 until 1920, the religious-nationalistic movement which he led struggled against the Italians, Ethiopians, and, most persistently, the British. Following his death in 1920, the colonial authorities reasserted control. We have already described the British and Italian colonial styles in Chapter 2. In the case of British Somaliland, the British confined themselves to doing as little as possible. The Italians did introduce plantation agriculture to Somalia and developed a modest physical infrastructure, but their resources and energies were diverted into their Ethiopian operations after 1935. After the conquest of Ethiopia, the Italians administered the Somali-inhabited Ogaden from Mogadiscio, Italian Somaliland. When they likewise occupied British Somaliland after the outbreak of World War II, the Italians brought the Somalis under a single government for the first time in their history. Thus, despite the colonial overtones, this brief period is remembered by the Somalis as evidence of their essential unity as a people.

A British counterattack eventually regained the area during 1941. Uninspiring as subsequent British rule was economically, it did permit, even encourage, political activity, particularly of an anti-Italian variety. The Somali Youth Club and the Patriotic Benefit Union sprang up in 1943 and became the Somali Youth League and the Hisbia Digil Mirifle respectively in 1947. The British, in the person of Ernest Bevin, then Foreign Secretary, also stimulated Somali ambitions by proposing the creation of a "Greater Somalia" to unite all the Somalis in the Horn of Africa. However desirable this plan might have been from the Somali point of view, it was opposed by the other colonial powers (as well as by the British Colonial Office) and undercut by the British-Ethiopian agreements of 1942 and 1944 and the beginnings of the cold war.[3]

Eventually the Ogaden region was returned to Ethiopia (1948) and it was decided to likewise cede the Haud and the Reserved Area of British Somaliland to the same power in 1954, control of the area of British Somaliland having reverted to Great Britain in 1941. When a Four Power Commission could not agree on the future course of the former Italian area, the matter was turned over to the United Nations. During 1949, the General Assembly approved a trusteeship agreement whereby Italy would administer the territory, now known as Somalia, for ten years under United Nations supervision. The instructions to the administering authority, the *Amministrazione Fiduciaria Italiana della Somalia* (AFIS) were clear:

Foster the development of free political institutions and promote the development of the inhabitants of the Territory towards independence; and to this end shall give the inhabitants of the Territory a progressively increasing participation in the various organs of Government.[4]

Italy and the United Nations are widely credited with encouraging both political and economic development and with maintaining a stable arena within which multiparty democratic politics could take place.[5] Suffrage was even-

[3]C. P. Potholm, *Liberation and Exploitation: The Struggle for Ethiopia* (Washington, D.C.: University Press of America, 1976). See also the Somali point of view, *The Somali Peninsula: A New Light on Imperial Motives* (Mogadiscio: Government Printer, 1962); and Benjamin Rivlin, *The United Nations and the Italian Colonies* (New York: Carnegie Endowment for International Peace, 1950).

[4]United Nations, *Draft Trusteeship Agreement for the Territory of Somaliland Under Italian Administration,* Supplement #10 A/1294 (1950), p. 5.

[5]Those interested in an examination of this period should consult I. M. Lewis, *The Modern History of Somaliland* (New York: Praeger, 1965), chapter 7; A. A. Castagno, Jr., *Somalia* (New York: Carnegie Endowment for International Peace, 1959), chapters 1 and 2; and Saadia Touval, *Somali Nationalism: International Politics and the Drive for Unity in the Horn of Africa* (Cambridge, Mass.: Harvard University Press, 1963), chapter 7. See also Laurence S. Finkelstein, *Somaliland under Italian Administration: A Case Study in United Nations Trusteeship* (New York: Woodrow Wilson Foundation, 1955); Mark Karp, *The Economics of Trusteeship in Somalia* (Boston: Boston University Press, 1960); Gilbert Ward, "Somalia: From Trust Territory to Nation 1950–1960," *Pylon,* vol. 26, no. 2, pp. 173–86; and Robert Gavin, "Economic and Social Conditions in Somaliland Under Italian Trusteeship," *International Labor Review,* vol. 66, no. 3 (September 1952), pp. 25–26. See also the works listed on pages 286–287 of the Bibliography.

tually extended to all and Somalis gradually took over control of the army, police and the civil service. Politics throbbed and a plethora of parties sprang up.

In the series of municipal, district, and national elections which took place during the decade from 1950–60, the Somali Youth League emerged as the most powerful and widely supported of the parties. One of its leaders, Abdullahi Issa, headed the first Somali government and served as prime minister during the period of internal self-government (1956–60). At independence, July 1, 1960, the former Italian area merged with British Somaliland (which had attained independence five days before) to form the Republic of Somalia.

At the time of independence, the Somali political system was led by a president who was chosen by the National Assembly (which consisted of 122 members who were elected for five-year terms by universal adult suffrage). There was also a prime minister, likewise chosen by the National Assembly. In this context, the individualistic, polyarchal, outspoken nature of the Somali people was given free reign. No less than 130 political parties sprang up over the next six years and electoral politics became a highly competitive, constantly shifting kaleidoscope of alliances, factionalism, and political intrigue, in which clan and lineage concerns dominated. Corruption was widespread.

In all of this, kinship groups were of as much significance as the parties themselves. For, although Somalis see themselves as a true and homogenous people, they are also cognizant of divisions among themselves, divisions of a genealogical and an occupational nature. There is, for example, a pronounced distinction between the Somalis who think of themselves as Samaales and those who think of themselves as Sabs. The majority Samaales are essentially nomads who occupy the areas north of the Uebi Scebelli river and south of the Giuba. The Sabs are the descendants of those Somalis who settled between the rivers, intermarried with the Bantu-speaking and Galla peoples, and became, over time, farmers who kept livestock rather than true pastoralists. The broad distinction between Samaale and Sab can be overdrawn, however. There are, for example, among the Samaales some sedentary Hawiyes and farming Isaqs. Overall, 70 percent of all Somalis are pastoralists, 20 percent are primarily engaged in agriculture, and 10 percent are in commerce.

The Sabs and the Samaales are themselves broken down into clan families, clans, primary lineage units, and dia-paying groups.[6] There are two major Sab clan families—the Digil and the Rahanweyn—and four Samaale groups—the Darod, Hawiye, Dir, and Isaq. Generally speaking, each clan family is able to trace its ancestors back 30 generations and ranges in size from 500,000 persons (Dir) to over 1.5 million (Darod).

[6]For further detail, the interested reader should consult I. M. Lewis, *A Pastoral Democracy* (London: Oxford University Press, 1961); and Castagno, *Somalia,* from which the following section is drawn.

Somali clans are smaller, ranging in size from 10,000 to 100,000 persons, and can trace their common ancestry back perhaps 20 generations. Examples of clans would be the Dulbahante of the Darod clan family, the Iise of the Dir, and the Galgial of the Hawiye. Although many of the Sab clans have a territorial base, Samaale clans do not have as rigidly defined territory and move across the Horn of Africa in search of grazing land and water. Clans are further divided into primary lineage groups or subclans. These are able to trace their lineage back 6 to 10 generations. As was outlined in Chapter 1, there are seldom formal offices of leadership among the primary lineage groups. Marriage usually takes place outside the primary lineage group but within the clan or clan family. Society is basically patrimonial and patrilocal although the husband often uses the grazing and water rights of his wife's lineage.

Below the subclan is the dia-paying group. Depending upon its location and the ecological situation, the dia-paying group may range in size from 120 to 9,000 males. By the late 1950s there were over 950 recognized dia-paying groups in Somalia, plus 361 in Somaliland.[7] Dia-paying groups were originally fighting units of Somali males, consisting of "close kinsmen united by a specific contractual alliance whose terms stipulate that they should pay and receive blood compensation (Arabic, *diva;* Somalia, *mag*) in consort."[8]

In the harsh struggle for life in the Horn of Africa, where the margin of survival was seldom wide and every able-bodied man was needed, the Somalis tended to use compensation of camels and other livestock wherever possible. Joining a band to reduce one's liability was essential. By accepting a common share of the fortunes of a dia-paying group an individual would no longer stand alone, he would have protection, status, and a place in the society. The process of identification with one's dia-paying group is centuries old and has not died out with the thrust of modernity, for the dia-paying group represents the primary building block of Somali society.

Quite obviously, in Somalia kinship is of vital concern in placing an individual in society and providing him with a reference point. To this extent, the Somali system was essentially ascriptive. But there was—and is—another side to life as a Somali. Somali males are born into genealogies over which they have no control, but they also enter into contracts or compacts (which bind them to other persons) and social clusters (which join societal segments by specifying the kind and degree of interaction). Contracts are made, and broken, between individuals and groups and between groups. Allegiances shift, alliances are formed and dissolved. There is also a strong achievement orientation to Somali life even though ascriptive elements place broad limits on the process. Struggling in a hostile environment, the Somalis are highly competitive. They are,

[7]I. M. Lewis, "The Northern Pastoral Somali of the Horn," p. 517. General Barre "outlawed" the practice of dia-paying in 1976.

[8]Lewis, *Modern History of Somaliland* (New York: Praeger, 1965), pp. 166–67.

generally speaking, active rather than passive, and conditioned to accept achievement as well as birth as social determinants.

With this qualification, and it is an important one, clan and kinship may well be viewed as the primary forces which shape Somali social and political life. The links of kinship are both vital and pervasive:

> No other single line of communication and common interest connected so directly and incontrovertibly the pastoral nomad in the interior with his kinsman in the civil service, in the National Assembly, or in the Cabinet itself. No other bond of mutual interest had so many far-reaching ramifications in all aspects of private and public life.[9]

In this context, the clan and lineage loyalties stimulated the formation of political parties and tended to perpetuate the societal cleavages along kinship lines.

Aden Abdullah Osman, who was the first president of the Republic, was a Hawiye, while the prime minister, Dr. Abdirashid Ali Shermarke, was from the Darod clan. Dr. Shermarke served as prime minister from 1960–64 and president from 1967–69 (until his assassination). Abdirzag Haji Husseyn, also a Darod, was prime minister from 1964–67; Mohammad Haji Ibrahim Egal served as prime minister from 1967–69. Not surprisingly, General Siad Barre, army commander from 1965–69, was also a Darod.

Somalia's Political Parties

During its polyarchal phase (preindependence until 1969) Somalia's political system was exemplified by a vibrant party system with a great variety of individual parties and complex electoral politics. Of the 130 parties (many of them ephemeral) which sprang up during this period, there were 3 or 4 major ones that attracted relatively wide support.

The most important of these was the Somali Youth League (SYL). Formed in the 1940s, it underwent a period of Hawiye-Darod hegemony to become a national coalition encompassing a wide variety of ethnic groups. During its initial formation, it enjoyed British support, not only in British Somaliland, but in Italian Somaliland and Kenya as well. In contrast to British policy in Tanganyika, civil servants were allowed, even encouraged, to participate in politics. When the Somali Youth League publicly pressed for Four Power (U.S., British, French, and Russian) rather than purely British control over Somalia, however, Great Britain banned the SYL in Kenya and incarcerated its leaders.

The Somali Youth League was initially led by the more progressive towns-

---

[9]Touval, *Somali Nationalism,* p. 95.

men in the territory and opposed "tribalism" even though it subsequently modified its stand on this issue and adopted a policy of "ethnic balance." It stood categorically for the union of all Somalis irrespective of existing international frontiers:

> We wish our country to be amalgamated with the other Somalilands and to form one political, administrative and economic unit with them. We Somalis are one in every way. We are the same racially and geographically, we have the same culture, we have the same language and the same religion. There is no future for us except as part of a Greater Somalia.

It was always the most national of the parties and its strong showing in the early elections of the 1950s enabled the SYL to form the first Somali government in 1956. From 1956 until the *coup* in 1969, the SYL leadership generally formed the majority of the decision-making elite although it has shown a remarkable ability to change that elite internally and to absorb a variety of counter-elites and leaders of would-be pressure groups. In fact, the internal dynamics of the SYL have provided as much a basis for national politics in Somalia as has the interplay between the SYL and the other parties (thus giving it something of the flavor of TANU or KANU). Each president and every prime minister since independence has belonged to the SYL at the time of their selection even though several came from other parties initially. The SYL relies heavily on the clan organizations to provide its party organization at the local level.

A second party of note and the one Somali party with a transnational rhetoric and ideology was the Somali Democratic Union. Formed by Haji Muhammad Hussein in 1962, the Somali Democratic Union (SDU) has adopted a basically socialist platform and would seek to replace the tribe with the state as the basic welfare institution in Somali society. In this regard, it has generally espoused a position urging the confiscation of foreign investment in Somalia and opposed Somali contact with the European Economic Community. Haji Hussein was himself a president of the SYL during 1956–57, but for personal as well as ideological reasons, he quarreled with the then prime minister, Abdullahi Issa, and the chairman of the legislative council (and later president of the Republic), Aden Abdullah Osman. Haji Hussein then formed the Greater Somali League (GSL) which, in turn, was split over Hussein's militant espousal of pan-Arabism and socialism. Haji Hussein was subsequently joined by some members of the Somali National League and the United Somali Party (each of which was a coalition of parties from the former British Somaliland). The new party was called the Somali Democratic Union.

The GSL won 36 seats in the municipal elections of 1958 but boycotted the National Assembly elections of the next year, charging political harassment. The SDU won 15 seats in the March 1964 general elections but lost support by 1969. Even though the SDU was unable to match the appeal of the SYL in the countryside, it played the important role of devil's advocate and offered policy alternatives to the electorate. Because it challenged some of the fundamental assumptions of the ruling coalition, the political context of Somalia was undoubtedly richer for its existence.

A third major party was the Somali Independent Constitution Party, or the *Hisbia Destour Mustaquil Somali* (HDMS). Founded as the *Hisbia Digil Mirifle* (HDM) in 1947, this party has acted as a major pressure group, representing the interests of the Sabs. Based among the riverine peoples, it originally urged the administering authority to adopt a federal constitution for Somalia, one which would have protected its agricultural interests against pastoral hegemony. When this effort failed, the HDMS party attempted to broaden its appeal to non-Sab groups and changed its name to the Somali Independent Constitution Party.

This tactic was not an outstanding success and it did not enlarge its political position since it won 13 national seats in 1956. Along with the GSL, the HDMS boycotted the 1959 elections, but some of its leaders ran for public office, were elected, and subsequently joined the SYL-dominated government of 1960. Although the HDMS did win 9 seats in the 1964 national elections, its strength decreased further as it continued to function primarily as a Sab-oriented pressure group, gaining 3 seats in the 1969 elections. It voted for or against government proposals depending upon how they would impinge upon the area between the Uebi Scebelli and the Giuba.

Another major party was the Socialist National Congress (SNC). It is the heir to the Somali National League which emerged as the dominant party in British Somaliland and which originated as the Somaliland National Society of 1947. The SNC won 20 of 33 seats and 52 percent of the vote in the preindependence election of 1960, defeating the northern branch of the SYL, the National United Front, and the Darod- and Dir-based United Somali party. After the union of the Somaliland and Somalia, the leaders of the SNC played major roles in various governments.

Ibrahim Egal, for example, who was prime minister of Somaliland during the June 26 to July 1, 1960 period subsequently became Minister of Defense and later Minister of Education during the Somalia government of Abdirashid Ali Shermarke (1960–64). Egal left the government in 1962 along with the other principal northern politicians such as Jama Abdullahi Galib in a protest over the "second class" treatment accorded the north after the merger. These northern dissidents eventually aided in the downfall of the SYL government under Abdirizak Haji Hussein in 1967. Under the new president of the Republic, Abdirashid Ali Shermarke, Egal formed a new government and this "national" coalition was elected by the largest majority ever attained by any Somali government (119–2). In the March 1969 elections, the SNC won only 11 seats.

Postindependence Politics and Elections

A brief description of the course of politics in Somalia since independence is necessary in order to see how the Somali Youth League emerged to play a dominant role in the political life during the polyarchal phase of the nation and to illustrate the continuing patterns of widespread participation, regime alteration, and political divisiveness. The growth of political awareness and the expansion of participation in the decision-making process proceeded quite rapidly during the 1950s and 1960s.[10] During the 1954 municipal elections, 37,697 men voted. Two years later, over 614,904 participated and, after suffrage was extended to women in 1958, over one million Somalis voted in the 1964 general election. The number of political parties increased from 8 in 1950 to 21 in 1954 to over 100 by 1968. The United Nations observers, who had feared for the democratic process if the suffrage was too rapidly extended, were both surprised and pleased:

The high degree of political party activity throughout the Territory is without doubt one of the most unique and impressive aspects the Territory's political life.[11]

In Somalia, the Somali Youth League demonstrated early that it had a national following, winning 141 out of 281 seats and 48 percent of the vote in the 1954 municipal council elections. The HDM party captured 57 seats, while the Somali African Union and the Somali National Union won 28 and 5 seats respectively. Smaller local parties won the rest.

In British Somaliland, meanwhile, politics were stimulated by the developments in Somalia and by the British decision in 1954 to return the Haud and the reserved area to Ethiopia the following year. Ethiopian claims to these regions had been established on the basis of the 1897 treaty with Great Britain and reaffirmed in the 1942 and 1944 agreements. The British government was itself divided over the return, the Foreign Office being in favor of it and the Colonial Office generally opposing it. The Colonial Secretary himself seemed to be chagrined by the provisions of the 1897 treaty but found that it was "impossible to undo it."[12]

Reaction was not long in coming. The northern branch of the SYL, with its support among the Darods and the newly formed Somali National League,

---

[10]Lewis, *Modern History of Somaliland,* chapters 7 and 8; and Castagno, "Somali Republic," in *Somalia,* pp. 524–58 analyze in some detail the course of party politics. For more descriptive accounts of Somalia in this period, see E. A. Bayne, *Four Ways of Politics* (New York: American University Field Staff, 1965), and the earlier account by Margaret Lawrence, *New Wind in a Dry Land* (New York: Knopf, 1964).

[11]United Nations, T/1344, p. 16.

[12]Lewis, *Modern History of Somaliland,* p. 152.

which drew its strength from the Isaqs, cooperated briefly in the Somaliland National Front in a vain attempt to oppose the British action. After the first flush of unity, both groups went their own ways, although the Front lingered on as a separate entity. Despite the fact that all Somaliland parties opposed the British action and all championed the unification of all Somalis, the Somali National League emerged as the most organized and effectively led organization combining with its allies in the United Somali Party to form the independence government in 1960.

The 1956 national elections in the trust territory of Somalia concerned the newly created Territorial Assembly which succeeded the older, largely appointed Territorial Council. Some distillation of the parties took place due, in part, to the perceived need to compete across the country as a whole. The SYL emerged as the major force in national politics, winning 43 of the 70 elected seats and 54 percent of the vote. Ten seats in the Assembly were reserved for various other ethnic groups, 4 Italians, 4 Arabs, 1 Indian, and 1 Pakistani. The renamed HDMS party captured 13 seats, the Somali Democratic Party 3, and the Marehan Union 1.

The Somali Democratic Party is illustrative of the process which occurred in Somalia during the 1950s and 1960s whereby political parties formed, split, coalesced, and reformed, changing names all the while. The Somali Democratic Party was itself a union of four smaller parties—the Somali Progressive League, the Somali African Union, the National Somali Union, and the Somali Patriotic Union—which had won 66 seats among themselves during the 1954 elections. Led by Muhammed Sheik Osman and Abdullahi Hagi Mohammed, it amassed 80,000 votes in the 1956 general elections and later merged with two smaller parties to form the Liberal Somali Youth Party. Yet, by independence, the party had melted away, some of its supporters gravitating toward the Greater Somali League, others to the SYL. Despite the fact that its program approximated that of the SYL, the greater organizational power of the SYL and its position at the center of the decision-making process attracted many of its members, particularly after Abdullahi Issa of the SYL became acting prime minister and Aden Abdullah Osman became president of the Territorial Assembly.

Yet, the very tendencies toward amalgamation, in the personal and ethnic ethos of Somali politics, produced tensions within the SYL as new members joined and diluted the already loose control which the leaders of the SYL were able to maintain over the rank and file. After the disagreements outlined above, Haji Muhammad Hussein formed the Greater Somali League prior to the 1958 municipal elections and gained a measure of Darod support. Despite these defections, however, the SYL won 51 percent of the vote and 416 seats to 175 for the HDMS, 36 for the Greater Somali League, and 27 for the Liberal Somali Youth Party. These successes were followed by the strong showing of the SYL in the Territorial Assembly elections of 1959. It won 61 seats uncontested and 22 of the 29 contested. The Liberal Somali Youth Party captured 2 and the HDMS dissidents 5. As mentioned earlier, the HDMS and GSL parties boycotted the election on the grounds of SYL harassment and voting fraud, but individual members of the HDMS gathered 40,857 votes to 35,769 for the Liberal Party and 237,134 for the SYL.

Despite their commanding majority in parliament, the leadership of the SYL made overtures to the HDMS personnel in an attempt to unify the country behind the government. Two prominent leaders of the HDMS, Muhammad Abdi Nur ("Juju") and Abdulcadir Muhammad Aden ("Zoppo"), did in fact join the government.

Castagno feels that this was due to Sab fear of eventual Darod hegemony and the perceived need to work with the Hawiye elements in the SYL, elements which were now in control following the Haji Hussein defection.[13] It could also have been due to a realization of where personal political power lay. The parliament was itself roughly divided into one-third Sab, one-third Darod, and one-third Hawiye. The overtures by the SYL did cause some discontent within the Darod wing of the SYL and among those SYL leaders such as Dr. Abdirashid Ali Shermarke, who opposed "tribalism." It is interesting to note, however, that when Dr. Shermarke formed several governments during the 1960–64 period, he judiciously applied the much maligned principle of "ethnic balance."

Early in 1960, as previously agreed by the SYL and SNC, the Legislative Council of Somaliland and the Territorial Assembly of Somalia voted for unification of the two areas and on July 1, 1960, the two states became the United Republic of Somalia. The 33 members of the Somaliland council joined the 90 members of the Somalia assembly to form the National Assembly of the Republic, and political developments continued at a rapid rate following independence and unification. Aden Abdullah Osman, a former president of the SYL, became provisional president of the Republic until he defeated Sheik Ali Jumale in the presidential elections of July, 1961. Dr. Abdirashid Ali Shermarke formed a new government which was in effect a coalition between the SYL and the two dominant northern groups, the Somali National League and the United Somali Party.

The entrance of the northerns into the cabinet did not eliminate the general sense of dissatisfaction which grew in the former British territories. The difficulties centered around the differing colonial backgrounds, legal codes, tariff rates, and languages as well as around the sense of power deflation which accompanied the shift of the capital from Hargeisa in the north to Mogadiscio in the south. The June 1961 plebiscite to approve the union showed that a large number of northerners opposed the merger even though, overall, it was approved by a vote of 1,760,540 to 182,911.

[13]Castagno, "Somali Republic," in *Somalia,* pp. 538–39.

Later in the year, during December, there was an army mutiny among northern officers stationed at Hargeisa. Strictly speaking, the disturbance was not an attempted *coup* as there was no effort made to take over the government and by the time troops arrived from the south, the disorders were over. The incident served, however, to underscore the dissatisfaction rife in the north, as did the resignations of Egal and the other northern politicians in 1962. Their formation in 1963 of the Somali National Congress signalled the existence of formidable opposition in that region. They were joined by the SYL followers of Sheik Ali Jumale, the defeated candidate for president.

Although Prime Minister Shermarke was able to form a new government, opposition continued until after the 1964 elections. These were, by Somali standards, a massive exercise, involving 21 parties, 973 candidates for 123 seats, and over a million voters. Competition was keen and the SYL faced its strongest opposition to date as the northern-based Somali National Congress won 22 seats, the Somali Democratic Union 15, the HDMS 9, and the various other parties 8. There was a high turnover of deputies, with 68 new members elected out of 123. Soon after the elections, 20 members elected under other party banners crossed the aisle and joined the SYL forces. Despite the commanding lead enjoyed by the SYL, President Osman apparently felt that the nation was ready for a change and urged Abdirizak Haji Hussein to form a government.

Abdirizak Haji Hussein then sought to interject a more "progressive" (i.e., detribalized) ethos into the operations of the government, but opposition coalesced around his plans to enlarge the cabinet and curtail the expansion of the army. A SYL faction led by Dr. Shermarke and Secretary General Yassin Nur Hassan joined with members of the SDU and SNC to bring down the government after only six weeks in office. Inner turmoil within the SYL led to a protracted governmental crisis and Abdirizak Haji Hussein was unable to form a government which was acceptable to all sides for two months. Eventually, that government lasted three years but was constantly under attack. The crossing and recrossing of party lines and the shifts of personal and ethnic loyalties occurred throughout the life of the government.

Ironically enough, Abdirizak Haji Hussein was chosen secretary general of the SYL in February 1967, becoming the first man ever to hold the two offices of secretary general and prime minister simultaneously. Six months later, he was voted out of office. He then formed a new party, the Democratic Action Party, with some SYL dissidents. In the presidential elections of 1967, the National Assembly chose Dr. Abdirashid Ali Shermarke to replace Aden Abdullah Osman, and Shermarke in turn asked Muhammad Ibrahim Egal to form a government. The inclusion of Egal brought in many former members of the SNC and the Egal government received the largest vote of confidence ever accorded a Somali government. The Egal government, both in terms of personnel and domestic policy, did not differ markedly from previous governments. Only in the area of foreign policy did the government seem to move in new directions and even here it seemed to be less a change in goals than in tactics.

Without renouncing the goal of eventual union of all Somalis, the Egal government sought a detente with Kenya and Ethiopia in an attempt to gain by negotiations what Somalia had been unable to accomplish by supplying various Somali insurgent groups in both countries. Following the Arusha accords during October 1967, Somalia has attempted to normalize relations with Kenya and Ethiopia. This development will be analyzed in detail under the section on goals, but it should be mentioned in this connection that there was widespread opposition to this change in tactics.

In the 1969 elections, the SYL led the pack by a conclusive margin, attaining 73 out of 122 seats as over 1,000 candidates vied for the National Assembly. The SNC won 11 and the HDMS only 3. Dr. Shermarke again asked Muhammad Ibrahim Egal to form the government and the predominance of the SYL became overwhelming as many members of the SNC, HDMS, and other minor parties joined the SYL. As Lewis has so aptly put it, "Thus with surprizingly little fuss or clamour, the Somali Republic had as last joined the ranks of African one-party states."[14]

The Military Takeover

It is interesting to speculate what might have happened had the army leadership not moved to overthrow the government in October of 1969. Certainly, the stage was set for the continuation of polyarchal politics within the framework of the single-party SYL government, and under civilian authority it would have been unthinkable to deny the average Somali his right to participate in national elections. But a number of factors were already undercutting civilian government.

Corruption had been widespread for many years and the 1969 elections indicated that the most blatant methods for buying and selling votes had been employed. The armed forces had grown in size and strength during the previous decade until they were absorbing fully 38 percent of the operating budget. But the military were unhappy with the accords Dr. Shermarke had signed with Kenya and Ethiopia and, more importantly, the head of the national police (which had served as a counterweight to the army), General Abshir, resigned prior to the elections, charging political interference with his work.

Thus, when a dissident policeman shot President Shermarke on October 15, the stage was set for a military takeover. While there is no evidence that the military hierarchy was involved in the assassination (the assassin was tried and executed), they moved quickly in the interregnum to establish themselves in

[14]I. M. Lewis, "The Politics of the 1969 Somali Coup," *The Journal of Modern African Studies,* vol. 10, no. 3 (October 1972), p. 397.

power before the National Assembly could choose a new president. On October 21, the army moved and arrested the politicians. A new Supreme Revolutionary Council (SRC), headed by General Muhammad Said Barre, was formed. Railing against "corruption, bribery, nepotism, theft of public funds, injustice"[15] and the like, the SRC attacked the policies of the previous regime.

In 1970, the political system's name was changed to the Somali Democratic Republic. The SRC began a number of self-help schemes designed to improve the quality of rural life, and declared that the country would follow "socialist" goals and abolish tribalism. Considerable infighting within the SRC—both vice presidents, General Korshell and General Mohammad Ainanshe, were arrested for promoting "imperialist plots"—and the severe drought of 1971–74 delayed the formation of a new revolutionary Marxist party until 1976, but the movement toward the left was steady and discernible from the beginning.

On June 28, 1976, the Somali Socialist Revolutionary Party (SSRP) was formed from the old SRC. General Barre became secretary general of the party, and head of the 73-member Supreme Council and the vital 5-man Political Bureau. The main ideology of the SSRP was "scientific socialism," and three key members of the Political Bureau were Marxist ideologists. General Barre urged that the SSRP become a "vanguard" movement to (1) form political cadres capable of carrying out the revolution, (2) activate the process of economic development, and (3) liberate and unify all Somali peoples wherever they are found. The 15,000-member SSRP was to spread out into every district and "into the villages" in an effort to make the revolution an actuality.

Observers of the Somali scene have commented on the effective job done by the new government in resettling over 100,000 nomads stricken by the drought, in the promotion of local self-help schemes which have involved the masses in constructive activities, and in the sharp decrease in official corruption so long a conspicuous feature of the Somali scene. And, thus far, the revolution has reached out and touched many lives. For example, a decades-long controversy over what script should be used in writing Somali was quickly settled (Latin was chosen over Arabic and Osymania). New schools, new roads, a rise in literacy, and increased emphasis on social mobilization are all part of it. Equal rights for women "compatible with our socialist principles" have been pushed since 1975. The government has nationalized the oil-marketing companies, banks, and land, but not petty trading. Agricultural production is up, progress is being made.

At the same time, Somalia has a long way to go. It remains one of the poorest countries in the world. And the strong Somali State Security System has shown no reluctance to use violence or arbitrary imprisonment to "defend

[15]Mayamed [Muhammad] Siyad Barre, *My Country and My People* (Mogadiscio, Somalia: Government Printer, n. d.).

the revolution." There are also certain crosscurrents which make the ultimate outcome of the Somali experience less clear. For one thing, the amount of Soviet influence declined rapidly after the USSR began to support Ethiopia. Although General Barre was initially pleased with Russian (and Chinese) assistance, he and the other leaders of the SSRP are very concerned with Soviet involvement in Ethiopia. Ethiopian and Somali aims in the area are incompatible, irrespective of the current similarities in their ideologies. Somalia wants control of the Ogaden region of Ethiopia and the more than 500,000 Somalis who live there, while Ethiopia is bound and determined to hold onto both. Somali commitment to Marxism may well extend beyond interaction with the Soviets, but their enthusiasm may well diminish now that the Soviets were expelled in November 1977 and vigorously supported Ethiopia in early 1978.

There is also the element of Islam. Although the SSRP has gone far to indicate that Marxism and the Koran are compatible, there are obviously some strains here as well. Islam currently provides a good deal of cohesion in the society. The basic cultural values of Islam are accepted and most Somalis are devout members of the orthodox *shafi'i* school of the Sunnite sect. Most adult men belong to one of the many dervish orders. Although it is true that because of their ecological setting, the Somalis are often pragmatic about some aspects of their religion (the women, for example, seldom wear veils), still the Somalis are deeply religious. This adds to their feeling of oneness and separates them (in their eyes at least) from the "Christian" and "pagan" groups which exist in Ethiopia and Kenya.

Despite the fact that Arabic is the medium of expression in religious training, the Somali language is of great importance in solidifying Somali society and facilitating political communication within the political system. Somali is spoken by nearly four million persons and its oral traditions are of significance in portraying a sense of shared culture. The *gabays,* or long epic poems, are recited over and over and the lessons of Somali society are transmitted by means of the spoken word with a feeling that borders on reverence. Moreover, the Somali language both reflects and helps to promote the democratic and egalitarian ethos so intrinsic to Somali society. It is a blunt language and its few polite words and formal forms of address are largely recent borrowings from Arabic and other languages.

It is in this context that Saudi Arabia and Kuwait have recently become interested in Somalia and its problems. The conservative, Islamic governments of these two states clearly see Islam and Marxism as incompatible and they would like to replace Moscow as the chief aid suppliers to the Somalis. They would like to have the Somalis look to them for assistance and guidance and to temper the revolution which is occurring in the Horn of Africa.

Whatever the ultimate influx of the exogenous influences, there is also the constant of Somali nationalism. The Somalis are a fiercely proud, intensely nationalistic people who see themselves as a nation ordained by God, or First

Cause, or whatever, to maintain themselves in the face of all manner of political competition.

For the Somalis, there must be unity. Despite the clan feuds, the "tribalism," the individualism, and the petty infighting, they are all Somalis. The common culture, *xeer*, unites them and, in their eyes at least, unification must come. The present boundaries of the Somali Republic are "provisional." There are the Somalis in Ethiopia and Kenya and in the newly independent Djibuti to be gathered in. The provisional boundaries must be altered. This overriding concern, far more than the type of ideology the Somalis espouse at a given moment in time, is paramount. And, in the last analysis, Marxism is a blueprint for societal change, not a method of mitigating the conflicts which must invariably arise from this drive.

Thus, Marxism, like Islam before it, is likely to be tempered by the fact of Somali nationalism. Currently, "scientific socialism," which means one thing to communists and noncommunists elsewhere, is translated by the Somalis as *hantiwadaaga cilmiga ku dhisan,* or "livestock sharing which is based on knowledge."[16] How much of the Somali revolution will ultimately be laid to Marxism and how much will simply be labeled "modernization" remains to be seen. For the moment, however, Somalia continues to chart its own course for the future—one based on a diverse heritage and a strong sense of nationhood.

ETHIOPIA

Ironically, it is the centuries-old enemy of Somalia, Ethiopia, which alone of the neighboring countries is also pursuing a Marxist course in its politics. This large (395,000 square miles) and populous (28 million people) country occupies an important strategic position in the Horn of Africa. For centuries a series of peoples from north, north central, and east Africa, as well as from the Arabian peninsula, moved into the area. In the center of these movements was an Amharic-speaking Christian core which was surrounded by hostile Islamic and pagan peoples.[17]

During the nineteenth century, especially under the leadership of Menelik II, this Amharic core expanded to subjugate many of the surrounding peoples. In 1930, Haile Selassie became emperor of Ethiopia and its "modern era" began. Ethiopia was invaded in 1936 by the Italians and the emperor was forced to flee to England. During World War II, the British and their Com-

[16]David Laitin, "The Political Economy of Military Rule in Somalia," *Journal of Modern African Studies,* vol. 14, no. 3 (September 1976), p. 463.

[17]For the convoluted and often exciting history of the region, see the books listed on pages 286–287 of the Bibliography.

monwealth allies, aided by indigenous Ethiopian patriots, recaptured the countries of Ethiopia, Eritrea, and Somalia from the Italians.

The former Italian colonies were eventually divided, with Ethiopia getting control over Eritrea in what was supposed to be a federation, but which in fact was a centralized political system dominated by the Ethiopian government. Despite an abortive military *coup* in 1960 and a simmering revolt in Eritrea which developed in the early 1960s, Ethiopia remained overwhelmingly conservative and dominated by its Amharic-speaking people. The aging emperor gradually lost touch with reality. A severe drought in 1972 gripped most of the country and over 250,000 people eventually died. Refugees poured into the urban areas. Inflation and corruption were widespread and the government seemed almost powerless to take action.

The "Creeping *Coup*"

In this setting, a "creeping *coup*" developed over the course of several years, ultimately bringing to power young army officers who were determined to make a Marxist revolution and to totally transform the country. Unlike Somalia, where the revolutionary activity came as a surprise to most observers, Ethiopia had long been considered ripe for violent social upheaval.[18] The autocratic emperor was committed to the continuation of a feudal system which sharply divided the society into those who owned land and those who did not, those who spoke Amharic or Tigren and those who did not, those who were prominent in the Coptic Ethiopian Orthodox Church and those who were not. In many provinces revolts against the central authority simmered and, as will be seen in the following pages, "liberation" movements abounded.

The "creeping *coup*" began in January of 1974 as army units stationed at Negelle mutinied and demanded pay increases to keep up with inflation. Haile Selassie had always relied on the various branches of the armed forces to keep one another in check and, in the past, the emperor had not hesitated to use force quickly and ruthlessly to punish disobedience. This time, however, he—or those around him—hesitated, then met the demands of the mutineers. The "negelle flu," as it was called, spread as more and more army units demanded increases in pay and/or refused to obey orders. In February, the government of Prime Minister Aklilu Habte Wolde resigned. There continued to be widespread unrest in the 50,000-man army, and troops were called out to control events in the capital, Addis Ababa. During April and May, the government continued to make concessions, including the acceptance of a demand for a constitutional monarchy. Mutinies continued. There was a series of strikes and violence mounted. In September, the army moved to depose the 82-year-old

[18]Perhaps the best capsule portrait of Ethiopian society on the brink of conflagration is Edmund Murray, *Kulubi* (New York: Crown Publishers, 1973).

monarch who had ruled his country for 43 years. The army leaders chose Crown Prince Asfa Wossen as "king designate" as if to hedge their bets against the future. Their own shadowy ruling group, called the *Dergue* (Amharic for "committee") engaged in an internal power struggle.

Marxist Modernizers: The *Dergue*

This struggle erupted in November of 1974, when the first leader of the *Dergue*, Lt. General Aman Andom, was killed and 60 top military officials and civilians were massacred. General Tafari Bante was chosen as the titular head of the new 120-man Provisional Military Council. The *Dergue* continued to be wracked by internal divisions, but the leadership proclaimed "Ethiopian socialism." Calling for social and economic equality, the *Dergue* nationalized all major industries and, in the Nationalization of Rural Lands Proclamation of March 4, 1975, confiscated all land and called for its redistribution. During the same month, the *Dergue* obviously felt strong enough to do away with the monarchy; it simply "abolished" it and "canceled" royalty.

Later during 1975, Haile Selassie died and the *Dergue* stepped up its attacks on the military and economic presence of the United States, which had provided the Ethiopian armed forces with virtually all of their heavy weapons.[19] During September and October, opposition to the *Dergue* mounted among students, workers and many former landowners and peasants. The *Dergue* moved swiftly and ruthlessly, purging large numbers of intellectuals, students, and workers in the urban areas, then turning on the rightists. Several thousand people were killed during these waves alone.

In 1976 there was a further swing to the left and an acceptance of Marxism as the primary ideological guidepost for the maturing revolution. In April, the Provisional Military Government (PMG) officially formed the People's Democratic Republic of Ethiopia and issued its detailed program. It called for the "total eradication of feudalism, bureaucratic capitalism and imperialism," and declared itself to be totally "Marxist-Leninist in approach." Power struggles within the *Dergue* continued and in February 1977 Brigadier General Tafari Bante was killed, along with many of his key supporters; Col. Mengistu Haile Miriam, the slender Oromo, emerged as leader of the ruling group. Mengistu became Commander-in-Chief of the Armed Forces and Chairman of the Provisional Military Administrative Government, as well as head of the 16-person standing committee and the 32-person central committee. The revolution, he vowed, would continue.

Yet, there remains widespread opposition to both the *Dergue* and the revolution. In Eritrea alone, there are three distinct groups struggling to free

[19]For a pre-*coup* assessment of Selassie rule, see Andrew Jaffe, "Haile Selassie's Remarkable Reign," *African Report* (May 1971), pp. 16–18.

the province from Ethiopian rule. First, there is the Eritrean Liberation Front (ELF), led by Ahmed Nasser and supported by many Moslems in the area as well as by Syria and Saudi Arabia. Second, there is its initially Christian breakaway competitor, the Eritrean People's Liberation Front (EPLF). Curiously enough, the EPLF is also strongly Marxist in terms of ideology, but determined to seek an independent nation under its leader, Ramadan Mohammed Nur. A third anti-Ethiopian group, the Eritrean Liberation Front–Popular Liberation Forces (ELF-PLF) brings yet another ingredient to the scene and all three movements probably have as many as 30,000 people under arms against the Ethiopians. An initial movement toward unity took place in October, 1977 when the leaders of the ELF and EPLF announced a political and military merger.

In addition, there is the right wing and traditional leadership who oppose the *Dergue*. United under an umbrella organization called the Ethiopian Democratic Union (EDU) and led by General Iyassu Mengesha and Nega Tegegne, it is located in Bagemder, Tigre, and Gojjam, although the Ethiopian army has driven its principal units into the Sudan on several occasions. Although it remains a moderate alternative to the *Dergue,* its calls for democratic elections and peace talks seem overrun by events.

The *Dergue* is also opposed by the urban-based Ethiopian People's Revolutionary Party (ERPP) which opposed the monarchy even before there was a *Dergue* and argues that the *Dergue* has not gone far enough and therefore has "betrayed" the revolution. Urban guerrilla warfare waged by students, workers, and disaffected intellectuals on the behalf of the ERPP has led to large-scale killings in retaliation by the *Dergue.*

As if these groups were not enough, there are the Somali Western Somali Liberation Front (WSLF), the Afar Liberation Front (ALF), and the Tigre People's Liberation Front (TPLF) all seeking freedom from the control of the *Dergue* and whoever is in Addis Ababa. As of 1978, there were widespread rebellions in no less than 10 of Ethiopia's 14 provinces.

Yet, despite the opposition and the turmoil, the civil war, and the impending international conflicts,[20] the Marxist modernizers in Ethiopia continue to carry out their revolution. Like the Bolsheviks in the Russia of 1918, they are beset on all sides by right-wing and left-wing opposition, by separatism and internal dissension, but they continue to be bent on massive societal transformation, both for the cause of revolution and for their own preservation. The revolution has become their *raison d'être* and the legitimizing ingredient in their repression of all those who would replace them.

Thus far, the Marxist modernizers have carried the revolution into a num-

---

[20]The best of the recent spate of books on the conflicts in the Horn is Tom J. Farer, *War Clouds on the Horn of Africa: A Crisis for Detente* (New York: Carnegie Endowment for International Peace, 1976).

ber of key structures: the ruling class, the system of land tenure, important sectors of the economy, and critical social mobilization. With regard to the ruling class, the *Dergue* have simply decapitated the old order. Thousands have been executed and virtually the entire family is dead or in exile. The old aristocracy is no more. The "congruence of class and ethnicity" has been rent asunder.[21] The Amharic domination of the government and army has been broken and the Coptic Church, so long a bulwark of the old order has been "nationalized." The *Dergue* simply dismissed the Patriarch of the Ethiopian Orthodox Church, Abun Tewoflos, and replaced him with a prelate supportive of the revolution.

Perhaps the most revolutionary aspect of the *Dergue* approach has been in the area of land reform. In pre-*coup* Ethiopia, status, wealth, and power depended on one's control over land.[22] Land tenure was a very complicated affair, with as many as 111 different land tenures in Wollo province alone.[23] In many areas, the rate of absentee landlordship ran as high as 40 to 50 percent. Feudal levies were high and peasants often worked their entire lives simply to keep even with their rents. In a country where 85 percent of the total population was involved in subsistence agriculture, land reform was an extremely popular idea. In fact, ". . . the peasants received the new land reform initially as liberation from colonial exploitation as well as from social injustice."[24]

But land reform has not gone smoothly. Early peasant enthusiasm has cooled somewhat and many former land owners in the more traditional areas armed their peasants against the governmental intrusion (often in the form of students and union members). Because the government was unable to send out trained cadres, the land reform act, initially at least, led to great waste, confusion, and violent societal upheaval. Not surprisingly, agricultural production was down markedly in 1975 and 1976. Beset on all sides by opponents, the *Dergue* has simply not been able to devote the time, energy and manpower to the resolution of all the ramifications of land reform. Irrespective of how long it takes the system to get agriculture moving again, however, the old feudal patterns of land tenure are gone and, with them, the societal order that was the old Ethiopia.

In addition to the *Dergue's* action with regard to the old social order, its leaders have also adopted a Marxist set of propositions for the economy with nationalization of key industries, banks, and the like, and severe limits on

[21]John Markakis, "Social Formation and Political Adaptation in Ethiopia," *Journal of Modern African Studies,* vol. 11, no. 3 (September 1973), p. 365.

[22]Marina Ottaway, "Social Classes and Corporate Interests in the Ethiopian Revolution," *The Journal of Modern African Studies,* vol. 14, no. 3 (1976), pp. 469–86.

[23]Paul Brietzke, "Land Reform in Revolutionary Ethiopia," *Journal of Modern African Studies,* vol. 14, no. 4 (1976), pp. 637–60.

[24]John Harbeson, "Ethiopia: Whither the Revolution," *Africa Report* (July-August 1976), p. 50.

private ownership of even small business. A complete balance sheet on the success or failure of these measures is not yet possible, although there have been some attempts at such a tally.[25] The government is trying to maintain its power and the impetus of the revolution by massive social mobilization. By mid-1977, fully 100,000 Ethiopians had been marshalled into a People's Militia. Armed with Soviet weapons and destined to march against the various secessionist groups, the militia also serves as a social conduit for the ideals and goals of the revolution which are imparted along with military training. Whether this group will be able to recapture the Ogaden region from the Somalis remains to be seen.

Thus, it remains to be seen just how far the Marxist modernizers will be able to carry the revolution in contemporary Ethiopia. There is no mass party as yet and the revolutionary leadership is beset on all sides by a host of enemies. In fact, it is by no means certain that Ethiopia will continue to exist as an integral whole.[26] The revolution may stave off disintegration or hasten it. The *Dergue* may find itself in the uninviting position (again, like the Bolsheviks of 1918 Russia) of having to give up territory in order to gain time—time to secure the revolution and crush internal opposition. Just as the Soviet Union under Lenin made a separate peace with Germany in order to safeguard the revolution, the Ethiopian leaders may well have to give up Eritrea and the Ogaden in order to insure that their revolution is not countervailed. On the other hand, a defeated and discredited *Dergue,* having lost several of Ethiopia's provinces might well feel a backlash from the very elements it now commands, especially the regular army.

This helps to explain the *Dergue's* willingness to rely on thousands of Cubans and Russians to fight its battles against Somalia and the Eritrean Freedom Fighters.

GUINEA-BISSAU

If the chaotic situation in Ethiopia militates against any facile judgments about the future course of the revolution, if the multifaceted civil war is still in progress, then there is an interesting set of contrasts across the continent in Guinea-Bissau. There, other Marxist modernizers are seeking to reconstruct their society following a long and bloody liberation struggle which took on many aspects of a civil war since many inhabitants fought on the side of the

[25]See William Lee, "Ethiopia: A Review of the Dergue," *Africa Report,* vol. 22, no. 2 (March-April 1977), pp. 7–11.

[26]The opposite point of view, namely, that in fact Ethiopia has a set of shared experiences which will tend to hold the empire together in the face of these upheavals, is expressed by Donald Levine, "The Roots of Ethiopia's Nationhood," *Africa Report* (May 1971), pp. 12–15.

Portuguese to prevent their takeover. In addition, the Marxist modernizers in both Guinea-Bissau and Mozambique have a much more extensive body of belief outlined in their pursuit of Afro-communism.

In Chapter 3 we outlined the political views of Amilcar Cabral, founder and leader of the *Partido Africano de Independencia da Guiné e Cabo Verde* (PAIGC) until his assassination in January 1973. In that section, we outlined the extent to which his basic Marxian views were translated into the African context during the struggle for liberation and how, with only minor modifications, they continued to form the major corpus of ideological principles. Thus, when the Portuguese finally acknowledged the fact of Guinean independence in September 1975, the PAIGC not only had accomplished a good deal of their revolution already, they had the working guidelines for their new society.[27]

As Thomas Henriksen has pointed out, the Guinean revolution (and that of Mozambique) ". . . were the first successful indigenous Marxist-inspired revolutions not growing directly from the conditions of major wars."[28] Moreover, Guinea (and to a lesser extent Mozambique) were the only African countries which had obtained their independence primarily on the battlefield. Certainly, these parties were the only ones which at the time of independence stood as *bona fide* alternatives to the colonial power and had developed a self-contained, functioning, administrative structure in the liberated areas. That is to say, when the PAIGC declared the independence of Guinea-Bissau in September 1974, and when the Portuguese acknowledged that independence a year later, the PAIGC was already a government in being.[29]

How did this come to pass? The process was a slow and painful one. This small (14,000 square miles) country with 700,000 people has been under the control of the Portuguese since the fifteenth century and its administration followed the classical Portuguese pattern outlined in Chapter 2. PAIGC was not organized until 1956 and undertook no military action until 1961, following the bloody Portuguese suppression of a critical dock strike in Bissau. Founded by Amilcar Cabral and Raphel Barbosa, the PAIGC took to the countryside and began to harass the Portuguese.

For over a decade, its forces struggled in small group actions, consolidating their control over the countryside and gradually escalating the war. Supported by arms from the Soviet Union and China, and in the later years the recipient of medical and financial support from the Scandinavian countries, PAIGC gradually became the government-in-being for half the territory and half the population.

[27]For historical background on the area, see page 278 of the Bibliography.

[28]Thomas H. Henriksen, "People's War in Angola, Mozambique and Guinea-Bissau," *The Journal of Modern African Studies,* vol. 14, no. 3 (1976), p. 399.

[29]Accounts of life in the liberated areas are to be found in Gerard Chaliand, *Armed Struggle in Africa* (New York: Monthly Review Press, 1969); and Basil Davidson, *The Liberation of Guiné* (Baltimore: Penguin Books, 1969).

By 1971, PAIGC was able to establish a civilian administration in the liberated areas and the next year, elections were held in these freed territories. At that time, a 120-person National Assembly was selected, consisting of 40 members of PAIGC and 80 "from the masses." In 1973 Amilcar Cabral was assassinated and Aristides Pereira became Secretary General of PAIGC; Luis Cabral, Amilcar's younger brother, became Deputy Secretary General. That same year, the congress of PAIGC adopted a constitution which, in turn, was ratified by the National Assembly. Its tenets established the basic outlines of the Guinean state as it now exists.

Under the constitution of 1973, the PAIGC is the vanguard of the revolution and the only political organization permitted. Its 24-member Executive Committee and its 85-person High Council for the Struggle are organized along the Marxist-Leninist principle of "democratic centralism," with every citizen over the age of 15 permitted to vote for the PAIGC slate of candidates for the National Assembly. In turn, the National Assembly chooses the governmental Council of State, which serves for three-year terms and selects the president, who is chief of state. Luis Cabral was chosen the first president in 1973 and reelected in 1977.

Thus, the PAIGC government was able to actualize portions of its revolution and to engage in administration prior to taking over at the time of independence. It is just as well that the party had the opportunity to test itself against the tasks which lay ahead, for at the time of independence there was a wide range of problems which called for skillful and careful handling.

First, the Cape Verde Islands were, by and large, not enthusiastic about becoming an integral part of Guinea. Many inhabitants feared the submersion of their culture and life styles if there was a union with the mainland (although, conversely, many on the mainland feared the predominance of Cape Verdians within the PAIGC hierarchy). Also, with 300,000 Cape Verdians living overseas under a variety of cosmopolitan influences, neither the PAIGC nor the revolution initially had widespread support.

Second, the war against the Portuguese became over time a bitter and divisive civil war, with thousands of Africans serving with the Portuguese army and a number of atrocities committed by both sides. This, coupled with the traditional leaders in the Bafata and Gabu regions who opposed the "modernizers" as much as the Marxists, meant that at the time of independence many were apprehensive about the control the PAIGC militants would have over their lives.

Third, the guerrilla army of over 10,000 people would have to be integrated into civilian life and the many skills which had been developed to pull down the colonial edifice would have to be redirected toward the rebuilding of the country. In addition, the nearly 200,000 refugees who had fled the fighting and settled in Guinea and Senegal would likewise have to be integrated into the society and the economy of the new nation.

Fourth, as a result of the war, the economy of Guinea-Bissau, never robust, had been devastated. Over a decade of war and strife had completely disrupted normal patterns. Food, especially rice, had to be imported in large quantities. With little industry, agricultural development would have to be a primary focus of the new regime.

Finally, the revolutionary doctrine which had served the PAIGC so well in the liberated areas would have to be transferred to the areas previously under Portuguese control. The enthusiasm for the PAIGC which had sustained the people in the liberated portions of the country would have to be translated to the population which had, at the least, been passive toward PAIGC successes. Indeed, the excitement of liberation and success on the battlefield would also have to be institutionalized through the political process if the revolutionary ideals were to continue.

Thus far, the PAIGC has made considerable progress with these problems. The victorious PAIGC worked hard to make the merger with the Cape Verde islands as palatable as possible. In 1976, both territories agreed to form a united territory, at least with regard to the legal system, and the PAIGC on both the islands and the mainland continues to set a successful merger as a priority goal. In fact, it may well take the eventual form of a modified federation as obtained between Tanganyika and Zanzibar from 1964 to 1976.

The results to date of national unification seem more clear-cut. The PAIGC imprisoned a number of African soldiers, especially officers, who had fought with the Portuguese, but in September 1976 they announced a general amnesty which covered the majority of Africans. The amnesty did not cover people who were charged with treasonous acts which led to a loss of life during the conflict —thereby giving the PAIGC reasonably wide latitude in dealing with specific cases. In 1977, however, this amnesty was extended and all death sentences were commuted to 15 years hard labor.

With the help of the United Nations High Commissioner for Refugees, most of the exiles in Guinea and Senegal were returned and they, together with the bulk of the armed forces, had been fairly well integrated socially by the end of 1977. And many army militants have been "seconded" to civilian jobs to replace the departing Portuguese.

Less progress has been made in the economic sector. The People's Stores *(Armazéns do Povo),* which were so successful in the liberated areas, have not been as readily accepted in the newly freed territories. The PAIGC insisted that the state control internal trade in the basic products; instituted strict price controls; nationalized land, the banks, and existing industry; and engaged in strict state planning for the economy. Private enterprise has been "supervised and integrated."

Attempts to develop worker's cooperative farms have moved slowly and there continues to be considerable opposition to them, although significant progress on the production of rice has been made. It seems likely that there will continue to be strains and tensions within the PAIGC itself between the moderate pragmatists who want to get the economy moving again (and let Marxist principles lie fallow for a while) and the militants such as Vasco Cabral, the Commissioner of Economic Planning, and Dr. Jose Arauyo, Commissioner of Party Affairs, who are concerned that the revolution move ahead along more strictly obeyed principles.

Not surprisingly, the transition to peace has brought about some faltering interest in the PAIGC. During the 1976 elections for the National Assembly, there was a very low voter turnout, with the PAIGC getting less than 50 percent of the vote in a variety of areas. In fact, the results were so disappointing that elections were held again—without a marked increase in participation. Clearly, the party will have to redouble its efforts at social mobilization and political participation if the popular involvement in the revolution is not to diminish.

The PAIGC has long felt that although the revolution is based on the masses, it is not to be led by them. The real revolutionary vanguard, according to Cabral and others within the movement, has been the educated lower-middle class, the petty bourgeoisie, although the unemployed urban dwellers also accepted this message. During the war, it was possible to generate support for the goals of the PAIGC, especially independence, rather easily. But now, with the Portuguese gone, greater efforts at political socialization will be required to sustain enthusiasm for the revolution. The party has become the state, but it clearly must not wither away before the revolution is complete.[30]

The PAIGC leadership seems dedicated and less doctrinaire than their counterparts in Somalia, Ethiopia, or Mozambique. This may be due in part to the less threatening position they occupy. External threats seem substantially lower than in the other three countries, and opposition to PAIGC rule seems far less widespread. The leadership also seems more committed to meaningful political participation than in the other territories. It is, of course, too early to tell, but Guinea-Bissau would seem to have the potential to become the first at least partially polyarchal of the Marxist regimes if the present leadership—or some future leadership—were to make it a priority item for the nation.

MOZAMBIQUE

In Mozambique, the Marxist-modernizer flavor is very strong, perhaps the strongest of the four systems under review. This 303,000-square-mile territory

---

[30]For an overview of the PAIGC in action, see Lars Rudebeck, "Political Mobilization for Development in Guinea-Bissau," *Journal of Modern African Studies,* vol. 10, no. 1 (May 1972), pp. 1–18; and T. H. Henrikson, "Some Notes on the National Liberation Wars in Angola, Mozambique and Guinea-Bissau," *Military Affairs,* vol. 16, no. 1 (February 1977).

of nearly 10 million people was under Portuguese control for nearly five centuries. For much of that time, a great deal of the area was only nominally under the control of Lisbon, and the local feudal *prazzo* system held sway.[31] Although the Portuguese made a variety of attempts to modify their colonial system in order to maintain their hold on the African territories, many Africans preferred total independence.

In 1962, Dr. Eduardo Mondlane, an American-trained anthropologist, and a number of Mozambiquens formed the *Frente de Libertação de Moçambique* (FRELIMO). After guerrilla training in Algeria and Tanzania, FRELIMO launched a series of attacks on the northern province of Cabo Delgado. From these modest beginnings, FRELIMO grew in size and importance until, like the PAIGC in Guinea-Bissau, it had total administrative control over vast liberated zones. In 1969, Dr. Mondlane was assassinated by a bomb, and a triumvirate of Urio Simango, Marcelino dos Santos, and Samora Machel inherited the leadership of the group.

The uneasy alliance fell apart in November 1969, and Simango was expelled. Dos Santos settled for vice president of FRELIMO, and Machel became president in May 1970. Machel, a former male nurse, who had met Mondlane in 1961, was a product of the FRELIMO organization, having worked his way up the ranks to become defense secretary in 1966. Under Machel's direction, FRELIMO expanded its scope of attacks until by 1974 it was threatening the Portuguese in over half the country, especially in the area north of Deira. The situation, although not as advanced as that in Guinea-Bissau, nevertheless indicated that FRELIMO was in the process of winning the battle for independence even before the Portuguese *coup* in Lisbon. Following the *coup* in Portugal, a shaky ceasefire developed between FRELIMO and the Portuguese as Portuguese soldiers refused to fight on. An agreement was soon reached which called for the independence of Mozambique in September 1975.

During 1974 and early 1975, the situation in the territory was confused. Some Portuguese officials tried to create political alternatives to FRELIMO; the territory's 250,000 Portuguese settlers, increasingly concerned over the impending takeover, created a number of right-wing organizations such as *Fico* (Portuguese for "I stay"). There was some violence and mutiny among several army units. In the end, however, the Portuguese turned control of the territory over to FRELIMO without national elections and all but 20,000 of the Portuguese left, fearing that life would be very different under the new government.

And life was different indeed. Not only was there now an African government in place of the Portuguese, but that government took on an increasingly radical and Marxist tenor as time went on. Since its inception, FRELIMO has

---

[31]For accounts of this period see pages 263, 271, 278, and 283 of the Bibliography.

had three party congresses, the first, in 1962, established the organization. The second, held in 1968, took place in Mozambique for the first time. The third took place in February 1977, on the eighth anniversary of the death of Dr. Mondlane. It was at the second party congress that the shape of Mozambique's future was clearly underscored, and the ascendancy of the Marxist modernizers within the party firmly established.

At the congress, FRELIMO was converted into a "vanguard party faithful to the principles of scientific socialism." Espousing the doctrine of what it termed Afro-Communism, FRELIMO charged itself with making a full-fledged revolution, eliminating "all types of exploitation" and pledging itself to the "destruction of capitalism." Henceforth, FRELIMO was to be an elite party with a small membership (as opposed to the struggle period, when recruitment was widespread), and an alliance of workers and peasants (but only those peasants who joined the new collectives could be eligible for membership).

Openly Marxist, the party continued to be led by Samora Machel, who was elected president (both of FRELIMO and the country) to serve a five-year term running to 1982. The office of vice president was abolished. There was a 9-person permanent Political Committee and a 66-member Central Committee. Other key people in the party and the government included Jorge Rebelo, Minister of Information, and Jose Oscar Monterior, FRELIMO party secretary for organization. The Afro-Communism of FRELIMO is nationalistic in intent but in its own words, "Marxist, hard and pure."

The problems it faces are enormous and there has been far less progress in solving them than in the case of Guinea-Bissau. The economy virtually collapsed during the 1974–75 period with agricultural and industrial production falling by over 75 percent. In fact, it is the modest hope of FRELIMO that by 1980, production can get up to where it was in 1973.

Part of the collapse was due to the wholesale disengagement of the Portuguese who left the country with virtually everything they could carry with them. Since they had long held the most important administrative and economic posts in the country, their withdrawal undoubtedly added greatly to the trauma of independence (in fact, the situation was so acute in the ports of Maputo and Beira that South Africans had to be brought in to replace the departing Portuguese).

Unlike Guinea-Bissau, Mozambique also had to deal with considerable outside pressure. Rhodesian forces, seeking to destroy the liberation movements in that country, have engaged in hot pursuit, often deep into Mozambique. Mozambique has closed its border to traffic from Rhodesia (thereby losing considerable revenues) and is actively supporting the liberation forces.

Furthermore, the revolution has not been universally welcomed. Machel called for People's Tribunals to try "bandits and reactionaries" and by 1977 there were numerous political prisoners held in "re-education centers." Foreign commentators (including South Africans) have put the figure as high as 40,000 (which is probably too high) and FRELIMO puts the number at 3,000 (which is probably too low). FRELIMO has had to call on Tanzania for 2,500 troops to guard the important Cabora Bassa dam (which, ironically enough, FRELIMO spent a great deal of effort trying to blow up when it was in Portuguese hands) and to put down uprisings in the Makonde area. Since the Makonde formed the bulk of FRELIMO's army, this put considerable strain on the government. In addition, there has been a few nuisance raids by dissidents calling themselves the Mozambique United Front.

Thus far, FRELIMO has nationalized land, rental properties, the legal profession, *The Banco National Ultra Marino* and the health and education sectors. Much of the industrial capacity has passed to the state by default as the Portuguese have withdrawn. The FRELIMO leadership is concentrating on the formation of communal villages and collective farms, to be followed by the development of heavy industry, although private enterprise remains a feature of Mozambiquen life as of 1978.

As of 1977, there were widespread food shortages and, although coal, iron, cashews, cotton, sugar, tea, and copra offer some hope for the future, the present economic situation is acute, with imports in 1976 exceeding exports by $400 million to $176 million. Again, it is ironic to note that Mozambique continued to export labor to South Africa (100,000 workers a year) until June 1977. Mozambique was the recipient of 60 percent of the workers' salary, payable in gold at $42 an ounce, which it then sold on the open market for $130 to $140 an ounce. This expediency was without critics within FRELIMO, and is being phased out under considerable criticism.

The revolution in Mozambique, like those in Guinea-Bissau, Somalia, and Ethiopia, is far from complete. It is not totally clear whether the Marxist modernizers will succeed in making the kind of social and economic changes which they are now calling for. Marxism is still a blueprint, a design, not an actuality. All these countries face considerable challenges in the years ahead.

But the start has been made. The Marxist modernizers now represent an in-place, ongoing alternative to the polyarchal and authoritiarian types outlined in the previous chapters. How relevant will the Marxist modernizers' approach ultimately be for the rest of Africa? Much remains to be seen. With the exception of Somalia, all have developed in the course of armed struggle and an often brutal civil war. The manner of their "birth," then, is not without consequences for those who would imitate this particular process. In the case of Somalia, the fact that the leadership came to power in a fashion similar to dozens of other governments would seem to suggest that the Somali approach could be more easily duplicated. Whether it will or not is unclear at this moment, for the making of a genuine revolution remains tough, hard, often brutal work. Eggs are smashed to make omelets. We do not know how much appeal a genuine revolution (as opposed to the mere posturing about revolution) will have for Africa's leaders of tomorrow but, for the moment at least, the Marxist modernizers do offer a relevant alternative to the previous patterns of governing in Africa.

SUMMARY AND CONCLUSIONS

In this work, we have canvassed the various political trends which are operative in contemporary Africa. We have looked at the elements of African traditional life which are such an important part of the African experience. We have looked at the colonial overlay which provided so many of the initial political frameworks and we have examined the African political thought and its content, not only as put forth by leaders and statesmen, but by African writers as well. All of these strands, as well as the actual course of politics in Africa today suggest a variety of conclusions.

1. The first of these is the inherent fragility of polyarchal politics in the Africa context. We have seen the difficulties that the polyarchal systems have faced. We have indicated the reasons why many of them have collapsed. In fact, the widespread destruction of the polyarchal systems throughout contemporary Africa has been one of its most prominent features.

But there is a corollary to the fragility of the polyarchal system and that is that the polyarchal approach retains a persistent popularity, particularly for those citizens who have been able to participate. Wherever genuine polyarchal systems have functioned, there has been widespread and enthusiastic involvement in the process. Generally speaking, only those governments and leaders voted out of office have found it necessary to rail against the polyarchal form. What we have consistently noted, however, is that polyarchal systems require time and effort as well as governmental commitment to function properly. It is for Africans themselves to decide whether the effort in a particular country and a particular situation is worth the struggle to maintain such systems.

2. Another recurring theme in both the politics of Africa and the writing about such politics is the tendency toward authoritarianism. One simply cannot look at the contemporary African political scene, or read African writers on the subject, without concluding that authoritarianism in both its civilian and military guises, is an almost ubiquitous feature of the political landscape. It appears irrespective of colonial heritage or traditional antecedents (as well it should since it is a recurring theme in both as well). It is widespread and persistent. It appears in a variety of forms across time and space. There is nothing in the current context to suggest that it will either vanish or even diminish.

3. The present political climate of Africa suggests that there is a definite and growing appeal which Marxism and revolutionary theory have for many

of Africa's elites. It already exists in at least five African states and conceivably could be adopted by various other governments. The creation of new party structures, increased citizen participation (often in the form of mobilization), and the redistribution of wealth, services, and opportunities all have considerable appeal.

So, too, does the notion of Marxist doctrine per se since it gives a body of belief as legitimacy for regimes often lacking in legitimacy other than that of the gun. To be tied into a world force which other countries have adopted, to be a part with others who share your ideology is reassuring, even comforting. The Marxist modernizers offer a blueprint for society (however appropriate or inappropriate) and an opportunity to espouse a set of goals which are attractive (often far more attractive than the process by which the goals are to be reached). It seems likely that at least this level of appeal will continue affected only in part by the "success" or "failure" of the experiments already underway.

4. There remains the persistent theme of diversity. The diversity of the traditional African forms, the diversity of the colonial overlay and the African responses to it, the diversity of existing political forms all attest to the human richness of African political life. The value-spread and broad spectrum of relevant utopias suggests that political diversity will remain as much an intrinsic part of Africa's future as its past and present. And this is how it should be. All political systems have benefits, both real and imagined; all demand costs. Which system is "best" clearly depends on circumstances and these are always changing. As Solon put it, "What government is best? The answer is, For What People and For What Age?" It is clear that what will endure in the African context is the polycentrism of political forms. There will be no African solution, only African solutions.

three

COMPREHENSIVE BIBLIOGRAPHY

As an introductory text, this work is designed to bring the student in contact with the basic patterns of political behavior and thought in contemporary black Africa. In this type of enterprise it is not possible to cover all the issues raised or topics suggested by the vast number of materials dealing with Africa. Moreover, since the major thrust of this work is political, many historical, anthropological, and economic dimensions have only been skirted.

Therefore, in the sections that follow, we have put together what is the most extensive bibliography of Africana to be found in any basic text. We have taken the vast outpouring of literature that has developed in the past several decades and organized it in two ways: by topic and by country. The interested reader will therefore be able to probe deeply those aspects that most interest her or him.

African Politics
in Perspective

In this section, we attempt to take the more important book length treatments of African subjects and break them down by topics. Obviously, these categories are neither mutually exclusive nor rigid. Instead we have tried to include relevant material where appropriate, even if that material appears more than once.

The student may suggest that there could be more or fewer categories, but these seem adequate to help set the context for African politics. They are most helpful in enabling the interested reader to bridge the gap between the traditional political patterns outlined in Chapter 1 and the existing patterns covered in Chapters 5 through 7.

Any adequate treatment of the history of Africa and that of the interaction between Africans and Europeans would obviously take several volumes the size of this one. But for the readers concerned with the historical dimensions, there are topics listed ranging from "The History of Africa" to the "European Penetration" and "Decolonization."

THE PHYSICAL FRAME

BOYD, A. and P. VAN RENSBURG. *An Atlas of African Affairs* (New York: Praeger, 1965).

CLIFFORD, M. L. and E. S. ROSS. *The African Environment: Portrait of a Continent* (New York: Barnes and Noble, 1971).

DEBLIJ, HARM J. *A Geography of Subsaharan Africa* (Chicago: Rand McNally, 1964).

FITZGERALD, W. *Africa: A Social, Economic and Political Geography of Its Major Regions* (London: Methuen, 1968).

FORDHAM, PAUL. *The Geography of African Affairs* (Baltimore: Penguin Books, 1965).

FREEMAN-GRENVILLE, G. S. P. *A Modern Atlas of African History* (Totowa, N.J.: Rowman & Littlefield, 1976).

GROVE, A. T. *Africa South of the Sahara* (Oxford: Oxford University Press, 1967).

HANCE, W. *Geography of Modern Africa* (New York: Columbia University Press, 1964).

HODGSON, R. D. and E. A. STONEMAN. *The Changing Map of Africa* (Princeton, N.J.: Van Nostrand, 1963).

MOUNTJOY, A. and C. EMBLETON. *Africa: A New Geographical Survey* (New York: Praeger, 1967).

OMINDE, S. H. (ed.). *Studies in East African Geography and Development* (Los Angeles: University of California Press, 1971).

Oxford Regional Economic Atlas (Oxford, England: Clarendon Press, 1965).

PROTHERO, R. M. *People and Land in Africa South of the Sahara* (London: Oxford University Press, 1972).

SOMMER, JOHN. *Bibliography of African Geography, 1940–1964* (Hanover, N.H.: Dartmouth University Press, 1966).

DIVERSITY AND ETHNICITY IN TROPICAL AFRICA

FLAHUS, OLIVIA. *African Beginnings* (New York: Viking Press, 1967).

GIBBS, JAMES (ed.). *Peoples of Africa* (New York: Holt, Rinehart and Winston, 1965).

LEAKEY, L. S. B. and V. M. GOODALL. *Unveiling Man's Origins* (Cambridge, England: Schenkman Publishing, 1969).

MAQUET, JACQUES. *Civilizations of Black Africa* (London: Oxford University Press, 1972).

———. *Power and Society in Africa* (New York: McGraw-Hill, 1971).

MIDDLETON, JOHN (ed.). *Black Africa: Its Peoples and Their Culture Today* (New York: Macmillan, 1970).

MONTAGU, ASHLEY (ed.). *The Concept of Race* (New York: Macmillan, 1964).

MURDOCK, GEORGE. *Africa: Its Peoples and Their Culture History* (New York: McGraw-Hill, 1959).

OTTENBERG, S. and P. (eds.). *Cultures and Societies of Africa* (New York: Random House, 1965).

SELIGMAN, C. G. *Races of Africa* (London: Oxford University Press, 1930).

SKINNER, E. P. *Peoples and Cultures of Africa* (Garden City, N.Y.: Doubleday, 1973).

TRADITIONAL AFRICAN POLITICAL SYSTEMS

(F)* AMADI, E. *The Concubine* (New York: Humanities Press, 1966).

BALANDIER, G. *Daily Life in the Kingdom of the Kongo* (New York: Random House, 1968).

*(F) indicates fiction.

COHEN, R. and J. MIDDLETON (eds.). *Comparative Political Systems* (Garden City, N.Y.: Natural History Press, 1967).

DALTON, GEORGE (ed.). *Tribal and Peasant Economies* (Garden City, N.Y.: Natural History Press, 1967).

DOUGLAS, M. and P. KABERRY (eds.). *Man in Africa* (Garden City, N.Y.: Doubleday, 1971).

EISENSTADT, S. N. "Primitive Political Systems: A Preliminary Comparative Analysis," *American Anthropologist,* 61 (1959), 200–220.

FAIRSERVIS, W. A. *The Ancient Kingdoms of the Nile* (New York: Mentor Books, 1962).

FORDE, D. and P. M. KABERRY (eds.). *West African Kingdoms in the 19th Century* (London: Oxford University Press, 1969).

FORTES, M. and E. E. EVANS PRITCHARD. *African Political Systems* (London: Oxford University Press, 1940).

GAY, JOHN. *Red Dust on the Green Leaves* (Thompson, Conn.: Inter-Culture Associates, 1973).

GLUCKMAN, M. "The Rise of the Zulu Empire," *Scientific American,* vol. 202, no. 4 (1960), pp. 157–69.

——. *Politics, Law and Ritual in Tribal Society* (Chicago: Aldine-Atherton, 1968).

HALLETT, R. "African Politics in the Middle of the 19th Century," *Africa to 1875* (Ann Arbor: University of Michigan Press, 1969).

HERSKOVITS, M. J. *Dahomey, An Ancient West African Kingdom,* 2 vols. (New York: J. J. Augustin, 1938).

HULL, RICHARD W. African Cities and Towns Before the European Conquest (New York: Norton, 1977).

JULY, ROBERT. *Precolonial Africa* (New York: Scribner's Sons, 1975).

LEUTZION, NEHEMIA. *Ancient Ghana and Mali* (London: Methuen, 1973).

LEWIN, JULIUS. *Studies in African Law* (Philadelphia: University of Pennsylvania Press, 1947).

MAIR, LUCY. *Primitive Government* (Baltimore: Penguin Books, 1964).

MAQUET, JACQUES. *Civilizations of Black Africa* (London: Oxford University Press, 1972).

MIDDLETON, JOHN and DAVID TAIT. *Tribes Without Rulers* (London: Routledge & Kegan Paul, 1958).

MURPHY, JEFFERSON. *The Bantu Civilization of Southern Africa* (New York: Thomas Y. Crowell, 1974).

OCHOLLA, AYAYO. *Traditional Ideology and Ethics Among the Southern Luo* (Uppsala, Sweeden: Scandinavian Institute of African Studies, 1976).

OMER-COOPER, J. D. *The Zulus Aftermath* (Evanston, Ill.: Northwestern University Press, 1969).

(F) OUOLOGUEM, Y. *Bound to Violence* (New York: Harcourt Brace Jovanovich, 1971).

RADCLIFFE-BROWN, A. R. and DARYLL FORDE (eds.). *African Systems of Kinship and Marriage* (London: Oxford University Press, 1950).

——. *Structure and Function in Primitive Society* (New York: Free Press, 1952).

SCHAPERA, I. *Government and Politics in Tribal Societies* (New York: Schocken, 1967).

(F) SELLASSIE, S. *The Afersata* (New York: Humanities Press, 1969).

(F) ——. *Warrior King* (London: Heinemann, 1974).

SKINNER, E. P. *The Mossi of the Upper Volta* (Stanford, Calif.: Stanford University Press, 1964).

THOMAS, ELIZABETH MARSHALL. *Warrior Herdsmen* (New York: Random House, 1965).

THOMPSON, L. *African Societies in Southern Africa* (New York: Praeger, 1969).

TURNBULL, COLIN. *Man in Africa* (Garden City, N.Y.: Doubleday, 1976).

TYRELL, BARBARA. *Tribal Peoples of Southern Africa* (Capetown, South Africa: Books of Africa, 1971).

VANSINA, S. *Kingdoms of the Savanna* (Madison: University of Wisconsin Press, 1966).

HISTORY OF AFRICA

AJAYI, A. F. and MICHAEL CROWDER (eds.). *History of West Africa*, vol. 1 (New York: Columbia University Press, 1972).

———. *History of West Africa*, vol. 2 (New York: Columbia University Press, 1976).

BENNETT, NORMAN. *Africa and Europe: From Roman Times to the Present* (New York: Africana Publishing, 1975).

BOAHEN, ADU. *Topics in West African History* (London: Longmans, 1966).

BROOKS, LESTER. *Great Civilizations of Ancient Africa* (New York: Four Winds Press, 1971).

CARY, M. and E. H. WARMINGTON. *The Ancient Explorers* (Baltimore: Penguin Books, 1963).

CLARK, J. DESMOND. *The Prehistory of Africa* (New York: Praeger, 1970).

COLE, SONIA. *The Prehistory of East Africa* (New York: Macmillan, 1963).

———. *Leakey's Luck* (New York: Harcourt Brace Jovanovich, 1975).

COLLINS, R. O. (ed.). *African History* (New York: Random House, 1971).

———. *Problems in African History* (Englewood Cliffs, N.J.: Prentice-Hall, 1968).

DAVIDSON, B. *The Lost Cities of Africa* (Boston: Little, Brown, 1959).

———. *A Guide to African History* (Garden City, N.Y.: Doubleday, 1965).

———. *A History of West Africa* (Garden City, N.Y.: Doubleday, 1966).

———. *The African Past* (New York: Grosset & Dunlap, 1967).

———. *A History of East and Central Africa* (Garden City, N.Y.: Doubleday, 1968).

———. *The African Genius* (Boston: Little, Brown, 1969).

———. *Africa in History* (New York: Macmillan, 1969).

DEGRAFT-JOHNSON, J. C. *African History* (New York: Walker, 1954).

FAGE, J. D. *A History of West Africa* (London: Cambridge University Press, 1969).

GAILEY, H. A. *History of Africa from 1800 to Present* (New York: Holt, Rinehart and Winston, 1972).

———. *The History of Africa in Maps* (Chicago: Donoyer-Geppert, 1971).

GANN, L. H. and PETER DUIGNAN. *Africa and the World: An Introduction to the History of Sub-Saharan Africa from Antiquity to 1840* (San Francisco: Chandler Publishing Company, 1972).

HALLETT, R. *Africa to 1875* (Ann Arbor: University of Michigan Press, 1969).

HARRIS, J. E. *Africans and Their History* (New York: Mentor Books, 1972).

HOWE, R. W. *Black Africa*, 2 vols. (New York: Walker, 1966).

INGHAM, K. *A History of East Africa* (New York: Praeger, 1962).

JULY, ROBERT. *A History of the African People* (New York: Scribner's Sons, 1970).

KINGSNORTH, G. *Africa South of the Sahara* (Cambridge, England: Cambridge University Press, 1966).

KLEIN, M. A. and G. W. Johnson (eds.). *Perspectives on the African Past* (Boston: Little, Brown, 1972).

LABOURET, HENRY. *Africa Before The White Man* (New York: Walker, 1962).

MARSH, Z. A. and G. W. KINGSNORTH. *An Introduction to the History of East Africa* (Cambridge, England: Cambridge University Press, 1965).

MCCALL, DANIEL. *Africa in the Time-Perspective* (London: Oxford University Press, 1969).

MOUNTFIELD, DAVID. *A History of African Exploration* (Northbrook, Ill.: Domas Books, 1976).

OLIVER, ROLAND. *An Atlas of African History* (London: Edward Arnold, 1958).

———. *The Middle Ages of African History* (London: Oxford University Press, 1967).

———. *Africa Discovers Her Past* (London: Oxford University Press, 1970).

OLIVER, ROLAND and A. ATMORE. *Africa Since 1800* (Cambridge, England: Cambridge University Press, 1967).

OLIVER, ROLAND and J. D. PAGE. *A Short History of Africa* (Baltimore: Penguin Books, 1962).

—— (eds.). *Papers in African Prehistory* (Cambridge, England: Cambridge University Press, 1970).

OLIVER, ROLAND and GERVASE MATHEW, (eds.). *History of East Africa* (London: Oxford University Press, 1963).

OSAE, T. A., S. N. NWABARA, and A. T. O. ODUNSI. *A Short History of West Africa: A.D. 1000 to the Present* (New York: Hill & Wang, 1973).

ROTBERG, ROBERT. *A Political History of Tropical Africa* (New York: Harcourt Brace Jovanovich, 1965).

SAMKANGE, STANLAKE. *African Saga* (Nashville, Tenn.: Abingdon Press, 1971).

TINDALL, P. E. N. *A History of Central Africa* (New York: Praeger, 1968).

WALKER, ERIC A. *A History of Southern Africa* (London: Longmans, 1962).

WARD, W. E. F. *A History of Africa* (Nashville, Tenn.: Aurora Publishers, 1970).

—— and L. WHITE. *East Africa: A Century of Change* (New York: Africana Publishing Corp., 1971).

WEBSTER, J. B. and A. BOAHEN. *History of West Africa* (New York: Praeger, 1967).

WIEDNER, DONALD L. *A History of Africa South of the Sahara* (New York: Random House, 1962).

WILLS, A. J. *An Introduction to the History of Central Africa* (London: Oxford University Press, 1964).

WILSON, DEREK. *A History of South and Central Africa* (Cambridge, England: Cambridge University Press, 1975).

THE AGE OF SLAVERY AND THE BLACK DIASPORA

BAKER, S. *Ismailia* (New York: Harper and Brothers, 1875).

BASTIDE, ROGER. *African Civilizations and the New World* (New York: Harper & Row, 1971).

BAYLISS, J. F. (ed.). *Black Slave Narratives* (New York: Macmillan, 1970).

BEACHEY, R. *The Slave Trade of Eastern Africa* (New York: Barnes & Noble, 1976).

CAIRNES, J. E. *The Slave Power* (New York: Harper & Row, 1969).

CANOT, THEODORE. *Twenty Years of an African Slaver* (New York: Appleton and Company, 1854). See also the original manuscript by Theophilas Conneau, *A Slaver's Log Book* (Englewood Cliffs, N.J.: Prentice-Hall, 1976).

CHINWEIZU, V. *The West and the Rest of Us* (New York: Random House, 1975).

CLARKE, JOHN H. and VINCENT HARDING. *Slave Trade and Slavery* (New York: Holt, Rinehart and Winston, 1970).

COUPLAND, R. *East Africa and Its Invaders* (Oxford: Clarendon Press, 1938).

(F) COURLANDER, HAROLD. *The African* (New York: Crown Publishers, 1967).

CURTIN, PHILIP D. (ed.). *Africa Remembered* (Madison: University of Wisconsin Press, 1967).

——. *The Atlantic Slave Trade* (Madison: University of Wisconsin Press, 1969).

DAVIDSON, B. *Black Mother* (Boston: Little, Brown, 1961).

DAVIS, DAVID. *The Problem of Slavery in Western Culture* (Ithaca, N.Y.: Cornell University Press, 1966).

DuBois, W. E. B. *The Suppression of the Slave Trade* (New York: Shocken Books, 1968, ed. 1896).

DUFFY, J. *A Question of Slavery* (Cambridge, Mass.: Harvard University Press, 1967).

DUMONT, P. J. *Narrative of Thirty-four Years Slavery and Travels in Africa* (London: Richard Phillips, 1819).

ELKINS, S. M. *Slavery* (Chicago: University of Chicago Press, 1968).

FALCONBRIDGE, ALEXANDER. *An Account of the Slave Trade of the Coast of Africa* (London: S. Phillips, 1788).

FISHER, A. and H. FISHER. *Slavery and Muslim Society in Africa* (Garden City, N.Y.: Doubleday, 1972).

FOSTER, HERBERT. *From the African Slave Trade to Emancipation* (Milburn, N.J.: R. F. Publishing, 1974).

HALEY, ALEX. *Roots* (Garden City, N.Y.: Doubleday, 1976).

(F) HERSEY, JOHN R. *White Lotus* (New York: Knopf, 1965).

MANNIX, DANIEL P. and MALCOLM COWLEY. *Black Cargoes: A History of the Atlantic Slave Trade, 1518–1865* (New York: Viking Press, 1962).

NWULIA, MOSES D. E. *Britain and Slavery in East Africa* (Washington, D.C.: Three Continents Press, 1975).

POPE-HENNESSY, J. *A Study of the Atlantic Slave Traders (1441–1807)* (New York: Random House, 1967).

REDDING, SAUNDERS. *They Came in Chains* (Philadelphia: Lippincott, 1950).

RICHARDSON, PATRICK. *Empire and Slavery* (London: Longmans, 1968).

(F) SCHWARZ-BART, ANDRE. *A Woman Named Solitude* (New York: Atheneum, 1973).

(F) SINGER, ISAAC BASHEVI. *The Slave* (New York: Avon, 1968).

WARD, W. E. *The Royal Navy and the Slavers* (New York: Random House, 1969).

THE EUROPEAN PENETRATION

ARNOT, F. S. *Garenganze* (London: Frank Case, 1969).

BAKER, ANNE. *Morning Star* (London: William Kimber, 1972).

BAKER, SAMUEL W. *Albert N'Yanza* (Philadelphia: Lippincott, 1868).

———. *Exploration of the Nile Tributaries of Abyssinia* (Hartford: O. D. Case and Company, 1868).

BARBAZON, JAMES. *Albert Schweitzer* (New York: G. P. Putnam's, 1975).

BARTH, HENRY. *Travels and Discoveries: North and Central Africa,* (Philadelphia: J. W. Bradley, 1859).

BLAKE, ROBERT. *Disraeli* (Garden City, N.Y.: Doubleday, 1967).

BRODIE, F. W. *The Devil Drives* (New York: W. W. Norton, 1967).

BURTON, RICHARD F. *First Footsteps in East Africa* (New York: E. P. Dutton, 1856).

CAMERON, V. L. *Across Africa* (New York: Harper and Bros., 1877).

CHURCHILL, W. S. *The River War* (New York: Award Books, 1964).

CLARK, LEON E. (ed.). *Through African Eyes*, vols. 3, 4 (New York: Praeger, 1970).

COLLINS, R. O. *Europeans in Africa* (New York: Random House, 1971).

———. *Problems in the History of Colonial Africa* (Englewood Cliffs, N.J.: Prentice-Hall, 1970).

COOLEY, W. D. *The Negroland of the Arabs* (New York: Barnes & Noble, 1841).

CURTIN, P. (ed.). *Africa and the West: Intellectual Responses to European Culture* (Madison: University of Wisconsin Press, 1972).

———. *The Image of Africa: British Ideas and Action, 1780–1850,* 2 vols. (Madison: University of Wisconsin Press, 1964).

DEGRAMONT, SANCHE. *The Strong Brown God: The Story of the Niger River* (Boston: Houghton Mifflin, 1976).

DIKE, K. O. *Trade and Politics in the Niger Delta* (London: Oxford University Press, 1956).

DuChaillu, Paul. *Explorations and Adventures* (New York: Harper and Bros., 1862).

———. *My Apong Kingdom* (New York: Harper and Bros., 1874).

Edwards, A. B. *A Thousand Miles Up the Nile* (New York: A. L. Burt, 1888).

Garrison, W. L., *Thoughts on African Colonization* (New York: Arno Press, 1969).

Gollwitzer, Heinz. *Europe in the Age of Imperialism* (New York: Harcourt Brace Jovanovich, 1969).

Hall, Richard, *Stanley: An Adventurer Explored* (Boston: Houghton Mifflin, 1975).

Hallett, Robin (ed.). *The Niger Journal of Richard and John Lander* (New York: Praeger, 1966).

Jeal, Tim. *Livingston* (New York: G. P. Putnam's, 1973).

Johnson, Jean. *Africa and the West* (Hinsdale, Ill.: Dryden Press, 1974).

Livingston, David. *Missionary Travels* (New York: Harper and Bros., 1858).

———. *Perilous Adventures and Extensive Discoveries in the Interior of Africa* (Philadelphia and Boston: Hubbard Brothers, 1872).

———. *Lost and Found, or Africa and Its Explorers* (Hartford: Mutual Publishing Co., 1873).

Livingston, David and H. M. Stanley. *Livingston's Africa* (Philadelphia: Hubbard Bros., 1872).

Livingstone, W. P. *Mary Slessor of Calabar* (London: Hodder and Stoughton, 1915).

MacKay, H. J. *MacKay of Uganda* (New York: A. C. Armstrong, 1890).

McEwan, P. J. *Nineteenth Century Africa* (London: Oxford University Press, 1968).

Moffat, Robert. *Missionary Labours and Scenes* (New York: Robert Carter, 1848).

Moorehead, Alan. *The White Nile* (New York: Harper & Row, 1960).

———. *The Blue Nile* (New York: Harper & Row, 1962).

Moorhouse, Geoffrey. *The Missionaries* (Philadelphia: Lippincott, 1973).

Mounteney-Jephson, A. J. *Emin Pasha* (New York: Scribner's Sons, 1890).

Nicol, Davidson (ed.). *Africanus Horton* (New York: Africana Publishing Corp., 1969).

Ogot, Bethwell (ed.). *War and Society in Africa* (London: Frank Cass, 1974).

Omer-Cooper, J. D. et al. *Making of Modern Africa* (London: Longmans, 1968).

Park, Mungo. *Life and Travels in Africa* (New York: Dodd & Mead, 1795).

Peters, Carl. *New Light on Dark Africa* (London: Ward, Lock, 1891).

Pinto, Serpa, *How I Crossed Africa*, 2 vols. (London: Sampson Low, Marston, Searle, and Rivington, 1881).

(F) Shaw, George Bernard. *The Black Girl in Search of God* (New York: Dodd, Mead, 1959).

Simmons, Jack. *Livingston and Africa* (New York: Collier Books, 1962).

Speke, John. *Journal of the Discovery of the Source of the Nile* (New York: Harper and Bros., 1864).

Stanley, H. M. *Through the Dark Continent*, 2 vols. (New York: Harper and Bros., 1879).

———. *Coomassie and Magdala* (New York: Harper and Bros., 1874).

———. *In Darkest Africa*, 2 vols. (New York: Scribner's Sons, 1891).

Strachey, Lytton. *Eminent Victorians* (New York: Capricorn Books, 1963).

Taylor, Bayard. *Journey to Central Africa* (New York: G. P. Putnam, 1854).

Thompson, Joseph. *To the Central African Lakes and Back,* 2 vols. (Boston: Houghton Mifflin, 1881).

———. *Through Masai Land,* (London: Franc Cass, 1885).

Thunberg, C. P. *Travels* (London: F. and C. Rivington, 1795).

Tyler, Josiah (ed.). *Livingston Lost and Found* (Hartford: Mutual Publishing, 1873).

Walker, F. Deaville. *William Carey* (Chicago: Moody Press, 1925).

Wasserman, Jacob. *Bula Matari* (New York: Liveright, 1933).

IMPERIALISM: THE "SCRAMBLE FOR AFRICA" AND AFRICAN RESISTANCE

(F) ACHEBE, C. *Things Fall Apart* (New York: Humanities Press, 1958).

(F) AKPAN, N. U. *The Wooden Gong* (London: Longmans, 1965).

AUSTEN, R. A. *Modern Imperialism: Western Overseas Expansion and Its Aftermath, 1776–1965* (Boston: D. C. Heath, 1969).

BERESFORD, CHARLES. *The Memoirs of Admiral Lord Charles Beresford* (Toronto: S. B. Gundy, 1914).

BETTS, R. (ed.). *The "Scramble" for Africa* (Boston: D. C. Heath, 1966).

CARTEY, WILFRED and M. KILSON (eds.). *Colonial Africa* (New York: Random House, 1970).

CHAMBERLAIN, M. E. *The Scramble for Africa* (London: Longmans, 1974).

COFFEY, THOMAS. *Lion By the Tail* (New York: Viking Press, 1974).

CROWDER, M. *West African Resistance to Colonial Rule* (London: Hutchinson, 1971).

FIELDHOUSE, D. K. *The Colonial Empires* (New York: Delacorte Press, 1965).

GALLAGHER, J. and R. ROBINSON. *Africa and the Victorians* (London: Macmillan, 1965).

GARDNER, B. *The African Dream* (New York: G. P. Putnam, 1970).

GIFFORD, P. and W. R. LOUIS. *Britain and Germany in Africa* (New Haven: Yale University Press, 1967).

HALIBURTON, G. M. *The Prophet Harris* (London: Oxford University Press, 1973).

HARGREAVES, J. *Prelude to the Partition of West Africa* (London: Macmillan, 1963).

HARRIS, W. B. *France, Spain, and the Rif* (London: Edward Arnold, 1927).

HEGGOY, A. A. *The African Policies of Gabriel Hanotaux, 1894–1889* (Athens: University of Georgia Press, 1972).

HOBSON, J. A. *Imperialism* (London: Allen & Unwin, 1938).

HUTTENBACK, R. A. *The British Imperial Experience* (New York: Harper & Row, 1966).

KILLINGRAY, DAVID. *A Plague of Europeans* (Baltimore: Penguin Education, 1973).

LICHTHEIM, G. *Imperialism* (New York: Praeger, 1971).

MAGNUS, P. *Kitchener: Portrait of an Imperialist* (New York: E. P. Dutton, 1968).

MILLER, CHARLES. *Battle for the Bundu* (New York: Macmillan, 1974).

MILLIN, S. G. *Cecil Rhodes* (New York: Harper & Row, 1933).

MOREL, E. D. *The Black Man's Burden* (New York: Monthly Review Press, 1970).

NADEL, G. and P. CURTIS. *Imperialism and Colonialism* (New York: Macmillan, 1964).

(F) NGUBANE, JORDAN K. *USHABA: The Hurtle to Blood River* (Washington, D.C.: Three Continents Press, 1974).

PENROSE, E. F. (ed.). *European Imperialism and the Partition of Africa* (London: Frank Cass, 1976).

ROTBERG, R. and A. MAZRUI (eds.). *Protest and Power in Black Africa* (London: Oxford University Press, 1970).

(F) SAMKANGE. *On Trial for My Country* (New York: Humanities Press, 1966).

STEVENS, G. W. *With Kitchener to Khartum* (New York: Dodd, Mead, 1898).

STRANGE, Mark. *Cape to Cairo: Rape of a Continent* (New York: Harcourt Brace Jovanovich, 1973).

TWAIN, MARK. "To the Person Sitting in Darkness," in Charles Neider (ed.), *The Complete Essays of Mark Twain* (Garden City, N.Y.: Doubleday, 1963).

WEST, RICHARD. *Congo* (New York: Holt, Rinehart and Winston, 1972).

WINKS, R. (ed.). *British Imperialism* (New York: Holt, Rinehart and Winston, 1965).

WRIGHT, H. M. *The New Imperialism* (Boston: D. C. Heath, 1961).

ZIEGLER, PHILIP. *Omdurman* (New York: Knopf, 1974).

COMPARATIVE COLONIAL SYSTEMS

(F) ACHEBE, C. *Arrow of God* (Garden City, N.Y.: Doubleday, 1967).

(F) AKPAN, N. U. *The Wooden Gong* (London: Longmans, 1965).

ANDERSON, SUSAN. *May Perry of Africa* (Nashville, Tenn.: Broadman Press, 1966).

BALANDIER, GEORGES. *Ambiguous Africa* (New York: Random House, 1966).

BEBEY, FRANCIS. *Agatha Moudio's Son* (New York: Lawrence Hill, 1973).

BETHAM-EDWARDS M. *In French-Africa* (London: Chapman and Hall, 1912).

BETTS, R. *Assimilation and Association in French Colonial Theory* (New York: Columbia University Press, 1961).

BRUNSCHWIG, H. *French Colonialism, 1871–1914: Myths and Realities* (London: Pall Mall, 1964).

CESAIRE, AIMÉ. *Discourse on Colonialism* (New York: Monthly Review Press, 1972).

COHEN, WILLIAM. *Rulers of Empire* (Stanford, Calif.: Stanford University Press, 1971).

CROWDER, M. *West Africa under Colonial Rule* (Evanston, Ill.: Northwestern University Press, 1968).

DUFFY, J. *Portugal in Africa* (Baltimore: Penguin, 1962).

———. *Portuguese Africa* (Cambridge, Mass.: Harvard University Press, 1959).

DUIGNAN, PETER and GANN, L. H. *Colonialism in Africa, 1870–1960* (Cambridge, England: Cambridge University Press, 1973).

(F) ECHEWA, T. O. *The Lands Lord* (Westport, Conn.: Lawrence Hill, 1976).

FYFE, C. *Africanus Horton* (London: Oxford University Press, 1972).

(F) GREENE, G. *The Heart of the Matter* (New York: Viking Press, 1961).

HAILEY, LORD. *An African Survey* (London: Oxford University Press, 1956).

HODGKIN, T. *Nationalism in Colonial Africa* (New York: New York University Press, 1956).

MANNONI, C. *Prospero and Caliban* (New York: Praeger, 1956).

MARSHALL, D. BRUCE. *The French Colonial Myth and Constitution-making in the Fourth Republic* (New Haven: Yale University Press, 1973).

(F) NWAPA, F. *Efuru* (New York: Humanities Press, 1966).

(F) OYONO, F. *Houseboy* (New York: Humanities Press, 1960).

(F) ———. *The Old Man and the Medal* (New York: Humanities Press, 1956).

RAM, V. *Comparative Colonial Policy* (London: Longmans, 1929).

ROBERTS, S. *History of French Colonial Policy* (London: King and Company, 1929).

SCHWEITZER, ALBERT. *On the Edge of the Primeval Forest* (New York: Macmillan, 1948).

SMITH, B. S. *But Always as Friends* (Durham, N.C.: Duke University Press, 1969).

TURNER, VICTOR (ed.). *Colonialism in Africa: 1870–1960* (Cambridge, England: Cambridge University Press, 1971).

VARLEY, D. *A Bibliography of Italian Colonization in Africa with a Section on Abyssinia* (London: Pall Mall, 1970).

WEINSTEIN, BRIAN. *Eboué* (London: Oxford University Press, 1972).

WILFRED, CARTEY and MARTIN KILSON (eds.). *The African Reader: Colonial Africa* (New York: Random House, 1970).

PAN-AFRICANISM AND NEGRITUDE

ABRAHAM, W. E. *The Mind of Africa* (Chicago: University of Chicago Press, 1962).

AJALA, ADEKUNLE. *Pan-Africanism: Evolution, Progress and Prospects* (New York: St. Martin's Press, 1973).

AMODA, MOYIBI. *Black Power and Black Vision* (Philadelphia: Westminister Press, 1972).

ANDEMICAEL, BERHANYKUN. *The OAU and the UN* (New York: Africana Publishing Corp., 1976).

BARRETT, LEONARD. *Soul-Force: African Heritage in Afro-American Religion* (Garden City: Doubleday, 1974).

BETTS, RAYMOND (ed.). *The Ideology of Blackness* (Boston: D. C. Heath, 1971).

CAUTE, DAVID. *Frantz Fanon* (New York: Viking Press, 1970).

CERVENKA, Z. *The Organization of African Unity* (New York: Praeger, 1969).

CLARKE, JOHN HENRIK (ed.). *Malcolm X, The Man and His Times*, 3rd ed. (New York: Collier Books, 1970).

———. *Marcus Garvey and the Vision of Africa* (New York: Random House, 1974).

CRONON, E. D. *Black Moses* (Madison: University of Wisconsin Press, 1955).

——— (ed.). *Marcus Garvey* (Englewood Cliffs, N.J.: Prentice-Hall, 1973).

DIOP, C. A. *The African Origin of Civilization* (New York: Lawrence Hill, 1974).

DuBOIS, W. E. B. *The Autobiography of W. E. B. DuBois* (New York: New World Publishers, 1968).

———. *Black Titan* (Boston: Beacon Press, 1970).

———. *The World and Africa* (New York: International Publishers, 1965).

FANON, FRANTZ. *The Wretched of the Earth* (New York: Grove Press, 1963).

———. *Black Skin, White Masks* (New York: Grove Press, 1967).

———. *A Dying Colonialism* (New York: Grove Press, 1965).

FERKISS, VICTOR. *Africa's Search for Identity* (Cleveland: World Publishing, 1966).

FOX, ELTON. *Garvey* (New York: Dodd, Mead, 1972).

FRANCK, T. M. (ed.). *Why Federations Fail* (New York: New York University Press, 1968).

GARVEY, A. *Garvey and Garveyism* (New York: Macmillan, 1963).

GEISMAN, PETER. *Fanon* (New York: Dial Press, 1971).

GENDZIER, IRENE L. *Frantz Fanon: A Critical Study* (New York: Vintage Press, 1974).

GREEN, R. and A. SEIDMAN. *Unity or Poverty* (Baltimore: Penguin Books, 1969).

HANSEN, EMMANUEL. *Frantz Fanon* (Columbus: Ohio State University Press, 1977).

HARRIS, SHELDON. *Paul Cuffe: Black America and the African Return* (New York: Simon & Schuster, 1972).

HERSKOVITS, M. J. *The Myth of the Negro Past* (Boston: Beacon Press, 1959).

HOOKER, J. *Black Revolutionary* (New York: Praeger, 1967).

———. *Henry Silvester Williams* (London: Rex Collins, 1975).

JACQUES-GARVEY, A. (ed.). *Philosophy and Opinions of Marcus Garvey* (New York: Atheneum, 1969).

JAHN, JANHEINZ. *Neo-African Literature* (New York: Grove Press, 1968).

KESTELOOT, LILYAN. *Intellectual Origins of the African Revolution* (Rockville, Md.: New Perspectives, 1968).

KILSON, M. and A. HILL (eds.). *Apropos of Africa* (Garden City, N.Y.: Doubleday, 1971).

KING, WOODIE and EARL ANTHONY (eds.). *Black Poets and Prophets* (New York: Mentor Books, 1972).

LEGUM, C. *Pan Africanism* (New York: Praeger, 1962).

LYNCH, H. *Edward Wilmot Blyden* (London: Oxford University Press, 1967).

MAQUET, JACQUES. *Africanity: The Cultural Unity of Black Africa* (London: Oxford University Press, 1972).

MARKOVITZ, I. *Leopold Senghor and the Politics of Negritude* (New York: Atheneum, 1969).

MEMMI, ALBERT. *The Colonizer and the Colonized* (Boston: Beacon Press, 1967).

MINOGUE, MARTIN and JUDITH MOLLEY (eds.). *African Aims and Attitudes* (Cambridge, England: Cambridge University Press, 1924).

MPHAHLELE, E. *The African Image* (New York: Praeger, 1962).

MUKASA, HAM. *Sir Apolo Kagua Discovers Britain* (New York: Humanities Press, 1975).

PADMORE, GEORGE. *Pan-Africanism or Communism* (Garden City, N.Y.: Doubleday, 1971).

QUAISON-SACKEY, ALEX. *Africa Unbound* (New York: Praeger, 1962).

REDLEY, E. *Black Exodus* (New Haven: Yale University Press, 1969).

REED, JOHN and CLIVE WAKE. *Senghor: Prose and Poetry* (London: Oxford University Press, 1965).

THOMPSON, V. B. *Africa and Unity: The Evolution of Pan-Africanism* (New York: Humanities Press, 1969).

TURNBULL, COLIN. *The Lonely African* (Garden City, N.Y.: Doubleday, 1962).

WELCH, C., *Pan Africanism: Dream of Unity* (Ithaca, N.Y.: Cornell University Press, 1967).

YONG, TABAN LO LI. *The Last Word* (Nairobi, Kenya: East African Publishing House, 1969).

DECOLONIZATION IN FRANCOPHONE AFRICA

ADLOFF, RICHARD. *West Africa: The French-Speaking Nations* (New York: Holt, Rinehart and Winston, 1964).

DELUSIGNAN, GUY. *French-Speaking Africa Since Independence* (New York: Praeger, 1969).

FOLTZ, WILLIAM. *From French West Africa to the Mali Federation* (New Haven: Yale University Press, 1969).

GERTEINY, A. *Maruitania* (New York: Praeger, 1967).

HARGREAVES, JOHN (ed.). *France and West Africa* (New York: Macmillan, 1969).

———. *West Africa: The Former French States* (Englewood Cliffs, N.J.: Prentice-Hall, 1967).

HATCH, J. *Africa: The Rebirth of Self-Rule* (London: Oxford University Press, 1957).

JALLOH, A. A. *Political Integration in French-Speaking Africa* (Berkeley: University of California Press, 1974).

MACRAE, D. *Parliament, Parties and Society in France, 1946–1958* (London: Macmillan, 1967).

MACRIDIS, R. *"France," Modern Political Systems: Europe* (Englewood Cliffs, N.J.: Prentice-Hall, 1963).

MORGENTHAU, R. S. *Political Parties in French Speaking West Africa* (London: Clarendon Press, 1964).

MORTIMER, E. *France and the Africans 1944–1960* (New York: Walker, 1969).

SALACUSE, J. W. *French Speaking Africa* (Charlottesville, Virginia: Michie, 1969).

THOMPSON, V. M. and R. ADLOFF. *French West Africa* (Stanford, Calif.: Stanford University Press, 1958).

WALLERSTEIN, IMMANUEL. *Africa: The Politics of Independence* (New York: Random House, 1961).

ZOLBERG, A. *One Party Government in the Ivory Coast* (Princeton, N.J.: Princeton University Press, 1964).

DECOLONIZATION IN ANGLOPHONE AFRICA

APTER, D. *Political Kingdom in Uganda* (Princeton, N.J.: Princeton University Press, 1965).

AUSTIN, DENNIS. *Politics in Ghana 1946–1960* (London: Oxford University Press, 1964).

BARBER, S. *Rhodesia: Background to Rebellion* (London: Oxford University Press, 1967).

CHURCH, R. J. HARRISON. *Environment and Politics in West Africa* (New York: Van Nostrand, 1967).

COLEMAN, J. *Nigeria: Background to Nationalism* (Los Angeles: University of California Press, 1958).

GAILEY, HARRY. *A History of the Gambia* (New York: Praeger, 1962).

GROTPETER, JOHN and WARREN WEINSTEIN. *The Pattern of African Decolonization: A New Interpretation* (Syracuse, N.Y.: The Maxwell School, 1973).

HALLETT, ROBIN. *People and Progress in West Africa* (New York: Pergamon Press, 1966).

ITOTE, W. *"Mau Mau" General* (Nairobi, Kenya: East Africa Publishing House, 1967).

JORDAN, ROBERT. *Government and Power in West Africa* (New York: Africana Publishing Corp., 1970).

KILSON, M. *Political Change in a West African State (Sierra Leone)* (Cambridge, Mass.: Harvard University Press, 1966).

LEWIS, W. ARTHUR. *Politics in West Africa* (London: Oxford University Press, 1965).

MULFORD, D. *Zambia: The Politics of Independence 1957–1964* (London: Oxford University Press, 1967).

MUNGEAM, G. H. *British Rule in Kenya* (London: Oxford University Press, 1967).

(F) NGUGI, J. *A Grain of Wheat* (New York: Humanities Press, 1967).

(F) ———. *Weep Not Child* (New York: Collier Books, 1968).

OHAEG BULAM, F. U. *Nationalism in Colonial and Post-Colonial Africa* (Washington, D.C.: University Press of America, 1977).

POST, KEN. *The New States of West Africa* (Baltimore: Penguin Books, 1964).

POST, KEN and GEORGE JENKINS. *The Price of Liberty: Personality and Politics in Colonial Nigeria* (Cambridge, England: Cambridge University Press, 1973).

PRICE, J. H. *Political Institutions of West Africa* (New York: Humanities Press, 1967).

STEVENS, H. *The Political Transformation of Tanganyika* (New York: Praeger, 1968).

WILSON, H. S. (ed.). *Origins of West African Nationalism* (New York: St. Martin's Press, 1969).

THE DIPLOMACY OF INDEPENDENCE

AKPAN, MOSES E. *African Goals and Diplomatic Strategies in the United Nations* (North Quincy, Mass.: Christopher Publishing House, 1976).

(F) AYNOR, H. S. *Notes from Africa* (New York: Praeger, 1969).

BURKE, F. *Africa's Quest for Order* (Englewood Cliffs, N.J.: Prentice-Hall, 1964).

CARTEY, WILFRED and MARTIN KILSON (eds.). *The African Reader: Independent Africa* (New York: Random House, 1970).

CERVENKA, Z. *The Organization of African Unity* (New York: Praeger, 1969).

GEIGER, T. *The Conflicted Relationship* (New York: McGraw-Hill, 1967).

HOVET, THOMAS. *Africa in the United Nations* (Evanston, Ill.: Northwestern University Press, 1962).

MARVIN, D. (ed.). *Emerging Africa in World Affairs* (San Francisco: Chandler, 1965).

MAZRUI, A. *Towards a Pax Africana* (Chicago: University of Chicago Press, 1967).

———. *A World Federation of Cultures: An African Perspective* (New York: Free Press, 1976).

McKAY, V. *African Diplomacy* (New York: Praeger, 1966).

NIELSON, W. *The Great Powers and Africa* (New York: Praeger, 1969).

PADELFORD, NORMAN and RUPERT EMERSON (eds.). *Africa and World Order* (New York: Praeger, 1962).

SHEPARD, GEORGE. *Nonaligned Black Africa* (Boston: D. C. Heath, 1970).

THOMPSON, VIRGINIA. *West Africa's Council of the Entente* (Ithaca, N.Y.: Cornell University Press, 1972).

WALLERSTEIN, I. *Africa: The Politics of Unity* (New York: Random House, 1967).

WIDSTRAND, C. G. (ed.). *African Boundary Problems* (Uppsala, Sweden: Scandinavian Institute of African Studies, 1969).

ZARTMAN, I. W. *International Relations in the New Africa* (Englewood Cliffs, N.J.: Prentice-Hall, 1964).

POLITICS OF CONSENSUS AND DIRECTION

APTER, D. *The Gold Coast in Transition* (Princeton, N.J.: Princeton University Press, 1955).

————. *The Politics of Modernization* (Chicago: University of Chicago Press, 1965).

BUSIA, K. A. *Africa in Search of Democracy* (New York: Praeger, 1967).

CARTER, G. (ed.). *National Unity and Regionalism in Eight African States* (Ithaca, N.Y.: Cornell University Press, 1967).

————. *African One Party States* (Ithaca, N.Y.: Cornell University Press, 1962).

————. *Five African States* (Ithaca, N.Y.: Cornell University Press, 1968).

COLEMAN, J. and C. ROSBERG. *Political Parties and National Integration in Tropical Africa* (Berkeley: University of California Press, 1965).

HACHTEN, W. *Muffled Drums* (Ames: Iowa State University Press, 1971).

JOHNSON, W. *The Cameroon Federation* (Princeton, N.J.: Princeton University Press, 1970).

(F) KAYIRA, LEGSON. *The Detainee* (New York: Humanities Press, 1974).

LOFCHIE, M. (ed.). *The State of the Nations* (Berkeley: University of California Press, 1971).

(F) PALANGYO, P. *Dying in the Sun* (New York: Humanities Press, 1968).

SKLAR, R. *Nigerian Political Parties* (Princeton, N.J.: Princeton University Press, 1963).

SNYDER, F. *One Party Government in Mali* (New Haven: Yale University Press, 1965).

ZOLBERG, A. *One Party Government in the Ivory Coast* (Princeton, N.J.: Princeton University Press, 1964).

————. *Creating Political Order* (Chicago: Rand McNally, 1967).

"THINGS FALL APART"

(F) ACHEBE, C. *No Longer At Ease* (New York: Astor-Honor, 1961).

(F) ————. "The Voter," in C. Achebe, *Girls at War and Other Stories* (New York: Collier Books, 1970).

ANDRESKI, A. *The African Predicament* (Chicago: Aldine-Atherton, 1968).

(F) ARMAH, AYI KWEI. *The Beautyful Ones Are Not Yet Born* (Boston: Houghton Mifflin, 1968).

BRETTON, H. *The Rise and Fall of Swame Nkrumah* (New York: Praeger, 1966).

(F) CESAIRE, A. *A Season in the Congo* (New York: Grove Press, 1968).

DUMONT, R. *False Start in Africa* (New York: Praeger, 1966).

(F) DUODU, CAMERON. *The Gab Boys* (New York: Fontane Books, 1969).

FITCH, R. and M. OPPENHEIMER. *Ghana: End of an Illusion* (New York: Monthly Review Press, 1966).

(F) GOLDING, WILLIAM. *Lord of the Flies* (New York: G. P. Putnam, 1959).

HUNTINGTON, S. "Political Development and Political Decay," *World Politics,* vol. 17, no. 3 (1965), pp. 386–430.

NKRUMAH, K. *Dark Days in Ghana* (New York: International Publishers, 1966).

ODINGA, OGINGA. *Not Yet Uhuru* (New York: Hill & Wang, 1967).

OJUKWU, ODUMEGWU. *Biafra* (New York: Harper & Row, 1969).

———. *Random Thoughts* (New York: Harper & Row, 1969).

RIVKIN, ARNOLD. *Nation-Building in Africa* (New Brunswick, N.J.: Rutgers University Press, 1969).

(F) SERUMAGA, ROBERT. *Return to the Shadows* (New York: Atheneum, 1970).

SOYINKA, WOLE. *Kongi's Harvest* (London: Oxford University Press, 1967).

———. *The Interpreters* (New York: Macmillan, 1965).

THE PRAETORIAN IMPULSE

(F) ACHEBE, CHINUA. *A Man of the People* (Garden City, N.Y.: Doubleday, 1965).

AFRIFA, A. *The Ghana Coup* (London: Frank Cass, 1966).

(F) ALUKO, T. M. *Chief the Honourable Minister* (New York: Humanities Press, 1970).

BEBLER, ANTON (ed.). *Military Rule in Africa* (New York: Praeger, 1973).

BIENEN, H. (ed.). *The Military Intervenes* (New York: Russell Sage, 1970).

DECALO, SAMUEL. *Coups and Army Rule in Africa* (New Haven: Yale University Press, 1976).

FEIT, EDWARD. *The Armed Bureaucrats* (Boston: Houghton Mifflin, 1973).

FIRST, RUTH. *Power in Africa* (Baltimore: Penguin Books, 1972).

GRUNDY, K. *Conflicting Images of the Military in Africa* (Nairobi, Kenya: East African Publishing House, 1968).

GUTTERIDGE, W. *The Military in African Politics* (London: Methuen, 1969).

HUNTINGTON, SAMUEL. *The Soldier and the State* (Cambridge, Mass.: Harvard University Press, 1957).

———. *Changing Patterns of Military Politics* (New York: Free Press, 1962).

KELLEY, G. *Lost Soldiers: The French Army and Empire in Crisis, 1947–1962* (Cambridge, Mass.: MIT Press, 1965).

LEE, J. M. *African Armies and Civil Order* (New York: Praeger, 1969).

LEFEVER, E. *Spear and Scepter* (Washington, D.C.: Brookings Institute, 1970).

LUTTWAK, E. *Coup d'Etat* (New York: Fawcett Books, 1968).

MAZRUI, ALI. "Soldiers as Traditionalisors," *World Politics,* vol. 28, no. 2 (January 1976), pp. 246–72.

MINERS, N. J. *The Nigerian Army 1956–1966* (London: Methuen, 1971).

OCRAN, A. K. *A Myth is Broken* (London: Longmans, 1968).

PYE, L. "Armies in the Process of Political Modernization," in J. J. Johnson, *Role of the Military in Underdeveloped Countries* (Princeton, N.J.: Princeton University Press, 1962).

WEEKS, G. "The Armies of Africa," *Africa Report* (January 1, 1964).

WELCH, C. (ed.). *Soldier and State in Africa* (Evanston, Ill.: Northwestern University Press, 1970).

RACIAL AND CULTURAL DICHOTOMIES
IN THE AFRICAN CONTEXT

ABRAHAMS, P. *Tell Freedom* (New York: Collier Books, 1970).

(F) ACHEBE, CHINUA. "Marriage is a Private Affair," in C. Achebe, *Girls at War and Other Stories* (New York: Collier Books, 1970).

BESHIR, M. O. *The Southern Sudan: Background to Conflict* (New York: Praeger, 1968).

BILL, JAMES A. and CARL LEIDEN. *The Middle East: Politics and Power* (Boston: Allyn & Bacon, 1974).

(F) EKWENSI, C. *Iska* (New York: Humanities Press, 1961).

GERTEINY, A. *Mauritania* (New York: Praeger, 1967).

GLUBB, J. *A Short History of the Arab Peoples* (New York: Stein & Day, 1970).

(F) HEAD, B. *Maru* (New York: McCall Publishing, 1971).

HISKETT, MERVYN. *The Sword of Truth: The Life and Times of Shehu Usuman Dan Fodio* (London: Oxford University Press, 1973).

HUTTENBACK, ROBERT A. *Racism and Empire* (Ithaca, N.Y.: Cornell University Press, 1976).

KING, NOEL Q. *Christian and Muslim in Africa* (New York: Harper & Row, 1971).

KRITZECK, J. and W. LEWIS (eds.). *Islam in Africa* (New York: Van Nostrand, 1969).

KUPER, L. and M. G. SMITH (eds.). *Pluralism in Africa* (Los Angeles: University of California Press, 1969).

MELADY, T. P. *Burundi: The Tragic Years* (Maryknoll, Md.: Orbis Books, 1974).

ODUHO, W. and W. DENG. *The Problem of the Southern Sudan* (London: Oxford University Press, 1962).

OLORUNSULA, V. (ed.). *The Politics of Cultural Sub-Nationalism in Africa* (Garden City, N.Y.: Doubleday, 1972).

SEGAL, R. *The Race War* (New York: Viking Press, 1966).

TOYNBEE, A. *Between the Niger and the Nile* (London: Oxford University Press, 1962).

TRIMINGHAM, J. *Islam in West Africa* (London: Oxford University Press, 1964).

AFRICAN SOCIALISM

BUSIA, K. A. "African Socialism," *Africa in Search of Democracy* (New York: Praeger, 1967).

NNOLI, O. "The Meaning of Self-Reliance for Africa," *Africa Report* (January 1971), pp. 23–25.

NYERERE, J. *Freedom and Socialism* (London: Oxford University Press, 1968).

———. *Ujamaa: Essays on Socialism* (London: Oxford University Press, 1968).

REPUBLIC OF KENYA. *African Socialism,* Sessional Paper No. 10 of 1963/65 (Nairobi, Kenya: Government Printer, 1966).

ROSBERG, C. and W. FRIEDLAND (eds.). *African Socialism* (Stamford, Conn.: Hoover Institute Press, 1965).

SENGHOR, L. *On African Socialism* (New York: Praeger, 1964).

THOMAS, L. V. *Le Socialisme et L'Afrique* (Paris: Le Livre Africain, 1966).

ECONOMIC DEVELOPMENT:
HOPES AND IMPEDIMENTS

AMIN, SAMIR. *Unequal Development: An Essay on the Social Formations of Peripheral Capitalism* (New York: Monthly Review Press, 1977).

CERVENKA, Z. (ed.). *Land-Locked Countries of Africa* (Uppsala, Sweden: Scandinavia Institute of African Studies, 1973).

DUMONT, R. *False Start in Africa* (New York: Praeger, 1966).

HANCE, W. *African Economic Development* (New York: Praeger, 1967).

HAPGOOD, D. *Africa: From Independence to Tomorrow* (New York: Atheneum, 1970).

HUNTER, G. *The Best of Both Worlds?* (London: Oxford University Press, 1967).

————. *Modernizing Peasant Societies* (London: Oxford University Press, 1969).

KAMARCK, A. *The Economics of African Development* (New York: Praeger, 1967).

MEISTER, ALBERT. *East Africa: The Past in Chains, the Future in Pawn* (New York: Walker, 1968).

MILLIKEN, M. F. and DAVID HAPGOOD. *No Easy Harvest* (Boston: Little, Brown, 1968).

MLADEK, J. V. "The Evolution of African Currencies," *Africa Report* (May 1966), pp. 47–51.

MYRDAL, G. *Rich Lands and Poor* (New York: Harper & Row, 1957).

NURKSE, R. *Problems of Capital Formation in Underdeveloped Countries* (Oxford, England: Blackwell, 1957).

ROSTOW, W. *The Stages of Economic Growth* (Cambridge, England: Cambridge University Press, 1960).

STILLMAN, A. "Economic Cooperation in Africa," *Africa Report* (June 1967), pp. 20–26.

VITAKAZI, A. "Non-Governmental Agencies and Their Role in Development in Africa," *African Studies Review*, vol. 13, no. 2 (September 1970), pp. 169–202.

EXOGENOUS FACTORS OPERATIVE IN THE AFRICAN CONTEXT

International Communism

BRZENZINSKI, Z. *Africa and the Communist World* (Stanford, Calif.: Stanford University Press, 1963).

COOLEY, S. K. *East Wind Over Africa*, rev. ed. (New York: Walker, 1966).

KAUTSKY, J. *Political Change in Underdeveloped Countries* (New York: John Wiley, 1967).

LARKIN, B. *China and Africa, 1949–1970* (Berkeley: University of California Press, 1971).

LEGVOLD, R. *Soviet Policy in West Africa* (Cambridge, Mass.: Harvard University Press, 1970).

MORRISON, DAVID. *The USSR and Africa* (London: Oxford University Press, 1964).

TYAGUNENKO, V. L. *Industrialisation of Developing Countries* (Moscow: Progress Publishers, 1973).

UNITED STATES CENTRAL INTELLIGENCE AGENCY. *Communist Aid to Less Developed Countries of the Free World, 1975* (Washington, D.C.: Government Printing Office, 1976).

VAKHRUSHEV, VASILY. *Neocolonialism: Methods and Manoeuvres* (Moscow: Progress Publishers, 1973).

The United States and Western Europe

ANUMONYE, AMECHI. *African Students in Alien Cultures* (Buffalo, N.Y.: Black Academy Press, 1970).

ATWOOD, W. *The Reds and the Blacks* (New York: Harper & Row, 1967).

BALDWIN, D. *Foreign Aid and American Foreign Policy* (New York: Praeger, 1966).

CHESTER, EDWARD. *Clash of Titans* (Maryknoll, Md.: Orbis Books, 1974).

CLARK, JOHN PEPPER. *America, Their America* (New York: Africana Publishing Corp., 1964).

CROCKER, C. "France's Changing Military Interests," *Africa Report* (June 1968).

EMERSON, R. *Africa and U.S. Policy* (Englewood Cliffs, N.J.: Prentice-Hall, 1966).

HAYFORD, F. K. *Inside America: A Black Diplomat Speaks Out* (Washington, D.C.: Acropolis Books, 1972).

(F) Ike, Chukwuemeka. *The Naked Gods* (New York: Fontane Books, 1971).

JALLOH, ABDUL A. *Political Integration in French-Speaking Africa* (Berkeley: University of California Press, 1973).

LAKE, ANTHONY. *The "Tar Baby" Option: American Policy Toward South Africa* (New York: Columbia University Press, 1976).

LEMARCHAND, RENE. "The CIA in Africa," *The Journal of Modern African Studies,* vol. 14, no. 3 (1976), pp. 401–26.

LEVITT, LEONARD. *An African Season* (New York: Simon & Schuster, 1966).

LIYONG, TABAN LO. "Negroes are not Africans," in T. L. Liyong, *The Last Word* (Nairobi, Kenya: East African Publishing House, 1969).

McKAY, V. (ed.). *Africa in the United States* (New York: Bartell Books, 1967).

MORROW, JOHN. *First American Ambassador to Guinea* (New Brunswick, N.J.: Rutgers University Press, 1968).

NG'WENO, H. "The Whites and the Brown," *Daily Nation,* reprinted in *Africa Report* (October 1967), p. 75.

NIELSEN, W. *The Great Powers and Africa* (New York: Praeger, 1969).

SMITH, STEWART. *U.S. Neocolonialism in Africa* (Moscow: Progress Publishers, 1974).

(F) THEROUX, PAUL. *Fong and the Indians* (Boston: Houghton Mifflin, 1968).

———. *Girls at Play* (Boston: Houghton Mifflin, 1969).

UNITED STATES DEPARTMENT OF STATE. *National Security Study Memorandum* no. 39 (New York: Lawrence Hill, 1976).

WENNER, K. *Shamba Letu* (Boston: Houghton Mifflin, 1970).

WILLIAMS, G. MENEN. *Africa for the Africans* (Grand Rapids, Mich.: William Eerdmans, 1969).

WOLF, C. JR. *United States Policy and the Third World* (Boston: Little, Brown, 1967).

The Lusotropical Phenomenon

BENDER, GERALD. *Portugal in Africa: A Bibliography of the UCLA Collection* (Los Angeles: African Studies Center, University of California, 1972).

BOXER, C. R. *Four Centuries of Portuguese Expansion 1415–1825* (Los Angeles: University of California Press, 1969).

CHILCOTE, R. *Portuguese Africa* (Englewood Cliffs, N.J.: Prentice-Hall, 1965).

DUFFY, J. *Portugal in Africa* (Baltimore: Penguin Books, 1962).

GALVAO, H. *Santa Maria* (London: Oxford University Press, 1961).

NOGUEIRA, F. *The Third World* (London: Johnson and Company, 1967).

———. *The United Nations and Portugal: A Study of Anti-Colonialism* (London: Sedgwick and Jackson, 1963).

PELISSER, RENÉ. "Spain's African Sandboxes," *Africa Report* (February 1966), pp. 17–38.

TEIXEIRA, B. *The Fabric of Terror* (New York: Devin-Adiar Company, 1965).

REVOLUTIONARY CHANGE IN AFRICA

BARNETT, D. and R. HARVEY. *The Revolution in Angola* (Columbus, Ohio: Bobbs-Merrill, 1972).

CABRAL, AMILCAR. *Revolution in Guinea: An African People's Struggle* (London: State One Publications, 1969).

CHALIAND, GERALD. *Armed Struggle in Africa* (New York: Monthly Review Press, 1969).

CHILCOTE, R. "The Political Thought of Amilcar Cabral," *Journal of Modern African Studies,* vol. 6, no. 3 (1968), pp. 373–88.

CORNELL, BARBARA. *The Bush Rebels* (New York: Holt, Rinehart and Winston, 1972).

DAVISON, B. *The Liberation of Guinea* (Baltimore: Penguin Books, 1969).

———. *In the Eye of the Storm: Angola's People* (Garden City, N.Y.: Doubleday, 1973).

FANON, F. *Toward the African Revolution* (New York: Grove Press, 1967).

GIBSON, R. *African Liberation Movements* (London: Oxford University Press, 1972).

GRUNDY, KENNETH. *Guerrilla Struggle in Africa* (New York: World Order Books, 1971).

LEMARCHAND, R. "Rwanda," in Rene Lemarchand, *Rwanda and Burundi* (New York: Praeger, 1970).

LOFCHIE, M. *Zanzibar: Background to Revolution* (Princeton, N.J.: Princeton University Press, 1965).

MONDLANE, EDUARDO. *The Struggle for Mozambique* (Baltimore: Penguin Books, 1969).

NKRUMAH, KWAME. *Handbook of Revolutionary Warfare* (New York: International Publishers, 1969).

———. *Class Struggle in Africa* (New York: International Publishers, 1970).

———. *Revolutionary Path* (New York: International Publishers, 1973).

OKELLO, JOHN. *Revolution in Zanzibar* (Nairobi, Kenya: East African Publishing House, 1965).

MISCELLANEOUS WORKS: POLITICAL

ADAM, THOMAS. *Government and Politics in Africa* (New York: Random House, 1967).

BARNES, LEONARD. *Africa in Eclipse* (New York: St. Martin's Press, 1971).

BELASCO, M. et al. *Africa: History, Culture, People* (New York: Cambridge Book Company, 1966).

BOZEMAN, ADDA B. *Conflict in Africa: Concepts and Realities* (Princeton, N.J.: Princeton University Press, 1976).

BRETTON, HENRY. *Power and Politics in Africa* (Chicago: Aldine-Atherton, 1972).

CARTER, G. (ed.). *Politics in Africa* (New York: Harcourt Brace Jovanovich, 1966).

———. *Independence for Africa* (New York: Praeger, 1960).

CARTER, G. and W. O. BROWN (eds.). *Transition in Africa* (Boston: Boston University Press, 1954).

COHEN, RONALD and JOHN MIDDLETON (eds.). *From Tribe to Nation in Africa* (San Francisco: Chandler, 1970).

COWAN, L. G. *The Dilemmas of African Independence* (New York: Walker, 1964).

DAVIDSON, BASIL. *Which Way Africa?* (Baltimore: Penguin Books, 1964).

———. *Can Africa Survive?* (Boston: Little, Brown, 1974).

DODGE, DOROTHY. *African Politics in Perspective* (New York: Van Nostrand, 1966).

DORO, MARION and NEWELL STULTZ (eds.). *Governing in Black Africa* (Englewood Cliffs, N.J.: Prentice-Hall, 1970).

DOSTERT, P. E. *Africa 1974* (Washington, D.C.: Stryker-Post, 1974).

EMERSON, RUPERT and MARTIN KILSON (eds.). *The Political Awakening of Africa* (Englewood Cliffs, N.J.: Prentice-Hall, 1965).

HANNA, W. J. (ed.). *Independent Black Africa* (Chicago: Rand McNally, 1960).

———. *Politics in Black Africa* (East Lansing: Michigan State University Press, 1964).

HARRIS, RICHARD (ed.). *The Political Economy of Africa* (Cambridge, England: Schenkman, 1975).

HATCH, JOHN. *A History of Postwar Africa* (New York: Praeger, 1965).

——. *Africa Today And Tomorrow* (New York: Praeger, 1965).

——. *Africa: The Rebirth of Self Rule* (London: Oxford University Press, 1967).

HUXLEY, ELSPETH. *With Forks and Hope* (New York: William Morrow, 1964).

JONES, J. R. MAITLAND. *Politics in Africa: The Former British Territories* (New York: W. W. Norton, 1973).

KAHN, E. J. *The First Decade* (New York: W. W. Norton, 1972).

KEESING'S RESEARCH REPORTS, *Africa Independent* (New York: Scribner's Sons, 1972).

KOHN, H. and WALLACE SOKOLSKY. *African Nationalism in the Twentieth Century* (New York: Van Nostrand, 1960).

KOLEUZON, E. *Africa South of the Sahara* (Boston: Allyn & Bacon, 1970).

LEGUM, COLIN (ed.). *Africa: Contemporary Record* (London: Rex Collings, 1969 and yearly thereafter).

LYSTAD, ROBERT. *The African World* (New York: Praeger, 1965).

MARKOVITZ (ed.). *African Politics and Society* (New York: Free Press, 1970).

MAZRUI, ALI. *Cultural Engineering and Nation-building in East Africa* (Evanston, Ill.: Northwestern University Press, 1972).

McEWAN, P. J. M. (ed.). *Twentieth-Century Africa* (London: Oxford University Press, 1970).

McEWAN, P. J. M. and R. B. SUTCLIFFE (eds.). *Modern Africa* (New York: Thomas Y. Crowell, 1965).

MOORE, C. C. and A. DUNBAR. *Africa: Yesterday and Today* (New York: Bantam Books 1968).

NIELSON, WALDERMAR. *Africa* (New York: Atheneum, 1969).

OLORUNSOLA, V. A. (ed.). *The Politics of Cultural Sub-Nationalism in Africa* (Garden City, N.Y.: Doubleday, 1972).

OPOLOT, JAMES. *Criminal Justice and Nation Building in Africa* (Washington, D.C.: University Press of America, 1976).

PADEN, JOHN and EDWARD SOJA (eds.). *The African Experience* (Evanston, Ill.: Northwestern University Press, 1970).

POTHOLM, C. P. *Four African Political Systems* (Englewood Cliffs, N.J.: Prentice-Hall, 1970).

RUBIN, LESLIE and BRIAN WEINSTEIN. *Introduction to African Politics: A Continental Approach* (New York: Praeger, 1974).

"SCIPIO." *Emergent Africa* (New York: Simon & Schuster, 1965).

SEGAL, RONALD. *African Profiles* (Baltimore: Penguin Books, 1962).

SPIRO, HERBERT. *Africa: The Primacy of Politics* (New York: Random House, 1966).

——. *Politics in Africa* Englewood Cliffs, N.J.: Prentice-Hall, 1962).

——. *Patterns of African Development* (Englewood Cliffs, N.J.: Prentice-Hall, 1967).

SWARTZ, M., V. TURNER, and A. TUDEN (eds.). *Political Anthropology* (Chicago: Aldine-Atherton, 1966).

WALLBANK, W. (ed.). *Contemporary Africa* (New York: Van Nostrand, 1956).

——. *Documents on Modern Africa* (New York: Van Nostrand, 1956).

MISCELLANEOUS WORKS:
ECONOMIC, SOCIAL, AND CULTURAL

ALLEN, PHILIP M. and AARON SEGAL, *The Traveler's Africa* (New York: Hopkinson and Blake, 1973).

BASCOM, W. and M. J. HERSKOVITS (eds.). *Continuity and Change in African Cultures* (Chicago: University of Chicago Press, 1959).

BELASCO, M. J. et al. *The New Africa* (New York: Cambridge Book Company, 1966).

BLUMENTHAL, SUSAN. *Bright Continent* (Garden City, N.Y.: Doubleday, 1974).

BOHANNAN, PAUL. *Africa and Africans* (New York: Natural History Press, 1964).

—— (ed.). *African Homocide and Suicide* (New York: Atheneum, 1967).

CLARK, LEON E. *Continuity and Change*, vol. 1 (New York: Praeger, 1969).

COWAN, L. GRAY (ed.). *Education and Nation-Building in Africa* (New York: Praeger, 1966).

COX, THORNTON. *Traveller's Guide to Southern Africa*, 2nd ed. (New York: Hastings House, 1973).

DAVIDSON, BASIL et al. *African Kingdoms* (New York: Time-Life Books, 1971).

DAVIDSON, NORMAN. *Modern Exploration, Sport and Travel* (Philadelphia: Lippincott, 1932).

DAVIES, JOAN. *African Trade Unions* (Baltimore: Penguin Books, 1966).

DIBBLE, J. B. *In This Land of Eve* (New York: Abingdon Press, 1965).

EISELEN, ELIZABETH and MARGUERITE UTTLEY. *Africa* (New York: Ginn and Company, 1966).

EYER, EDWARD. *Primitive Peoples Today* (Garden City, N.Y.: Doubleday, 1959).

FORDE, DARYLL (ed.). *African Worlds* (London: Oxford University Press, 1954).

GREENBERG, J. H. *Anthropological Linguistics* (New York: Random House, 1968).

GUNTHER, JOHN. *Inside Africa* (New York: Harper & Row, 1953).

GUTKIND, PETER. *The Emergent African Urban Proletariat* (Montreal: McGill Center For Developing Areas Studies, 1974).

HAFKIN, NANCY J. and EDNA G. BAY (eds.). *Women in Africa: Studies in Social and Economic Change* (Stanford, Calif.: Stanford University Press, 1976).

HALLET, JEAN-PIERRE and ALEX PELLE. *Pygmy Kitabu* (New York: Fawcett, 1975).

HEMPSTONE, SMITH. *Africa—Angry Young Giant* (New York: Praeger, 1961).

HERSKOVITS, M. J. *The Human Factor in Changing Africa* (New York: Random House, 1958).

HILLMAN, EUGENE. *Polygamy Reconsidered* (Maryknoll, Md.: Orbis Books, 1975).

IRVINE, S. H. and J. T. SANDERS (eds.). *Cultural Adaptation Within Modern Africa* (New York: Teachers College Press, 1972).

JOHN, JANHEINZ. *Through African Doors* (New York: Evergreen Press, 1962).

JONES, E. C. *The Elizabethan Image of Africa* (Charlottesville: University Press of Virginia, 1971).

KAMARACK, ANDREW M. *The Tropics and Economic Development* (Baltimore: Johns Hopkins University Press, 1977).

KANE, ROBERT S. *Africa A–Z* (Garden City, N.Y.: Doubleday, 1961).

KITCHEN, HELEN (ed.). *A Handbook of African Affairs* (New York: Praeger, 1966).

LEGUM, COLIN (ed.). *Africa: Handbook to a Continent* (New York: Praeger, 1966).

LUDWIG, EMIL. *The Nile* (New York: Garden Publishing Co., 1938).

LYOD, P. C. *Africa in Social Change* (Baltimore: Penguin Books, 1967).

MADUBUIKE, IHECHUKWU. *A Handbook of African Names* (Washington, D.C.: Three Continents Press, 1976).

MAIR, LUCY. *Witchcraft* (New York: McGraw-Hill, 1969).

MALINOWSKI, B. *Magic, Science and Religion* (Garden City, N.Y.: Doubleday, 1948).

——. *Dynamics of Cultural Change* (New Haven: Yale University Press, 1945).

MBITI, JOHN S. *The Prayers of African Religion* (Maryknoll, N.Y.: Orbis Books, 1976).

NOLAN, BARBARA (ed.). *Africa is People* (New York: E. P. Dutton, 1967).

O'BARR, WILLIAM et al. (eds.). *Survey Research in Africa: Its Applications and Limits* (Evanston, Ill.: Northwestern University Press, 1973).

PAGE, MARTIN. *The Yam Factor* (Garden City, N.Y.: Doubleday, 1972).

PAULME, D. (ed.). *Women of Tropical Africa* (Los Angeles: University of California Press, 1971).

ROLAND, JOAN. *Africa: The Heritage and the Challenge* (New York: Fawcett, 1974).

SAID, ABDUL A. *The African Phenomenon* (Boston: Allyn & Bacon, 1968).

SANDBROOK, RICHARD and ROBIN COHEN (eds.). *The Development of an African Working Class* (Toronto: University of Toronto Press, 1976).

SORKIN, ALAN L. *Health Economics in Developing Countries* (Lexington, Mass.: Lexington Books, 1976).

SPENCER, ANNE. *An African Panorama* (New York: Friendship Press, 1970).

TESSLER, MARK et al. *Traditions and Identity in Changing Africa* (New York: Harper & Row, 1973).

VAN DEN BERGE, P. *Africa: Social Problems of Change and Conflict* (San Francisco: Chandler, 1965).

VAN DER POST, L. *The Dark Eye in Africa* (New York: Apollo, 1965).

AFRICAN WILDLIFE

ADAMSON, JOY. *Forever Free* (New York: Bantam Books, 1967).

AKELEY, M. J. *Carl Akeley's Africa* (New York: Blue Ribbon Books, 1929).

BROWN, LESLIE. *The Life of the African Plains* (New York: McGraw-Hill, 1972).

BURTON, JANE. *Animals of the African Year* (New York: Holt, Rinehart and Winston, 1972).

DOUGLAS-HAMILTON I. and O. DOUGLAS-HAMILTON. *Among the Elephants* (New York: Viking Press, 1975).

HEMINGWAY, ERNEST. *Green Hills of Africa* (Middlesex, England: Penguin Books, 1936).

HUNTER, J. A. *Hunter* (New York: Harper & Row, 1954).

LEWIS ETHELREDA (ed.). *Trader Horn* (New York: Simon & Schuster, 1928).

MATTHIESSEN, PETER and ELIOT PORTER. *The Tree Where Man was Born and the African Experience* (New York: E. P. Dutton, 1972).

MOOREHEAD, ALAN. *No Room in the Ark* (New York: Harper & Row, 1957).

MOSS, CYNTHIA. *Portraits in the Wild* (Boston: Houghton Mifflin, 1975).

ROBINS, ERIC. *The Ebony Ark* (New York: Taplinger, 1970).

ROOSEVELT, THEODORE. *African Game Trails,* 2 vols. (New York: Scribner's Sons, 1920).

RUARK, R. *Use Enough Gun* (New York: New American Library, 1966).

––––––. *Horn of the Hunter* (New York: Crest Publications, 1952).

SANDERSON, IVAN. *Animal Treasure* (New York: Pyramid Books, 1966).

SCHALLER, GEORGE. *The Serenget: Lion* (Chicago: University of Chicago Press, 1972).

TAYLOR, JOHN. *Pondoro* (New York: Simon & Schuster, 1955).

TOGAWA, YUKIO. *African Animals* (Tokyo: Kodansha International, 1968).

AFRICAN ARTS

BASCOM, WILLIAM. *African Art in Cultural Perspective* (New York: W. W. Norton, 1973).

BEBEY, FRANCIS. *African Music: A People's Art* (New York: Lawrence Hill, 1975).

BIEBUYCK, DANIEL (ed.). *Tradition and Creativity in Tribal Art* (Los Angeles: University of California Press, 1969).

BOAS, FRANZ. *Primitive Art* (New York: Dover Publications, 1955).

DELANGE, JACQUELINE. *The Art and Peoples of Black Africa* (New York: E. P. Dutton, 1967).

FAGG, WILLIAM and MARGARET PLASS. *African Sculpture* (New York: E. P. Dutton, 1964).

GORER, GEOFFREY. *African Dances* (New York: W. W. Norton, 1962).

LANDECK, BEATRICE. *Echoes of Africa* (New York: David McKay, 1961).

LAUDE, JEAN. *The Arts of Black Africa* (Berkeley: University of California Press, 1971).

MAKEBA, MIRIAM. *The World of African Song* (New York: Quadrangle Books, 1971).

OHN, STEVEN and REBECCA RILEY. *Africa from Real to Reel* (Waltham, Mass.: African Studies Association, 1976).

OLIVER, PAUL. *Savanna Syncopators* (New York: Stein & Day, 1970).

OTTEN, CHARLOTTE (ed.). *Anthropology and Art* (New York: Natural History Press, 1971).

PARRINDER, GEOFFREY. *African Mythology* (London: Paul Hamlyn, 1967).

SEGY, LADISLAS. *African Sculpture Speaks* (New York: Da Capo Press, 1975).

SERWADDA, W. M. *Songs and Stories from Uganda* (New York: Thomas Y. Crowell, 1974).

SWEENEY, J. J. *African Sculpture* (Princeton, N.J.: Princeton University Press, 1964).

WILLETT, FRANK. *African Art* (New York: Praeger, 1971).

WINGERT, P. S. *Primitive Art* (New York: Meridian Books, 1962).

Country by Country Analysis

In the previous section of the bibliography, we dealt with a number of topics whose works can enrich our understanding of how politics in Africa evolved. Here we are concerned with an analysis of each country in Africa. There are numerous books we have placed in their proper category; the list is self-explanatory, although both new and old names have been included if the country has changed names since independence.

In order to keep this section down to a manageable size, we have not included journal articles except in very rare instances. For articles and more recent information (because of the time lag between the writing of a book and its publication), the reader should also consult some of the standard periodicals dealing with Africa such as:

Africa
Africa Report

African Studies Review
Journal of Modern African Studies
Journal of Asian and African Studies
Africa Today
Africa Confidential
Issue
West Africa
Transition
African Forum
Journal of African History
Pan African Journal
African Research Bulletin
Afrique Nouvelle

ALGERIA

BARACI, A. HUM. *Algeria: A Revolution that Failed* (London: Pall Mall, 1966).

BEDJAOUI, M. *La Revolution Algerième et Le Droit* (Brussels: EAIJD, 1961).

BISHAI, W. *Islamic History of the Middle East* (Boston: Allyn & Bacon, 1968).

BLAIR, T. *The Land to Those Who Work It* (Garden City, N.Y.: Doubleday, 1970).

BOUDIAF, M. *Ouva L'Algeria* (Paris: Editions Librare de l'Etoile, 1964).

BRACE, RICHARD. *Morocco, Algeria, Tunisia* (Englewood Cliffs, N.J.: Prentice-Hall, 1964).

CHALIAND, G. *Algérie, Est-Elle Socialiste?* (Paris: François Maspero, 1964).

CLEGG, IAN. *Workers' Self-management in Algeria* (New York: Monthly Review Press, 1971).

HALPERN, M. *The Politics of Social Change in the Middle East and North Africa* (Princeton, N.J.: Princeton University Press, 1963).

HENISSART, P. *Wolves in the City: The Death of French Algeria* (New York: Simon & Schuster, 1970).

LEWIS, BERNARD. *The Arabs in History* (New York: Harper & Row, 1958).

MOORE, C. H. *North Africa* (Boston: Little, Brown, 1970).

OTTAWAY, D. and M. OTTAWAY. *Algeria: The Politics of a Socialist Revolution* (Berkeley: University of California Press, 1970).

PICKLES, D. *Algeria and France: From Colonialism to Cooperation* (New York: Praeger, 1963).

SMITH, W. C. *Islam in Modern History* (New York: New American Library, 1957).

STEEL, RONALD. *North Africa* (New York: H. W. Wilson, 1967).

U.S. DEPARTMENT OF DEFENSE. *Area Handbook for Algeria* (Washington, D.C.: Government Printing Office, 1965).

WILLIAMS, ANN. *Britain and France in the Middle East and North Africa* (New York: St. Martin's Press, 1968).

ZARTMAN, I. W. *Government and Politics in Northern Africa* (New York: Praeger, 1965).

——— (ed.). *Man, State and Society in the Contemporary Magrib* (New York: Praeger, 1973).

ANGOLA

ABSHIRE, DAVID and MICHAEL SAMUELS (eds.). *Portuguese Africa* (New York: Praeger, 1969).

BARNETT, D. and ROY HARVEY (eds.). *The Revolution in Angola: MPLA Life Histories and Documents* (Columbus, Ohio: Bobbs-Merrill, 1972).

BIRMINGHAM, DAVID. *The Portuguese Conquest of Angola* (London: Oxford University Press, 1965).

———. *Trade and Conflict in Angola, 1483-1790* (New York: Oxford University Press, 1966).

CHILCOTE, RONALD. *Portuguese Africa* (Englewood Cliffs, N.J.: Prentice-Hall, 1965).

DASILVA REGO, A. *Portuguese Colonization in the Sixteenth Century* (Johannesburg, South Africa: Juta and Sons, 1957).

DAVIDSON, BASIL. *In the Eye of the Storm: Angola's People* (Garden City, N.Y.: Doubleday, 1973).

DUFFY, JAMES. *Portugal in Africa* (Baltimore: Penguin Books, 1962).

———. *Portuguese Africa* (Cambridge, Mass.: Harvard University Press, 1962).

———. *A Question of Slavery* (Cambridge, Mass.: Harvard University Press, 1967).

ENGMARK, ANDERS and PETER WASTBEPS. *Angola and Mozambique: The Case Against Portugal* (New York: Roy Publishers, 1961).

FREYRE, GILBERTO. *The New World in the Tropics* (New York: Knopf, 1958).

———. *Le Portugaise et les Tropiques* (Lisbon: Government Printer, 1961).

GALVAO, HENRIQUE. *Santa Maria: My Crusade for Portugal* (New York and London: Oxford University Press, 1961).

GLASGOW, ROY. *Pragmatism and Idealism in Brazilian Foreign Policy in Southern Africa,* Munger Africana Library Notes #23 (Pasadena: California Institute of Technology, 1974).

HAMMOND, R. J. *Portugal and Africa 1815-1910* (Stanford, Calif.: Stanford University Press, 1966).

LEGUM, COLIN and TONY HODGES. *After Angola* (New York: Africana Publishing Corp., 1976).

LIVERMORE, H. *History of Portugal* (Cambridge, England: Cambridge University Press, 1947).

MARCUM, JOHN. *The Angolan Revolution* (Cambridge, Mass.: MIT Press, 1969).

MINTER, WILLIAM. *Portuguese Africa and the West* (New York: Monthly Review Press, 1972).

MOREIRA, ADRIANO. *A Policy of Integration* (Lisbon: Government Printer, 1961).

MPLA, *Revolution in Angola* (London: Merlin Press, 1972).

NEVINSON, HENRY W. *A Modern Slavery* (New York: Shocken Books, 1968).

NOGUEIRA, F. *The United Nations and Portugal: A Study of Anti-Colonialism* (London: Sidgwick & Jackson, 1963).

———. *The Third World* (London: Johnson & Johnson, 1967).

OKUMA, T. *Angola in Ferment* (Boston: Beacon Press, 1962).

SALAZAR, A. *Portugal and the Anti-Colonialist Campaign* (Lisbon: Government Printer, 1960).

TEIXEIRA, BERNARDO. *The Fabric of Terror* (New York: Devin-Adair Company, 1965).

WHEELER, DOUGLAS and RENÉ PÉLISSIER. *Angola* (New York: Praeger, 1971).

WILSON, E. *Angola Beloved* (Neptune, N.J.: Loizeaux Bros., Inc., 1967).

BOTSWANA

CERVENKA, Q., C. DONAT, H. LAB, and W. LONSKI. *Botswana, Lesotho and Swaziland* (Bonn: Neue Reihe, 1974).

HAILEY, LORD. *The Republic of South Africa and the High Commission Territories* (London: Oxford University Press, 1963).

HALPERN, J. *South Africa's Hostages* (Baltimore: Penguin Books, 1965).

HEAD, B. *A Question of Power* (New York: Parthenon Books, 1973).

(F)* ———. *When Rainclouds Gather* (New York: Simon & Schuster, 1969).

KHAME, TSHEDKEDI. *Bechuanaland, A General Survey* (Johannesburg: Institute of Race Relations, 1957).

———. *Beuchuanaland and South Africa* (London: Africa Bureau, 1955).

MUNGER, N. *Beuchuanaland: Pan African Outpost or Bantu Homeland* (London: (London: Oxford University Press, 1965).

SCHAPERA, ISAAC. *A Handbook of Tswana Law and Custom* (London and New York: Oxford University Press, 1938).

———. *Native Land Tenure in the Bechuanaland Protectorate* (Alice, South Africa: Lovedale Press, 1943).

———. *Tribal Legislation Among the Tswana of the Bechuanaland Protectorate* (London: Lund, Humphries, 1943).

———. *Migrant Labour and Tribal Life* (London and New York: Oxford University Press, 1947).

———. *The Ethnic Composition of the Tswana Tribes* (London: London School of Economics, 1952).

SILLERY, A. *The Bechuanaland Protectorate* (London and New York: Oxford University Press, 1952).

———. *Botswana: A Short Political History* (London: Methuen, 1974).

STEVENS, R. P. *Lesotho, Botswana and Swaziland* (New York: Praeger, 1967).

VENGROFF, RICHARD. *Botswana: Rural Development in the Shadow of Apartheid* (Cranbury, N.J.: Fairleigh Dickinson University Press, 1977).

BURUNDI

CLIFFORD, M. L. *Bisha of Burundi* (New York: Thomas Y. Crowell, 1973).

LEMARCHAND, R. *Rwanda and Burundi* (New York: Praeger, 1970).

MELADY, T. P. *Burundi: The Tragic Years* (Maryknoll, N.Y.: Orbis Books, 1974).

U.S. DEPARTMENT OF DEFENSE. *Area Handbook for Burundi* (Washington, D.C.: Government Printing Office, 1969).

WEINSTEIN, WARREN. *Historical Dictionary of Burundi* (Metuchen, N.J.: Scarecrow Press, 1976).

WINGERT, N. *No Place to Stop Killing* (Chicago: Moody Press, 1974).

CAMEROUN

AHIDJO, AHMADOU. *Contribution al la Construction Nationale* (Paris: Presence Africaine, 1964).

ARDENER, EDWIN. *Coastal Bantu of the Cameroons* (London: International African Institute, 1956).

ENGELBERT, MUENG. *L'Histoire du Cameroun* (Paris: Presence Africaine, 1963).

EYONGETAH, T. and R. BRAIN. *A History of Cameroon* (London: Longmans, 1974).

GARDINIER, D. *Cameroons: U.N. Challenge to French Policy* (London: Oxford University Press, 1963).

JOHNSON, W. *The Cameroon Federation* (Princeton, N.J.: Princeton University Press, 1970).

*We have indicated, with (F), those works that capture the flavor of a particular country.

LeVine, V. *The Cameroons: From Mandate to Independence* (Los Angeles: University of California Press, 1964).

———. *The Cameroons Federal Republic* (Ithaca, N.Y.: Cornell University Press, 1963).

Reyher, R. *The Fon and his Hundred Wives* (Garden City, N.Y.: Doubleday, 1952).

Ritzenthaler, P. *The Fon of Bafut* (New York: Thomas Y. Crowell, 1966).

Rubin, N. *Cameroun: An African Federation* (New York: Praeger, 1971).

Rudin, H. *Germans in the Cameroons 1854–1914* (London: Jonathan Cope, 1938).

CENTRAL AFRICAN REPUBLIC

Ballard, John. "Equatorial Africa," in G. Carter (ed.), *National Unity and Regionalism* (Ithaca, N.Y.: Cornell University Press, 1967).

Gide, Andre. *Retour au Tchad* (Paris: Gallmard, 1928).

———. *Voyage au Congo* (Paris: Gallmard, 1927).

Kalck, P. *Central African Republic: A Failure in Decolonization* (New York: Praeger, 1972).

(F) Maran, R. *Batouala* (Washington, D.C.: Black Orpheus Press, 1972).

Teulieres, A. *L'Oubanqui Face a l'Avenir* (Paris: Editions de l'Union Francaise, 1953).

Thompson, V. M. and R. Adloff. *The Emerging States of French Equatorial Africa* (Stanford, Calif.: Stanford University Press, 1960).

CHAD

Ballard, J. "Equatorial Africa," in G. Carter (ed.), *National Unity and Regionalism* (Ithaca, N.Y.: Cornell University Press, 1967).

Carbou, H. *La Region du Tchad et du Ouaddai* (Paris: E. Leroux, 1912).

Thompson, V. M. and R. Adloff. *The Emerging States of French Equatorial Africa* (Stanford, Calif.: Stanford University Press, 1960).

CONGO (BRAZZAVILLE)

Ballard, John. "Equatorial Africa," in G. Carter (ed.), *National Unity and Regionalism* (Ithaca, N.Y.: Cornell University Press, 1967).

Gide, A. *Travels in the Congo* (Los Angeles: University of California Press, 1968).

Rouget, F. *L'Expansion Coloniale au Congo Français* (Paris: E. LaRose, 1906).

Thompson, V. M., and R. Adloff. *The Emerging States of French Equatorial Africa* (Stanford, Calif.: Stanford University Press, 1960).

U.S. Department of Defense. *Area Handbook for People's Republic of the Congo* (Washington, D.C. Government Printing Office, 1971).

DAHOMEY

Akindélé, A. and C. Aguessy. *Dahoney* (Paris: Editions Maritimes et Coloniales, 1955).

Gélé, M. A., *Naissance d'un État Noir: L'Evolution Politique et Constitutionelle du Dahomey* (Paris: Pichon and Durand Auzrás, 1969).

Herskovits, Melville. *Dahomey, An Ancient West African Kingdom* (Evanston, Ill.: Northwestern University Press, 1938).

Polanyi, Karl. *Dahomey and the Slave Trade* (Seattle: University of Washington Press, 1966).

Ronen, Dov. *Dahomey: Between Tradition and Modernity* (Ithaca, N.Y.: Cornell University Press, 1975).

(F) Yerby, Frank. *The Dahomean* (New York: Dial Press, 1971).

EGYPT (UNITED ARAB REPUBLIC)

Abdel-Fadil, Mahmoud. *Development, Income Distribution and Social Change in Rural Egypt (1952–1970): A Study in the Political Economy of Agrarian Transition* (Cambridge, England: Cambridge University Press, 1975).

Abdel-Nalek, Anouar. *Egypt: Military Society* (New York: Vintage Books, 1968). Originally published as *Egypte Société Militare* (1962).

Aldred, Cyril. *The Egyptians* (New York: Praeger, 1963).

———. *Egypt to the End of the Old Kingdom* (New York: McGraw-Hill, 1965).

Ammar, Hamed. *Growing Up in an Egyptian Village* (London: Routledge & Kegan Paul, 1954).

Ayrout, Henry. *The Egyptian Peasant* (Boston: Beacon Press, 1936).

Berger, M. *Bureaucracy and Society in Modern Egypt* (Princeton, N.J.: Princeton University Press, 1957).

Bowie, Robert R. *Suez, 1956* (New York: Oxford University Press, 1974).

Bulliet, R. W. *The Camel and the Wheel* (Cambridge, Mass.: Harvard University Press, 1975).

Copeland, Miles. *The Game of Nations* (New York: Simon & Schuster, 1969).

Fakhouri, Hani. *Kafr El-Elow: An Egyptian Village in Transition* (New York: Holt, Rinehart and Winston, 1972).

Harbison, Frederick H. and Ibrahim A. Ibrahim. *Human Resources For Egyptian Enterprise* (New York: McGraw-Hill, 1958).

Hussein, Taha. *The Future of Culture in Egypt* (New York: Octagon Books, 1975).

(F) Ibrahim, Sonallah. *The Smell of It* (New York: Humanities Press, 1971).

Janssen, P. and K. Scherer. *Egypt* (Chicago: Follett Publishing, 1967).

Kay, Shirley. *The Egyptians: How They Live and Work* (New York: Praeger, 1975).

Kilpatrick, Hilary. *The Modern Egyptian Novel* (London: Ithaca Press, 1974).

Leiden, C. and K. M. Schmitt. *The Politics of Violence: Revolution in the Modern World* (Englewood Cliffs, N.J.: Prentice-Hall, 1968).

Little, Tom. *Modern Egypt* (New York: Praeger, 1967).

Ludwig, Emile. *The Nile* (New York: Garden City Publishing Co., 1939).

(F) Mahfouz, Naguib. *Midag Alley* (London: Heinemann, 1975).

Mansfield, Peter. *Nasser's Egypt* (Baltimore: Penguin Books, 1963).

Mayfield, James. *Rural Politics in Nasser's Egypt* (Austin: University of Texas Press, 1971).

Mead, Donald. *Growth and Structural Change in the Egyptian Economy* (New Haven: Yale University Press, 1967).

Mertz, Barbara. *Red Land, Black Land* (New York: Delta, 1966).

Millard, Anne. *Egypt* (New York: Putnam's Sons, 1971).

Rejwan, Nissim. *Nasserist Ideology: Its Exponents and Critics* (New York: John Wiley, 1974).

Safran, Nadav. *Egypt in Search of Political Community* (Cambridge, Mass.: Harvard University Press, 1961).

Smith, Wilfred Cantwell. *Islam in Modern History* (New York: Mentor, 1963).

Tignor, Robert L. and R. O. Collins. *Egypt and the Sudan* (Englewood Cliffs, N.J.: Prentice-Hall, 1967).

U.S. Department of Defense. *Area Handbook for the United Arab Republic (Egypt)* (Washington, D.C.: Government Printing Office, 1964).

Vatikiotis, Panayiotis J. *The Egyptian Army in Politics* (Bloomington: Indiana University Press, 1961).

Wendell, Charles. *The Evolution of the Egyptian National Image: From Its Origins to Ahmad Lutfi Al-Sayyid* (Los Angeles: University of California Press, 1972).

White, J. M. *Everydaylife in Ancient Egypt* (New York: Capricorn Books, 1967).

ETHIOPIA

Bender, M. L. *Language in Ethiopia* (New York: Oxford University Press, 1976).

———— (ed.). *The Non-Semitic Languages of Ethiopia* (East Lansing: The African Studies Center, Michigan State University, 1976).

Bruce, James. *Travels to Discover the Source of the Nile in the Years 1768, 1769, 1770, 1771, 1772, and 1773* (Glasgow: W. Falconer, 1818).

Cheesman, R. E. *Lake Tana and the Blue Nile: An Abyssinian Quest* (London: Frank Cass, 1968).

Clapham, C. *Haile-Selassie's Government* (New York: Praeger, 1970).

Coffey, Thomas. *Lion By the Tail* (New York: Viking Press, 1974).

Gamst, Frederick C. *The Qemant* (New York: Holt, Rinehart and Winston, 1969).

Greenfield, R. *Ethiopia: A New Political History* (New York: Praeger, 1965).

Hess, R. *Ethiopia: The Modernization of Autocracy* (Ithaca, N.Y.: Cornell University Press, 1970).

Hidaru, Alula and Dessalegn Rahmato (eds.). *A Short Guide to the Study of Ethiopia* (Westport, Conn.: Greenwood Press, 1976).

Huntingford, G. W. B. *The Glorious Victories of Amda Seyon, King of Ethiopia* (London: Oxford University Press, 1965).

Jesman, C. *The Ethiopian Paradox* (London: Oxford University Press, 1963).

Last, Geoffrey and Richard Pankhurst. *A History of Ethiopia in Pictures* (London: Oxford University Press, 1972).

Legesse, Asmaron. *GADA* (New York: Free Press, 1973).

Levine, V. *Wax and Gold* (Chicago: University of Chicago Press, 1967).

Lewis, Ian Myrrdin. *Peoples of the Horn of Africa* (London: International African Institute, 1955).

Longrigg, Stephen A. *A Short History of Eritrea* (Oxford: Clarendon Press, 1945).

Lord, Edith. *Queen of Sheba's Heirs* (Washington, D.C.: Acropolis Books, 1970).

Mosley, L. *Haile-Selassie, The Conquering Lion* (London: Oxford University Press, 1964).

(F) Murray, Edmund. *Kulubi* (New York: Crown Publishers, 1973).

Nesbitt, L. M. *Hell Hole of Creation* (New York: Knopf, 1933).

Nicol, C. W. *From the Roof of Africa* (New York: Knopf, 1972).

Perham, M. *The Government of Ethiopia* (London: Oxford University Press, 1964).

Potholm, C. P. *Liberation and Exploitation: The Struggle For Ethiopia* (Washington, D.C.: University Press of America, 1976).

Reddon, Kenneth R. *The Legal System of Ethiopia* (Charlottesville, Va: Michie, 1968).

Reid, J. M. *Traveller Extraordinary* (New York: W. W. Norton, 1968).

Rosenfeld, Chris Prouty. *The Chronology of Menilek II of Ethiopia, 1844–1913* (East Lansing: African Studies Center, Michigan State University, 1976).

SCHAEFER, LUDWIG F. (ed.). *The Ethiopian Crisis: Touch-Stone of Appeasement?* (Boston: D. C. Heath, 1961).

(F) SCHOLEFIELD, ALAN. *The Hammer of God* (New York: William Morrow, 1973).

SELASSIE, HAILE. *Selected Speeches of His Imperial Majesty Haile Selassie I* (Addis Ababa: Government Printer, 1967).

(F) SELASSIE, S. *Warrior King* (London: Heinemann, 1974).

(F) ———. *The Afersata* (New York: Humanities Press, 1968).

ULLENDORFF, E. *The Ethiopians* (New York: Oxford University Press, 1965).

U.S. DEPARTMENT OF DEFENSE. *Area Handbook for Ethiopia* (Washington, D.C.: Government Printing Office, 1971).

(F) WORKU, DANIACHEW. *The Thirteenth Sun* (New York: Humanities Press, 1973).

GABON

DUCHAILLU, P. B. *Explorations and Adventures in Equatorial Africa* (New York: Harper and Bros., 1862).

THOMPSON, V. M. and R. ADLOFF. *The Emerging States of French Equatorial Africa* (Stanford, Calif.: Stanford University Press, 1960).

WEINSTEIN, BRIAN. *Gabon: Nation Building on the Ogoué* (Cambridge, Mass.: MIT Press, 1967).

GAMBIA

GAILEY, H. *A History of the Gambia* (New York: Praeger, 1962).

RICE, B. *Enter Gambia* (Boston: Houghton Mifflin, 1967).

GHANA

AFRIFA, A. *The Ghana Coup* (London: Frank Case, 1967).

(F) AIDOO, AMA. *No Sweetness Here* (Garden City, N.Y.: Doubleday, 1972).

ALUKO, OLAJIDE. *Ghana and Nigeria, 1957–1970* (New York: Barnes & Noble, 1976).

APTER, D. *The Gold Coast in Transition* (Princeton, N.J.: Princeton University Press, 1955).

(F) ARMAH, AYI KWEI. *The Beautyful Ones Are Not Yet Born* (Boston: Houghton Mifflin, 1968).

AUSTIN, D. *Politics in Ghana 1946–1960* (London: Oxford University Press, 1965).

———. *Ghana Observed: Essays on the Politics of a West African Republic* (New York: Holmes and Meier, 1976).

BARKER, P. *Operation Cold Chop* (Accra: Ghana Publishing Corporation, 1969).

BECKMAN, BJÖRN. *Organising the Farmers: Cocoa Politics and National Development in Ghana* (Uppsala, Sweeden: The Scandinavian Institute of African Studies, 1976).

BRETTON, HENRY. *The Rise and Fall of Kwame Nkrumah* (New York: Praeger, 1966).

BUSIA, K. A. *Africa in Search of Democracy* (New York: Praeger, 1967).

DAVIDSON, BASIL. *Black Star: A View of the Life and Times of Kwame Nkrumah* (New York: Praeger, 1973).

DICKSON, K. B. *A Historical Geography of Ghana* (Cambridge, England: Cambridge University Press, 1969).

(F) DUODU, CAMERON. *The Gab Boys* (New York: Fontana Books, 1969).

FAGE, J. D. *Ghana: A Historical Interpretation* (Madison: University of Wisconsin Press, 1959).

FIELD, M. J. *Search for Security* (New York: W. W. Norton, 1970).

FITCH, R. and M. OPPENHEIMER. *Ghana: End of an Illusion* (New York: Monthly Review Press, 1966).

FLINT, JOHN. *Nigeria and Ghana* (Englewood Cliffs, N.J.: Prentice-Hall, 1966).

FOSTER, P. and ARISTIDE ZOLBERG (eds.). *Ghana and the Ivory Coast* (Chicago: University of Chicago Press, 1971).

FYNN, J. K. *Asante and Its Neighbors: 1700–1807* (Evanston, Ill.: Northwestern University Press, 1971).

GARLICK, PETER C. *African Traders and Economic Development in Ghana* (London: Oxford University Press, 1971).

GENOUD, ROGER. *Nationalism and Economic Development in Ghana* (New York: Praeger, 1969).

GRINDAL, BRUCE. *Growing Up in Two Worlds: Education and Transition Among the Sisala of Northern Ghana* (New York: Holt, Rinehart and Winston, 1972).

GRUNDY, KENNETH W. "The Political Ideology of Kwame Nkrumah," in W. A. E. Skurnik (ed.), *African Political Thought* (Denver: University of Denver, 1968).

JACOBSON, DAVID. *Itinerant Townsmen: Friendship and Social Order in Urban Ghana* (Menlo Park, Calif.: Cummings Publishing, 1973).

KRAUS, J. "Arms and Politics in Ghana," in Claude Welch (ed.), *Soldier and State in Africa* (Evanston, Ill.: Northwestern University Press, 1970).

LeVINE, VICTOR T. *Political Corruption: The Ghana Case* (Stanford, Calif.: Hoover Institution Press, 1975).

McKOWN, RUBIN. *Nkrumah* (Garden City, N.Y.: Doubleday, 1973).

NKRUMAH, K. *Ghana, The Autobiography of Kwame Nkrumah* (London: Nelson, 1957).

———. *I Speak of Freedom* (London: Heinemann, 1961).

———. *Towards Colonial Freedom* (London: Heinemann, 1962).

———. *Africa Must Unite* (London: Heinemann, 1963).

———. *Consciencism* (London: Heinemann, 1964). (Probably written by 4 or 5 persons, including Habib Niang and Massanga of the UPC—Cameroun.)

———. *Neocolonialism, the Last State of Imperialism* (London: Heinemann, 1965).

———. *Dark Days in Ghana* (New York: International Publishers, 1968).

———. *Handbook of Revolutionary Warfare* (New York: International Publishers, 1968).

———. *Class Struggle in Africa* (New York: International Publishers, 1970).

OCRAN, A. K. *A Myth is Broken* (London: Longmans, 1968).

OMARI, T. P. *Kwame Nkrumah: The Anatomy of an African Dictatorship* (New York: Africana Publishing Corp., 1970).

PINKNEY, ROBERT. *Ghana Under Military Rule 1966–1969* (London: Methuen, 1972).

THOMPSON, W. S. *Ghana's Foreign Policy 1957–1966* (Princeton, N.J.: Princeton University Press, 1969).

U.S. DEPARTMENT OF DEFENSE. *Area Handbook for Ghana* (Washington, D.C.: Government Printing Office, 1971).

WARD, W. E. F. *Government in West Africa* (London: Allen & Unwin, 1965).

———. *A History of Ghana* (New York: Praeger, 1963).

WOLFSON, FREDA. *Pageant of Ghana* (London: Oxford University Press, 1965).

WORONOFF, JON. *West African Wager* (Metuchen, N.J.: Scarecrow Press, 1972).

GUINEA

ADAMOLEKUN, LAPIPO. *Sekou Touré's Guinea* (New York: Barnes & Noble, 1976).

AMEILLON, B. *La Guinée: Bilan d'une Independance* (Paris: François Maspero, 1964).

(F) LAYE, CAMARA. *The African Child* (London: Collins, 1965).

————. *A Dream of Africa* (New York: Collier Books, 1968).

TOURÉ, SEKOU. *L'Action Politique de Parti Démocratique de Guinée* (Paris: Presence Africaine, 1959).

————. *La Guinée et L'Emancipation Africaine* (Paris: Presence Africaine, 1959).

————. *The International Policy of the Democratic Party of Guinea*, vol. 7 (Cairo: Société Orientale de Publicité, 1960).

————. *The Political Action of the Democratic Party of Guinea for the Emancipation of Guinean Youth*, vol. 8 (Cairo: Société Orientale de Publicité, 1960).

————. *Experience Guineenne et Unité Africaine* (Paris: Presence Africaine, 1961).

GUINÉ (BISSAU)

CABRAL, AMILCAR. *Return to the Source: Selected Speeches of Amilcar Cabral* (New York: Monthly Review Press, 1973).

————. *Revolution in Guiné: An African People's Struggle* (London: Stage One Publications, 1969).

CHALIAND, GERALD. *Armed Struggle in Africa* (New York: Monthly Review Press, 1969).

CORNWALL, BARBARA. *The Bush Rebels* (New York: Holt, Rinehart and Winston, 1972).

DAVIDSON, B. *The Liberation of Guiné* (Baltimore: Penguin Books, 1969).

DAVIS, JENNIFER. *The Republic of Guinea-Bissau* (New York: The Africa Fund, 1974).

INSTITUTO CUBANO DEL LIBRO. *Portuguese Colonies: Victory or Death* (Havana: Urselia Diaz Baez, 1971).

TOKYO, TADAHIRO OGAWA. *No Pintcha* (Tokyo: Taimatsu-sha, 1972).

VENTER, A. J. *Portugal's Guerrilla War* (Capetown, South Africa: John Malherbe, 1973).

————. *Portugal's War in Guiné-Bissau* (Pasadena, Calif.: Munger Africana Library Notes, 1973).

IVORY COAST

ALLAND, ALEXANDER. *When The Spider Danced* (Garden City, N.Y.: Doubleday, 1976).

ANGOULVANT, G. *La Pacification de la Côte d'Ivoire 1908–1915* (Paris: Larose, 1916).

COHEN, MICHAEL. *Urban Policy and Political Conflict in Africa: A Study of the Ivory Coast* (Chicago: University of Chicago Press, 1974).

D'ABY, F. J. AMON. *La Côte d'Ivoire dans la Cité Africaine* (Paris: Larose, 1951).

(F) DADIÉ, B. *Climbé* (New York: Africana Publishing, 1971).

FOSTER, P. and A. ZOLBERG (eds.). *Ghana and the Ivory Coast* (Chicago: University of Chicago Press, 1971).

GUERRY, VINCENT. *Life With the Baoulé* (Washington, D.C.: Three Continents Press, 1975).

STANILAND, MARTIN. "Single-Party Regimes and Political Change: The P.D.C.I. and Ivory Coast Politics," in Colin Leys (ed.), *Politics and Change in Developing Countries* (Cambridge, England: Cambridge University Press, 1969).

WORONOFF, JON. *West African Wager* (Metuchen, N.J.: Scarecrow Press, 1972).

ZOLBERG, A. *One Party Government in the Ivory Coast,* rev. ed. (Princeton, N.J.: Princeton University Press, 1969).

KENYA

BARNETT, D. and K. NJAMA. *Mau-Mau from Within* (New York: Monthly Review Press, 1966).

BENNETT, G. and CARL ROSBERG. *The Kenya Election: Kenya 1960–1961* (London: Oxford University Press, 1961).

BIENEN, HENRY. *Kenya: The Politics of Participation and Control* (Princeton, N.J.: Princeton University Press, 1974).

CELL, JOHN W. *By Kenya Possessed: The Correspondence of Norman Leys and J. H. Oldham, 1918–1926* (Chicago: University of Chicago Press, 1976).

COLE, SONIA. *Leakey's Luck* (New York: Harcourt Brace Jovanovich, 1975).

COX, R. *Kenyatta's Country* (New York: Praeger, 1965).

DIAMOND, S. and F. G. BURKE (eds.). *The Transformation of East Africa: Studies in Political Anthropology* (New York: Basic Books, 1966).

DINESEN, ISAK. *Out of Africa* (New York: Random House, 1938).

———. *Shadows on the Grass* (New York: Random House, 1961).

GATHERU, R. MUGO. *A Child of Two Worlds* (Garden City, N.Y.: Doubleday, 1965).

GHAI, D. P. (ed.). *Portrait of a Minority: Asians in East Africa* (Nairobi, Kenya: Oxford University Press, 1965).

HANLEY, GERALD. *Warriors and Strangers* (New York: Harper & Row, 1971).

HENDERSON, L. *Man Hunt in Kenya* (Garden City, N.Y.: Doubleday, 1958).

HOLMAN, DENNIS. *Mau-Mau Manhunt* (New York: Pyramid Books, 1965).

HUXLEY, ELSBETH. *The Flame Trees of Thika* (New York: William Morrow, 1959).

———. *A New Earth* (New York: William Morrow, 1960).

———. *White Man's Country: Lord Delamere and the Making of Kenya* (New York: Praeger, 1967).

ITOTE, W. *"Mau-Mau" General* (Nairobi, Kenya: East African Publishing House, 1967).

KAHIGA, SAMUEL. *The Girl From Abroad* (New York: Humanities Press, 1974).

KARIUKE, J. *"Mau-Mau" Detainee* (London and Baltimore: Penguin Books, 1963).

KENYATTA, JOMO. *Facing Mt. Kenya* (London: Seeking & Warburg, 1938).

———. *Suffering Without Bitterness* (Nairobi, Kenya: East African Publishing House, 1968).

LEAKEY, L. S. R. *Adam's Ancestors* (New York: Harper & Row, 1960).

———. *Kenya: Contents and Problems* (Nairobi, Kenya: East African Publishing House, 1967, reprint).

———. *White Africa* (Nairobi, Kenya: East African Publishing House, 1967).

LEVINE, R. and B. LEVINE. *Nyansongo: A Gusii Community in Kenya* (New York: John Wiley, 1966).

MACPHEE, A. M. *Kenya* (New York: Praeger, 1968).

MBOYA, T. *Freedom and After* (Boston: Houghton Mifflin, 1963).

MEISTER, A. *East Africa: The Past in Chains, The Future in Pawn* (New York: Walker, 1968).

MUNGEAM, G. H. *British Rule in Kenya* (London: Oxford University Press, 1967).

MURRAY-BROWN, JEREMY. *Kenyatta* (New York: E. P. Dutton, 1973).

MUTHIANI, JOSEPH. *Akamba from Within* (Jericho, N.Y.: Exposition Press, 1973).

MWANGI, MEJA. *Kill Me Quick* (New York: Humanities Press, 1973).

————. *Carcase for Hounds* (New York: Humanities Press, 1974).

(F) NGUGI, JAMES. *A Grain of Wheat* (New York: Humanities Press, 1968).

(F) ————. *Weep Not Child* (New York: Collier Books, 1969).

ODINGA, O. *Not Yet Uhuru* (New York: Hill & Wang, 1967).

OJANY, F. F. and R. B. OGENDO. *Kenya: A Study in Physical and Human Geography* (London: Longmans, 1973).

OSOGO, JOHN. *A History of the Baluyia* (London: Oxford University Press, 1966).

(F) REID, V. S. *The Leopard* (New York: Collier Books, 1971).

ROELKER, JACK. *Mathu of Kenya* (Stanford, Calif.: Hoover Institution Press, 1976).

ROSBERG, C. and R. NOTTINGHAM. *The Myth of the Mau-Mau* (New York: Praeger, 1967).

(F) RUARK, R. *Something of Value* (Garden City, N.Y.: Doubleday, 1955).

(F) ————. *Uhuru* (New York: McGraw-Hill, 1962).

SHEFFIELD, JAMES. *Education in Kenya* (New York: Teachers College Press, 1973).

SORENSON, M. P. K. *Origins of European Settlements in Kenya* (Nairobi, Kenya: Oxford University Press, 1968).

WASSERMAN, GARY. *Politics of Decolonization: Kenya Europeans and the Land Issue, 1960–1965* (New York: Cambridge University Press, 1976).

WERLIN, HERBERT. *Governing an African City: A Study of Nairobi* (New York: Africana Publishing Corp., 1974).

LESOTHO

ASHTON, E. *The Basuto* (London: Oxford University Press, 1952).

HAILEY, LORD. *The Republic of South Africa and the High Commission Territories* (London: Oxford University Press, 1963).

HALPRIN, J. *South Africa's Hostages* (Baltimore: Penguin Books, 1965).

KHAKETLA, B. M. *Lesotho 1970: An African Coup Under the Microscope* (Los Angeles: University of California Press, 1972).

LANGDON, G. *The Basutos* (London: Hutchinson, 1909).

(F) MOPELI-PAULUS, A. S. and PETER LANHAM. *Blanket Boy* (New York: Thomas Y. Crowell, 1953).

(F) MURRAY, A. A. *The Blanket* (New York: Vanguard Press, n.d.).

PALMER, V. V. and S. M. POULTER. *The Legal System of Lesotho* (Charlottesville, Va.: Michie, 1972).

POULTER, SEBASTIAN. *Family Law and Litigation in Basotho Society* (New York: Oxford University Press, 1976).

SPENCE, J. E. *Lesotho: The Politics of Dependence* (London: Oxford University Press, 1968).

STEVENS, R. P. *Lesotho, Botswana and Swaziland* (New York: Praeger, 1967).

THOMPSON, LEONARD. *Survival in Two Worlds: Moshoeshoe of Lesotho 1786–1870* (London: Oxford University Press, 1975).

TILTON, G. *The Rise of the Basuto* (Cape Town, South Africa: Juta Press, 1950).

WILLIAMS, J. G. *Moshesh, the Man on the Mountain* (London: Oxford University Press, 1950).

LIBERIA

BUELL, R. L. *Liberia, A Century of Survival* (Philadelphia: Liberty Hall, 1947).

CLIFFORD, M. L. *The Land and People of Liberia* (Philadelphia: Lippincott, 1970).

CLOWER, E. et al. *Growth Without Development* (Evanston, Ill.: Northwestern University Press, 1966).

GAY, JOHN. *Red Dust on the Green Leaves* (Thompson, Conn.: Interculture, 1973).

GREEN, GRAHAM. *Journey Without Maps* (New York: Viking Press, 1967).

HOLDEN, E. *Blyden of Liberia* (New York: Vintage Press, 1967).

LIEBENOW, G. *Liberia* (Ithaca, N.Y.: Cornell University Press, 1969).

LOWENKOPF, MARTIN. *Politics in Liberia* (Stanford, Calif.: Hoover Institution Press, 1976).

MARINELLI, L. *The New Liberia* (New York: Praeger, 1964).

MCLAUGHLIN, R. U. *Foreign Investment and Development in Liberia* (New York: Praeger, 1966).

TOLSON, M. B. *Libretto for the Republic of Liberia* (New York: Macmillan, 1970).

U.S. DEPARTMENT OF DEFENSE. *Area Handbook for Liberia* (Washington, D.C.: Government Printing Office, 1964).

WARNER, ESTER. *New Song in a Strange Land* (Boston: Houghton Mifflin, 1948).

WILSON, C. M. *Liberia: Black Africa in Microcosm* (New York: Harper & Row, 1971).

WREH, TUAN. *The Love of Liberty: The Rule of President William vs. Tubman in Liberia, 1944–1971* (London: C. Hurst and Co., 1976).

YOUNG, E. *The Republic of Liberia* (London: Ruskin House, 1959).

LIBYA

Books listed under *Algeria* dealing generally with North Africa or Islam

FIRST, RUTH. *Libya: The Elusive Revolution* (New York: Africana Publishing Corp., 1975).

HABIB, HENRY PIERRE. *Politics and Government of Revolutionary Libya* (Montreal: Le Cercle du Livre de France, 1975).

KHADDURI, M. *Modern Libya* (Baltimore: Johns Hopkins University Press, 1963).

REYNOLD, JOYCE (ed.). *Libyan Studies* (London: Paul Elek Books, 1976).

U.S. DEPARTMENT OF DEFENSE. *Area Handbook for Libya* (Washington, D.C.: Government Printing Office, 1969).

WRIGHT, J. *Libya* (New York: Praeger, 1968).

ZARTMAN, I. W. *Government and Politics in Northern Africa* (New York: Praeger, 1963).

——— (ed.) *Man, State and Society in the Contemporary Maghrib* (New York: Praeger, 1973).

MALAGASY REPUBLIC

KENT, R. *From Madagascar to the Malagasy Republic* (London: Thames and Hudson, 1962).

RALAIMIHOATRA, E. *Histoire de Madagascar* (Tanaanarive, Malagasy Republic: Imprint Government, 1965).

THOMPSON, V. and R. ADLOFF. *The Malagasy Republic* (Stanford, Calif.: Stanford University Press, 1965).

MALAWI

GANN, LEWIS. *Central Africa: The Former British States* (Englewood Cliffs, N.J.: Prentice-Hall, 1971).

(F) KAYIRA, LEGSON. *The Looming Shadow* (New York: Collier Books, 1970).

(F) ———. *The Detainee* (New York: Humanities Press, 1974).

MASON, PHILIP. *Year of Decision: Rhodesia and Nyasaland 1960* (London: Oxford University Press, 1960).

McMASTER, CAROLYN. *Malawi; Foreign Policy and Development* (New York: St. Martin's Press, 1974).

PACHAI, BRIDGLAL. *Malawi: The History of the Nation* (London: Longmans, 1973).

PIKE, J. *Malawi* (New York: Praeger, 1968).

READ, MARGARET. *Children of Their Fathers* (New York: Holt, Rinehart and Winston, 1962).

ROTBERG, R. I. *The Rise of Nationalism in Central Africa: The Making of Malawi and Zambia, 1873–1964* (Cambridge, Mass.: Harvard University Press, 1965).

MALI

FOLTZ, W. *From French West Africa to the Mali Federation* (New Haven: Yale University Press, 1965).

GARDNER, B. *The Quest for Timbuctoo* (New York: Harcourt Brace Jovanovich, 1968).

IMPERATO, P. J. *A Wind in Africa* (St. Louis: Warren Green, 1975).

JONES, WILLIAM I. *Planning and Economic Policy: Socialist Mali and Her Neighbors* (Washington, D.C. Three Continents Press, 1976).

MAUGHAM, R. *The Slaves of Timbuktu* (London: Longmans, 1961).

MINER, H. *The Primitive City of Timbuctoo* (Garden City, N.Y.: Doubleday, 1965).

MOORHOUSE, GEOFFREY. *The Fearful Void* (Philadelphia: Lippincott, 1974).

SEABROOK, WILLIAM. *The White Monk of Timbuctoo* (New York: Harcourt Brace Jovanovich, 1934).

SNYDER, F. *One Party Government in Mali* (New Haven: Yale University Press, 1965).

MAURITANIA

GERTEINY, A. *Mauritania* (New York: Praeger, 1967).

MOORHOUSE, GEOFFREY. *The Fearful Void* (Philadelphia: Lippincott, 1974).

MAURITIUS

BENEDICT, B. *Mauritius* (New York: 1965).

MOROCCO

COHEN, I. and L. HAHN. *Morocco, Old Land, New Nation* (New York: Praeger, 1966).

HALPERN. *The Politics of Social Change in the Middle East and North Africa* (Princeton, N.J.: Princeton University Press, 1963).

HALSTEAD, J. P. *Rebirth of a Nation* (Cambridge, Mass.: Harvard University Press, 1968).

LANDAU, ROM. *Morocco Independent* (London: Allen & Unwin, 1961).

MIKESELL, MARVIN W. *Northern Morocco: A Cultural Geography* (Berkeley: University of California Press, 1961).

RABINOW, PAUL. *Symbolic Domination: Cultural Form and Historical Change in Morocco* (Chicago: University of Chicago Press, 1975).

U.S. DEPARTMENT OF DEFENSE. *Area Handbook for Morocco* (Washington, D.C.: Government Printing Office, 1965).

WOOLMAN, DAVID S. *Rebels in the Rif: Abdel Karim and the Rif Rebellion* (Stanford, Calif.: Stanford University Press, 1968).

ZARTMAN, I. WILLIAM. *Government and Politics in Northern Africa* (New York: Praeger, 1963).

————. *Destiny of a Dynasty: The Search for Institutions in Morocco's Developing Society* (Columbia, S.C.: Studies in International Affairs, 1964).

————. *Problems of New Power: Morocco* (New York: Atherton Press, 1964).

———— (ed.). *Man, State and Society in the Contemporary Maghrib* (New York: Praeger, 1973).

MOZAMBIQUE

COUPLAND, R. *East Africa and Its Invaders* (London: Oxford University Press, 1938).

————. *The Exploitation of East Africa, 1856–1890* (London: Oxford University Press, 1939).

HASTINGS, ADRIAN. *Wiriyamu: My Lai in Mozambique* (Maryknoll, N.Y.: Orbis Books, 1974).

LIVINGSTON, D. *Narrative of an Expedition to the Zambezi and Its Sources* (London: Oxford University Press, 1966).

MONDLANE, E. *The Struggle for Mozambique* (Baltimore: Penguin Books, 1969).

NAMIBIA (SOUTHWEST AFRICA)

BLEY, HELMUT. *South West Africa under German Rule, 1894–1914* (London: Heinemann, 1971).

BRUWER, J. P. *South West Africa: The Disputed Land* (Johannesburg, South Africa: Nasionale Boekhandel Beperk, 1966).

COCKRAM, G. M. *South West African Mandate* (Capetown, South Africa: Juta Press, 1976).

DUGARD, JOHN. *The South West Africa/Namibia Dispute* (Los Angeles: University of California Press, 1973).

FIRST, RUTH. *South West Africa* (Baltimore: Penguin Books, 1963).

HALL, RICHARD (ed.). *South West Africa (Namibia)* (London: The Africa Bureau, 1970).

(F) HELFMAN, E. S. *The Bushmen and Their Stories* (New York: Seabury Press, 1971).

LEJEUNE, ANTHONY. *The Case for Southwest Africa* (London: Tom Stacey, 1971).

LOWENSTEIN. A. K. *Brutal Mandate* (New York: Macmillan, 1963).

MOLNAR, T. *South West Africa: The Last Pioneer Country* (New York: Fleet Publishing Company, 1966).

RHOODIE, ESCHEL. *South West: The Last Frontier in Africa* (New York: Twin Circle, 1967).

(F) SCHOLEFIELD, ALAN. *The Eagles of Malice* (London: Heinemann, 1969).

SLONIM, SOLOMON. *South West Africa and the United Nations: An International Mandate in Dispute* (Baltimore: Johns Hopkins University Press, 1973).

(F) STANDER, SIEGFRIED. *The Fortress* (Boston: Houghton Mifflin, 1973).

THOMAS, ELIZABETH M. *The Harmless People* (New York: Vintage Press, 1959).

VAN DER POST, LAURENS. *The Heart of the Hunter* (New York: William Morrow, 1961).

————. *The Lost World of the Kalahari* (New York: William Morrow, 1958).

WELLINGTON, J. H. *South West Africa and Its Human Issues* (London: Oxford University Press, 1967).

NIGER

BONARDI, P. *La Republique du Niger, Naissance d'un Etat* (Paris: Ed. A. P. D., 1960).

DE RIVIERES, E. S. *Le Niger* (Paris: Société d' Editions, 1952).

THOMPSON, VIRGINIA. "Niger," *National Unity and Regionalism* (Ithaca, N.Y.: Cornell University Press, 1966).

NIGERIA

(F) ALUKO, T. M. *His Worshipful Majesty* (New York: Humanities Press, 1973).

(F) AMADI, ELECHI. *Sunset in Biafra* (New York: Humanities Press, 1973).

(F) ANIEBO, I. N. C. *The Anonymity of Sacrifice* (New York: Humanities Press, 1974).

ARIKPO, OKIO. *The Development of Modern Nigeria* (London: Penguin Books, 1967).

ARNOLD, GUY. *Modern Nigeria* (London: Longmans, 1977).

(F) ATTAWAY, ROBERT. *I Think of Warri* (New York: Harper & Row, 1974).

AWOLOWO, OBAFEMI. *The Autobiography of Chief Obafemi Awolowo* (London: Cambridge University Press, 1960).

AZIKIWE, NNAMDI. *Zik: A Selection from the Speeches of Nnamdi Azikiwe* (London: Cambridge University Press, 1961).

BASCOM, W. *The Yoruba* (New York: Holt, Rinehart and Winston, 1969).

BELLO, AHMADU. *My Life* (London: Cambridge University Press, 1962).

BLITZ, L. FRANKLIN (ed.). *The Politics and Administration of Nigerian Government* (New York: Praeger, 1965).

BRETTON, H. *Power and Stability in Nigeria* (New York: Praeger, 1962).

COHEN, RONALD. *The Kanuri of Bornu* (New York: Holt, Rinehart and Winston, 1967).

COLEMAN, J. *Nigeria: Background to Nationalism* (Berkeley: University of California Press, 1958).

CROWDER, MICHAEL. *A Short History of Nigeria* (New York: Praeger, 1965).

DE ST. JORRE, JOHN. *The Brother's War: Biafra and Nigeria* (Boston: Houghton Mifflin, 1972).

DIKE, K. O. *Eminent Nigerians of the Nineteenth Century* (Cambridge, England: Cambridge University Press, 1960).

EZERA, K. *Constitutional Developments in Nigeria* (Cambridge, England: Cambridge University Press, 1960).

FLINT, J. *Nigeria and Ghana* (Englewood Cliffs, N.J.: Prentice-Hall, 1966).

FORSYTH, FREDERICK. *The Biafra Story* (Baltimore: Penguin Books, 1969).

GREEN, M. M. *The Village Affairs* (New York: Praeger, 1964).

HISKETT, MERVYN. *The Sword of Truth: The Life and Times of the Shehu Usuman Dan Fodio* (London: Oxford University Press, 1973).

IDANG, G. J. *Internal Politics and Foreign Policy, 1960–1966* (Ibadan, Nigeria: Ibadan University Press, 1974).

IGBOZURIKE, MARTIN. *Problem-Generating Structures in Nigeria's Rural Development* (Uppsala, Sweden: The Scandinavian Institute of African Studies, 1976).

IGIEHON, NUSER. *To Build A Nigerian Nation* (Elmscourt, England: Arthur Stockwell, 1975).

LEIS, PHILIP E. *Enculturation and Socialization in Ijaw Village* (New York: Holt, Rinehart and Winston, 1972).

LINDFORS, BUNTH (ed.). *Critical Perspectives on Nigerian Literature* (Washington, D.C.: Three Continents Press, 1976).

MACKINTOSH, JOHN P. *Nigerian Government and Politics* (Evanston, Ill.: Northwestern University Press, 1966).

(F) MEZU, S. O. *Behind the Rising Sun* (London: Heinemann, 1971).

MINERS, N. J. *The Nigerian Army 1956–1966* (London: Methuen, 1971).

NWANKWO, ARTHUR and SAMUEL IFEJIKA. *The Making of a Nation: Biafra* (London: Christopher Hurst, 1969).

OJUKWU, C. ODUMEGWU. *Biafra*, 2 vols. (New York: Harper & Row, 1969).

OSTHEIMER, J. M. *Nigerian Politics* (New York: Harper & Row, 1973).

OYEWOLE, FOLA. *Reluctant Rebel* (London: Rex Collings, 1975).

OYINBO, JOHN. *Nigeria: Crisis and Beyond* (London: Charles Knight, 1971).

PANTER-BRICK, S. K. (ed.). *Nigerian Politics and Military Rule: Prelude to the Civil War* (London: Athlone Press, 1970).

SCHWARZ, WALTER. *Nigeria* (New York: Praeger, 1968).

SKLAR, R. *Nigerian Political Parties* (Princeton, N.J.: Princeton University Press, 1963).

UCHENDU, V. *The Igbo* (New York: Holt, Rinehart and Winston, 1965).

WHITAKER, C. S. *The Politics of Tradition: Continuity and Change in Northern Nigeria 1946–1966* (Princeton, N.J.: Princeton University Press, 1970).

WILLIAMS, GAVIN. *Nigeria: Economy and Society* (London: Rex Collings, 1976).

RWANDA

LEMARCHAND, R. *Rwanda and Burundi* (New York: Praeger, 1970).

U.S. DEPARTMENT OF DEFENSE. *Area Handbook for Rwanda* (Washington, D.C.: Government Printing Office, 1969).

SENEGAL

BEHRMAN, L. *Muslim Brotherhoods and Politics in Senegal* (Cambridge, Mass.: Harvard University Press, 1970).

CROWDER, M. *Senegal* (London: Oxford University Press, 1962).

DELEUSSE, HERBERT. *Léopold Sédar Senghor L'Africain* (Paris: Hatier, 1967).

FOLTZ, W. *From French West Africa to the Mali Federation* (New Haven: Yale University Press, 1965).

GUIBERT, ARMAND. *Léopold Sédar Senghor: L'Homme et L'Oeuvre* (Paris: Presence Africaine, 1962).

——— (ed.). *Léopold Sédar Senghor: Poetes d'Aujord'hui* (Paris: Editions Seghers, 1969).

KLEIN, M. *Islam and Imperialism in Senegal* (Stanford, Calif.: Stanford University Press, 1967).

MILCENT, ERNEST and MONIQUE SORDET. *Léopold Sédar Senghor et la Naissance de l'Afrique Moderne* (Paris: Editions Seghers, 1969).

O'BRIEN, RITA CRUISE. *White Society in Black Africa: The French of Senegal* (Evanston, Ill.: Northwestern University Press, 1972).

(F) OUSMANE, SEMBENE. *Xala* (New York: Lawrence Hill, 1976).

REED, JOHN and CLIVE WAKE (eds.). *Senghor: Prose and Poetry* (New York: Humanities Press, 1976).

ROUS, JEAN. *Lépold Sédar Senghor* (Paris: John Didier, 1967).

SENGHOR, LÉOPOLD SÉDAR. *Nation et Voie Africaine du Socialisme* (Paris: Editions, 1961).

SIERRA LEONE

BANTON, MICHAEL. *West African City* (London: Oxford University Press, 1957).

CARTWRIGHT, J. H. *Politics in Sierra Leone* (Toronto: University of Toronto Press, 1970).

CLAPMAN, CHRISTOPHER S. *Liberia and Sierra Leone* (New York: Cambridge University Press, 1976).

CLIFFORD, M. L. *The Land and People of Sierra Leone* (Philadelphia: Lippincott, 1972).

COLE, ROBERT W. *Kossoh Town Boy* (Cambridge, England: Cambridge University Press, 1969).

COLLIER, GERSHON. *Sierra Leone* (New York: New York University Press, 1970).

(F) CONTON, WILLIAM. *The African* (Boston: Little, Brown, 1960).

COX, THOMAS. *Civil-Military Relations in Sierra Leone* (Cambridge, Mass.: Harvard University Press, 1976).

FYFE, CHRISTOPHER. *A Short History of Sierra Leone* (to 1898) (London: Oxford University Press, 1962).

KILSON, MARTIN. *Political Change in a West African State: A Study of the Process of Modernization in Sierra Leone* (Cambridge, Mass.: Harvard University Press, 1966).

PORTER, ARTHUR. *Creoledom* (London: Oxford University Press, 1963).

LEWIS, ROY. *Sierra Leone* (London: H. M. S. Stationery Office, 1954).

SOMALIA

BARRE, MAJOR-GENERAL MOHAMED SIAD. *My Country and My People* (Mogadishu: Ministry of Information and National Guidance, 1970).

CASTAGNO, A. A. JR. "Somalia," *International Conciliation,* vol. 522 (1959).

CONTINI, PAOLO. *The Somali Republic: An Experiment in Legal Integration* (London: Frank Cass, 1969).

DOOB, LEONARD W. *Resolving Conflict in Africa* (New Haven: Yale University Press, 1970).

DRYSDALE, JOHN. *The Somali Dispute* (New York: Praeger, 1964).

(F) FARAH, NURRUDDIN. *From a Crooked Rib* (New York: Humanities Press, 1970).

HANLEY, GERALD. *Warriors and Strangers* (New York: Harper & Row, 1971).

HESS, ROBERT. *Italian Colonialism in Africa* (Chicago: University of Chicago Press, 1966).

HOSKYNS, C. *The Ethiopia-Somali-Kenya Dispute 1960–67* (Dar Es Salaam: Oxford University Press, 1969).

KARP, M. *The Economics of Trusteeship in Somalia* (Boston: Boston University Press, 1960).

LAITIN, DAVID. "The Political Economy of Military Rule in Somalia," *The Journal of Modern African Studies,* vol. 14, no. 3 (1976), pp. 449–68.

LAURENCE, MARGARET. *New Wind in a Dry Land* (New York: Knopf, 1964).

LEWIS, I. M. *The Modern History of Somaliland* (London: Praeger, 1965).

————. *A Pastoral Democracy* (London: Oxford University Press, 1961).

————. *Peoples of the Horn of Africa* (London: International Institute, 1955).

MUHAMMAD, HAJI NOOR. *The Legal System of the Somali Democratic Republic* (Charlottesville, Va.: Michie, 1972).

THOMPSON, V. and R. ADLOFF. *Djibouti and the Horn of Africa* (Stanford, Calif.: Stanford University Press, 1968).

TOUVAL, SAADIA. *Somali Nationalism* (Cambridge, Mass.: Harvard University Press, 1963).

SOUTH AFRICA

(F) ABRAHAMS, PETER. *Wild Conquest* (Garden City, N.Y.: Doubleday, 1971).

ADAM, HERIBERT. *Modernizing Racial Domination: The Dynamics of South African Politics* (Los Angeles: University of California Press, 1971).

————. *South Africa: Sociological Perspectives* (London: Oxford University Press, 1970).

AFRICA RESEARCH GROUP. *Race to Power* (Garden City, N.Y.: Doubleday, 1974).

ANDREWS, H. T. et al. (eds.) *South Africa in the Sixties* (Capetown: South African Foundation, 1962).

BALLINGER, MARGARET. *From Union to Apartheid: A Trek to Isolation* (New York: Praeger, 1969).

BARBEE, JAMES. *South Africa's Foreign Policy 1945–1970* (London: Oxford University Press, 1973).

BENSON, MARY. *South Africa: The Struggle for a Birthright* (New York: Minerva Press, 1969).

(F) BOETIE, DUGMORE. *Familiarity is the Kingdom of the Lost* (New York: Fawcett Books, 1970).

BRAITHWAITE, E. R. *Honorary White* (New York: McGraw-Hill, 1975).

BROOKES, EDGAR H. *Apartheid: A Documentary Study of Modern South Africa* (London: Routledge & Kegan Paul, 1968).

BROTZ, HOWARD. *The Politics of South Africa* (London: Oxford University Press, 1977).

BROWN, DOUGLAS. *Against the World: Attitudes of White South Africa* (Garden City, N.Y.: Doubleday, 1968).

BROWN, W. H. *On the South African Frontier* (New York: Scribner's Sons, 1899).

BUNTING, BRIAN. *The Rise of the South African Reich* (Baltimore: Penguin Books, 1969).

BUTLER, JEFFREY, ROBERT RUTBERG, and JOHN ADAMS. *The Black Homelands of South Africa: The Political and Economic Development of Bophuthatswana and Kwazulu* (Los Angeles: University of California Press, 1977).

BUTLITSKY, A. V. "South Africa: The Explosion Must Come," in *Races and Peoples* (Moscow: Progress Publishers, 1974).

CALDWELL, THEODORE C. *The Anglo-Boer War* (Boston: D. C. Heath, 1965).

(F) CARIM, ENVER. *The Golden City* (New York: Grove Press, 1969).

CARLSON, JOEL. *No Neutral Ground* (New York: Thomas Y. Crowell, 1973).

CARTER, GWENDOLYN M. *The Politics of Inequality: South Africa Since 1948* (New York: Praeger, 1962).

CARTER, GWENDOLYN, THOMAS KARIS, and NEWELL STULTZ. *South Africa's Transkei: The Politics of Domestic Colonialism* (Evanston, Ill.: Northwestern University Press, 1967).

CARTER, GWENDOLYN M. and THOMAS KARIS (eds.). *From Protest to Challenge: A Documentary History of African Politics in South Africa 1882–1964,* 3 vols. (Stanford, Calif.: Hoover Institution Press, 1971, 1973).

CHURCHILL, WINSTON. *London to Ladysmith and Ian Hamilton's March* (New York: Harcourt Brace Jovanovich, 1962).

CLAMMER, DAVID. *The Zulu War* (Cape Town, South Africa: Purnell, 1973).

(F) CLIVE, WILLIAM. *The Tune That They Play* (New York: Simon & Schuster, 1973).

COLVIN, IAN D. (ed.). *The Cape of Adventure* (London: T. C. and E. C. Jack, 1912).

COWLES, RAYMOND. *Zulu Journal* (Los Angeles: University of California Press, 1959).

CRAFFORD, F. S. *Jan Smuts* (London: Allen & Unwin, 1945).

DANIELS, GEORGE M. *Southern Africa: A Time for Change* (New York: Friendship Press, 1964).

DAVENPORT, T. R. *The Africaner Bond 1880–1911* (London: Oxford University Press, 1967).

DAVIS, J. A. and J. K. BAKER (eds.). *Southern Africa in Transition* (New York: Praeger, 1966).

DEKIEWIET, C. W. *A History of South Africa: Social and Economic* (London: Oxford University Press, 1967).

DENOON, DONALD. *Southern Africa Since 1800* (New York: Praeger, 1973).

DESMOND, C. *The Discarded People* (Baltimore: Penguin Books, 1971).

DEVILLIERS, H. H. W. *Ruvonia: Operation Mayibuye* (Johannesburg, South Africa: Afrikaanse Pers-Boekhandel, 1964).

DRURY, ALLEN. *A Very Strange Society* (New York: Trident Press, 1967).

(F) EDEN, DOROTHY. *Siege in the Sun* (London: Hodder Paperbacks, 1967).

FARWELL, BYRON. *The Great Anglo-Boer War* (New York: Harper & Row, 1976).

FEIT, EDWARD. *African Opposition in South Africa* (Stanford, Calif.: Hoover Institution Press, 1967).

———. *South Africa: The Dynamics of the African National Congress* (London: Oxford University Press, 1962).

———. *Urban Revolt in South Africa 1960–1964* (Evanston, Ill.: Northwestern University Press, 1971).

FISHER, J. *The Afrikaners* (London: Cassell, 1969).

FRYE, WILLIAM. *In Whitest Africa: The Dynamics of Apartheid* (Englewood Cliffs, N.J.: Prentice-Hall, 1968).

FUGARD, ATHOL. *Statements* (London: Oxford University Press, 1974).

FURNEUX, R. *The Zulu War: Isandhlwana and Rorke's Drift* (Philadelphia: Lippincott, 1963).

GARDNER, BRIAN. *Mafeking* (New York: Harcourt Brace Jovanovich, 1966).

GOVERNMENT OF SOUTH AFRICA. *State of South Africa Yearbook* (Johannesburg: Da Gama Publishers, yearly).

———. *Stepping into the Future* (Johannesburg: Erudita, 1975).

———. *South Africa: A Visual History* (Johannesburg: Perskor Publishers, 1976).

———. *Multi-National Development in South Africa* (Pretoria: State Department of Information, 1974).

———. *Black Development in South Africa* (Johannesburg: Benbo, 1976).

GRUNDY, KENNETH W. *Confrontation and Accommodation in Southern Africa: The Limits of Independence* (Los Angeles: University of California Press, 1973).

HANCE, W. et al. *Southern Africa and the United States* (New York: Columbia University Press, 1968).

HARTMANN, HEINZ. *Enterprize and Politics in South Africa* (Princeton, N.J.: Princeton University Press, 1962).

HEARD, KENNETH. *General Elections in South Africa, 1943–1970* (London: Oxford University Press, 1974).

HEPPLE, ALEX. *South Africa: A Political and Economic History* (New York: Praeger, 1966).

———. *Verwoerd* (London: Penguin Books, 1967).

HILL, CHRISTOPHER R. *Bantustans: The Fragmentation of South Africa* (London: Oxford University Press, 1964).

HOAGLAND, JIM. *South Africa: Civilizations in Conflict* (Boston: Houghton Mifflin, 1972).

HOFMEYR, JAN. *South Africa* (New York: McGraw-Hill, 1952).

HORWITZ, RALPH. *The Political Economy of South Africa* (New York: Praeger, 1967).

HUDSON, W. et al. *Anatomy of South Africa* (Cape Town, South Africa: Purnell, 1966).

INFORMATION SERVICE OF SOUTH AFRICA. *South African Tradition* (New York: Information Service of South Africa, 1974).

———. *Homelands, the Role of Corporations* (New York: Information Service of South Africa, 1974).

JUTA, JAN. *Background in Sunshine* (New York: Scribner's Sons, 1972).

KAHN, E. J. JR. *The Separated People: A Look at Contemporary South Africa* (New York: W. W. Norton, 1968).

KANTOR, JAMES. *A Healthy Grave* (London: Hamish Hamilton, 1967).

KRUGER, D. W. *The Making of a Nation* (Johannesburg, South Africa: Macmillan, 1969).

KRUGER, PAUL. *The Memoirs of Paul Kruger Told by Himself* (New York: The Century Company, 1902).

———. *The Memoirs of Paul Kruger (1902)* (London: T. F. Unwin, 1902).

KUPER, LEO. *An African Bourgeoisie: Race, Class, and Politics in South Africa* (New Haven: Yale University Press, 1965).

LA GUMA, ALEX (ed.). *Apartheid: A Collection of Writings on South African Racism by South Africans* (Berlin: Seven Seas Publishers, 1971).

———. *The Stone Country* (London: Heinemann, 1974).

(F) ———. *A Walk in the Night* (New York: Humanities Press, 1967).

LAURENCE, JOHN. *The Seeds of Disaster* (New York: Taplinger, 1968).

LEGUM, COLIN and MARGARET LEGUM. *South Africa: Crisis for the West* (New York: Praeger, 1964).

LEISS, AMELIA (ed.). *Apartheid and United Nations Collective Measures: An Analysis* (New York: Prepared under the auspices of the Carnegie Endowment for International Peace, 1965).

LeMAY, G. H. L. *Black and White in South Africa* (New York: American Heritage Press, 1971).

LEVER, H. *The South African Voter* (Cape Town, South Africa: Juta Press, 1972).

LICHTENSTEIN, W. H. C. (translated by Dr. O. H. Spohr). *Foundation of the Cape About the Buchuanas* (Cape Town, South Africa, A. A. Balkema, 1973).

LUTHULI, ALBERT. *Let My People Go* (New York: Meridian, 1962).

MACKLER, IAN. *Pattern for Profit in Southern Africa* (Boston: D. C. Heath, 1972).

MALHERBE, PAUL. *Multistan* (Cape Town, South Africa: David Philip, 1974).

MANDELA, N. *No Easy Walk to Freedom* (London: Heinemann, 1965).

MARQUARD, LEO. *A Federation of Southern Africa* (London: Oxford University Press, 1971).

———. *The Peoples and Policies of South Africa* (London: Oxford University Press, 1962).

———. *A Short History of South Africa* (New York: Praeger, 1968).

MASON, G. H. *Life With the Zulus of Natal* (London: Frank Cass, 1968).

MBEKI, GOVAN. *South Africa: The Peasants Revolt* (Baltimore: Penguin Books, 1964).

McBRIDE, ANGUS. *The Zulu War* (London: Osprey Publishing, 1976).

(F) McMENEMY, NICKIE. *Assegai* (London: Macmillan, 1973).

MEINTJES, JOHANNES. *General Louis Botha* (London: Cussell, 1970).

———. *The Anglo-Boer War 1899–1902* (Capetown, South Africa: C. Struik, 1976).

MOKGATLE, NABOTH. *The Autobiography of an Unknown South African* (Los Angeles: University of California Press, 1971).

MOODIE, DUNBAR. *The Rise of Afrikanerdom* (Los Angeles: University of California Press, 1975).

MOORE, BASIL (ed.). *The Challenge of Black Theology in South Africa* (Atlanta: John Knox Press, 1973).

MORRIS, DONALD. *The Washing of the Spears* (New York: Simon & Schuster, 1965).

MORTON, H. V. *In Search of South Africa* (London: Methuen, 1948).

MPHAHLELE, E. *Down Second Avenue* (Garden City, N.Y.: Doubleday, 1971).

(F) ———. *The Wanderers* (New York: Macmillan, 1971).

MULLER, C. F. (ed.). *500 Years: A History of South Africa* (Pretoria, South Africa: Academia Press, 1969).

MUNGER, EDWIN. *Afrikaner and African Nationalism* (London: Oxford University Press, 1967).

NGUBANE, JORDAN K. *An African Explains* Apartheid (New York: Praeger, 1963).

(F) ———. *Ushaba* (Washington, D.C.: Three Continents Press, 1974).

NIELSEN, WALDEMAR A. *African Battleline: American Policy Choices in Southern Africa* (New York: Harper & Row, for the Council in Foreign Relations, 1965).

(F) PATON, ALAN. *Cry, The Beloved Country* (New York: Scribner's Sons, 1948).

(F) ———. *Too Late the Phalarope* (New York: Scribner's Sons, 1953).

(F) ———. *Tales From a Troubled Land* (New York: Scribner's Sons, 1961).

———. *South African Tragedy: The Life and Times of Jan Hofmeyr* (New York: Scribner's Sons, 1965).

———. *The Long View* (New York: Praeger, 1968).

———. *Apartheid and the Archbishop: The Life and Times of Geoffrey Clayton* (New York: Scribner's Sons, 1973).

POTHOLM, C. P. and RICHARD DALE (eds.). *Southern Africa in Perspective: Essays in Regional Politics* (New York: Free Press, 1972).

RHOODIE, ESCHEL. *The Paper Curtain* (Johannesburg, South Africa: Vortrekkerpens, 1969).

———. *The Third Africa* (New York: Twin City, 1968).

RIDPATH, J. C. and E. S. ELLIS. *The Story of South Africa* (Chicago: J. H. Moore, 1899).

RITTER, E. A. *Shake Zulu: The Rise of the Zulu Empire* (New York: Mentor, 1973).

(F) RIVE, RICHARD. *Emergency* (New York: Macmillan, 1970).

(F) ——— (ed.). *Quartet* (New York: Humanities Press, 1963).

ROBERTSON, JANET. *Liberalism in South Africa: 1948-1963* (London: Oxford University Press, 1971).

ROUX, EDWARD. *Time Longer than Rope: A History of the Black Man's Struggle for Freedom in South Africa,* 2nd ed. (Madison: University of Wisconsin Press, 1964).

RUSSELL, D. E. H. *Rebellion, Revolution, and Armed Force: A Comparative Study of Fifteen Countries with Special Emphasis on Cuba and South Africa* (New York: Academic Press, 1974).

SACHS, ALBIE. *Justice in South Africa* (Los Angeles: University of California Press, 1973).

SACHS, WULF. *Black Anger* (New York: Grove Press, 1957).

SACKS, BENJAMIN. *South Africa: An Imperial Dilemma* (Albuquerque: University of New Mexico Press, 1967).

SCHAPERA, I. *The Bantu Speaking Tribes of South Africa* (London: S. Routledge Sons, 1937).

(F) SCHREINER, O. *The Story of an African Farm* (New York: Fawcett Books, 1968).

SETAI, BETHUEL. *The Political Economy of South Africa* (Washington, D.C.: University Press of America, 1977).

SIMONS, H. J. and R. E. SIMONS. *Class and Colour in South Africa* (Baltimore: Penguin Books, 1969).

SMITH, K. W. *From Frontier to Midlands: A History of the GRAAF-Reinet District 1786-1910* (Grahamstown, South Africa: Rhodes University, 1976).

SMUTS, J. C. *Holism and Evolution* (New York: Viking Press, 1926).

SMUTS, J. C. JR. *Jan Christian Smuts* (New York: William Morrow, 1952).

South Africa 1974 (Official Yearbook of the Republic of South Africa) (Johannesburg: South African Department of Information, 1973).

SOUTH AFRICAN INSTITUTE OF RACE RELATIONS. *A Survey of Race Relations in South Africa* (Johannesburg: South African Institute of Race Relations, yearly).

Southern Africa Problems and U. S. Alternatives (New York: Center for War/Peace Studies, 1972).

SOWDEN, LEWIS. *The Land of Afternoon: The Story of a White South African* (New York: McGraw-Hill, 1968).

SPENCE, J. E. *Republic Under Pressure: A Study of South African Foreign Policy* (London: Oxford University Press, for the Royal Institute of International Affairs, 1965).

STEWARD, ALEXANDER. *The World, the West and Pretoria* (New York: David McKay, 1977).

STOCKHOLM INTERNATIONAL PEACE RESEARCH INSTITUTE. *Southern Africa: The Escalation of a Conflict* (Stockholm: Almquist and Wiksell, 1976).

STOKKE, OLAV and CARL WIDSTRAND (eds.). *Southern Africa,* 2 vols. (Uppsala, Sweden: Scandinavian Institute of African Studies, 1973).

STULTZ, NEWELL M. *Afrikaner Politics in South Africa, 1934–1948* (Los Angeles: University of California Press, 1974).

(F) Themba, Can. *The Will to Die* (New York: Humanities Press, 1972).

THOMPSON, LEONARD. *African Societies in Southern Africa* (New York: Prager, 1969).

———. *Politics in the Republic of South Africa* (Boston: Little, Brown, 1966).

THOMPSON, LEONARD and JEFFRY BUTLER. *Change in Contemporary South Africa* (Los Angeles: University of California Press, 1975).

TYRRELL, BARBARA. *Tribal Peoples of Southern Africa* (Cape Town, South Africa: Books of Africa, 1971).

UNESCO. *Apartheid, Its Effects on Education, Science, Culture, and Information* (Paris: UNESCO, 1967, 1972).

VAN DEN BERGHE, PIERRE L. *South Africa: A Study in Conflict* (Middletown, Conn.: Wesleyan University Press, 1965).

VANDENBOSCH, AMRY. *South Africa and the World: The Foreign Policy of Apartheid* (Lexington: University Press of Kentucky, 1970).

(F) VAN DER POST, LAURENS. *A Story Like the Wind* (New York: William Morrow, 1972).

VISUAL PUBLICATIONS. *South Africa: A Visual History* (Johannesburg, South Africa: Visual Publications, 1972).

WALKER, ERIC. *A History of South Africa, the Great Trek* (London: Longmans, 1962).

WALL, PATRICK (ed.). *The Indian Ocean and the Threat to the West* (London: Stacey International, 1975).

———. *Prelude to Détente* (London: Stacey International, 1975).

WALSHE, PETER. *The Rise of African Nationalism in South Africa* (Los Angeles: University of California Press, 1971).

WERE, GIDEON. *A History of South Africa* (New York: Africana Publishing Corp., 1974).

WILLIAMS, A. F. B. *Botha, Smuts and South Africa* (New York: Collier Books, 1962).

WILSON, FRANCIS. *Migrant Labour in South Africa* (Johannesburg: Christian Institute of South Africa, 1972).

WILSON, M. and L. THOMPSON (eds.). *The Oxford History of South Africa,* 2 vols. (London: Oxford University Press, 1969, 1971).

WOLSELEY, GARNET. *The South African Journal of Sir Garnet Wolseley 1879–1880* (Cape Town, South Africa: A. A. Balkema, 1973).

WORALL, DENIS (ed.). *South Africa: Government and Politics* (Pretoria, South Africa: J. L. Van Schaik, 1971).

WORTH, C. B. *Mosquito Safari* (New York: Simon & Schuster, 1971).

(F) ZWELONKE, D. M. *Robben Island* (London: Heinemann, 1973).

SUDAN

ALBINO, O. *The Sudan: A Southern Viewpoint* (London: Oxford University Press, 1970).

BAKER, ANNE. *Morning Star* (London: William Kimber, 1972).

BECHTOLD, PETER. *Politics in the Sudan Since Independence* (New York: Praeger, 1976).

BERNATZIK, H. A. *Gari-Gari* (New York: Henry Holt, 1936).

BESHIR, M. O. *Southern Sudan: Background to Conflict* (London: Hurst & Co., 1968).

COLLINS, R. O. *The Southern Sudan 1883–1898* (New Haven: Yale University Press, 1964).

COLLINS, R. O. and R. L. TIGNOR. *Egypt and the Sudan* (Englewood Cliffs, N.J.: Prentice-Hall, 1967).

DENG, FRANCIS M. *Tradition and Modernization* (New Haven: Yale University Press, 1971).

DUGMORE, A. R. *The Vast Sudan* (New York: Frederick Stokes, 1926).

DUNCAN, T. S. R. *The Sudan's Path to Independence* (London: Heinemann, 1957).

EL MAHDI, MANDOUR. *A Short History of the Sudan* (London: Oxford University Press, 1965).

EPRILE, CECIL. *War and Peace in the Sudan: 1955–1972* (London: David and Charles, 1974).

EVANS-PRITCHARD, E. E. *The Nuer* (London: Oxford University Press, 1940).

FARWELL, BYRON. *Prisoners of the Mahdi* (New York: Harper & Row, 1967).

GRAY, RICHARD. *A History of the Southern Sudan, 1839–1889* (London: Oxford University Press, 1961).

HENDERSON, K. D. *The Sudan* (New York: Praeger, 1966).

———. *Sudan Republic* (New York: Praeger, 1965).

HOLT, P. M. *A Modern History of the Sudan* (London: Weidenfeld and Nicolson, 1961).

HOWELL, JOHN (ed.). *Local Government and Politics in the Sudan* (Khartoum, Sudan: Khartoum University Press, 1974).

ISMAIL, SALAH KHOGALI. *Sudan: In Pictures* (New York: Sterling Publishing Co., 1976).

ODUHO, J. and WILLIAM DENG. *The Problems of the Southern Sudan* (London: Oxford University Press, 1963).

SAID, B. M. *The Sudan: Cross Roads of Africa* (London: Bodley Head, 1965).

(F) SALIH, TAYEB. *Season of Migration to the North* (New York: Humanities Press, 1969).

SLATIN, R. *Fire and Sword in the Sudan* (London: E. Arnold, 1896).

TONIOLO, E. and RICHARD HILL (eds.). *The Opening of the Nile Basin: Writings by Members of the Catholic Mission to Central Africa on the Geography and Orthonography of the Sudan, 1842–1881* (New York: Barnes & Noble, 1975).

TRIMINGHAM, S. *Islam in the Sudan* (London: Oxford University Press, 1958).

U. S. DEPARTMENT OF DEFENSE. *Area Handbook for the Republic of the Sudan* (Washington, D. C.: Government Printing Office, 1964).

WINGATE, RONALD. *Wingate of the Sudan: The Life and Times of General Sir Reginald Wingate, Maker of the Anglo-Egyptian Sudan* (Westport, Conn.: Greenwood Press, 1975).

SWAZILAND

BARKER, DUDLEY. *Swaziland* (London: Her Majesty's Stationery Office, 1965).

BEST, ALAN. *The Swaziland Railroad* (East Lansing: Michigan State University Press, 1966).

GROTPETER, JOHN J. *Historical Dictionary of Swaziland* (Metuchen, N.J.: Scarecrow Press, 1975).

HALPERN, J. *South Africa's Hostages* (Baltimore: Penguin Books, 1965).

HOLEMAN, J. F. (ed.). *Experiment in Swaziland* (Cape Town, South Africa: Oxford University Press, 1964).

KUPER, HILDA. *An African Aristocracy* (London: Oxford University Press, 1947).

————. *A Uniform of Color* (Johannesburg: Witwatersrand University Press, 1947).

————. *The Swazi* (London: International African Institute, 1952).

————. *The Swazi: A South African Kingdom* (New York: Holt, Rinehart and Winston, 1963).

(F) ————. *Bite of Hunger* (New York: Harcourt Brace Jovanovich, 1966).

(F) ————. *A Witch in My Heart* (London : Oxford University Press, 1970).

LEISTNER, G. M. E. and P. SMIT. *Swaziland: Resources and Development* (Pretoria: South African Institute, 1969).

MARWICK, B. A. *The Swazi* (London: Frank Cass, 1940; reissued 1966).

MATSEBULA, J. S. M. *A History of Swaziland* (Cape Town: Longmans Southern Africa, 1972).

(F) MILLER, ALLISTER. *Mamisa, The Swazi Warrior* (Pietermaritzburg, South Africa: Shuter & Shooter, 1963).

POTHOLM, C. P. *Swaziland: The Dynamics of Political Modernization* (Los Angeles: University of California Press, 1972).

STEVENS, R. P. *Botswana, Lesotho, Swaziland* (New York: Praeger, 1967).

VAN WYK, A. J. *Swaziland: A Political Study* (Pretoria: South African Institute, 1969).

TANZANIA

BENNETT, NORMAN. *Mirambo of Tanzania* (London: Oxford University Press, 1971).

BIENEN, H. *Tanzania: Party Transformation and Economic Development* (Princeton, N.J.: Princeton University Press, 1967).

BURKE, FRED. *Tanganyika: Preplanning* (Syracuse, N.Y.: Syracuse University Press, 1965).

CAMERON, D. C. *My Tanganyika Service and Some Nigeria* (London: Allen & Unwin, 1939).

CAMERON, J. and W. A. DODD. *Society, Schools and Progress in Tanzania* (New York: Pergamon Press, 1970).

CHIDZERO, B. T. G. *Tanganyika and International Trusteeship* (London: Oxford University Press, 1961).

CLIFFE, L. (ed.). *One Party Democracy: The 1965 Tanzania General Elections* (Nairobi, Kenya: East African Publishing House, 1967).

COLE, SONIA. *The Prehistory of East Africa* (London: Penguin Books, 1954).

DIAMOND, S. and F. C. BURKE (eds.). *The Transformation of East Africa: Studies in Political Anthropology* (New York: Basic Books, 1966).

DON NANJIRA, DANIEL. *The Status of Aliens in East Africa: Asians and Europeans in Tanzania, Uganda, and Kenya* (New York: Praeger, 1976).

DUGGAN, W. R. and J. R. CIVILLE. *Tanzania and Nyerere* (Maryknoll, N.Y.: Orbis Books, 1976).

FOX, LORENE. *East African Childhood* (London: Oxford University Press, 1967).

GHAI, D. P. (ed.). *Portrait of a Minority: Asians in East Africa* (Nairobi, Kenya: Oxford University Press, 1965).

HATCH, JOHN. *Tanzania: A Profile* (New York: Praeger, 1972).

HEUSSLEE, ROBERT. *British Tanganyika* (Durham, N.C.: Duke University Press, 1971).

HOPKINS, RAYMOND. *Political Rules in a New State* (New Haven: Yale University Press, 1971).

INGLE, CLYDE. *From Village to State in Tanzania* (Ithaca, N.Y.: Cornell University Press, 1972).

KIMAMBO, I. N. and A. J. TEMU. *A History of Tanzania* (Evanston, Ill.: Northwestern University Press, 1969).

LARDEN, ROBERT. *Oman Since 1856* (Princeton, N.J.: Princeton University Press, 1967).

LIEBENOW, J. GUS. *Colonial Rule and Political Development in Tanzania: The Case of the Makonde* (Evanston, Ill.: Northwestern University Press, 1971).

MacDONALD, A. *Tanzania: Young Nation in a Hurry* (New York: Hawthorne, 1966).

MAGUIRE, G. ANDREW. *Toward 'Uhuru' in Tanzania* (Cambridge, England: Cambridge University Press, 1969).

MEISTER, A. *East Africa: The Past in Chains, the Future in Pawn* (New York: Walker, 1968).

NELLIS, JOHN R. *A Theory of Ideology: The Tanzanian Example* (Nairobi, Kenya: Oxford University Press, 1972).

NYERERE, JULIUS. *Freedom and Unity* (London: Oxford University Press, 1967).

––––––. *Ujamaa Essays on Socialism* (London: Oxford University Press, 1968).

)GOT, B. A. and J. A. KIERAN (eds.). *Zamani: A Survey of East African History* (Nairobi, Kenya: East African Publishing House, 1968).

RICHARDS, AUDREY. *The Multicultural States of East Africa* (Montreal: McGill University Press, 1969).

RUTHENBERG, HANS. *Smallholder Farming and Smallholder Development in Tanzania* (Munchen, Germany: Weitforum Verlag, 1968).

SMITH, W. E. *We Must Run While They Walk* (New York: Random House, 1971).

STEPHENS, H. W. *The Political Transformation in Tanganyika: 1920–1967* (New York: Praeger, 1968).

SWENDSEN, K. E. and M. TEISEN (eds.). *Self-Reliant Tanzania* (Nairobi, Kenya: East African Publishing House, 1969).

TORDOFF, W. *Government and Politics in Tanzania* (Nairobi, Kenya: East African Publishing House, 1967).

U.S. DEPARTMENT OF DEFENSE. *Area Handbook for Tanzania* (Washington, D.C.: Government Printing Office, 1968).

TOGO

THOMPSON, V. M. and R. ADLOFF. *The Emerging States of French Equatorial Africa* (Stanford, Calif.: Stanford University Press, 1960).

TUNISIA

BROWN, L. CARL. *The Tunisia of Ahmad Bay (1837–1855)* (Princeton, N.J.: Princeton University Press, 1975).

DWIGNAUD, JEAN. *Change at Shebka* (New York: Pantheon Books, 1970).

LING, DWIGHT L. *Tunisia, From Protectorate to Republic* (Bloomington: Indiana University Press, 1967).

MOORE, CLEMENT HENRY. *Tunisia Since Independence: The Dynamics of One-Party Government* (Berkeley: University of California Press, 1965).

ZARTMAN, I. W. (ed.). *Man, State and Society in the Contemporary Maghrib* (New York: Praeger, 1973).

UGANDA

APTER, D. *Political Kingdom in Uganda* (Princeton, N.J.: Princeton University Press, 1965).

BARBER, JAMES. *Imperial Frontier* (Nairobi, Kenya: East African Publishing House, 1968).

BEATTIE, JOHN. *Bunyoro* (New York: Holt, Rinehart and Winston, 1961).

BURKE, F. *Local Government and Politics in Uganda* (Syracuse, N.Y.: Syracuse University Press, 1964).

CENTRAL OFFICE OF INFORMATION. *Uganda: The Making of a Nation* (London: Her Majesty's Stationery Office, 1962).

FALLERS, L. *Bantu Bureaucracy* (Chicago: University of Chicago Press, 1956).

FRANCK, THOMAS. "East African Federation," in Thomas Franck, *Why Federations Fail* (New York: New York University Press, 1968).

GHAI, D. P. (ed.). *Portrait of a Minority: Asians in East Africa* (Nairobi: Oxford University Press, 1965).

GUKIINA, P. M. *Uganda: A Case Study in African Political Development* (Notre Dame, Ind.: Notre Dame University Press, 1972).

HUGHES, A. J. *East Africa* (Baltimore: Penguin Books, 1963).

IBINGIRA, G. S. K. *The Forging of an African Nation* (New York: Viking Press, 1973).

INGHAM, K. *The Making of Modern Uganda* (London: Allen & Unwin, 1958).

INGRAMS, HAROLD. *Uganda* (London: Her Majesty's Stationery Office, 1960).

JOHNSON, SIR H. *The Story of My Life* (Columbus, Ohio: Bobbs-Merrill, 1923).

————. *The Uganda Protectorate* (London: Hutchinson & Co., 1902).

KASFIR, NELSON. *The Shrinking Political Arena* (Los Angeles: University of California Press, 1976).

LAMPHEAR, J. J. *The Traditional History of the Jie of Uganda* (New York: Oxford University Press, 1976).

LUGARD, SIR F. D. *The Rise of Our East African Empire* (London: Blackwood and Sons, 1893).

MACKAY, J. H. *A. M. Mackay of Uganda* (New York: A. C. Armstrong, 1890).

MAMDANI, MAHMOOD. *Politics and Class Formation in Uganda* (New York: Monthly Review Press, 1976).

MARTIN, DAVID. *General Amin* (London: Faber & Faber, 1974).

MEISTER, A. *East Africa: The Past in Chains, the Future in Pawn* (New York: Walker, 1968).

MELADY, MARGARET and THOMAS MELADY. *Uganda: the Asian Exiles* (Maryknoll, N.Y.: Orbis Books, 1976).

MIDDLETON, JOHN. *The Lugbara* (New York: Holt, Rinehart and Winston, 1965).

NYAKATURA, J. W. *Anatomy of An African Kingdom* (Garden City, N.Y.: Doubleday, 1973).

OSOGO, JOHN. *A History of the Baluyia* (London: Oxford University Press, 1966).

SCHWARTZ, B. (ed.). *Caste in Overseas Indian Communities* (San Francisco: Chandler, 1967).

TURNBULL, COLIN. *The Mountain People* (New York: Simon & Schuster, 1972).

VINCENT, JOAN. *African Elite: The Big Men of a Small Town* (New York: Columbia University Press, 1971).

WEST, HENRY W. *Land Policy in Buganda* (Cambridge, England: Cambridge University Press, 1972).

WINTER, E. H. *Beyond the Mountains of the Moon* (Urbana: University of Illinois Press, 1965).

WRIGHT, MITCHAEL. *Buganda in the Heroic Age* (London: Oxford University Press, 1973).

UPPER VOLTA

BASSOLET, F. D. *Evolution DeLa Haute Volta de 1898 au 3 Janvier 1966* (Ouagadougou, Upper Volta: Imprierie Nationale Haute Volta, 1968).

ZAIRE (formerly CONGO: KINSHASA)

Bouscaren, Anthony. *Tshombe* (New York: Twin Circle Publishing, 1967).

Bouvier, Paul. *L'Accession du Congo Belge a l'Independance* (Brussels: Editions de l'Institut de Sociologie, 1965).

Centre de Recherches et d'Information Socio Politiques (CRISP). *Congo Yearly Reports* (Princeton, N.J.: Princeton University Press, yearly).

(F) Conrad, J. *The Heart of Darkness* (New York: New American Library, 1956).

Cornevin, *Histoire au Congo* (Paris: Gerger-Levault, 1963).

Crabb, John. *The Legal System of Congo-Kinshasa* (Charlottesville, Va.: Michie, 1970).

Dayal, R. J. *Mission for Hammarskjöld: The Congo Crisis* (Princeton, N.J.: Princeton University Press, 1976).

Gerard-Libois, Jules. *Katanga Secession* (Madison: University of Wisconsin Press, 1966).

(F) Greene, G. *A Burnt-Out Case* (New York: Viking Press, 1961).

Gunther, John. *Meet the Congo* (New York: Harper & Row, 1959).

Heinz, G. and H. Donnay. *Lumumba: The Last Fifty Days.* (New York: Grove Press, 1969).

Hilton-Simpson, M. W. *Land and Peoples of Kasai* (London: Constable and Company, 1911).

Hoare, M. *Congo Mercenary* (London: Allen & Unwin, 1967).

Hoskyns, C. *The Congo Since Independence* (London: Oxford University Press, 1965).

Kanza, Thomas. *Conflict in the Congo* (Baltimore: Penguin Books, 1972).

Kenny, Lona. *Mbooka* (New York: Crown Publishers, 1972).

LeFever, E. *Crisis in the Congo: A U.N. Force in Action* (Washington, D.C.: Brookings Institution, 1965).

LeMarchand, R. *Political Awakening in the Congo* (Berkeley: University of California Press, 1965).

Lumumba, P. *Congo, My Country* (London: Chapman and Hall, 1962).

Mockler, A. *The Mercenaries* (New York: Collier Macmillan, 1969).

(F) O'Brien, C. C. *Murderous Angels* (Boston: Little, Brown, 1968).

————. *To Katanga and Back* (New York: Simon & Schuster, 1963).

Reed, D. *111 Days in Stanleyville* (New York: Harper & Row, 1966).

Scott, Ian. *Tumbled House: The Congo at Independence* (London: Oxford University Press, 1969).

Tshombe, Moise. *My 15 Months in Government in the Congo* (Pland, Texas: University of Pland, 1967).

Turnbull, Colin. *The Forest People* (Garden City, N.Y.: Doubleday, 1962).

Vansine, Jan. *Kingdoms of the Savanna* (Madison: University of Wisconsin Press, 1968).

Weiss, H. *Political Protest in the Congo* (Princeton, N.J.: Princeton University Press, 1967).

Willame, Jean-Claude. *Patrimonialism and Political Change in the Congo* (Stanford, Calif.: Stanford University Press, 1972).

Young, Crawford. "Domestic Violence in Africa: the Congo," in C. W. Anderson, Fred von der Mahden, and Crawford Young, *Issues of Political Development* (Englewood Cliffs, N.J.: Prentice-Hall, 1967).

————. *Politics in the Congo* (Princeton, N.J.: Princeton University Press, 1965).

ZAMBIA

Bates, R. *Unions, Parties and Political Development* (New Haven: Yale University Press, 1971).

Cervenka, Zdenek and R. Weiss. *Zambia, the First Ten Years 1964–1974* (Stockholm: Swedish-Zambian Association, 1974).

COLEMAN, FRANCIS L. *The Northern Rhodesia Copperbelt* (Manchester, England: The University Press, 1971).

FAGAN, BRIAN M. (ed.) *A Short History of Zambia from the Earliest Times Until A.D. 1900* (Nairobi and New York: Oxford University Press, 1966).

GANN, L. H. *A History of Northern Rhodesia* (London: Chatto and Windus, 1964).

GRAY, RICHARD. *The Two Nations: Aspects of the Development of Race Relations in the Rhodesias and Nyasaland* (London: Oxford University Press, 1960).

HALL, R. *The High Price of Principles: Kaunda and the White South* (New York: Africana Publishing Corp, 1969).

————. *Zambia* (New York: Praeger, 1967).

HITCHCOCK, BOB. *Bwana-Go Home* (Cape Town, South Africa: Howard Timmins, 1973).

HOWARTH, D. *The Shadow of the Dam* (London: Collins, 1961).

KAPFERER, BRUCE. *Strategy and Transaction in an African Factory* (Manchester, England: The University Press, 1973).

KAUNDA, KENNETH. *A Humanist in Africa* (London: Longmans, 1966).

————. *Zambia Shall Be Free* (London: Heinemann, 1962; New York: Praeger, 1963).

LEYS, COLIN and CRANFORD PRATT. *A New Deal in Central Africa* (London: Heinemann, 1960).

MACPHERSON, FERGUS. *Kenneth Kaunda of Zambia* (London: Oxford University Press, 1974).

MARKS, STUART A. *Large Mammals and a Brave People: Subsistence Hunters in Zambia* (Seattle: University of Washington Press, 1976).

MEEBELO, HENRY. *Reaction to Colonialism* (Manchester, England: The University Press, 1971).

MULFORD, D. *Zambia: The Politics of Independence* (New York: Oxford University Press, 1968).

PETTMAN, JAN. *Zambia; Security and Conflict* (New York: St. Martin's Press, 1974).

(F) POWNALL, DAVID. *The Raining Tree War* (London: Faber & Faber, 1974).

ROBERTS, ANDREW. *A History of the Bemba* (Madison: University of Wisconsin Press, 1973).

ROTBERG, R. I. *The Rise of Nationalism in Central Africa: The Making of Malawi and Zambia, 1873–1964* (Cambridge, Mass.: Harvard University Press, 1965).

SKLAR, RICHARD L. *Corporate Power in an African State: The Political Impact of Multinational Corporation in Zambia* (Berkeley and Los Angeles: University of California Press, 1975).

TORDOFF, WILLIAM (ed.). *Politics in Zambia* (Berkeley and Los Angeles: University of California Press, 1974).

TURNER, V. *The Forest of Symbols* (Ithaca, N.Y.: Cornell University Press, 1967).

ZANZIBAR

LOFCHIE, M. *Zanzibar: Background to Revolution* (Princeton, N.J.: Princeton University Press, 1965).

MIDDLETON, J. and J. CAMPBELL. *Zanzibar: Its Society and Its Politics* (London: Oxford University Press, 1965).

OKELLO, S. *Revolution in Zanzibar* (Nairobi, Kenya: East African Publishing House, 1967).

ZIMBABWE (RHODESIA)

ARRIGHI, G. *The Political Economy of Rhodesia* (The Hague: Mouton, 1967).

BARBER, J. *Rhodesia* (London: Oxford University Press, 1967).

BOWMAN, LARRY W. *Politics in Rhodesia* (Cambridge, Mass.: Harvard University Press, 1973).

BULL, T. *Rhodesia: Crisis of Color* (Chicago: Quadrangle Books, 1968).

—— (ed.). *Rhodesian Perspective* (Chicago: Quadrangle Books, 1968).

CLEGG, E. M. *Race and Politics: Partnership in the Federation of Rhodesia and Nyasaland* (London: Oxford University Press, 1960).

CLEMENTS, F. *Rhodesia: A Study of the Deterioration of a White Society* (New York: Praeger, 1969).

DAY, JOHN. *International Nationalism: The Extra-Territorial Relations of Southern Rhodesian African Nationalists* (London: Routledge and Kegan Paul, 1968).

GOOD, ROBERT. *UDI* (Princeton, N.J.: Princeton University Press, 1973).

HOLE, HUGH. *Old Rhodesian Days* (London: Frank Cass, 1928).

JOHNSON, FRANK. *Great Days* (Bulawayo: Books of Rhodesia, 1972).

KAPUNGA, LEONARD T. *Rhodesia: The Struggle for Freedom* (Maryknoll, N.Y.: Orbis Books, 1974).

KEATLEY, P. *The Politics of Partnership* (London: Penguin Books, 1963).

(F) LESSING, D. *African Stories* (New York: Ballantine, 1966).

(F) ——. *Going Home* (New York: Ballantine, 1968).

(F) ——. *The Grass is Singing* (New York: Ballantine, 1964).

LEYS, COLIN. *European Politics in Southern Rhodesia* (Oxford: Clarendon Press, 1959).

LONEY, MARTIN. *Rhodesia: White Racism and Imperial Response* (Baltimore: Penguin Books, 1975).

MASON, PHILIP. *Year of Decision: Rhodesia and Nyasaland 1960* (London: Oxford University Press, 1960).

MAXEY, KEES. *The Fight for Zimbabwe* (London: Rex Collins, 1975).

MTSHALI, B. VULINDLELA. *Rhodesia: Background to Conflict* (New York: Hawthorne, 1967).

MURRAY, D. J. *The Governmental System in Southern Rhodesia* (Oxford: Clarendon Press, 1959).

O'MEARA, PATRICK. *Rhodesia: Racial Conflict or Coexistence?* (Ithaca, N.Y.: Cornell University Press, 1975).

(F) SAMKANGE, S. *On Trial for My Country* (New York: Humanities Press, 1966).

——. *The Mourned One* (New York: Humanities Press, 1975).

SHAMUYARIRA, N. *Crisis in Rhodesia* (London: Andre Deutsch, 1965).

SITHOLE, N. *African Nationalism* (London: Oxford University Press, 1954).

SMITH, D. *Rhodesia: The Problem* (London: Maxwell, 1969).

STRAUSS, FRANCES. *My Rhodesia* (Boston: Gambit, 1969).

SYMONDS, A. *Southern Rhodesia: Background to Crisis* (London: Oxford University Press, 1965).

TIPPETTE, GILES. *The Mercenaries* (New York: Delacorte Press, 1976).

TODD, JUDITH. *The Right to Say No* (New York: The Third Press, 1973).

TREDGOLD, R. *The Rhodesia That Was My Life* (London: Allen & Unwin, 1969).

VAMBE, LAWRENCE. *An Ill-Fated People* (Pittsburgh: University of Pittsburgh Press, 1972).

——. *From Rhodesia to Zimbabwe* (Pittsburgh: University of Pittsburgh Press, 1976).

WELENSKY, SIR R. *4,000 Days* (London: Collins, 1964).

YOUNG, K. *Rhodesia and Independence* (London: Eyre and Spittiswoode, 1967).

INDEX